Dream of a Nation

Inspiring Ideas for a Better America

Published by SEE Innovation

www.seeinnovation.org

The views contained within reflect the perspectives of individual
authors and organizations and are not necessarily shared by all
contributors. Additionally, the editor's boxes contained throughout
were authored by SEE Innovation staff and not the authors. Likewise,
placement of photos within the book does not constitute agreement
with or endorsement of perspectives contained within them.

Original cover photo courtesy Jay L. Clendenin, copyright © 2009,
Los Angeles Times, Reprinted with Permission
Tyson Miller's cover photo courtesy Shannon Binns, *ifyouwonder.com*
Kelly Spitzner's photo courtesy Johnny Adamic

A portion of Alice Walker's contribution was excerpted from *We
Are the Ones We Have Been Waiting For: Light in a Time of Darkness*.
Copyright © 2006 by Alice Walker. Reprinted by permission of The
New Press. www.thenewpress.com.

Project Developer/Editor in Chief: Tyson Miller
Design/Production Director: Kelly Spitzner
Editor: Gretel Hakanson
Design Associate: Casey Bass
Researcher: Allen Law

This book was printed in the USA on 100% Postconsumer
Recycled Paper, Processed Chlorine Free Paper, Certified by the
Forest Stewardship Council™ (FSC®).

All climate impacts relative to the printing and distribution of
this book will be offset by Native Energy.

ISBN: 978-0-615-48226-2

The Story of this Book and Project

Dream of a Nation is more than a book. It is an evolving project that is dedicated to amplifying awareness of social, environmental and economic issues while drawing attention to the solutions. If you purchased a copy of *Dream of a Nation*, we greatly appreciate it and want you to know that it will be used to support:

- Distribution to every member of Congress
- A national tour that reaches individuals throughout the US
- Maintenance of Dreamofanation.org as a dynamic web community
- Curricular resources for teachers and students
- Outreach efforts to engage citizens in sharing their ideas and projects online
- A national Dreaming a Nation contest for young people
- Seed funding to help citizens bring ideas into action
- A documentary film version of the book

... and more!

So aside from deepening your knowledge, you're supporting a movement.
Don't forget to visit www.dreamofanation.org for music playlists, action items, resources and to share your dream. And please, tell a friend and spread the word.

Go to www.dreamofanation.org to be a part of a growing community and open a door to a world of more information and inspiration.

Dream of a Nation is a project of SEE Innovation, a national non-profit working to build awareness, capacity and structures for social and environmental transformation. This project would not have been possible without the support and generosity of the following foundations: Herb Block Foundation, FSI Foundation, Park Foundation and the Shumaker Family Foundation.

Green Press Initiative works with the book industry to reduce its environmental impact. In an effort to model environmental stewardship, this book is printed on 100% post-consumer recycled paper, which was processed without chlorine. The paper is also certified by the Forest Stewardship Council (FSC) and all climate impacts from production and distribution are offset through Native Energy annually. Green Press Initiative is another project of SEE Innovation.

"The world is as beautiful as it ever was.
It is changing, but then it always has been.
This is a good time to change,
and remain beautiful, with it."

⋗ Alice Walker, *pg. 408*

For Ayden and Kyle and all of the young ones

Contents

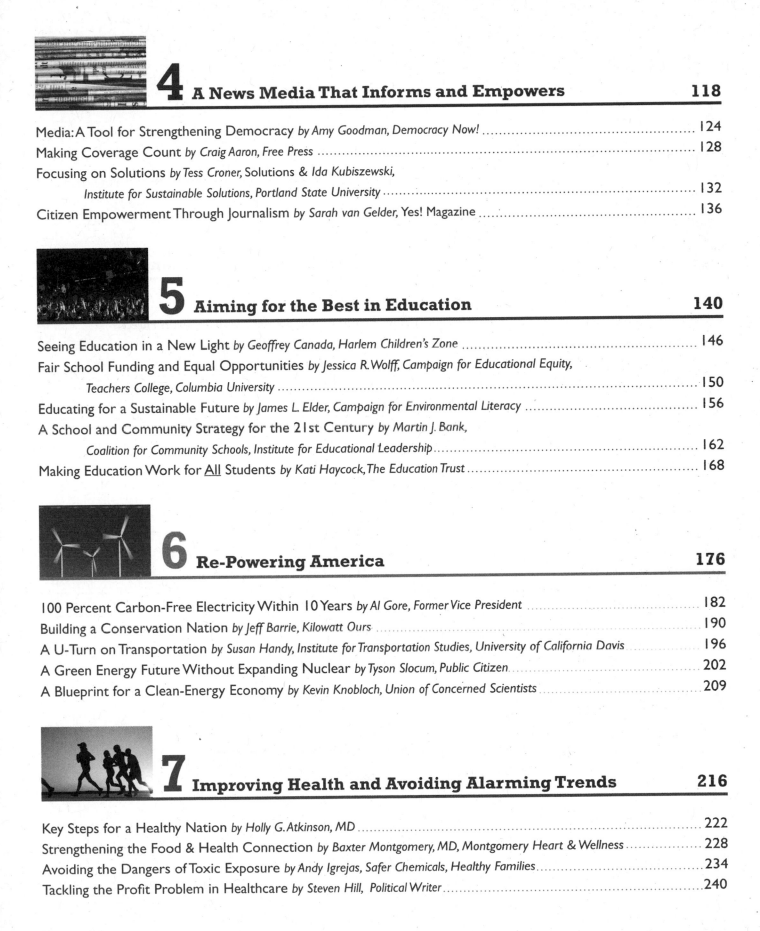

11 Waging Peace 354

12 A Nation That Shines 382

Foreword

by Paul Hawken

I once gave an interview to a journalist at *Fortune* magazine, and after he turned off the microphone he told me I was dreaming, that reality was different. I replied that of course I am dreaming, that someone has to dream in America because dreams of a livable future are not coming from politicians, bankers, and the media. It is our right to dream, and it is something we owe our children's children; it is a gift to the future and the future is begging.

It is not for any one group or individual to describe what a nation's dream *should* be for that is ideology. But it is the responsibility of citizens to have a dream that *could* be. A consuming and animating dream is a way of seeing the unknown that is possible, and in the case of *Dream of a Nation*, seeing with eyes wide open, feet on the ground, heart fully operative.

What distinguishes a dream from ideology is that it encompasses all people. It does not divide; it includes. A dream contains the multitudinous facets of human brilliance and caring. In *Dream of a Nation*, we see what is occluded and hidden within America, this vibrant, imaginative, inventive streak in our backbone that has gumption, street smarts and common sense. These qualities did not go away, but have been buried by fear, numbing polemics, pervasive greed and a culture of erosive individualism.

The book arrives at a calamitous point in American history that will no doubt enlarge and grow before we wake up as a nation. The multiple crises of poverty, indebtedness, corruption, climate change, income polarization, obesity, failing schools, abandoned elders, children, veterans and joblessness all have solutions that go beyond the nostrums that are mooted about in Washington DC.

The way to restore the vitality and health of an ecosystem or immune system is to connect more of a system to itself. The way to restore society is to restore the lost and severed connections between people and place, between livelihood and production, between food and farmer, to re-knit the commonwealth. A society is too complex for any one person to understand or dictate. It needs the same interventions that healing a disease requires, which is to create the conditions wherein the organism can heal itself. This book underlines the idea that rather than being adrift in America, our potential and capacity to adapt, grow, and prosper in a fair and just way is alive and in desperate need of forward momentum.

Inspiration is not garnered from the litanies of what may befall us; it resides in humanity's willingness to restore, redress, reform, rebuild, recover, reimagine, and reconsider. The fresh, sensible and ingenious proposals that *Dream of a Nation* puts forth are about creating the conditions that are conducive to life, to quote Janine Benyus, the author of *Biomimicry*. This discussion is not occurring on a national level to the extent it needs to. The exchanges we often hear on the airwaves or read in the popular press are not only boring; they are harmful. It is not just the way we are talking past each other when the microphones are on (and off), it is the abject lack of literacy about the nature of our problems and the sources of the solutions. *Dream of a Nation* includes new and known visionaries who together create the idea, in poet Denise Levertov's words, that "we have only begun to know the power that is in us if we would join our solitudes in the communion of struggle."

Dream of a Nation contains some of the most potent and powerful voices in our nation. Fears you may hold about the future of America or Americans can be vanquished here. You can read *Dream* from the middle out, from the back forwards, or from the beginning; it makes no difference. Everywhere there is mettle, ingenuity and heart in clear declarative prose, backed up by facts. This volume may be the equivalent of a tool Gary Snyder once proposed: a Tibetan Army knife with a patented mind opener to pry open the stale consciousness of power. Stale consciousness is within us, too, if we fall prey to despair. This book constitutes a blessing to us all.

Paul Hawken is an environmentalist, entrepreneur, journalist and author. Starting at age 20, he dedicated his life to sustainability and changing the relationship between business and the environment. His practice has included starting and running ecological businesses, writing and teaching about the impact of commerce on living systems, and consulting with governments and corporations on economic development, industrial ecology and environmental policy. His most recent book is Blessed Unrest. *For more on Hawken, visit www.paulhawken.com*

Introduction

"When the story of these times gets written, we want it to say that we did all we could, and it was more than anyone could have imagined." ⇾ Bono

Dream of a Nation as a book and project was born out of faith and frustration. Faith in human ingenuity, common sense and compassion. Frustration with the fact that sometimes we get so bogged down in the fight and the spectacle that there is a collective blindness to our shared purpose and society's real needs. But thankfully, it is ordinary people doing extraordinary things who are keeping the flame alive and charting a different path for our future. They are students and CEOs, political leaders and hip-hop artists, entrepreneurs and teachers, volunteers and big-thinkers who are rooted in creativity, positivity and hope.

Paul Hawken said, "Inspiration is not garnered from the litanies of what may befall us; it resides in humanity's willingness to restore, redress, reform, rebuild, recover, reimagine and reconsider." In a sense, this is what this book explores. When you flip the pages of *Dream of a Nation* they are meant to be both sobering and inspiring. Sobering because we face monumental challenges and don't have a lot of time or infinite resources. Inspiring because there are people and organizations throughout the land that are dedicated to the virtues of stewardship and fairness, and future generations. The dreams of ordinary citizens and visionaries are what have made and still make this great country of ours. Ultimately, in this shared and ever-evolving society, our greatest strength lies in our ability to work together toward a collective purpose that is grounded in our common humanity.

As one of the most prosperous and free countries on the planet, we have a strong foundation from which to keep the dream alive and growing. At the same time, there are a multitude of compounding challenges that require vital focus, new ways of thinking, bold actions and greater unity in order to solve.

Many of the problems and related solutions that we face are interconnected. As we reprioritize what we spend on the military, for example, it frees up resources for education, health, job creation and building the green economy. As we support local living economies, it prevents the off-shoring of opportunity and serves to reduce the growing economic divide. As the news media focuses more on constructive journalism and solutions, the spirit of collaboration is bolstered. As citizens are further empowered, communities across the land and democracy are strengthened.

Dream of a Nation reflects a growing movement that is relevant whatever your political persuasion or station in life. The work is full of contributions from visionaries and pioneering organizations that are committed to a common cause and to quickening the pace of change. While it doesn't cover every important issue and covers some not nearly deep enough, it is a starting place. You won't read it in a weekend; plan on weeks or months. And remember that the dream lives on in what you do with it.

More than a book, *Dream of a Nation* is an invitation. An invitation to explore issues that affect us all. An invitation to be open to possibility, to be part of the progress and the dream that is always unfolding.

Tyson Miller, *Editor*

Photo courtesy Shirley Gaca

A Dream of Our Country

Neosha Hampton
Ninth Grade Student
Milwaukee, WI

As a Nation we sometimes stand alone,
But one person can be **strong**.

So if we stand like we are one,
Then we can be a **shield against**

The poverty that calls the names of many,
And the hunger that grabs us by the neck,
The hate that chases love away,
While pride holds courage by the throat
And chokes it till there's no hold.

Painted with emotions

Chained with trivial views

Doesn't mean we cannot be one.

Be one like the molecules that
Run through our bodies
And all meet at an agreeing point.

Like the blood that courses through
Our veins.

The blood that is a velvety red
And supplies us with life.

Be one like the
Stars,
Sun,
Moon
And the Sky.
Be one like
We were made to be.

A People-Centered and Accountable Government

one

A look at the numbers...

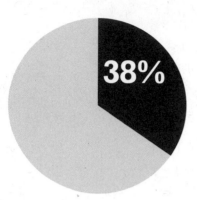 **38%** of US citizens believe that the government generally **"cares what people like me think."**

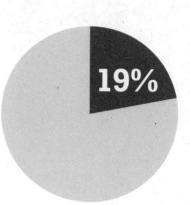 **19%** trust Washington to **"do what is right"** most of the time.

Participatory budgeting: One study found there is **greater transparency and more equitable spending** when citizens have a direct voice.

In Porto Alegre, Brazil, **participatory budgeting** led to a:

SPENDING

400% increase in school spending

300% increase in healthcare spending

4,000

Number of New Orleans citizens who participated in a council to prepare a $200 million rebuilding plan after Hurricane Katrina. 92% of the group supported the plan.

Training citizenship: **Citizens should do more than just vote** and can be empowered to take a more active role.

2x

Likelihood that New Leaders principals in Chicago would oversee 20+ point gains in student proficiency scores after developing the New Leaders for New Schools program (to train highly effective principals) in 2000.

Graduates to College

20%

70%

In Hocking, OH, Principal George Wood gives his students more say in their education. Within a decade, the percentage of graduates going on to college climbed from 20% to 70%.

While health, education and other budgets fall short, defense **spending totaled $690 billion** in 2010.

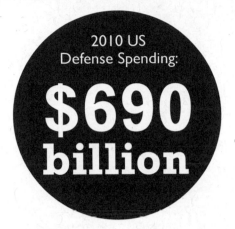

2010 US
Defense Spending:

$690 billion

Federal Education Spending:

$73 billion

Natural Resources and Environment Spending:

$43 billion

During the last presidential election cycle, elected officials solicited **$5 billion in total campaign contributions,** an average of $600,000 per hour.

$5 billion
total campaign contributions in 2008

$600,000
per hour

$300 million

Amount Canada spent during the last presidential election cycle with spending limits and donation caps.

Between 1989 and 2009, the healthcare industry gave a total of **$313.8 million in campaign contributions** to members of Congress.

HEALTHCARE INDUSTRY

$313.8 million

MEMBERS OF CONGRESS

$100 maximum

Using Fair Elections public financing, candidates receive a 4:1 match from the state on donations of $100 or less, but cannot accept any larger donations.

81%

Percentage of Connecticut state legislators who use the Fair Elections system voluntarily.

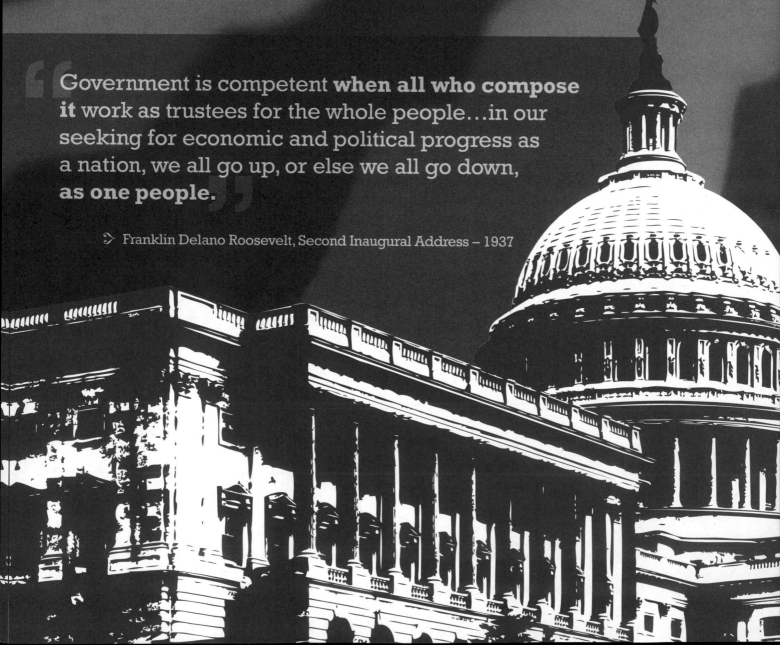

What is the measure of good government? . . . .

We can recognize whether government is operating in its highest form by looking at the results produced. We know we're on the right track when democracy is strengthened, and equality and opportunity touch every person. When common sense and long-term thinking are the norm, government is at its best. Propelled by shared values, good government lives in the hearts of open-minded citizens and leaders who build unity and serve the common good. A strong and effective government breathes when we get money and corrupting interests out of politics and when the spirit of collaboration is its guiding force.

Our government is moving forward. It's alive and unfolding across this land, growing stronger with each engaged citizen and sound decision. But there is still a need for new energy and creative ideas, a revived commitment to core principles and a return to the fundamentals.

"Government is competent **when all who compose it** work as trustees for the whole people…in our seeking for economic and political progress as a nation, we all go up, or else we all go down, **as one people.**"

> Franklin Delano Roosevelt, Second Inaugural Address – 1937

Committed
to the Right
Priorities

Post-
Partisan

Open
and
Transparent

Grounded
in Common
Purpose

Of the
People &
for the
People

Solutions-
Oriented

Bold and
Innovative

Toward a
Living Democracy

Frances Moore Lappé
Small Planet Institute
and Small Planet Fund

Most Americans grow up absorbing the notion that democracy boils down to just two things—elected government and a market economy. So, all that seems expected of us is to vote and to shop.

This stripped-down duo I call "thin democracy."

While thin democracy proves itself unable to meet today's challenges, another understanding of democracy is emerging: Democracy that is practiced as a way of life, no longer something done to us or for us but what we ourselves create. I call it "Living Democracy." In it, democracy is no longer merely a formal government construct, but something embedded in a wide range of human relationships. So its values apply just as much in economic life or in cultural life as in political life. Put very practically, Living Democracy means infusing the power of citizens' voices and values throughout our public relationships.

Photo courtesy David Ploenzke.

"All that seems expected of us is to vote and to shop"

> I call it "Living Democracy." In it, democracy is no longer merely a formal government construct, but something embedded in a wide range of human relationships. So its values apply just as much in economic life or in cultural life as in political life.

Rest assured, Living Democracy isn't a new fixed ism, blueprint or utopian end-state. Rather, democracy "becomes us" in both meanings of the phrase. It requires a shift in our focus from democracy as a thing we "have"—elections, parties and a market—to democracy as intricate relationships of mutuality that we create daily.

This shift in goals and expectations of both our government's role and of our role as citizens is already perceptible, if we look beyond our existing thin democracy to see the many facets of Living Democracy that are living, growing and changing lives. Examples are diverse and far-reaching; grassroots groups, individuals, conscious corporations, schools and local governments are creating Living Democracy in their communities.

A Citizens' Democracy

Grassroots-led reforms for voluntary public financing, called Clean Elections,[1] have significantly purged private wealth from elections in Maine, Arizona and Connecticut. Removing money from politics suddenly feels a lot more urgent to many Americans as they work through the worst economic collapse since the Great Depression, and they realize the root of crisis: the financial industry's political clout, via political contributions and lobbying, which got the rules changed to allow the dangerous risk-taking. Now, a national effort, with bipartisan-supported "Fair Elections" legislation pending in both houses of Congress, would take us a long way to truly publicly held government.

Americans realize the root of the crisis: the financial industry's political clout, via political contributions and lobbying, which got the rules changed to allow the dangerous risk taking.

STOP CORPORATE LOBBYISTS

www.FinishReformRight.com

> **The challenge is to leave behind the knee-jerk contempt for government and learn how to make the government our essential and powerful tool for creating the world we want.**

Proactive Government

Living Democracy depends on citizens shaping and trusting government as their tool. And that starts with exposing the misleading big-versus-small government frame and recognizing that what really matters is whether government is accountable to citizens. Accountable government, setting fair standards and rules, actually reduces the need for "big" government to clean up after human and environmental damage. From this frame, we can see with new eyes the cost of government action to end poverty or to clean up our environment. We can see that the real cost is government, not acting.

For example, look to the 1960s War on Poverty. With it launched hugely successful programs like Head Start, food stamps, work study, Medicare and Medicaid, which still exist today, as well as numerous other efforts. And during that decade, Americans cut the poverty rate almost in half.[2]

Now, as the threats of global climate change and world poverty become increasingly acute, more and more people realize that restoring our planet and its people depends on citizens reclaiming government from private interests. The challenge is to leave behind knee-jerk contempt for government and learn how to make government our essential and powerful tool for creating the world we want.

Engaging Citizens in Strengthening Democracy

The public's engagement in democracy is more than voting and shopping. A Living Democracy encourages ordinary citizens to be involved in identifying, discussing and deciding upon public policy and budgets. One way to engage citizens is through participatory budgeting where citizens have a direct say in the local budget. This process of democratic decision-making has been in place in many Brazilian cities since 1989. Ten years later, Chicago's 49th Ward launched the first participatory budgeting project in the US. In a series of public meetings over a six-month period, community members decided which community projects would be funded with the ward's $1.3 million capital infrastructure discretionary budget.[3] A study of Brazil found that, with more citizens' eyes on the budgeting process, there is less graft, greater government transparency and more equitable public spending, along with increased public participation.

The non-profit America*Speaks* has been working to increase citizen participation in democracy.
The organization aims to develop a national infrastructure for democratic deliberation that links decision-makers and citizens in determining public policy.

Citizens participate in an AmericaSpeaks meeting in Philadelphia.

Photos courtesy Erin & Joe/flickr

The non-profit America*Speaks* has been working to increase citizen participation in democracy. The organization aims to develop a national infrastructure for democratic deliberation that links decision-makers and citizens in determining public policy. Its work has engaged more than 147,000 people in all 50 states in large-scale citizen participation on issues such as the redevelopment of the World Trade Center site, the rebuilding of post-Katrina New Orleans, statewide healthcare reform in California and the national childhood obesity epidemic.

Organic Valley was started in Wisconsin in the 1980s and is now owned by over a thousand farmers in 32 states.

Photo courtesy Robert Eddy

Another example is the Citizens' Jury, pioneered by the Jefferson Center in Minnesota. This approach to collaborative problem-solving brings one to two dozen randomly selected citizens together over several days to weigh a critical issue and come to agreement on a direction. Hundreds of Citizens' Juries have been convened around the world to work toward solutions to challenges from sewage treatment to climate change.

Democracy Where Many Benefit As Opposed to Just a Few

Democracy is grounded in the notion of a "common good"—an understanding that our individual well being depends on the well being of the whole society. Businesses that close the gap between owners and workers for the common good are growing fast. Cooperatives are one example of a democratic business organization, where owners are also the business' workers or users of its services. In all their varieties—from finance to housing, farming, manufacturing and more—equitable sharing of responsibilities and benefits is a key value. Co-op membership jumped ten-fold in the last half century, now providing 100 million jobs worldwide. That's one-fifth more jobs than multinational corporations offer, according to the International Co-operative Alliance.

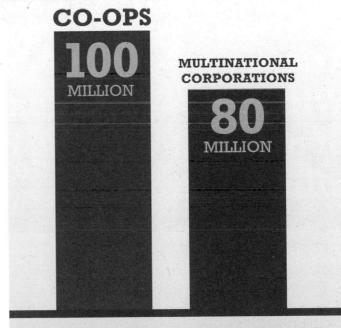

CO-OPS
100 MILLION

MULTINATIONAL CORPORATIONS
80 MILLION

Number of Jobs Worldwide

Cooperatives provide more than 100 million jobs worldwide. That's about 1/5 more jobs than multinational corporations offer.

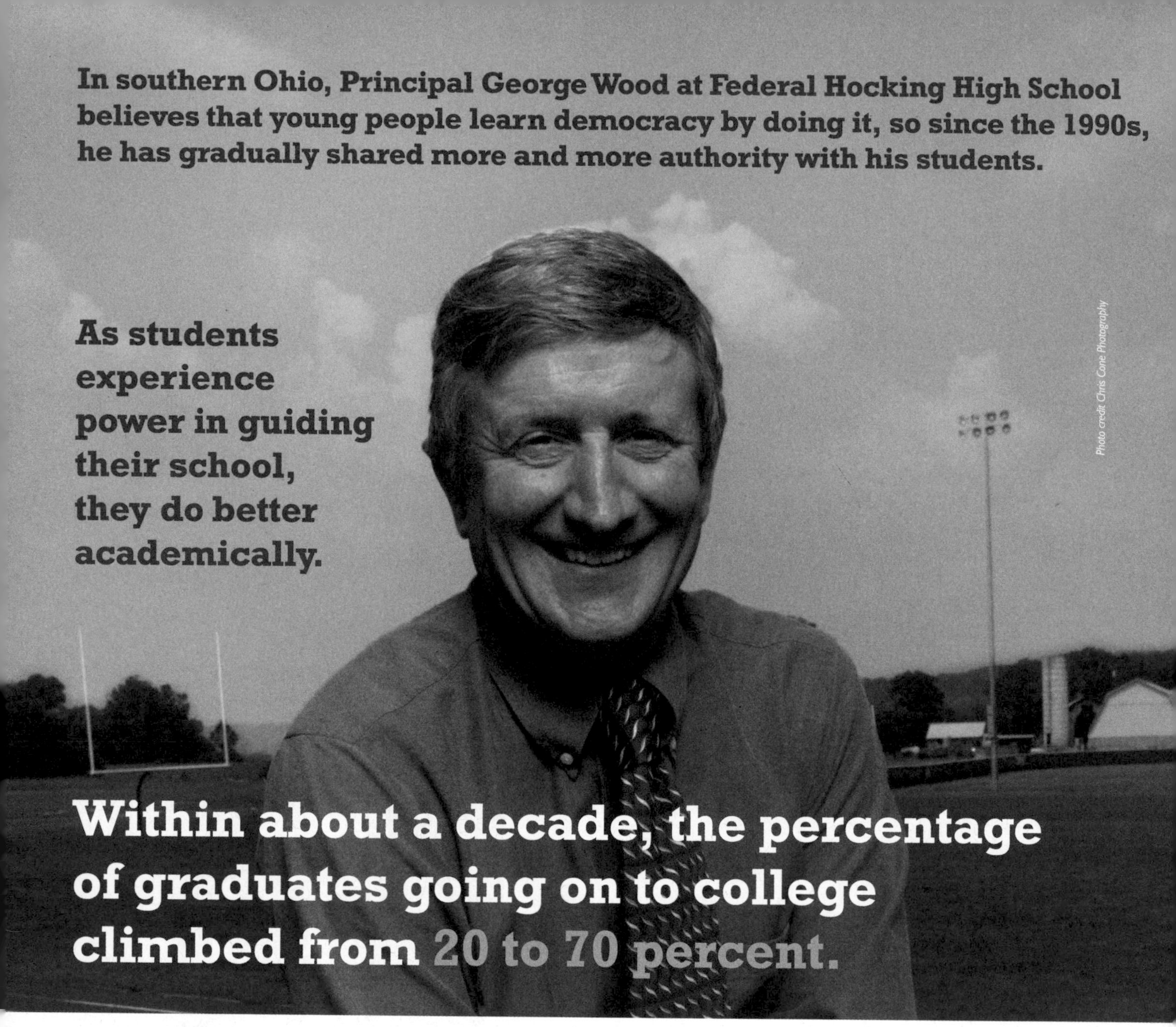

In southern Ohio, Principal George Wood at Federal Hocking High School believes that young people learn democracy by doing it, so since the 1990s, he has gradually shared more and more authority with his students.

As students experience power in guiding their school, they do better academically.

Within about a decade, the percentage of graduates going on to college climbed from 20 to 70 percent.

One example is Organic Valley, a dairy cooperative formed in the late 1980s by a handful of Wisconsin dairy farmers distressed that their neighbors' farms were folding while profits were going everywhere but to farmers. I would never have predicted that in two decades their determination would birth a half-billion-dollar company owned by over a thousand family farmers in 32 states. Organic Valley still lives by its democratic values, with profits returning to farmers and rural communities.

And some companies are proving that sky-high CEO pay isn't necessary for business success. While the average

US CEO-to-worker pay ratio has been greater than 200-to-1 since the mid-90s,[4] the green home-supplies company Seventh Generation caps its CEO total compensation at 14 times that of its average worker.[5]

Policies that benefit many are increasing as well, such as living wage ordinances that require businesses with public contracts to pay employees enough to live in dignity. Not only do such policies benefit the employees and their families; they also benefit the entire community since individuals have more disposable income to invest in their community. More than 120 cities and counties have adopted living wage ordinances, and the Obama

> **From political life to economic life to education, Living Democracy is taking shape as a set of system values that evolve with us.**

administration may soon be giving companies with living wage policies an advantage when seeking government contracts.[6]

Empowering the Next Generation

Students are moving from "community service," in which adults are in charge, to "apprentice citizenship," in which young people take ownership in hands-on learning. Most importantly, they experience their own power to make real, lasting improvements in their communities. From environmental restoration to improving their school food service, grade schoolers in 40 school districts in New England are learning by becoming community problem solvers as part of a movement led by Maine's KIDS Consortium.

In southern Ohio, Principal George Wood at Federal Hocking High School believes that young people learn democracy by doing it, so since the 1990s, he has gradually shared more and more authority with his students, ultimately including equal voice with teachers in hiring faculty. Students also serve on what is called the site-based committee, governing most aspects of school life. As students experience power in guiding their school, they do better academically. Within about a decade, the percentage of graduates going on to college climbed from 20 to 70 percent.[7]

From political life to economic life to education, Living Democracy is taking shape, not as a set system, finished once and for all, but as a set of system values that evolve with us: values of inclusion, mutual accountability

Citizens' Councils:
An Idea to Strengthen Democracy

Participating in democracy could become akin to jury duty and voting. The notion of a "national citizens' council" would be the pinnacle of citizen engagement in democracy. Similar to jury duty, members of the public would be randomly selected and financially compensated for their time to evaluate current issues and legislation. The general public could then be invited to review the votes and analysis of the citizen's council. Free from influence by special interests, the need to stay in office or pressure from legislators, citizens' councils would represent the public's best interest.

from the editor

and fairness, among others. On this journey, our expectations of the capacities and essential roles of regular citizens change. In contrast to thin democracy's reductive view of human beings, Living Democracy reflects and builds on what philosopher Erich Fromm described as the deep human drive to make an "imprint on the world, to transform and to change, and not only to be transformed and changed."[8]

•••••

Frances Moore Lappé is the author of 18 books, from Diet for a Small Planet *in 1971 to* EcoMind: Changing the Way We Think, to Create the World We Want *(Nation Books, 2011). With Anna Lappé, she leads the Small Planet Institute and Small Planet Fund (www. smallplanet.org). She is the recipient of 18 honorary degrees and is cofounder of Food First, the Institute for Food and Development Policy.*

Redefining Security
for Strong Communities and a Safer World

Former Republican President and Five-Star General Dwight D. Eisenhower once said, "Every gun that is made, every warship launched, every rocket fired signifies, in the final sense, a theft from those who hunger and are not fed, those who are cold and not clothed."

He understood fully the challenges of balancing priorities and the need for our country to focus on taking care of people instead of building a bigger war chest or achieving unending global military superiority. Yet despite his call for change, military spending has only continued to rise.

The US spends 42 percent of all world military expenditures—more than $690 billion in 2010[1]—including the military operations in Iraq and Afghanistan. Surprisingly, military spending is expected to increase,[2] even as our nation faces a five-year freeze or cap on what has been called non-security discretionary spending.[3] Where will military spending funds come

Greg Speeter
National Priorities Project

"Every **gun** that is made, every **warship** launched, every **rocket** fired signifies in the final sense a **theft** from those who **hunger** and are not fed, those who are **cold** and not clothed."

▷ Former Republican President and Five-Star General Dwight D. Eisenhower

from and how will we adequately fund our schools, infrastructure and communities, especially in the face of a freeze? Even in a weak economy, in 2011 we will spend twice as much on the military as we will spend on education, science, the environment, housing and transportation combined.[4]

A national mandate for a broadened definition of security calls for decent jobs, strong communities and a strong economy, and an end to war.

A national mandate for a broadened definition of security calls for decent jobs, strong communities, a strong economy and an end to war. To achieve that security will mean a paradigm shift in spending priorities, away from the military and toward our communities.

In fact, President Obama, Secretary of Defense Robert Gates and others have noted that the nature of the security threats to the US and the world have changed significantly in recent years, requiring non-military approaches and international cooperation.[5] Yet 87 percent of what we spend on "national security" goes to the military, with just 8 percent going to homeland security and 5 percent to such preventive measures as peacekeeping, diplomacy, non-proliferation, development assistance, alternative energy and methods to address global climate change.[6]

Funding the Right Priorities

The federal government used to prioritize ongoing public investments, and the results paid off. The Federal Housing Act and the GI bill after World War II increased home ownership and made college available to millions of people. The War on Poverty in the 1960s helped reduce poverty by 40 percent.[7] Federal environmental policies have substantially cleaned up the water, the air and toxic wastes. Despite some of these past successes, the threats to our communities and our international competitiveness are still overwhelming. For example:

ACCORDING TO THE **2011** U.S. BUDGET: we will spend twice as much on the **MILITARY** as we will spend on: + **EDUCATION** + **SCIENCE** + ENVIRONMENT + **HOUSING** + TRANSPORTATION COMBINED

In the last decade military spending has soared from **$300 billion to nearly $700 billion,** according to the White House's Office of Management and Budget.

The US ranks poorly
in many critical categories of human security:

20th in percent of students graduating from college

|||||||||||||||||||||||||||||||||||||||||||||||||||||||||||||||||||||||||||||||||||||||||||||||||||||

29th in infant mortality

|||||||||||||||||||||||||||||||||||||||||||||||||||||||||||||||||||||||||||||||||||||||||||||||||||||

31st in life expectancy

|||||||||||||||||||||||||||||||||||||||||||||||||||||||||||||||||||||||||||||||||||||||||||||||||||||

72nd in the gap between the rich and the poor

|||||||||||||||||||||||||||||||||||||||||||||||||||||||||||||||||||||||||||||||||||||||||||||||||||||

73rd in use of alternative energy

|||||||||||||||||||||||||||||||||||||||||||||||||||||||||||||||||||||||||||||||||||||||||||||||||||||

Child poverty:
We have the highest child poverty rates in the indus-trialized world. More than 15.4 million children—20.7 percent—live in poverty.[8] Nearly 60 of our major and mid-sized cities have child poverty rates of one-third or more.[9] Economists calculate child poverty costs the economy $500 billion a year in added healthcare costs, loss of productivity, earnings and taxation.[10]

Education:
Today children in the US are less likely to graduate from high school than their parents.[11] A major reason for this is that schools in low-income areas, especially in our largest cities, have fewer teachers, larger class size and are more overcrowded and in need of repair.[12]

Infrastructure:
The American Society of Civil Engineers ranked most of our infrastructure a D, noting one-third of our roads, one-quarter of our bridges and water systems affecting 10 percent of the population are in serious need of

With adequate funding, many people believe that the nation's social, environmental, and economic problems can be solved.

repair.[13] The American Federation of Teachers estimates it will cost $234 billion to repair our deteriorating public schools.[14]

The environment:
With less than 5 percent of the world's population, the US consumes 25 percent of the world's oil and produces 20 percent of the world's CO_2 emissions.[15] Eighty-seven percent of our energy comes from fossil fuels; only 7 percent from alternatives.[16]

A global context:
While we are by leaps and bounds number one in military spending, we rank poorly in many critical categories of human security. For example, the US ranks:[17]

- 29th in infant morality
- 31st in life expectancy
- 20th in percent of students graduating from college
- 72nd in the gap between the rich and the poor
- 73rd in use of alternative energy

Other countries with modern militaries, such as Japan, Australia, France and Canada, spend far less on their militaries (both in dollars and as a percentage of GNP)[18] and rank higher in categories of human development.[19]

TWO WAYS

to cut **billions of dollars a year** in Pentagon spending:

Saving Billions to Invest in Our Communities

With adequate funding, many believe that the nation's social, environmental and economic problems can be solved. But doing so will require new money and different spending priorities. Much of that money could come from responsible cuts in unneeded military spending. Here are just two ways to cut trillions of dollars a year in unnecessary Pentagon spending that could be invested in our communities:

Safely cut unneeded Cold War weapons and reduce waste and inefficiency.
Savings: $75 billion this year.

The Unified Security Budget Task Force, a group of national security experts, has identified $75 billion that could be saved in the current federal budget through cuts in nuclear forces, cuts in Cold War-era conventional or poorly performing weapons systems, reductions in non-essential force structure and reducing waste and inefficiency in the Pentagon.[20]

That $75 billion saved could be used to rebuild one-third of our deteriorated schools;[21] or more than double our federal commitment to elementary, secondary and higher education;[22] or provide 85 percent of college students in the US with Pell grants for one year.[23]

Make military operations a last resort.
Savings: trillions.

While our military slowly withdraws some troops from Iraq and plans to do the same in Afghanistan, it is now increasingly leading military interventions on a global scale. What we need to do is end the existing operations and in the future turn to military force only as a last resort after all peaceful alternatives have been exhausted. Between 2001 and 2010, the US spent more than $1 trillion on military operations for the occupation of Iraq and Afghanistan.[24] The $169.4 billion we spent in 2010 in Iraq and Afghanistan is 2.6 times what

1 Safely cut unneeded Cold War weapons; reduce waste & inefficiency

Photo courtesy US Navy Mass Communication Specialist Seaman Daniel A. Barker

SAVINGS:
$75 billion

WHAT COULD THIS MONEY DO?

- **Rebuild one-third** of our **deteriorated schools**
- **More than double** our commitment to **all levels of education**
- Provide **85% of college students** in the US with **Pell grants for one year**

2 Make military operations **a last resort.**

Photo courtesy Cpl. Brian M. Henner, US Marine Corps

SAVINGS:
Trillions

Representative **Barney Frank** along with others who are working on financial regulation reforms assembled **a bipartisan task force** that identified nearly **$1 trillion in savings** that could be **extracted** from the Pentagon budget through 2020.

Representative Barney Frank and his 16-member task force are working to garner the support of other members of Congress to include military spending cuts in any national deficit reduction plan.

we spent on all preventive measures—peacekeeping, international aid, alternative energy and non-proliferation combined![25]

We have to remember too that the cost of war is greater than dollars and cents. More than 7,000 soldiers lost their lives in the Iraq and Afghanistan wars[26] and the number of civilian casualties is estimated to be over 150,000.[27]

Signs of Promise

Representative Barney Frank, along with others who are working on financial regulation reforms, assembled a bipartisan task force that identified nearly $1 trillion in savings that could be extracted from the Pentagon budget through 2020. The 16-member task force produced a detailed report that outlines explicit cuts to military spending including reductions to the US

nuclear arsenal, shrinking the number of naval ships, spending less on research and cutbacks to big weapons programs.[28]

Building a Movement for New Priorities

We can substantially change our national priorities by cutting unnecessary military spending and investing in our communities. Here's how a movement might begin:

Bring social spending and peace advocates together around a long-term campaign to cut specific weapons and policies and invest in our communities.

For years social spending advocates have struggled with each other for smaller and smaller slices of the federal budget pie. A collaboration with the peace community and national security experts around efforts

We can substantially change our national priorities by cutting unnecessary military spending and investing in our communities.

to cut military spending would lead to a downward military spending trend and more funds available to "grow" the domestic spending pieces of the pie.

Challenge Congress with an alternative, common–sense budget.

During the late 1970s, Congressman Ron Dellums of California offered a transfer amendment in Congress that called for cutting funds for specific weapons and putting that money into social programs. While the amendment didn't pass, it did generate substantial discussion about what was wrong with our military policies and how to rationally address critical social needs. It's time to revisit that discussion in Congress.

Show the local impacts of current priorities and create accountability campaigns around the country.

Organizers know the importance of making issues local and real to people. For 28 years, National Priorities Project (NPP) has made complex federal spending information more accessible by helping people understand the local impact of national priorities. In fact, in late 2010 the New Priorities Network, along with over 30 of the nation's major peace and justice organizations and local organizations throughout the country, began a multi-year campaign to produce state and local resolutions to cut military spending to fund local jobs and services.

In his farewell address to the nation, President Eisenhower called for an "alert and knowledgeable citizenry" to determine the proper combination of "military machinery…with our peaceful methods and goals."[29] The current combination of these priorities—embodied in our annual federal budget—has the US continuing to police the world while our communities suffer and we lose our competitive edge. This is not the dream of this nation. A budget priorities movement led by economic justice, environmental, peace and progressive national security experts could change that combination, so instead our nation would work with the rest of the world to address terrorism and its causes, rid the Pentagon of unneeded weapons and policies and invest the savings in our communities and our environment.

. . . . .

Building a Movement for New Priorities

① **Bring social spending and peace advocates together around a long-term campaign to cut specific weapons and policies and invest in our communities.**

② **Challenge Congress with an alternative, common-sense budget.**

③ **Show the local impacts of current priorities and create accountability campaigns across the country.**

Greg Speeter founded the National Priorities Project (www.nationalpriorities.org) in 1983 as a way for the general public to better understand and participate in the federal budget process, especially by realizing how it impacts one's local community. He has written and spoken extensively on federal, social, military and tax policies. In 2008, he stepped down as executive director to focus on training and networking NPP information. Speeter began his professional life in 1966 as a community organizer and has also written books on community organizing and public access to the political process.

Getting Money Out of Politics:
Putting the Public First

One of the basic principles of American democracy is that all voices should be represented fairly, regardless of race, gender, socio-economic background, sexual orientation or age. Our reliance on private financing for political campaigns, however, places fundamental inequalities at the heart of the democratic process.

Privately financed campaigns have been part of American democracy from its outset, but they give us a system in which elected officials are beholden not to the public interest, but rather to the special interests that fund their elections, which ultimately leads to undue influence in legislative process.

Bob Edgar
Common Cause

In the US, the ratio of lobbyists to legislators is 23:1.

A Core Problem: Elections Dominated by Money

First, *private financing of political campaigns magnifies the power of large donors in the political process.* When members of Congress rely on big checks from corporations, industry lobbyists, special interests or wealthy individuals to get elected, those donors expect—and often get—something in return. Under one-half of one percent (0.36 percent) of the American population currently donates over $200 to political campaigns. This small, wealthy minority provides around 90 percent of the money that funds political campaigns and, in exchange, receives more access to candidates and more influence in shaping policies and legislation.[1] This dynamic can be seen in a number of issues; healthcare and climate change are two examples.

It is hard to know the exact influence of special-interest money on the legislation passed by Congress, but we know it has a huge role—often hindering progress and innovation. Between 1989 and 2009, the healthcare industry gave $313.8 million in campaign contributions to members of Congress. Of that, $166.7 million, or 53 percent, went to members of the House and Senate who sit on one of the five committees with jurisdiction over healthcare reform, according to data from the Center for Responsive Politics.[2]

Campaign Contributions from Healthcare Industry (1989–2009)

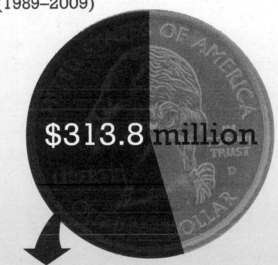

$313.8 million

$166.7 million (53%)
Given to members of Congress with jurisdiction over health reform

Despite a worldwide consensus on the harmful effects of carbon emissions, Congress only recently passed legislation to limit the discharge of greenhouse gases. The energy industry spent lavishly on lobbying and campaign contributions to fight any proposal.

Under one half of 1% (0.36%) of the American population currently donates over $200 to political campaigns. This small, wealthy minority provides around 90% of the money that funds political campaigns.

The energy industry is betting millions that they can buy influence in Congress and protect their profits.

According to lobby disclosure reports, 34 energy companies registered in the first quarter of 2009 to lobby Congress on legislation to limit greenhouse gases, known as the American Clean Energy and Security Act of 2009. These companies spent $23.7 million—or $260,000 per day—lobbying members of Congress in January, February and March of 2009. Many of these companies also made large contributions to members of the Senate Environment and Public Works Committee, which had jurisdiction over the legislation. Oil and gas companies, mining companies and electric utilities combined gave more than $2 million to the 19 members of the Senate Environment and Public Works Committee from 2007 to 2009.[3]

The energy industry is betting millions that it can buy influence in Congress and protect its profits, even if that means blocking an important step toward clean, renewable energy and a healthier planet. Tackling problems like global warming must start by ending the flow

of the industry's "Black Gold" of campaign contributions and lobbying cash to the most influential members of Congress.

It is impossible to say how each of these issues and many others would have been resolved in Congress if members were not dependent on these same companies for campaign contributions. What is clear, however, is that money and their willingness to invest it in campaigns gives these companies undue influence in the process of addressing national problems.

Second, private financing of political campaigns limits opportunities for qualified but unconventional candidates to run for and win elected office. Nine out of ten campaigns are won by the candidate who spends the most money. That drives candidates to focus more on fundraising and large donors than on mobilizing voters around ideas and issues. In 2010, the average winning House candidate spent $1.3 million, and the average winning Senate candidate spent $8.3 million.[4] The astronomical cost of campaigns has made it increasingly difficult for citizens who are not independently wealthy and whose platforms do not appeal to wealthy donors to mount competitive campaigns against well-funded incumbents or well-connected political insiders. The

Thirty-four energy companies registered in the first quarter of 2009 to lobby Congress on the American Clean Energy and Security Act of 2009 to limit greenhouse gases.

This group of companies spent a total of **$23.7 million**, or **$260,000 a day**, lobbying members of Congress in **January, February,** and **March.**

9 out of 10

political campaigns are won by the candidate who spends the most money

$$$$$$$$$ $

In 2010: Average winning **House** candidate spent:

$1.3 million

Average winning **Senate** candidate spent:

$8.3 million

need to raise enormous amounts of campaign cash creates barriers for huge segments of the population.

Third, private financing of campaigns forces members of Congress to spend too much time on fundraising, and not enough time on serving their constituents. US Representatives in contested elections spend 34 percent of their time, while in office, raising money for their next campaign rather than reading bills, responding to constituent concerns and meeting with voters to discuss legislative issues. And fundraising doesn't end with a successful election; when new members of Congress and Senators enter the world of Washington politics, they are immediately asked to set fundraising goals not only for their future campaigns, but for their party's fundraising arm as well.

For these reasons, many citizens feel locked out of their democracy and are cynical about the political process. America has one of the lowest voter turnout rates among the world's democracies—54 percent during presidential elections and roughly 40 percent in off-year elections—because people simply don't believe voting will change anything. They can see that

their elected officials are more beholden to campaign contributors than to their constituents. In order for a democracy to thrive and for the political process to produce outcomes that advance the interests of the public, citizens must have faith that the system works and adheres to the ideals under which their democracy was founded.

One Solution: Fair Elections

The key to strengthening America's democratic process is to reform the campaign financing system by implementing Fair Elections, a voluntary system of public financing for campaigns. This plan gives participating candidates $4 from a special public fund for each $1 they raise in private gifts of $100 or less. Candidates using this system are not allowed to spend any of their personal wealth or to accept any donations greater than $100. By creating a system that prioritizes small donors, Fair Elections levels the playing field, provides opportunities for citizens to have their voices heard and allows elected officials to better serve the public interest. A candidate elected under a Fair Elections system won't be beholden to a set of large campaign

With the costs of campaigns skyrocketing, it has become difficult for citizens who are not independently wealthy and whose platforms do not appeal to wealthy donors to mount a competitive campaign.

Janet Napolitano, former Arizona governor and now Secretary of Homeland Security, is one of the most outspoken supporters of Fair Elections.

To qualify for public funds, she gathered **4,000 contributions of $5 each** from Arizona residents. She sought and won Arizona's governorship twice using a Fair Elections–style public finance system.

Voters like public funding because it makes elected officials more accountable to them, reduces conflicts of interest and gives them more choice at the polls.

contributors, but rather to the general public, as America's founders intended.

Fair Elections has a proven track record of success and enjoys bipartisan support. Several states and cities have successfully implemented Fair Elections–style public financing. They have created an accountable government and restored confidence in the political process. Maine, Connecticut and Arizona all have Fair Elections at the statewide level. Eighty-five percent of Maine's legislature—Democrats and Republicans—was elected using a Fair Elections system of public financing. A recent poll found that 74 percent of Maine voters surveyed wanted candidates for governor to use the system, and 55 percent said they would be more likely to vote for a candidate who did.

In 2008, Connecticut became the first state to have Fair Elections public financing passed by its legislature

rather than through a voter referendum. Within two years, 81 percent of the Connecticut legislature was made up of politicians who used the system. By large margins, Connecticut voters believed that the influence of money on elected officials needed to be limited (82 percent) and that state politicians were more concerned with the needs of their campaign donors than the needs of the general public (62 percent).

Janet Napolitano, former Arizona governor and now Secretary of Homeland Security, is one of the most outspoken supporters of Fair Elections. To qualify for public funds, she gathered 4,000 contributions of $5 each from Arizona residents. She sought and won Arizona's governorship twice using a Fair Elections–style public finance system. Voters like public funding because it makes elected officials more accountable, reduces conflicts of interest and gives them more choice at the polls.

Roger Fulton, member of Washington Public Campaigns, stands with the Backbone Campaign's backbone puppet in front of Washington's state government building in Olympia rallying for clean elections.

Our problem with campaign finance is not so much the amount we spend, as it is who provides the money, what those donors get in return and how that distorts public policy and spending priorities. Keeping our elected officials dependent on the same wealthy, special interests they are supposed to regulate undermines public confidence in government and its ability to tackle the tough issues that face the nation. It's time to get our leaders out of the fundraising game and let them do the jobs we've elected them to do. Fair Elections is one possible solution. If your Representative supports Fair Elections, please thank him or her; if your Representative has not yet signed on, please ask him or her to do so.

. . . . .

Bob Edgar is the president and CEO of Common Cause (www.commoncause.org). Edgar arrived at Common Cause with a long history of leadership and public service that included 12 years in Congress. There, he led efforts to improve public transportation, fought wasteful water projects and authored the community Right to Know provision of Super Fund legislation. He also served on the House Select Committee on Assassinations that investigated the deaths of Dr. Martin Luther King Jr. and President John F. Kennedy. Edgar was the general secretary of the National Council of the Churches of Christ in the US for seven years immediately before arriving at Common Cause.

Common Cause is a national nonpartisan, non-profit citizens' lobby working to make government at all levels more honest, open and accountable, and to connect citizens with their democracy.

25

Citizens **Strengthening** Democracy

Democracy is fluid and dynamic, and its roots are deepened through the active participation of its citizens; not just when it comes time to vote, but all the time. Revitalizing democracy in America is not just a possibility—it's already happening. Innovative approaches to civic participation are making sure that citizens have a greater voice in public decisions across the United States and around the world.

Increased participation in democracy is a critical solution to the disconnectedness that many Americans feel from their officials and institutions of national government. Only 19 percent of Americans now expect Washington to "do what is right" most of the time.[1] Only 38 percent believe that government generally "cares what people like me think."[2] Americans are dismayed by the heightened partisanship that so often seems to get in the way of effective governance. They want their elected officials fighting against our greatest challenges, not each other.

Carolyn J. Lukensmeyer
America*Speaks*

Policy-makers, for their part, find it increasingly difficult to govern. They describe a political process defined by shallow media coverage, narrow-minded lobbying and turn to special interest campaigns and polls as a poor substitute for input from their constituents.

But, there is also very good reason— with proven means—to believe that civic engagement can be renewed. City budgets, disaster recovery plans, public policies and regional land-use plans have all been transformed by tapping the public's wisdom for better decision-making.

> "So many different folk came together and shared their voice. We felt someone was actually listening. That is really what is important, not just having a voice, but having your voice heard."
>
> ⊰ Participant of an America*Speaks* meeting

Connecting citizens and decision-makers throughout the policy-making process helps ensure these and other public decisions are made for the common good.

By convening the public at an appropriate scale and within the context of an actual decision-making process, it is possible to link policy-making, free of corrupting influences, with the will of the people. We know that citizens are eager to participate in public life and do have the ability to make informed judgments on complex policy issues, if they believe the government will listen.

Participative Democracy in Action

Even the most complex policy conversations, such as healthcare reform or disaster recovery, benefit from the guidance of thoughtful, informed input from a representative group of citizens. In fact, public participation can develop new solutions, increase public understanding of the issue and generate broad support for implementation.

Citizens Plan New Orleans' Recovery

Four thousand New Orleanians helped shape the city's recovery plan after Hurricane Katrina. New Orleans residents who had returned home, and those displaced

to 20 other locations around the nation, participated in simultaneous, interactive, video-connected meetings. Participants represented the city's pre-Katrina demographics by income, age, race and geography: 64 percent of participants of the Community Congress were African American, and 25 percent had annual household incomes below $20,000.

Participants successfully grappled with issues of flood protection, investments in education, land use and more. The Unified New Orleans Plan incorporated these public priorities, and at the end of the deliberations, 92 percent of participants agreed that the plan should go forward. The Unified New Orleans Plan was the first to get approval by all levels of local and state government, releasing over $200 million in much needed recovery funds.

A County Renews Its Future

Civic leaders in Owensboro-Daviess County, Kentucky, engaged citizens in developing—and implementing— solutions for the toughest questions facing their community.

A demographically representative group of 650 residents participated in a day-long meeting to discuss

Current and displaced residents of New Orleans met simultaneously in 21 locations to develop a unified plan for rebuilding the Hurricane Katrina ravaged city.

Demographically representative participants discuss key issues at small, facilitated discussion tables.

The community-led work groups continue to meet monthly, more than two years after the kick-off meeting, to work toward the community's vision. For example, the Region of Opportunity Action Group partnered with the city and county government to prepare a master plan for downtown, with unprecedented levels of public participation. The Healthy and Caring Community Action Group is expanding proven techniques to reduce substance abuse and coordinated a two-month volunteer program to help low-income families sign up for low-cost health insurance.

their community's pressing issues in economy, government, the environment, healthcare and education. The mayor, the county judge, all city commissioners, a state senator and two state representatives attended the We the People 21st Century Town Meeting and deliberated with citizens.

Action items were prioritized by participants, leading to public responses from elected and community leaders. Within weeks of the meeting, workgroups met to take action on these priorities, in which more than 300 area residents participated. More than 1,000 residents stayed informed about the process through regular communications and updates.

Healthcare Reform

Thousands of Californians came together at a daylong non-partisan conversation on healthcare reform to weigh in on critical policy options being considered by state leaders. Participants from every walk of life joined simultaneous conversations in eight locations across the state, all linked together by satellite. State lawmakers, including Governor Schwarzenegger, joined participants at the meeting.

Involving hundreds, or thousands, of people in a public meeting enables the outcomes to have greater visibility and credibility with policy-makers, the media, and the public as a whole.

As a result of the meeting, healthcare reform moved closer to the shared priorities of these citizen participants on three-quarters of issues in debate and strengthened the ultimate outcomes. For example, the two cost containment approaches that were most important to participants (prevention and wellness, with 62 percent support, and, streamlining administrative procedures, with 51 percent support) correlated with a stronger focus in these areas in the final compromise bill than was present in previous proposals. A cap on insurer profits was supported by 58 percent of participants, which had originally only been in the governor's proposal but was then embraced by other legislative leadership in the compromise bill.

Participants had more positive attitudes about state government, a greater belief in their own ability to be heard and make a difference and were significantly more likely to take political action on healthcare compared to those who did not attend. Policy-makers hailed California*Speaks* for bringing in fresh public perspectives and generating a sense of urgency for bipartisan change.

Participatory Budgeting

Municipal budget spending priorities are being determined with the input of residents in a process called participatory budgeting. Now used in cities around the world, a pioneering example of participatory budgeting was developed in Porto Alegre, Brazil. Since 1989, Porto Alegre has held neighborhood, regional and citywide assemblies where residents suggest, deliberate and decide on spending priorities. The resulting budget is binding, although the council can suggest changes and the mayor can veto the budget (although there is no record yet of this happening).

Importantly, participants are from diverse economic and political backgrounds, to ensure city spending helps address a severe inequality in living standards between the one-third of residents who live in slums and other residents with better access to public amenities.

A World Bank study shows that participatory budgeting in Porto Alegre has led to an increase in sewer and water connections, from 75 to 98 percent of households.

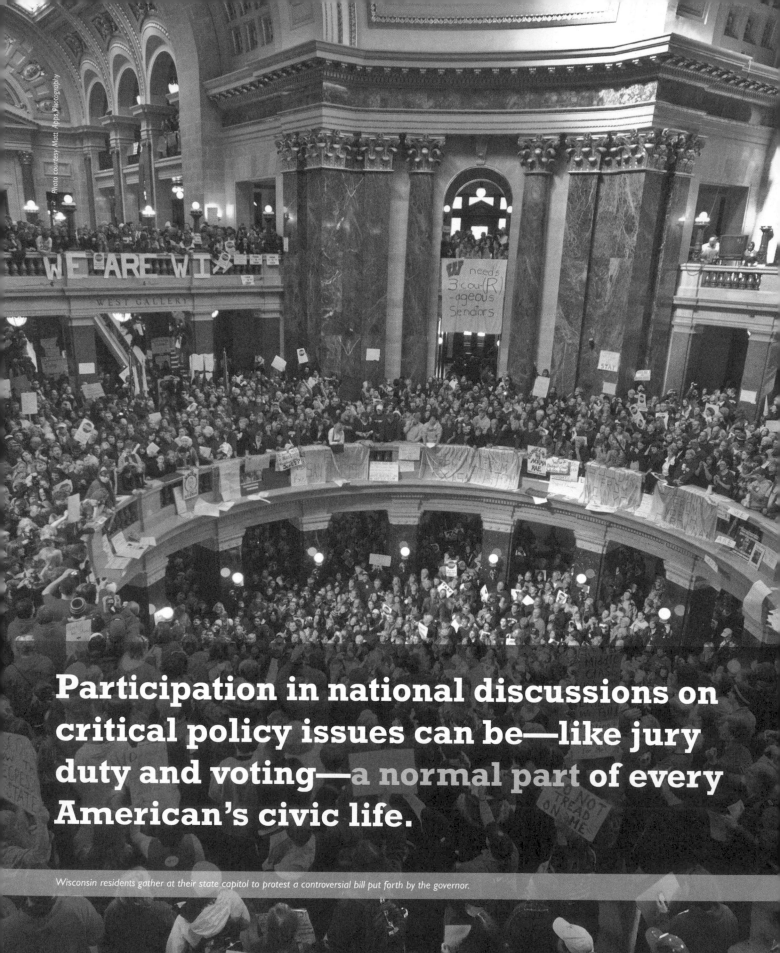

Participation in national discussions on critical policy issues can be—like jury duty and voting—a normal part of every American's civic life.

Wisconsin residents gather at their state capitol to protest a controversial bill put forth by the governor.

We now have an opportunity to transform the business of government so that citizens and residents are at the table.

The number of schools quadrupled, and the health and education budget increased from 13 percent to almost 40 percent.[3]

Successes in both large- and small-scale public participation projects, achieved over the past few decades, provide a road map for building a democracy in which citizens from every walk of life regularly meet and wrestle with tough policy questions, and then articulate their views to decision-makers.

This should not be a distant dream. Participation in national discussions on critical policy issues can be—like jury duty and voting—a normal part of every American's civic life. Our Founders created a system of governance that was brilliant in its simplicity—those who are governed must participate and give their consent. It is time to recapture that vision so American democracy can fulfill its aspirations.

Opening Our Government

On his first full day in office, President Barack Obama issued a Memorandum on Transparency and Open Government that calls for a new system of transparency, participation and collaboration. Later that year, the Obama administration issued an Open Government Directive to all federal agencies that specifies the steps they must take to become more open. President Obama has taken a first step to bring the American people closer into the public decision-making that most affects our lives.

We now have an opportunity to transform the business of government so that citizens and residents are at the table—collaborating on framing key policy issues, working through tough decisions and creating the future we want for our communities and our country. People are interested, they are capable and have growing expectations that government is listening.

If we will transform government in a way that is not episodic, that really changes the system at all levels, then it is imperative that all levels of government make an institutional commitment to greater citizen participation. A successful commitment to public participation in government requires a mandate in all levels of government, allocating sufficient funds, training and supporting staff, as well as a culture of experimentation that encourages innovation.

Citizens, too, carry deep responsibility for renewing our democratic system. Greater participation will require an increased public capacity to collaborate across difference, make commitments to action, stay informed and hold decision-makers accountable.

Reforms like these will ensure a more inclusive political process, which in turn will generate better policies, develop the public knowledge and will to carry them out, and lead not only to a more just and strong society, but to an upward cycle of economic, social and political progress.

.....

Dr. Carolyn J. Lukensmeyer is an innovator in deliberative democracy, public administration and organizational development. She is Founder and President of AmericaSpeaks (www.americaspeaks.org), a US-based non-profit that develops and implements innovative deliberative tools. AmericaSpeaks provides citizens a greater voice in local, regional and national decision-making on the most challenging public issues of the day. Over 150,000 people have participated in AmericaSpeaks' meetings where participants wrestle with complex issues, uncover shared priorities and offer recommendations to shape next steps. Lukensmeyer was Consultant (1993-1994) to the White House Chief of Staff and Chief of Staff (1986-1991) to Governor Celeste of Ohio. Lukensmeyer is author of numerous publications, including Public Deliberation: A Manager's Guide to Citizen Deliberation, Institutionalizing Large-Scale Engagements in Governance: A Link Between Theory *and* Practice *and* Beyond e-Government and e-Democracy: A Global Perspective *(2008).*

Innovation in Government

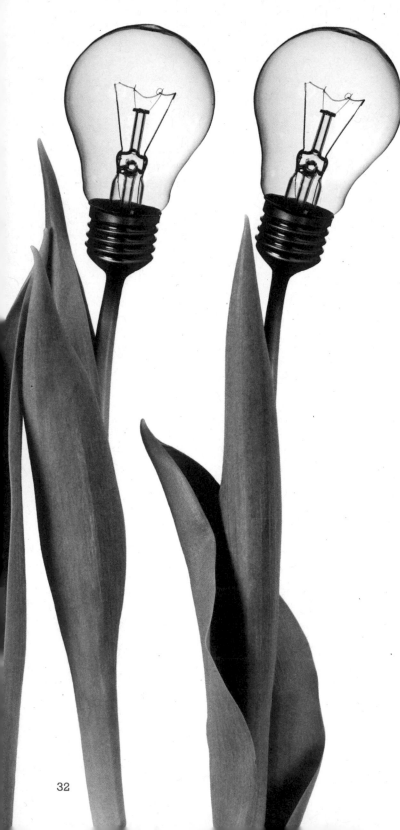

Karen Thoreson,
Alliance for Innovation and
James Svara,
Center for Urban Innovation,
Arizona State University

To many people, the idea of "government innovation" may qualify as an oxymoron. Governments are often viewed as plodding institutions that keep doing what they have always done and are unresponsive to ideas for change. In actuality, local governments can be seedbeds for new approaches. To be sure, more local governments could come up with new ideas and be more receptive to adopting new approaches developed in other settings, but many have a solid record of innovation.

Local governments may be more prone to innovation because they are different than their state and federal counterparts. They are closer to the people served and have a much greater potential for citizen engagement. Typically they are much less gripped by partisan conflict, and they are more likely to give professionals a chance to analyze problems and look for solutions.

Examples of Local Innovation

At the Alliance for Innovation, each year we see hundreds of examples of how cities and counties are remaking their communities for the better. The examples below are just a taste of what is happening across America.

Photo courtesy Troy Dilport

> **Local governments are closer to the people served and have a much greater potential for citizen engagement.**

Puget Sound, WA

In early 2000, the eCityGov Alliance was formed by a group of city managers who sensed the opportunity and the demand from citizens for online services. None of the communities had adequate budgets to develop robust websites. Working together, they pursued cross-boundary Internet service portals to access permits, parks and recreation activities, maps and property information. In 2009, the partnership added portals for shared procurement, government jobs and human services. From the original nine partner cities, the Alliance is now serving 39 organizations—34 cities, one county, a fire district, two economic development councils and an airport—with a combined population of 1.3 million citizens across a four-county region.[1]

Greensburg, KS

After a devastating tornado destroyed the entire town on May 4, 2007, the citizens, in partnership with their local government, decided to rebuild with sustainability principles governing all their actions. Three years later, the town has changed dramatically, with over 100 new homes, all of which are 40 percent more efficient than code, and many are aiming for LEED certification from the US Green Building Council. A wind farm with ten turbines produces enough power for over 4,000 households, making the town carbon neutral. Before the tornado, the town had little industry or economy to support the new generation. Now Greensburg is making its mark as one of the greenest towns in the nation.[2]

Washington, DC

In 2008, the DC Office of Technology hosted a contest to find new ways to the make the City's Data Catalog more useful for citizens. The Data Catalog, which contains open public data such as crime feeds, school test scores and poverty indicators, is considered the most comprehensive of its kind in the world. The contest resulted in the city having 47 different applications of iPhone, Facebook and other web applications that citizens could download or install. The cost of the competition was $50,000, but the value of the new applications is estimated to be in excess of $2,600,000.[3] Although Washington, DC discontinued future contests, the concept has been copied by other cities to advertise their transparency efforts and collaborate with citizens to address local issues.[4]

Photo courtesy: One Block Off the Grid, 1bog.org

San Francisco, CA

Embracing the notion of sustainable power, San Francisco has issued local municipal bonds to allow local homeowners to purchase rooftop solar systems. The city's incentives, combined with state and federal subsidies, pay up to half the cost or more of a residential solar system, providing many San Franciscans the initiative to go solar.[5] The city of San Francisco allocated $9.5 million to fund the first year of the solar program, which launched in 2008. Since then, over 1,100 applications have been received, resulting in over 3.8 megawatts of solar power installed or soon to be installed.[6]

2000 CALORIES A DAY
IS ALL MOST ADULTS SHOULD EAT

470 CALORIES

Photo courtesy: New York City Health Department

Giant apple raisin muffin

LOOK FOR THE NEW NYC
READ 'EM BEFORE YOU EAT 'EM!
CALORIE POSTINGS!

Healthy snack? Maybe not.

NYC Department of Health & Mental Hygiene

Michael R. Bloomberg
Thomas R. Frieden, M.D., M.P.H.

New York City, NY

Initiated by the office of Mayor Bloomberg, New York City has implemented some of the most cutting-edge health policies for food service establishments. Passed in 2006, the trans fat regulation prohibits restaurants from serving food with more than 0.5 grams of trans fat per serving.[7] To further support the goal of reducing obesity, heart disease, diabetes and other related diseases, the New York City Board of Health began requiring restaurants to list the calorie count for menu items.[8] In early 2010, the Bloomberg administration initiated a campaign to cut salt to reduce the incidence of high blood pressure, strokes, heart attacks and other related problems. The goal is to get Americans to reduce their salt intake by 25 percent over the next five years.[9]

Chicago, IL

Based on evidence that children from all communities can achieve at the highest levels with strong school leadership, the Chicago Public Schools developed New Leaders for New Schools, a program to recruit and train highly effective principals. Launched in 2000, the program recruits individuals from both academic and corporate sectors. Then a rigorous training program provides the tools and guidance needed to lead underserved and underperforming urban schools. Preliminary findings indicate that students in elementary and middle schools led by New Leaders principals for at least three years are academically outpacing their peers by statistically significant margins. New Leaders principals were twice as likely as other principals to oversee 20-plus point gains in student proficiency scores. And high schools led by New Leaders show higher graduation rates.[10]

Photo courtesy: New Leaders for New Schools

There are four shared elements that help spur innovation: aligning needs or opportunities with solutions, leadership, collaboration and partnership, and citizen engagement.

How to Expand Innovation?

These examples are the tip of the iceberg. Innovation is expressed in many different ways, but there are four shared elements that help spur innovation: aligning needs or opportunities with solutions, leadership; collaboration and partnership, and citizen engagement.

Taken alone, these elements that encourage innovation cannot promise success of a new venture. However, together they represent a willingness to solve tough problems, take advantage of new opportunities, get more people on board and produce new and amazing results.

. . . . .

Karen Thoreson is the president/chief operating officer for the Alliance for Innovation (www.transformgov.org). Prior to working for the alliance, she worked in local government in Glendale and Tucson, Arizona, and Boulder, Colorado. Thoreson also is a trainer and a speaker on public-private partnerships, community revitalization, innovation and strategic planning.

James Svara is professor of public affairs at Arizona State University and director of the Center for Urban Innovation (http://urbaninnovation.asu.edu). He is a member of the board of the Alliance for Innovation. Recent studies have focused on mayoral leadership in council-manager cities and referenda on form of government in large cities.

Bridging the Political Divide

Bradford Kane
The Bipartisan Bridge

Bipartisanship is necessary for our government to respond promptly and effectively to social and economic problems. It enables government to craft and implement a vision for long-term national success and is vital for strengthening our democracy.

Unfortunately, however, partisanship has become virulent in American politics. It gridlocks government and sets a tone of intransigence that aggravates cultural fragmentation and disenfranchises the electorate.

Whereas elections are designed to be combative, there is no need—or justification—for continuing that tenor once an election has determined the composition of our government. That is the time for bipartisanship, to enact sound policies, respect our elected leaders, re-assert our nation's moral high ground and reassert our global leadership. We do not need to abandon our party affiliations or principles. Instead, we just need to commit to collaborate for effective government and relegate combative partisanship to the few months preceding the next general election.

There are many instances of bipartisanship in Washington. Although most attention is drawn to contentious issues that showcase partisan actions, many other issues are addressed by lawmakers of both parties working together. Though challenging, bipartisanship can be advanced through steps that facilitate collaboration between officials with diverse political views and philosophies.

What Is Bipartisanship?

Although there are no official benchmarks, basically, bipartisanship is the willingness of officials to communicate, collaborate, compromise and act across party lines in good faith for "win-win" policies and decisions, on the merits, on a sustained basis. Bipartisanship does not mean equality, and does not dictate relinquishment of power to achieve collaboration for its own sake. It should not confine progress to positions with near-unanimous support, as a "lowest common denominator" among all officials. It does not mean that the President or a majority in Congress should capitulate to ultimatums from legislators that would forestall progress on their principal initiatives.

In Congress, bipartisanship has taken many forms, from specific actions to ongoing processes including:

• Joint Sponsorship of Bills: Legislation often has both Democratic and Republican sponsors, as well as many cosponsors from both parties. Past examples include the Kennedy-Kassebaum Health Insurance Portability and Accountability Act (HIPAA), the McCain-Feingold Bipartisan Campaign Reform Act and the Sarbanes-Oxley Public Company Accounting Reform and Investor Protection Act. Recently, food safety legislation was jointly developed by Senators Harkin, Enzi, Durbin, Gregg, Dodd and Burr; child nutrition legislation was jointly developed by Representatives Miller (CA), Platts and McCarthy (NY); a tax fairness and simplification bill was drafted by Senators Wyden and Gregg; and other bills on technology and innovation, oil spill prevention and transportation issues also have bipartisan sponsors and cosponsors.

WHAT BIPARTISANSHIP IS:

✔ The willingness of officials to **communicate, collaborate, compromise and act in good faith** on policies and decisions across party lines, on the merits, on a sustained basis.

✔ Transcending the traditional dialectic between the parties by deliberating as **long-term vested partners** on creative, diverse options.

WHAT IT'S NOT:

✗ **Relinquishing power** to achieve collaboration for its own sake.

✗ **Confining progress** to positions with near-unanimous support, as a "lowest common denominator" among all officials.

✗ Capitulation of the President or a majority in Congress to ultimatums from legislators that would **forestall progress** on their initiatives.

President Obama speaks with a bipartisan group of Congressional leaders in February of 2010.

During his campaign, President Obama expressed bipartisanship as an overarching tone based on mutual respect, receptivity to diverse opinions, openness to innovative yet practical solutions, debate that enhances understanding and decision-making based on facts rather than ideology.

Despite hurdles, he has crossed party lines and transcended partisan boundaries on many issues. For example, consensus building and compromise was evident in the president's deliberations over increasing the US troop presence in the Afghanistan War, his plan to increase teacher accountability in his education reform proposal, and the tax-cut extensions of December 2011, all of which appealed to Republicans. For the financial reform law of 2010, the President agreed to compromises that accommodated the views of both Republicans and Democrats. Even his healthcare reform proposals were initiated with a bipartisan approach, as President Obama convened bipartisan "summits," met with Republican lawmakers to hear their views and continued to adjust his proposals during the legislative process to accommodate Republicans. Since a hand that is extended must be reciprocated if bipartisanship is to be achieved, the assessment of health reform's bipartisan nature should focus on the President's efforts and the compromises inherent in his proposals, rather than the final vote.

• Coalitions: Occasionally, bipartisan groups form to address ongoing concerns. One case was the heralded Gang of 14, seven Republican and seven Democratic senators who collaborated to resolve differences on judicial appointments.

• Working Groups: Some issues are negotiated by small groups of legislators and can include packaging of provisions that appeal to legislators with diverse priorities. A high-profile example occurred during 2009 when a subgroup of senators from the Finance Committee (three Republicans and three Democrats) tried to resolve issues on healthcare reform. Although it was ultimately ill-fated, it did reach some points of agreement and refine the legislation for committee consideration. More recently, a "Gang of 6" senators, three Democratic and three Republican, began meeting in March 2011 to develop solutions to our nation's debt and deficit crises.

• Votes: In its most basic form, bipartisanship is exhibited by votes across party lines. Recently, Senators Snowe, Collins and Brown and the House Blue Dog Democrats have voted across party lines on prominent legislation, and many bills such as the Serve America Act receive broad bipartisan support.

Advancing Bipartisan/ Post-Partisan Collaboration

There is no definitive methodology to promote bipartisanship/post-partisanship, since it is a good faith process rather than a singular product or outcome. Although there is some bipartisanship even in today's charged political atmosphere, more must be done. The following ideas could further stimulate a bipartisan/post-partisan spirit and materialize into constructive outcomes:

• Discussion and Relationships: Congress should establish informal working groups for legislators with different philosophies to meet weekly to discuss and collaborate on issues of the day. The groups would convene senators and representatives who don't already spend time with each other and might not otherwise have reason to do so, to foster cross-party relationships and increase understanding of each other's positions. Discussions should seek diversity of opinions, honest critiques of one's own positions, innovative solutions that transcend entrenched party positions and consensus on specific issues that are delegated to them by the leadership.

• **District Tours:** To foster understanding of the conditions, concerns and needs of each other's districts that impact decision-making, legislators from opposite parties should pair up for reciprocal tours of each other's districts. By proverbially "walking a mile in each others' shoes," they could better appreciate the concerns that their colleagues address.

• **Objective Analyses:** To promote transparency and accountability, each bill[1] that comes to the House or Senate floor for a vote should be accompanied by an analysis from a non-partisan, objective office, e.g., Congressional Research Service. The analyses would include the qualitative impacts on various demographic groups (i.e., by income, geographic region and other factors where relevant, such as age, race/ethnicity, gender). Analyses should state the bills' fiscal impact and evaluate its short-term and long-term effects to encourage focus on long-term policy, which tends to deflate hot-button political issues.

• **Lobbying Reform:** Lobbyists should not be allowed to deliver a check one day and deliver views on legislation the next day. This nexus of money and policy, or campaign fundraising and legislation, is where many

For many years, Democratic Senator Ted Kenedy and Republican Senator Orrin Hatch were close friends, despite representing opposing parties. Their relationship can serve as a model to partisans into the future: that despite differing opinions and ideologies, it is possible to meet somewhere in the middle and forge lifelong friendships.

Photo courtesy Doug Mills/The New York Times/Redux

Jon Stewart and Steven Colbert's Rally to Restore Sanity and/or Fear brought together hundreds of thousands of people at the National Mall in Washington D.C. Its intent was to encourage and promote reasoned discussion in our country.

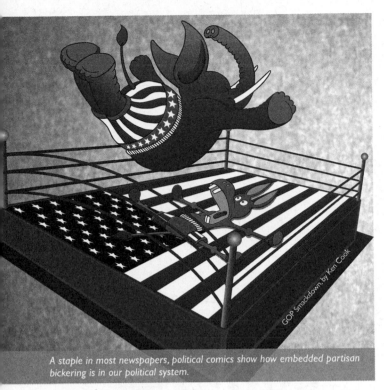

A staple in most newspapers, political comics show how embedded partisan bickering is in our political system.

GOP Smackdown, by Ken Cook

• **Win-Win Accommodation:** At the start of each Congress, lawmakers could be asked to take a seminar on mediation and dispute resolution, for use in resolving legislative disputes. The seminars can set a tone of cooperation and collaboration. Topics would include "benevolent negotiations" to build trusted, reliable, long-term partnerships for sustained bipartisanship. Through "benevolent negotiations," legislators would be encouraged to make good faith offers that address each others' main needs, rather than staking out hard-line positions and then nickel-and-diming each other toward a middle-ground settlement. It advances a climate of respect, trust and accommodation, like mediation without a mediator, nurturing long-term relationships while hurdling an impasse.

Bipartisanship Is Pragmatic and Is Rewarded by Voters

Some partisans may assail bipartisanship as being impossible, impractical or simply naive. Yet, such assertions are usually made out of a lack of effort, creativity or willingness to abandon cynical and malevolent perceptions of political advantage. Bipartisan/post-partisan action is distinct from naive notions of harmony because it enables pragmatic progress.

As polls about Congress indicate, those who step up and lead the healing process are the ones more likely to be rewarded by the electorate. To those who are bold enough to collaborate across traditional barriers to govern effectively and achieve results, the aura of leadership will be bestowed. Voters hunger for leaders who recognize that, despite their differences, all lawmakers can, should and must work together toward mutually agreeable policies that benefit the American people.

• • • • •

abuses occur, both subtly and overtly. The efforts to ban veiled earmarks responded to this but did not go far enough. Although lobbyists who provide campaign donations should be prohibited from directly discussing legislative matters with members, they are still entitled to communicate their views. To provide an appropriate channel, Congress should create a system of Congressional Interest Group Offices (CIGOs) that lobbyists could contact to offer their input. CIGOs would produce briefing materials on issues coming to a vote in committee or on the floor, and on other issues requested by a legislator. Members would receive objective information that includes the views of lobbyists and others, and a critique of them, without the foul play or undue influence of lobbyists who argue for their clients irrespective of the public interest. CIGOs would be non-partisan, with staff that is hired for objective analytical abilities and expertise, rather than political ties.

Bradford Kane created and leads The Bipartisan Bridge (www.bipartisanbridge.org), which advances bipartisanship and post-partisanship for effective government through ideas and solutions on which Americans with diverse political philosophies can collaborate. Kane served as legislative counsel to a member, counsel to a House subcommittee and both deputy controller and a deputy secretary in the state of California government. Kane also was the CEO of a non-profit that provides job skills training via e-learning, was a member of a nationwide task force on media issues and worked for organizations that advance effective use of technology solutions.

Citizen Stewardship

A look at the numbers...

8, 000, 000, 000 hours volunteered in 2009

by nearly **20%** of Americans.

8 billion

Number of hours that more than 63 million people (nearly 20% of Americans) volunteered in 2009.

$300 billion

Amount US citizens donated to charitable organizations in 2010 (about 2% of GDP)

If everyone in the world lived like Americans, **we would need 5 planets** to produce what we consume and absorb our waste.

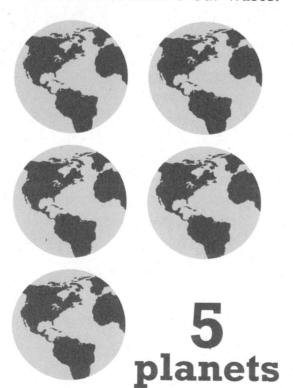

5 planets

Each year,
5.8 million tons of envelopes eventually end up as
450 thousand garbage trucks worth of waste.

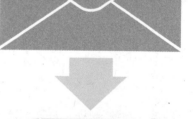
5.8 million tons

450,000 trucks

100 million

Number of trees that could be saved by eliminating all junk mail.

Millions of people and thousands of companies have opted out of junk mail through **donotmail.org and catalogchoice.org.**

US consumers buy more than **half a billion gallons of bottled water** every week, enough bottles to circle the globe 5 times.

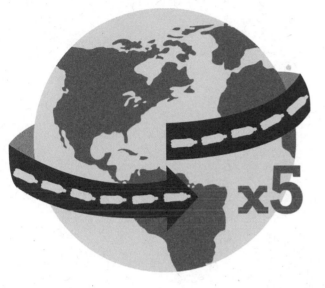

x5

17 million

Number of barrels of oil (used in manufacturing plastic water bottles) that would be saved by kicking the bottled water habit

100,000 cars

could run for a year on the oil saved.

20 tons

CO_2 emissions:

The average North American generates about **20 tons of CO_2 emissions** per year.

The world average is just under **4 tons**.

4 tons

1,100 lbs

Amount of CO_2 emissions that could be prevented by turning the thermostat down 3°F in the winter and up 3°F in the summer.

2,500 lbs

Amount of CO_2 emissions eliminated by getting rid of your second refrigerator.

1,040 lbs

Amount of CO_2 emissions that could be saved per year by using public transporation one day a week instead of driving.

"The most important office... that of private citizen."

> ➢ Supreme Court Justice Louis D. Brandeis

Justice Brandeis knew firsthand the potential that lies within each of us when we are inspired to act on behalf of the public good. He knew it from personal experience that helped to break up corporate monopolies, enact workplace safety and ensure freedom of speech.

Today, there are no shortages of problems that need fixing. Making progress toward solving the most pressing issues of our time requires us all to be stewards of each other and our planet.

Stewardship takes many forms. From implementing everyday actions that reduce one's footprint and organizing for veterans, to young people raising money to build wells and retirees revitalizing their community, the power of engaged citizens is immense.

Citizen stewardship is strong and needs to continue growing.

Paul Rieckhoff created the Iraq and Afghanistan Veterans of America (IAVA), which helps veterans become leaders, advocates for better care and increases awareness about the causes and consequences of war. By 2015, IAVA expects to have 175,000 veteran members and an additional 400,000 supporters.

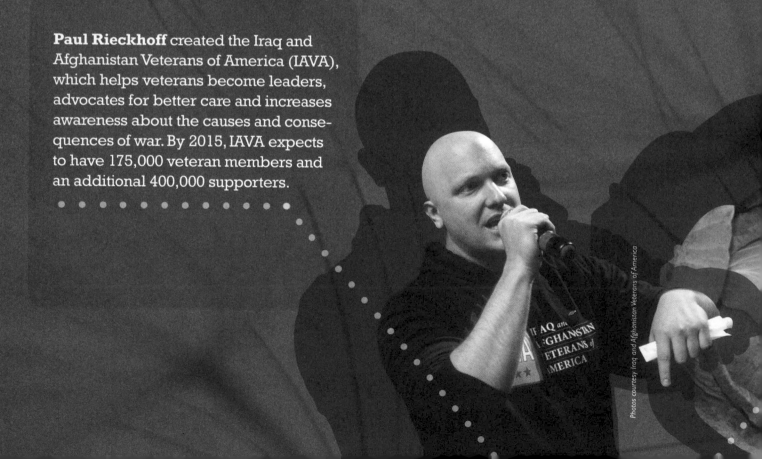

Photos courtesy Iraq and Afghanistan Veterans of America

Katie Stagliano rallied hundreds of people in her South Carolina town to create vegetable gardens that feed the hungry.

Ryan Hreljac started in first grade and raised $70 to help address clean water issues. Ten years later he created a network that built 630 water projects in 16 countries, bringing safe water and sanitation services to 700,880 people.

Unified
in Stewardship

Jerry M. Linenger
Former NASA Astronaut

Perched in space for five months aboard a Russian space station, I saw planet Earth in all its majesty.

White clouds swirling above the churning ocean currents. Brown, green and sometimes reddish continents poking their heads out of the predominance of blue. Fault lines cracking and moving the land masses. Wind storms denuding the topsoil of drought-stricken Sub-Saharan Africa and depositing that same soil on the leeward side of the Andes. Africa's loss, South America's gain. A thousand points of light shining through the deep green jungles of Brazil as the trees are burned to make way for more farms. Alive, dynamic, burning, swirling, spewing planet Earth.

I have heard other astronauts talk about the delicacy of the Earth and its many inhabitants. Indeed, when viewing the delimiter at Earth sunrise or sunset, the band of atmosphere is narrow, thin, seemingly clutching to the curvature of the Earth. I have heard them talk about the lack of political borders. One land, one Earth, all shared. True also. But my overwhelming impression after closely observing Earth for over 150 days was that the Earth is alive. Alive, breathing and buffering. A remarkably regenerative miracle, the Earth is ever-so dynamic. Ever changing, always adapting and renewing itself. The Earth is incredible, an extremely complex, closed ecosystem that for millions of years has supported life. A system so intrinsically intertwined, so time-tested and fine-tuned, that it is beyond our comprehension.

The over-consumption and individual insults to our planet do add up, and the consequences are beginning to show themselves at an alarming rate.

A space station essentially tries to mimic the processes of the Earth. We try to create a closed ecosystem that will support life. To be frank, we are not very good at it, and the only way that we can accomplish the task, even for short periods of time, is to cheat. That is, we supplement the life-support systems onboard by bringing along supplies taken from the planet. We are more like a modern-day camper than a forager of old who truly lived off of the land. To date, we have only been able to keep a few people alive in space at a time, and only at great cost and by bringing most of the gear and supplies with us.

Given the challenges associated with maintaining life without the benefit of the Earth's many life-supporting systems, we need to recognize the Earth as a miracle—a blessing to us. We must also shift our perspective and begin to see the Earth as a whole.

Forget the "kumbaya" feeling of looking down at an Earth with no borders between nations. Forget the chants of "can't we all just love one another?" But think if all of us on Earth could move toward a common perspective for one common problem that concerns us all. This common goal, in all of our interests, can perhaps move us beyond our differences, shift our perspective and make us realize that we are all in this closed ecosystem together. Can we be united in at least this one reality? Can we strive to keep Earth healthy and to expand our territorial boundary to the curved edge of the Earth? If not for us, then we must at least try for our children and our children's children.

For the record, I am not a fan of the "one world, one government" philosophy. A lot of our problems are local and need to be solved locally. Being cut off from mankind for five months taught me that one of the true blessings of the Earth is the diversity of our people and of our cultures. But after living in a closed ecosystem with two other people, all the while struggling to keep life-support systems functioning, I realized quickly that if we had one weak link in the chain, we would all suffer the consequences. One of the three of us not doing our job, one of us pushing the wrong button at the wrong time, one of us not "knowing our stuff" and improperly maintaining or repairing an oxygen generating system in a timely matter, and we all die. This underscored the importance of being there for each other as well.

In a closed ecosystem, with three on board, it is very easy to tell if you are the weak link in the chain. On our big, incredibly complex and self-correcting planet, populated with billions of people who for the most part are just trying to scratch out an existence, the effect of our individual actions are much more difficult to ascertain. But the consequences of our actions do exist. The over-consumption and individual insults to our planet do add up. And the consequences are beginning to show themselves at an alarming rate.

Indonesia is the most biodiverse region in the world, and unfortunately also has the highest rate of deforestation in the world, mainly due to our high demand for paper products and palm oil.

49

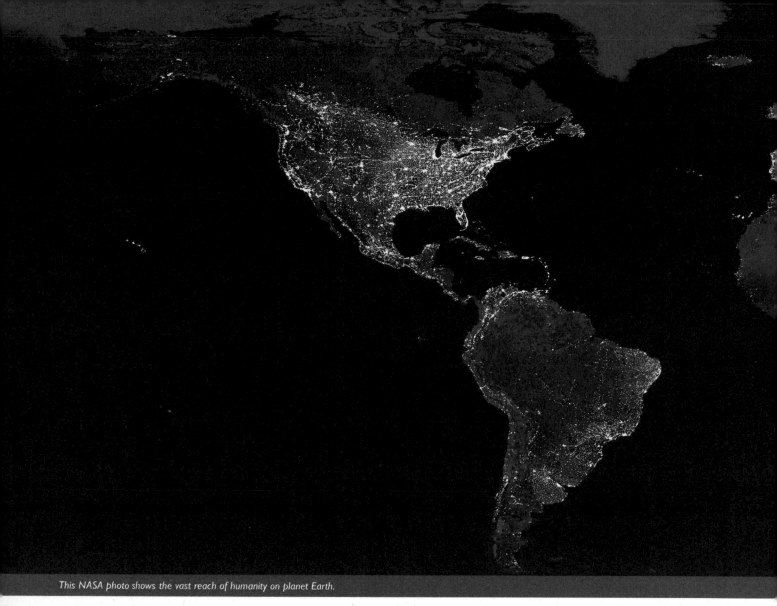

This NASA photo shows the vast reach of humanity on planet Earth.

It sure is easy to point fingers. But none of us should feel smug. We are the corporations, we are the governments, we are the citizens of our countries. We are the people of the Earth and taking action to conserve and live lighter on the planet can save forests, reduce climate impacts, prevent pollution, sustain communities, and preserve this planet's amazing diversity of life. Our voices and actions help to shape innovative government policies and business practices, and create a groundswell that will eventually permeate all of our institutions. Whether it's recycling or buying organic and local, helping to build a health clinic, getting rid of the second refrigerator and replacing light bulbs, driv-

ing less or not driving at all, eating less meat, serving those in need or being the environmental champion in a company or government position, or the myriad other options, every small or large step is meaningful. We as individuals can all be citizen-stewards.

And though the awareness and efforts to bring about these necessary changes are spreading, the pace of that unifying change is important as well. As individuals and as citizens of the nations of the world, we must quickly realize the balance needed on our planet before our efforts are too late. The pace of innovation needs to be laps ahead of the rate of degradation and extinction.

Taking action to conserve and live lighter on the planet can save forests, reduce climate impacts, prevent pollution & preserve this planet's amazing diversity of life.

Photo courtesy NASA

I can tell you plainly that our Earth and the diversity of life and cultures within it are special. If we shift our perspective and broaden our territorial boundary to encompass the planet as a whole, individually, we will do the right thing. We must let common sense be our guide, treating our closed Earth ecosystem with the same care that we would if we were an astronaut aboard a space station, a space station that we can only marvel at, that has functioned for millions of years and that we will never be able to replicate. The environment should not be a battleground between different political factions, nor should it be the cause of intergovernmental confrontation. Instead, it is a common ground that stretches across the entire political spectrum and, indeed, across all man-made boundaries. It is one issue that needs to unite us all.

.....

Dr. Jerry M. Linenger is a Naval Academy graduate holding a doctorate of medicine from Wayne State University and doctorate of philosophy from the University of North Carolina. In his mission on Mir, he logged 50 million miles in more than 2,000 orbits of Earth at 18,000 miles per hour. He was the first American to undock from the space station in Soyuz spacecraft and the first American to perform a spacewalk outside a foreign spacecraft; at the completion of the mission, he had spent more time in space than any American man.

51

Staying Within Our Limits

The last 200 years have transformed the American continent. Forests have given way to skyscrapers; fertile valleys bloomed with subdivisions and dot-com office parks; open plains have been cross-hatched with railway lines and interstates. Technology and industry have allowed us to vastly multiply the rate with which we can harvest nature's bounty. Yet, for all our 21st-century gadgetry and cyberspace-based commerce, we are still as dependent upon nature as the trappers and fisherman of our pre-industrial past—if not more so. And unfortunately, we have become so good at exploiting nature—not just as a country but as a species—that we are now reaping much more than what nature can renew.

Globally, humans use nature 50 percent faster than planet Earth can renew those resources and absorb the waste, such as CO_2.[1] This means that it takes the planet almost a year and a half to regenerate the resources humans use in one year. In the US, however, our demand on nature's services is much greater than the world average. According to Global Footprint Network's 2010 National Footprint Accounts, if everyone lived like an American, it would take almost five planets to produce what we consume and absorb our waste.

Mathis Wackernagel
Global Footprint Network

Globally, humans are now using nature 50 percent faster than planet Earth can renew those resources and absorb the waste, such as CO2.

The consequences of this overspending are dire. In the last two years, America has been wrestling with the biggest economic downturn in recent history, the result of years of living beyond our means. Yet for decades, we have also been living beyond our ecological means, and the risks of this debt dwarf those of the current financial crisis. With nature, unlike with the financial crisis, no bailout is possible.

The accounting is simple: We currently have only one planet that supports life. The surface of Earth is about 125 billion acres. But since most is ice, desert and deep ocean, only about one-quarter of it is productive (fishing grounds, forests, grazing land, crop land, etc.). With a world population of about 7 billion, this gives us roughly 5 acres per person. That's the budget.

Unfortunately, by the 1980s, human demand on resources was systematically exceeding the budget of what nature could renewably provide, a condition known as ecological overshoot. Overshoot has many manifestations: climate change is the most prominent and visible indicator that human pressure on the planet has reached a critical point. Particularly in the industrialized nations, carbon emissions from fossil fuel have become the dominant pressure exerted by humanity on nature. Yet it is certainly not the only pressure.

We are already seeing other disturbing signs of planetary overuse: peak energy, biodiversity loss, depleted fisheries, soil erosion and freshwater stress to name a few. We are facing a global supply-demand crunch of essential resources—an era that author and educator Richard Heinberg aptly calls "peak everything."[2]

In an era of multiple resource pressures, it makes little sense to argue which peak is more important. They are all part of the same phenomenon: we are simply putting more demand on nature's services than it can

handle. By addressing the common cause, we can rectify our path, rather than solving one problem at the expense of another.

To balance the books on our use of nature, we need clear metrics by which to understand and measure human pressures. The Ecological Footprint is one such tool, telling us how much nature we have, how much we use and who uses what.

What the Ecological Footprint Tells Us

Everything we consume—from a fresh tomato at the farmers' market to the plasma screen TV in the living room—originates in material that comes from nature. The Ecological Footprint tallies all the resources it takes to support a person's or population's lifestyle—the energy to power their homes, the cars they drive to work, the gifts they buy for their children's birthdays, etc.—and calculates the land and sea required to produce those resources and absorb the related waste, including CO2 emissions. The Ecological Footprint also includes each person's share of their society's infrastructure: schools, hospitals, military, highway systems and the like.

One planet and about 7 billion residents gives us roughly 5 global acres per person.

That's the budget.

It now takes the planet almost a year and six months to regenerate the resources humans use in one year.

The average person's footprint in the US is 20 global acres.*

* All data from Global Footprint Network
2010 National Footprint Accounts.

Ecological Footprint accounting enables us to compare human demand against biocapacity—what nature can supply—in the same way that financial accounting tracks expenditures against income. It allows us to look at nature's entire budget, rather than its separate components.

According to the most recent data, the average Ecological Footprint per capita was just under 7 acres per person. However, some countries' resource demands are significantly greater than average, and many are substantially smaller. In the US, the average person's Ecological Footprint is 20 global acres, the equivalent of 18 football fields.[3]

At the other end of the spectrum are countries like Haiti, Afghanistan and Malawi with Ecological Footprints of less than 1.3 global acres per capita—in most cases, too small to provide for the basic needs for food, housing and sanitation.

Resource consumption in the US breaks down as follows: How we get around—cars, airplanes, buses and trains—accounts for 24 percent of our Footprint. Housing and utilities account for 19 percent; food for 15 percent; services for 20 percent and goods for 11 percent. Our per capita share of government spending—infrastructure such as highways, bridges and dams—accounts for 11 percent.

For most activities in industrialized countries, the majority of the activity's Ecological Footprint is due to carbon emissions. In the US, the carbon Footprint (the amount of land and sea it would take to absorb all the carbon we emit) is 70 percent of our total Footprint. Worldwide, carbon accounts for half the Ecological Footprint and is its most rapidly growing component, having increased 700 percent since 1961.

Retooling Our Society for a Resource-Constrained Age

Although high-income nations tend to be clustered at the high end of the Footprint scale, nations with similar living standards—as measured by UN statistics on longevity, income, literacy rate, child mortality and other

A family and their belongings in Bhutan.

Photos courtesy Peter Menzel from his book, Material World.

In the US, the average person's Ecological Footprint is 20 global acres, the equivalent of 18 football fields.

And then there are countries like China, whose average Footprint is a little more than 5.1 global acres, close to the global budget.

In China, 5.1 global acres.*

factors—can have very different levels of resource consumption. The average resident of the European Union, for example, has a Footprint half that of the average American (although still well above what is replicable worldwide).

Why is this the case? The answer lies partially in the way our societies are structured. Consider Italy, which has a per capita Footprint of 12 acres.

Most people live in compact cities, where they can walk to work, school and shopping or use extensive bus and train systems. Public transportation is easily accessible and is often more convenient and cheaper than driving. People get much of their food from local markets and food producers and eat less packaged and frozen food.

Also, by being in more compact cities with less housing surface per person, the houses consume less energy for cooling and heating.

In the US, some of our Ecological Footprint is related to individual choices we make that affect our resource consumption. Much of our Ecological Footprint, however, is the result of infrastructure decisions made by business leaders and policy-makers, in some cases decades ago: decisions such as investing in highways rather than public transportation, and suburban growth over concentrated, urban development.

Considering the rapid escalation of overshoot and the slow rate at which human institutions, land-use patterns, infrastructure and populations change, the most

A family and their belongings in the US.

55

critical action steps must focus on decisions that affect us for many years. Human-made infrastructure—homes, roads, office structures, power plants, dams, transportation systems—may last 50 or 100 years and shape our way of living for their lifetime.

The Ecological Footprint can help leaders and policymakers understand what choices will have the farthest-reaching, most systemic positive or negative impact. As we decide where to put our money and efforts, we must ask—and press our leaders to ask—the following question: are we investing in resource opportunities that allow us to live efficiently or resource traps that force us into highly resource consumptive lifestyles?

Striving for Better

Each year, the amount of resources we demand per person increases. Meanwhile, the amount of people competing for these resources also increases. And as we continue to use up nature faster than it can renew itself, we liquidate our stocks of these resources, further tightening the budget of what is available.

Our five-planet level of resource consumption in the US is physically impossible to replicate worldwide. Yet

Here is how many planets we would need if everyone in the world consumed resources like a resident of each of these countries:

4.5 Earths

United States

3.1 Earths

United Kingdom

2.5 Earths

Germany

1.2 Earths

Argentina

> ## Our five-planet level of resource consumption in the US is **physically impossible** to replicate worldwide.

we all know there is a strong desire and urgency to live like Americans. As the world's resource debt grows, it becomes increasingly difficult to secure a higher level of resource consumption for vast segments of humanity. Therefore, we have a problem. If we continue to build our success on using ever more resources, we are preparing for our demise. At the same time, if we can push the ingenuity and revisioning needed to address our resource challenges, we can be best positioned to benefit from the future, rather than be steamrolled by it.

While the data may be shocking, there are key opportunities to reverse current trends, among them creating resource-efficient cities and infrastructure, fostering best-practice green technology and innovation and making resource limits central to decision-making at all levels of leadership. And the good news is future-proofing our economies has tremendous payback. Sustainability doesn't simply save the planet; it also ensures a long-term revenue stream for pioneer investors—those with the foresight to plan and make changes now for resource constraints in the future.

Human ingenuity has transformed the way we use nature. We must now put that talent toward another transformation: creating a society that provides prosperity and opportunity within the bounds of what the planet can provide.

• • • • •

Mathis Wackernagel, PhD, is a founder and president of Global Footprint Network (www.footprintnetwork. org), an international think-tank supporting the creation of a sustainable economy by advancing the use of the Ecological Footprint. Wackernagel has worked on sustainability issues and lectured at more than 100 universities on all continents except Antarctica. Wackernagel, along with Professor William Rees, created the "Ecological Footprint" concept, now a widely used sustainability measure. Wackernagel's awards include an honorary doctorate from the University of Berne, a 2007 Skoll Award for Social Entrepreneurship, a 2006 WWF Award for Conservation Merit and the 2005 Herman Daly Award of the US Society for Ecological Economics.

1.1 Earths

China

1 Earth

South Africa

0.4 Earths

India

What About YOUR Footprint?

Calculate your family's Footprint and make a commitment to **cut it in half.** Visit Global Footprint Network's website *www.footprintnetwork.org* to calculate now.

For steps on how you can **make the changes that matter,** see Center for a New American Dream's essay, *Key Steps For Living Lighter.* (page 58)

Living Lighter

For generations, the American way of life centered on freedom and opportunity—the American Dream. The dream was rooted in the belief that, in a peaceful and democratic society, citizens were free to pursue their goals and honest effort would result in a satisfactory degree of material comfort. The idealistic notion that in America one might reasonably aspire to a better life for oneself and one's family was a powerful symbol. It spoke not merely to personal aspirations but to our aim as a society as well.

Unfortunately, in the latter half of the 20th century, the traditional American Dream was overshadowed by a "more is better" focus that promoted not quality of life, but rather the unbridled production and consumption of stuff. While this simplified version of the dream successfully boosted our economy's material production and consumption, it has failed in more important ways. According to studies, all this material wealth didn't make us any happier than we were before the boom. Worse yet, shifting the prize from well-being to acquisition actually endangers some of the very things we cherish, such as leisure time, time spent with family and friends, along with clean air and water.

More than 90 percent of Americans agree that we are too focused on working and making money and not focused enough on family and community. Fewer than 30 percent of Americans say that having a bigger house or apartment or nicer things would make them much more satisfied with their lives, while more than half say that spending more time with family and friends and having less stress in their lives would make them much more satisfied. More than half of Americans also say they would be willing to trade a day's pay per week for an extra day off.[1]

Seán Sheehan
Center for a New American Dream

The "more is better" dream is unsustainable personally as it draws American families into a work-and-spend treadmill that depletes savings, clutters lives and decreases health due to increased stress and reduced exercise. It is unsustainable environmentally as it fuels a level of resource consumption with which the planet cannot keep up. The "more is better" dream, in fact, is denying our children their fair opportunity for comfort, security and a healthy environment.

Less Is More

Sustainable consumption is a new vision for our relationship with material resources that meets the needs of both present and future generations in ways that are economically, socially and environmentally sustainable. It's essential for a healthy global ecosystem and a just society offering all citizens the freedom, resources and personal security necessary to pursue their dreams, connect with the natural world and enjoy a high quality of life.

Students spend time out of the city at a retreat to learn about and connect with nature.

Some people jump into this new cultural vision with both feet. *Voluntary Simplicity* is an example of a social trend that emphasizes less is more. According to Duane Elgin, author of the book *Voluntary Simplicity,* the movement is defined as "living in a way that is outwardly simple and inwardly rich."[2]

Others make a conscious effort to infuse sanity into the hyper-commercialized "hot spots" of American life: holidays, weddings and moving day. These folks are pioneering alternative gift fairs, giving homemade meals and babysitting coupons rather than adding another tie to the overstuffed closet. They're refocusing the "big days" on the people and relationships that matter, rather than piling up debt and stuff for the sake of cultural expectation. They're choosing to live in more convenient, though often smaller, homes

Percentage of Americans who say...

...we're too focused on work and money and not enough on family & community: **90%**

...having a bigger house or nicer things would make them more satisfied in life: **30%**

...they would be willing to trade one day's pay per week for an extra day off: **50%**

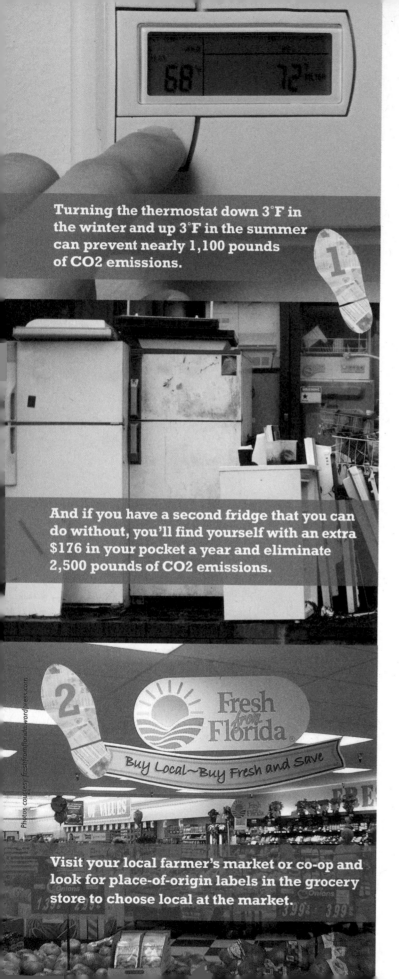

Turning the thermostat down 3°F in the winter and up 3°F in the summer can prevent nearly 1,100 pounds of CO2 emissions.

And if you have a second fridge that you can do without, you'll find yourself with an extra $176 in your pocket a year and eliminate 2,500 pounds of CO2 emissions.

Fresh *from* Florida®

Buy Local~Buy Fresh and Save

Photos courtesy freshfromflorida.wordpress.com

Visit your local farmer's market or co-op and look for place-of-origin labels in the grocery store to choose local at the market.

and apartments rather than "driving through traffic in a car that you are still paying for, in order to get to a job that you need so you can pay for the clothes, car and the house that you leave empty all day in order to afford to live in it," as columnist Ellen Goodman once put it.[3]

What We All Can Do: Steps for Living Lighter With Big Outcomes

What can we do every day to support and nurture an American Dream that upholds the spirit of the traditional dream—but with a new emphasis on sustainability and a celebration of non-material values? Seemingly small steps do matter and, when taken collectively with others, can really add up, for example:

1. **Trim your household energy use:** About half the energy use in an average home goes to space heating and cooling. Turning the thermostat down 3°F in the winter and up 3°F in the summer can prevent nearly 1,100 pounds of CO_2 emissions and save over $100 per year.[4] Replacing your inefficient refrigerator with an Energy Star model will save $665 over the next five years, and if you have a second fridge that you can do without, you'll find yourself with an extra $176 in your pocket a year and eliminate 2,500 pounds of CO_2 emissions.[5] Compact fluorescent light bulbs (CFLs) are four times more efficient and last up to ten times longer than incandescent bulbs. And light-emitting diodes (LEDs) last up to ten times as long as CFLs, use only two to ten watts of electricity and are mercury-free.[6]

2. **Eat local and sustainable:** Buying local food not only helps local farmers thrive, it also reduces energy consumption. The average food travels from pasture to plate an estimated 1,200 to 2,500 miles.[7] Even when they are not organic, small farms tend to be less aggressive than large factory farms about dousing their wares with chemicals. Visit your local farmer's market or co-op and look for place-of-origin labels in the grocery store to choose local at the market. Beyond supporting local farmers, look for organic products and humanely raised meat.

No Impact Man: Is Living a Zero-Waste Lifestyle Possible?

In today's society it's incredibly difficult to reduce the amount of trash we create. Look around and you will see trash everywhere (even before it's officially "trash"): paper towels, newspapers, throwaway coffee cups, disposable diapers, plastic water bottles, food packaging. In fact, 80 percent of the products sold in the US are designed to be used once and then thrown away.[1] Every American generates an average of four and half pounds of trash per day.

Reducing the amount of garbage we generate would require some extreme lifestyle shifts. One New York City resident wanted to see if it was possible. A self-described "liberal schlub," Colin Beavan, aka "No Impact Man," got tired of complaining about the world's problems without doing anything about them. Beavan and his family decided to attempt a zero-waste lifestyle for a year. His efforts to live without making any net impact on the environment were chronicled on his blog, in a book and film. No trash, no carbon emissions, no toxins in the water, no elevators, no subway, no products in packing, no plastics, no air conditioning, no TV were just a few of Beavan's goals.[2]

In order to reduce his family's trash output, Beavan introduced a number of lifestyle changes such as eliminating canned soda, bottled water, throwaway razors, food in takeout containers, paper coffee cups, disposable diapers, repackaged processed food and instead bought milk in returnable glass bottles, returning egg cartons to the market, carried reusable cloths instead of tissues and napkins, shopped from the bulk bins, used baking soda for toothpaste and deodorant, gave second-hand clothes to charities, and composted food scraps.[3]

It sounds extreme but Beavan said the project wasn't about becoming an ascetic or anti-materialist; rather it was about being "eco-effective" and finding the middle path.[4] "From the very get-go, the No Impact project was about a happier planet, happier people," said Beaven. "Far from depriving ourselves, reducing waste in our lives would move us closer to rather than farther from the lives we actually wanted."[5]

As a result, the Beavans not only prevented about 5,000 pounds of trash from going to the landfill, they also noticed they were happier, spent less money on "stuff" and were healthier from eating less processed, packaged and pre-prepared food.

from the editor

Photo courtesy of Oscilloscope Laboratories

Photo courtesy Marc Featherly, Illinois Wesleyan Photography

Recycling one aluminum can saves enough energy to run a TV for three hours, and each ton of copy paper recycled saves the equivalent of 26 trees.

Try taking public transportation, carpooling, or doing more things that don't require driving.

Look for healthier cleaning alternatives—often labeled as "non-toxic" and biodegradable."

The US is the top trash-producing country in the world at 1,609 pounds per person per year. This means that 5 percent of the world's people generate 40 percent of the world's waste.

3. **If you can't reuse it, recycle it and then buy recycled:** Recycling one aluminum can saves enough energy to run a TV for three hours, and each ton of copy paper recycled saves the equivalent of 26 trees.[8] On the other side of the recycling spectrum, choose products with recycled-content materials along with recycled and recyclable packaging. New products made from recycled materials are coming on the market every day, such as paper products, clothing, toothbrushes, razors, housewares and home improvement products.

4. **Downshift your driving:** The average American drives over 250 miles per week, burning more than a dozen gallons of gas, each of which releases roughly 20 pounds of CO_2 into the atmosphere.[9] Try taking public transportation, carpooling or doing more things that don't require driving. Taking public transportation instead of driving one day per week would reduce your CO_2 emissions by 1,040 pounds per year.[10]

5. **Get off the toxic train:** According to a US Environmental Protection Agency–funded project, the ingredients found in one out of every three commercial cleaning products are potentially harmful.[11] These chemicals can cause significant health problems and also find their way into lakes, streams and other water bodies (some of which may serve as drinking water sources). Look for healthier alternatives—often labeled as "non-toxic" and "biodegradable."[12]

6. **Watch your water:** The average residential water use in the US is 150 gallons per person per day. In response to the country's decade-long drought, urban areas of Australia were able to go as low as 34 gallons of water per person per day. Native and adaptive plants along with efficient irrigation systems can significantly cut outdoor water use. Look for the US EPA's new WaterSense label for toilets, faucets and shower

The average residential water use in the US is 150 gallons per person per day.

Each year more 100 million trees are turned into the 5.8 million tons of mail that end up as 450,000 garbage trucks worth of waste.

> **It's not an either-or situation; it's all hands on deck. And as Lao-Tsu said, "A journey of a thousand miles begins with a single step."**

heads which reduce water use as much as 35 percent.[13] It's time to take back the tap and say no to bottled water. US consumers buy more than half a billion gallons of bottled water every week, enough bottles to circle the globe more than five times. More than 17 million barrels of oil are used annually to manufacture water bottles—that translates to enough fuel for about 100,000 cars.[14]

7. **Junk your junk mail:** Credit card mailers and catalogs might seem insignificant, yet each year more than 100 million trees are turned into the 5.8 million tons of mail that end up as 450,000 garbage trucks worth of waste. And don't forget about the water and climate implications of paper manufacturing—the production and disposal of all this direct mail consumes more energy than 3 million cars![15] You can find forms online to opt out of junk mail and reduce your portion of this waste. Visit donotmail.org and catalogchoice.org for more.

Of course, these steps are just a few examples. Look around your community or online and you'll see dozens more. It's vital to keep one eye focused on tackling the hyper-commercialized hot spots and leveraging opportunities to evoke systemic change, but let's not let anyone tell us that small steps won't make a difference. It's not an either-or situation; it's all hands on deck. And as Lao-Tsu said, "A journey of a thousand miles begins with a single step."

.....

Seán Sheehan was an original staff member of the Center for a New American Dream (www.newdream.org), serving in a variety of management and communication capacities for more than a dozen years. He oversaw all of its online advocacy programs and campaigns, building a community of more than 100,000 individuals committed to shifting our cultural focus from "more is better" to one that inspires and empowers "more of what matters." Sheehan currently works as the e-Vermont Community Director for the Vermont Council on Rural Development.

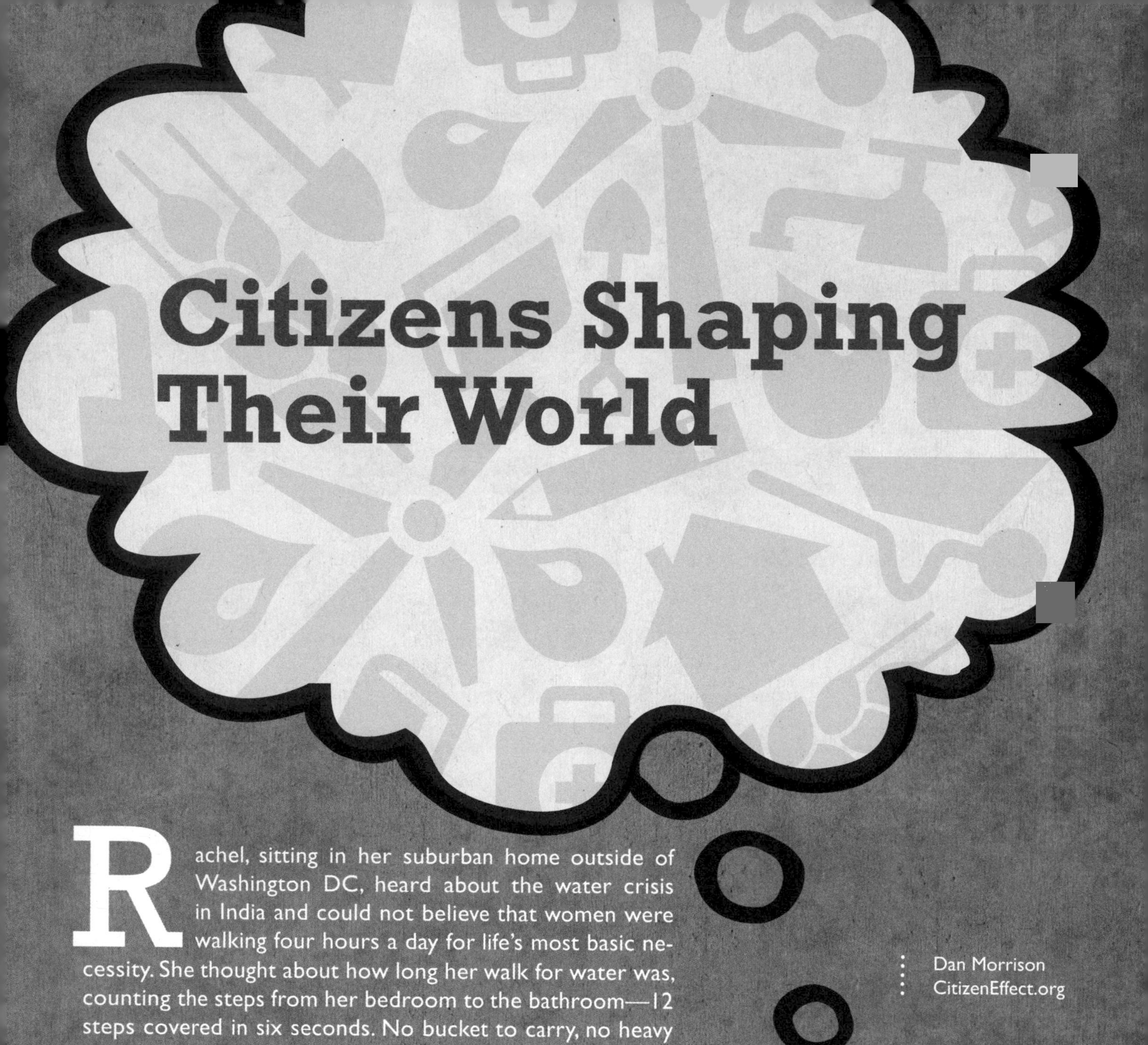

Citizens Shaping Their World

Dan Morrison
CitizenEffect.org

Rachel, sitting in her suburban home outside of Washington DC, heard about the water crisis in India and could not believe that women were walking four hours a day for life's most basic necessity. She thought about how long her walk for water was, counting the steps from her bedroom to the bathroom—12 steps covered in six seconds. No bucket to carry, no heavy pot balanced on her head. She simply needed to turn on the faucet, and safe drinking water flowed. The more she thought about it, the more it felt magical compared to the over two and a half billion people who lack access to sanitation and clean drinking water.[1]

Rachel decided to do something about it. She had never given money to a community overseas and knew nothing about "international development." As so many of us do when we don't know something, she went online and Googled "water India." A project to build a well in Sanganguna Village on CitizenEffect.org appeared.

Sanganguna Village is a rural community in Gujarat, India. Women not only needed to walk long distances for water, but the trek left them with no time to work, run a business or earn an income.

Rachel was determined to partner with Sanganguna Village and build that well. But Rachel had a problem. She did not have the $2,700 that Sanganguna Village needed. After all, she was only seven years old.

However, Rachel had the only things that really mattered—the passion to help a community in need and the desire to bring her friends and family together to help. She walked into her principal's office and said she wanted to organize Walk4Water Day at the school. On a beautiful spring day, Rachel brought together her community with the goal of raising enough money to build a well for a community halfway around the world. Her classmates came, learned about the water crisis in India, carried water jugs across a field, and together, they raised $3,700, $1,000 more than Rachel's goal.

Now Sanganguna Village has an accessible, sustainable source of clean water. Women have time to start businesses and earn an income. Children are attending school in greater numbers and for longer periods of time. Community health is improving. All because Rachel decided she had the power to act and be the change she wanted to see in the world.

Rachel was flexing her muscles as a citizen. She acted locally to organize her community to have an impact on a community in need of water. She defined herself much broader than just as a consumer and rejected the concept that the only duty of a citizen was to vote (even thought she can't vote for 11 years). She, like so many of her peers and elders in the Millennium generation, took an active role in creating the society she wants to live in.

No governments, no politics, no multilateral organizations and no corporations necessary. Rachel and Sanganguna Village are an example of citizens connecting with citizens to solve small but critical problems. Rather than focus on large unmanageable problems, Rachel and others are unlocking the potential of communities by completing small projects that empower people to be more self-reliant and in control of their own destiny. That is how the growing citizen effect movement works: small efforts and projects with direct visible impact.

Rachel brought together her community with the goal of raising enough money to build a well for a community halfway around the world.

A child walks for miles in order to get water for his family. Rachel (above, dark grey t-shirt) helped his community build a well.

Rachel had the only things that really mattered— the passion to help a community in need and the desire to bring her friends and family together to help.

Rachel's classmates (top) partnered with Sanganguna Village, raised the funds and built the well that the community needed.

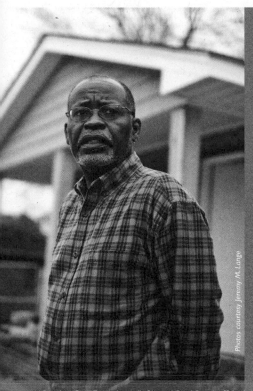

Today, citizens of all ages are not only looking to government, non-profits and international organizations to mitigate global water and food crises, stop genocides, fight HIV/AIDS and halt climate change and save the environment.

They are seeking ways to do it themselves.

Photos courtesy Jeremy M. Lange

Photos courtesy Iraq and Afghanistan Veterans of America

Brother Ray Eurguhart (left) and Paul Reickoff (right) are two citizens changing the world around them.

Today, citizens of all ages are not only looking to government, non-profits and international organizations to mitigate global water and food crises, stop genocides, fight HIV/AIDS and halt climate change and save the environment. They are seeking ways to do it themselves.

A lifelong resident of Durham, North Carolina, Ray Eurquhart has been a community activist for more than 40 years. Now in his 60s, the Air Force veteran and former city employee known as Brother Ray "is on a crusade to clean up the crime, replenish affordable housing and restore vitality" in his neighborhood. From picking up litter to running the local community center, Brother Ray is also a member of the community's redevelopment steering committee and is involved in a project to turn abandoned properties into livable, affordable homes. "Everything starts from self-interest," said Brother Ray. "I live over here, and so did my mother and father and father's mother. It was the village that brought us up. It taught us the value of community."[2]

In 2005, Dwight Owens suffered life-threatening injuries after being hit by a drunk driver. Although now confined to a wheelchair, Dwight is dedicated to serving others. Working with AmeriCorps' Linking Individuals into Neighborhoods and Communities project, he supports over 1,200 individuals with disabilities. He also works to ensure accessibility and independence by conducting Americans with Disabilities Act (ADA) site surveys and providing life skills training sessions. Dwight helps individuals transition from public institutions to their own homes and facilitates a support group for men with disabilities to encourage independence and leadership.[3]

Iraq War veteran Paul Rieckhoff wanted to improve the lives of Iraq and Afghanistan veterans and their families. After returning to the US from Baghdad in 2004, Rieckhoff created the Iraq and Afghanistan Veterans of America (IAVA). IAVA helps veterans become leaders in government, business and communities. The result is not just better care for veterans, but also a population

"Everything starts from self-interest," said Brother Ray. "I live over here, and so did my mother and father and father's mother. It was the village that brought us up. It taught us the value of community."

that understands the causes and consequences of war. By 2015, IAVA expects to have 175,000 veteran members and an additional 400,000 supporters.[4]

Rachel and others are ensuring that citizens will be the defining factor for 21st-century philanthropy. Microphilanthropy sites like Citizen Effect, GlobalGiving, Crowdrise and microfinance sites like Kiva are allowing citizens to partner with communities in need around the world and see the direct results of their efforts without the bureaucracy of large foundations and nonprofits. You give directly to a project and have a direct line of sight into the impact you have on the community. This was impossible 20 years ago; today Rachel can send money to Sanganguna Village, and a woman in Sanganguna can take a photo of the well with her phone and send it to Rachel.

Technology is a major reason why citizens are retaking control of society. You no longer need millions of dollars to connect with and support an entrepreneur or help a community in need. Technology, the Internet and mobile communication are connecting people of all income levels from all over the world to fund projects, solve problems and raise the voices of those that are oppressed and fighting for their rights and lives.

Recognizing the absurdity of wasted food, Jonathan Leung began recovering otherwise wasted food from his school cafeteria and delivering it to a homeless shelter in Philadelphia. He turned to technology to involve more students in the process of transporting food to those in need. Using a Google application, he created a volunteer sign-up form, which is exported to a spreadsheet and then to a map, allowing him to quickly determine how to best match volunteers with businesses for food pickup and shelters for deliveries. As the project expanded, Jonathan created Helping Hunger, a student-driven organization that has "rescued" nearly 7,500 pounds of food from caterers and restaurants, and transported it to soup kitchens and homeless shelters.[5]

Technology is a major reason why citizens are retaking control of society. You no longer need millions of dollars to connect with and support an entrepreneur or help a community in need.

High school students from Sugar Land, Texas partnered with their local supermarket to host a food drive.

Global problems are being redefined. Statistics that say "1.4 billion people live below $1.25 a day and 2.6 billion lack access to sanitation" are being replaced with "110 people in Sanganguna Village need $2,700 to build a sustainable well to access clean water." The first statistic is abstract and unsolvable for even the wealthiest philanthropist. The second is tangible and doable for a group of friends that get together and leverage their social network to raise the money and to transform the lives of a community.

Citizens will by no means replace the role of governments, political parties, venture capitalists, USAID or the Gates Foundation. These established organizations address crises and provide funding that large-scale problems require. However, citizens are beginning to take back control of these organizations that once worked for them, not on behalf of them like they do today. At Citizen Effect, we estimate that, in a few years, $1 spent on empowering citizen philanthropists will result in $15 raised for small but critical projects in the field. Citizens are force multipliers, and large organizations can leverage them to have a much greater impact at the community level where large programs are not as effective.

When Rachel set out to help Sanganguna Village, she did not know what "development" was. She did not have a master plan for Sanganguna and how to "lift them out of poverty." But she did have the passion to help people in need and wanted to do her part to be a positive change in the world. At the end of the day, she was just a citizen who decided she had a responsibility to others, and she could bring together other citizens to make a real difference and help build a more self-reliant and sustainable world. Rachel is a leader in the citizen effect movement that is transforming politics, entrepreneurial markets and philanthropy.

· · · · ·

Dan Morrison is the CEO and founder of Citizen Effect (www.citizeneffect.org), an entrepreneurial non-profit that empowers anyone to be a philanthropist. After a career as an innovation and brand strategy consultant, Morrison went to the University of Chicago and received a master's in Middle Eastern Studies. In 2006, Morrison was invited to India by the Self Employed Women's Association (SEWA), where he met a woman who needed to walk four hours for water. Morrison went home, sent a holiday card to friends and family and raised $5,000 to build a well in her village. Ever since, Morrison has been helping everyday citizens connect directly to communities in need around the world to build a more self-reliant and sustainable life.

Helping Others:
Finding the Will and the Way

There is a special power that is created when a young person learns to open his or her eyes and discover, in his or her own soul, the living, pulsing, breathing dreams of another. I believe that this discovery is the key to social change for people of any age or background, and it has been my quest to demonstrate this truth to girls and to the world.

It was in the summer of 2007 that this journey began. My idea then was simple: empower girls to fulfill their potential by training them to solve community problems—from sex trafficking to unequal access to education to health services inequities. I, along with the three friends I recruited for the project, soon realized that although no set of goals could include everything we might do—no program or organization or single individual could solve all of the issues we must confront—we could focus our energies on one idea and develop it really well. So we launched our first chapter in India, then Ghana, then Nigeria. Then almost surreally, we started receiving phone calls and emails from girls in other countries, like Turkey and Bangladesh, from girls who were itching to change realities but simply did not know how.

: Sejal Hathi
: Girls Helping Girls

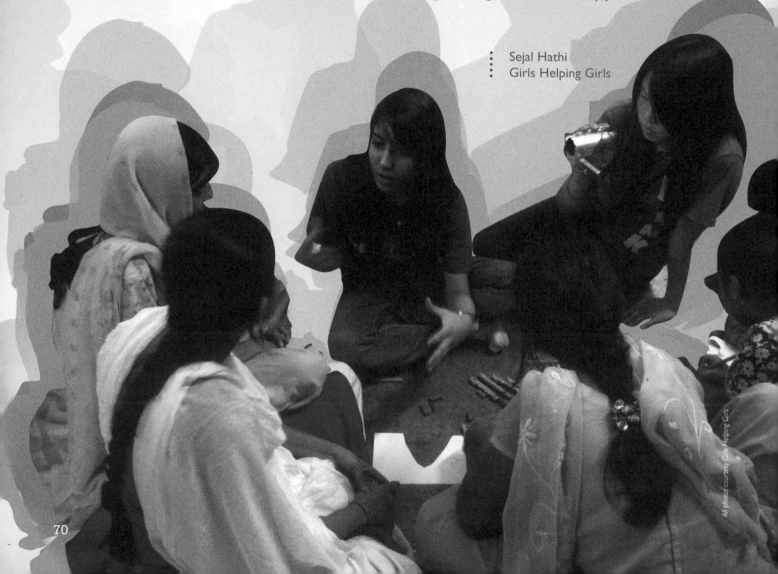

With help from Girls Helping Girls, this community in India was able to build a library to help continue the education of their girls.

Former Secretary-General of the United Nations Kofi Annan memorably declared that educating and empowering girls is the key to world peace and the most effective tool for global development. The World Bank demonstrated that investing in women raises economic productivity several-fold, empowering entire communities and countries. And Secretary of State Hillary Clinton this year insisted that the world cannot progress if women and girls are denied their rights and left behind. Yet, seven years after Annan's statement, millions of girls across the globe are not realizing their intrinsic power: Instead of saving the world, they are eroding their potential, falling victim to over 80 percent of human trafficking cases,[1] over 70 percent of illiteracy cases[2] and over 75 percent of sub-Saharan Africa's HIV cases in youth.[3] I could go on and on with the statistics, but the point is that, all across the globe, girls are losing self-dominion to a culture that decrees their duty is to cater to others and to mold themselves into casts set by society. We are trying to change this culture.

And like a viral message, our mission spread and spread and spread until it became a global movement unrestrained by a single director, but burgeoning with a mind of its own. Today, less than three years after first sketching our logo on a piece of scrap paper in the high-school library, our small team has mobilized and trained over 30,000 young women to create innovative and substantive change. With no hired advisors and not even a board of directors, we have provided girls from more than 20 countries the one-on-one mentorship, toolkits, funding and support network to build their own microenterprises, advocate against human rights abuses, construct holistic income-generation programs and create sustainable development initiatives in their communities. And we have raised over $60,000 to enable girls around the world to go to school.

Somehow, in some way, what we are doing is working, and girls are opening their eyes to their potential.

I want to tell you about Maria from California, who at age 17 belonged to an immigrant family without experience in the American education system. Maria told me that she often felt lost and hopeless and incapable of achieving anything worthwhile. Her family was falling apart, and her peers were dropping out of school in droves. Maria had become close to a schoolteacher, who showed her a newspaper article about our work to empower girls. Immediately, Maria said, "My attitude changed completely,

Statistics show that 94% of youth in America feel powerless to make a difference.

Girls Helping Girls proves that anything is possible.

I strive to empower this movement, by helping the world realize that our strengths lie in one another.

We are all a mosaic of gifts, and all of us possess the rich power to shape our globe and assert ourselves as ambassadors for change.

Mumtaz taught me that when we give to others what we care about the most, we allow ourselves to rebuild all that is broken within us, and thus to redefine our own potential.

With support from Girls Helping Girls, Mumtaz escaped an abusive relationship and along with her friends, started a food catering service, which allows her to support her family on her own.

because I finally felt like I could do something, be someone." Today, Maria is the first in her family to attend college and, through Girls Helping Girls' social entrepreneurship program, is creating her own initiative to prevent other youth from falling victim to depression and the dropout crisis in her community.

Maria showed me that every region of the world and every girl on this planet has something deep, tangible and worthwhile to offer. We can demonstrate this power to even the most battered girls by helping them to rebaptize their hardships as their strengths and leverage their challenges as their greatest assets for change.

I want to tell you about 25-year-old Mumtaz from India, who just five years ago was beaten constantly by her husband. One of our grassroots partners in India began helping her and providing free daycare for her daughter. When Girls Helping Girls visited Mumtaz's community, we worked with Mumtaz and her friends to develop a sustainable self-help group, training them in business enterprise and loaning the group $1,500 to create a food catering service. Now, Mumtaz is preparing to move into her own home with her daughter. And to heal from the abuses she suffered from her husband, she is sharing her own story and her own lessons with other women, thereby preventing them from falling into the same cycle of abuse she experienced.

Mumtaz taught me that when we give to others what we care about the most, rather than suffer more, we allow ourselves to rebuild all that is broken within us, and thus to redefine our own potential.

This is what I call self-transformation. And it is this spirit, this animus of collective self-awareness, that I seek to inspire in the swelling community of girls I work with every day.

I believe that all girls and all youth are a movement: a united and unstoppable force that can eradicate poverty, increase access to healthcare, reverse environmental degradation and solve the world's most pressing problems—if only they are given the tools and the opportunity. I strive to empower this movement, by helping the world realize that our strengths lie in one another and by energizing and equipping potential. We are all a mosaic of gifts, and all of us possess the rich power to shape our globe and assert ourselves as ambassadors for change. If I could do one thing to change the world, it would be to awaken this active consciousness in every individual.

.....

Sejal Hathi is a student at Yale University studying biology and international relations. An avid social entrepreneur, Sejal founded the international non-profit Girls Helping Girls at age 15 and, as CEO, has since trained thousands of girls worldwide to incubate entrepreneurial projects addressing global issues in more than 20 countries. Among several other projects, she has additionally served on the boards of several international non-profits, coauthored a monographic book and spoken for and advised political leaders, corporate executives and philanthropists from around the world on youth development issues and the benefits of investing in women and girls.

The Power of Young People to Change the World

T.A. Barron
Author and Prize Founder

If I could give today's young people three wishes, they would be:

More hugs.

More time outside in nature.

More belief in their own power to change the world.

While most people understand the importance of the first two wishes, the third one leaves some folks scratching their heads, wondering why young people's belief in their own power is so essential.

Let's start with the notion that all of us—especially young people—need heroes. We need them to be our guides on the twisting, sometimes difficult trail we call life. To show us just how far we can go, to help us know just how high we can climb.

> **Truth is, there is a potential hero, a future difference maker, in every young person. Each of them, from whatever background, is a bundle of untapped energy.**

And we need heroes today more than ever. Our modern society is terribly confused about the difference between a hero and a celebrity. And the difference is crucial.

A celebrity is all about fame—temporary, superficial fame, usually for qualities that are easy to see: a pretty face, a good hook shot, a great dance move. A hero, by contrast, is about character—qualities beneath the surface that aren't visible until they prompt action. Qualities like courage, hope, compassion and perseverance.

Heroes, real heroes, are all around us. They truly hold our world together, through their unselfish devotion to helping others, supporting families, teaching children, protecting the environment. They don't want fame, or glory, or even credit; they just want to help. In so many ways, these unsung heroes steer the boat in which all of us sail.

Yet young people hear a lot more about celebrities than about heroes, in every form of media. Worse yet, young people are treated too often as just another target market by advertisers. The underlying message they get from all this is that their self-worth comes from what they buy—which drink, which shoes, which cellphone—not who they are down inside.

What gets lost in this? Young people's sense of their own potential for heroic qualities—their own power to make a positive difference in the world.

Truth is, there is a potential hero, a future difference maker, in every young person. Each of them, from whatever background, is a bundle of untapped energy—a positive force who can do something to steer that communal boat that carries us all.

All it takes for that to be true is belief. For if young people believe in their own power, they will use it. And they will discover that any person—regardless of gender, age, race, cultural background or economic circumstance—can make a genuine, lasting impact.

How do we help skeptical young people believe in their own power?

The best way by far is simply to share examples of other young people who have made a difference. Those stories carry real inspiration, and they speak for themselves.

To turn the spotlight on such amazing young people and share their stories, I founded a national award, the Gloria Barron Prize for Young Heroes. Named after my mom, who was a quiet hero in my own life, this award, now in its tenth year, honors 25 young people annually. They come from every background, and they are as diverse as the youth of America. The one thing they all have in common is a belief in their own power to make a difference—and the dedication to make it happen.

This prize is really just a small thing, but its winners are shining examples of what young people can achieve. And I hope that those examples might inspire other young people to discover their own power to make a difference.

Here are a few of the winners from recent years:

Katie, age 10, has rallied hundreds of people in her town in South Carolina to help her create vegetable gardens to feed the hungry. How did she begin? As a third grader, she raised a tiny seedling into a huge 40-pound cabbage. When she saw how many people that cabbage fed at a local soup kitchen, she decided that she could do more. So far, she has donated more than 1,000 pounds of fresh produce to people in need.

Photos courtesy Katie's Krops

Anthony, age 12, created Heavenly Hats which has provided over 10,000 new hats to people who have lost their hair due to chemotherapy and other medical treatments. He started this project when his grandmother was diagnosed with cancer and lost her hair, motivating him to make her a hat to lift her spirits. Now, from his home in Wisconsin, he distributes hats donated from people around the world.

Photo courtesy Ryan and Ryan's Well Foundation

Ryan, age 11, has worked tirelessly to raise money to provide clean drinking water to African villages. When he first heard about the plight of African children who died from impure water, Ryan was only six years old. He decided to do something about it. In the next five years, he raised over $500,000—enough to build over 70 water wells.

Ellie, age 17, was volunteering at a center for Hispanic children in the Los Angeles area when she realized that many young people had difficulty speaking English clearly enough to succeed in school and find jobs. So she organized dozens of volunteers to create a website, RepeatAfterUs.com, to provide audio clips of over 5,000 texts to help anyone learn English as a second language.

Barbara, age 17, grew up on a farm in Texas. When she realized that local farmers were pouring their used motor oil into rivers and on the ground, causing pollution, she organized the creation of a recycling center for crude oil. Her project, called Don't Be Crude, has grown to include 18 recycling centers in Texas.

Shawn, age 18, founded Garden Angels at his high school in Brooklyn, New York, to transform an abandoned, trash-filled lot into a community garden. The hardest part of this task was to convince his peers that they could do better than hanging out with local gangs, that they could really change their community. His success leads Shawn to declare: "Every person, no matter how small, can make a difference."

Photo courtesy Ashoka

Chloe, age 17, founded the Climate Action Club at her school in Maine to help local residents do something to combat climate change. Overcoming resistance and skepticism, she persevered. Recently, the reusable bag campaign she initiated was adopted as the model for a statewide program to reduce waste.

Jaclyn, age 16, survived a bout with brain cancer as a child—and was encouraged by her friends on the University of Maryland Women's Lacrosse team. She decided to help other kids with cancer by creating an organization to pair those kids with college athletic teams whose support could aid the healing process. To date, more than 200 young people have been adopted by teams around the country.

Otana, age 15, discovered that the air purifier used by her asthmatic mother might actually be producing harmful levels of toxic ozone. She did her own scientific research after school; then began to share her findings with local and state officials. This culminated in her presentation to the California Air Resources Board, which then developed new regulations and became the first state to ban the sale of ozone-emitting air purifiers.

Ashley, age 16, visited Africa with her family and was deeply upset by the lack of educational opportunities for girls. When she returned home to Colorado, she started AfricAid, a non-profit organization to help provide schools for girls in Tanzania. In the years since its founding, AfricAid has helped educate over 40,000 young Africans.

The list could go on and on. These are but a few examples of young people who have discovered that they can build on their own energy and ideals to do something truly great.

And yet … maybe "great" isn't the right word. As Mother Teresa once said, "I have done no great deeds. But I have done many small deeds … with great love."

Let's all share such stories of empowered young people and do whatever we can to support the next generation in creating their vision for the future. The more we do that, the more those young people will steer our world's boat and fill its sails with love.

·····

T.A. Barron (www.tabarron.com), author of more than 20 books for young people and founder of the Gloria Barron Prize for Young Heroes (www.barronprize.org), lives in Colorado.

Creating a Stable and Equitable Economy

three

A look at the numbers...

The **richest 1%** of Americans own as much wealth as **all of those in the bottom 90%.**

RICHEST 1%

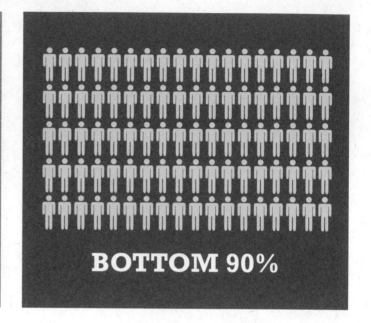

BOTTOM 90%

$980 billion:

Bush Administration tax cuts for the wealthiest 5% of households in America between 2001 and 2010.

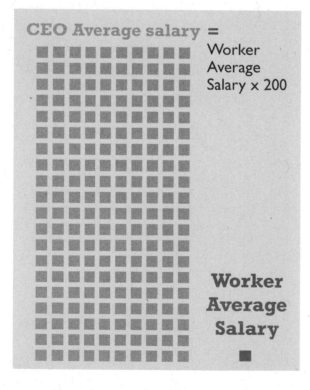

CEO Average salary = Worker Average Salary x 200

Worker Average Salary

200x

Amount that the top corporate CEOs in the US earn compared to the average worker.

10x

Amount that the top corporate CEOs in Japan earn compared to the average worker.

170

Number of full-time employees (with benefits) an American company could hire if the average top corporate CEO earned only 10 times the salary of the average employee.

Only **one-half** of work-ready
US adults have **full time jobs.**

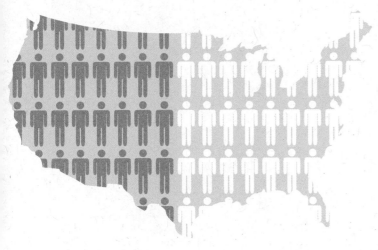

1.7 million

Number of new jobs in renewable power
generation, building retrofitting and renewable
transportation fuels that will be generated by 2018.

30 million

Number of permanent, full-time jobs that
would be created over the 15–20 years by
eliminating payroll taxes.

$100 spent at a **non–locally owned business:**

$33
stays
local

$100 spent at a **locally owned business:**

$78
stays
local

In a city with a
population of about
770,000 people,
shifting just

10%

of spending to locally
owned businesses
would create:

1,600
new jobs

$50 million
in new wages

$137 million
in new economic activity

81

The economy is a complex phenomenon that is best judged by the outcomes it creates. But when jobs go overseas and the gap between the rich and poor widens, when profits come before people, and when quality of life factors like happiness and environmental health are left out of the equation, then it seems as if we need something better. We need a new operating system. It's time for a new economy that's dedicated to building a better world, one that is life-supporting instead of a wealth-creation system that disproportionately benefits a narrow segment of society and mortgages our natural assets.

Economic transformation hinges upon changing the rules of the game so that...

Millions of green economy jobs get created in the next few years instead of the next few decades

Made in America and buying local become the norm again

The middle class gets widened instead of looking like an hour-glass between the ultra-rich and the poor

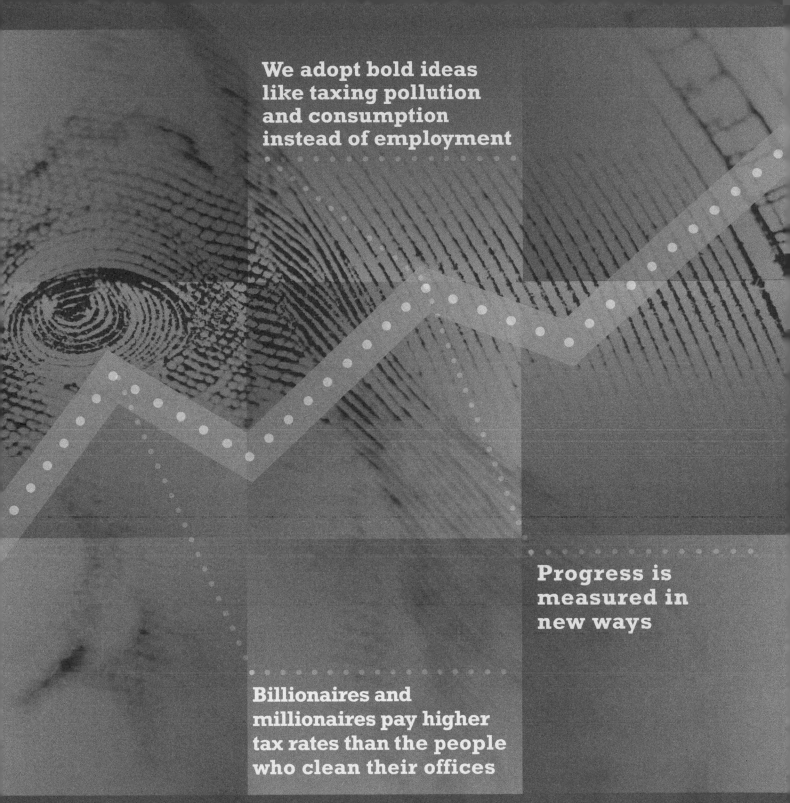

We adopt bold ideas like taxing pollution and consumption instead of employment

Progress is measured in new ways

Billionaires and millionaires pay higher tax rates than the people who clean their offices

"Concern for the **public good** must become the animating **force** of our economic order."

> Marjorie Kelly

Lighting the Way to a
New Economy

Life or money: that is our choice. The current system serves predominantly money. Our task is to replace it with a New Economy that serves life. My vision of the new economy is a global system of human-scale, interconnected Local Living Economies that function in harmony with local ecosystems, meet the basic needs of all people, support just and democratic societies and foster joyful community life.

Building a New Economy

We must shift the economic system's defining value from money to life; its focus of decision-making power from global corporations and financial markets to local people and communities; and its defining purpose from growing profligate consumption to supporting healthy, joyful living.

The goal is a New Economy that benefits all citizens and is based on real wealth. Real wealth has intrinsic value, as contrasted to mere exchange value. Life, not money, is the measure of real-wealth value. Examples include land, labor, knowledge and physical infrastructure. The most valuable examples of real living wealth are those that are beyond price: a healthy happy child, a meaningful living wage job, a healthy natural environment. Also called illusory wealth, phantom wealth is wealth that appears or disappears as if by magic. The term generally denotes money created by accounting entries or the inflation of asset bubbles unrelated to the creation of anything of real value or utility. The high-tech stock and housing bubbles are examples. Actualizing the New Economy vision requires a profound transformation of cultural values, institutional power and our ways of living.

David Korten
Living Economies Forum

84

Redefining Economic Indicators

Gross domestic product (GDP), a measure of the country's economic output, is often used as a measure of the economy's beneficial performance. But GDP is essentially a measure of how fast money is flowing through the economy. Using it as our leading economic indicator results in a vast range of distortions. Growth in expenditures on incarceration, toxic waste clean-up and weapons manufacture all contribute to GDP, but are reflections of social and economic failure—not success.

The problem begins with the practice of reducing everything to a financial metric. This puts the emphasis on the economy's financial performance, which often translates into its phantom-wealth performance, rather than its real-wealth, living world performance. Indices like the Genuine Progress Indicator modify GDP to correct for certain distortions and are a step in the right direction, but they retain the limitation of reducing life values to financial values.

We get what we measure, so let's measure economic performance against living wealth indicators of the health of people, communities and natural systems. Real economic performance is properly measured in terms of such things as improvements in air quality and

species extinction rates, decreasing length of the average commute and reduction of infant morality, childhood obesity, teen pregnancy and divorce rates. These are among the indicators of the real performance of the economy in terms of its contribution, or lack thereof, to the well-being of society. The idea that it is possible to reduce assessment of the health and performance of the complex economies of modern societies to a single financial metric is itself highly questionable.

If we must reduce this complexity to a single index, then let it be an index based on real living wealth indicators, for example, the Happy Planet Index compiled by the New Economics Foundation in London.[1] It is a composite of three indicators: life expectancy, life satisfaction or happiness and the ecological footprint, an indicator of the economy's per capita environmental burden. The result is an indicator of the ecological efficiency with which a society's economy is producing a given level of physical and emotional well-being. The results demonstrate that it is possible to live long, happy lives with a relatively small environmental impact.

As we replace financial indicators like GDP with living wealth indicators that focus attention on real economic performance, we can see more clearly the benefits of reallocating real-wealth resources from weapons to

Gross Domestic Product (GDP)

→ Measure of a country's economic output, or how fast money is flowing through the economy

→ Using it as our leading economic indicator results in a **vast range of distortions**—including positive growth associated with money spent on increased incarceration, toxic waste clean-up, weapons manufacture, etc.

Distorted

Genuine Progress Indicator (GPI)

→ Starts with same personal consumption data that the GDP is based on

→ Adjusts for factors such as: Income distribution

→ Adds factors such as: Value of household & volunteer work

→ Subtracts factors such as: Costs of crime & pollution

Holistic

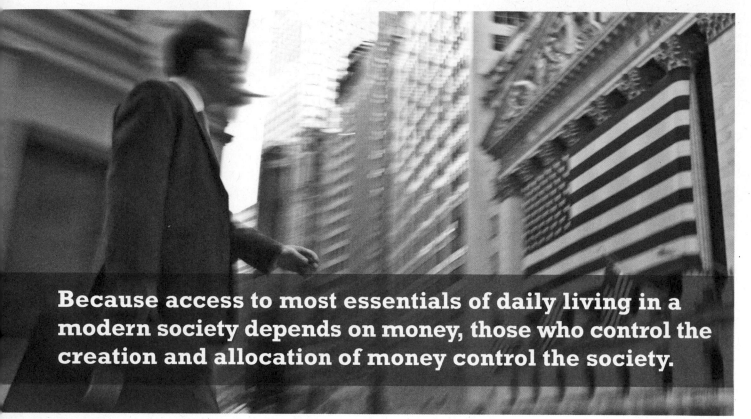

Because access to most essentials of daily living in a modern society depends on money, those who control the creation and allocation of money control the society.

healthcare and environmental rejuvenation, from prisons to rehabilitation, from suburban sprawl to compact communities, from automobiles to public transportation, from fossil fuels to energy conservation and development of sustainable energy sources, from mining to recycling, from advertising to education and from financial speculation to financing local entrepreneurship.

Changing the Money System

Money is merely a number of no intrinsic value created from nothing when a bank issues a loan. Yet, because access to most essentials of daily living in a modern society depends on money, those who control the creation and allocation of money control the society. We have allowed Wall Street to achieve monopoly control of the creation and allocation of money and thereby to make its values and priorities the values and priorities of the society.

We need a financial system that makes credit readily available at favorable rates to Main Street businesses that create family wage jobs producing real goods and services—and makes credit scarce and expensive for Wall Street speculators and predators. In short, we need to fundamentally restructure the money system

to look much like it did before the wave of deregulation that began in the late 1970s, based on locally owned independent, cooperative community banks and credit unions with a clear mandate to fund local homeowners and responsible businesses.

In the new money system, individual states would each have their own state-owned bank to issue credit for public investments. In addition the Federal Reserve would be a true federal central bank that operates transparently in the public interest to oversee money supply management and issue interest-free credit to the federal government rather than issuing it to private banks to in turn loan to the federal government at interest for purely private gain.

Wall Street's useful and essential functions—serving as a depository for savings, financing home ownership and business development, insuring against risk and clearing check and credit card transactions—can all be organized in ways that are more efficient, accountable and responsive than the current Wall Street model. The New Economy goal is a money system designed to assure transparency and public accountability, and a stable non-inflationary money supply responsive to community needs.

Creating Greater Equitability

In a finite world of limited real resources, the only way to meet the needs of everyone is for income and ownership to be equitably distributed through policies that support living wages, progressive taxation, quality public health and education service and broad participation in home and business ownership. The equitable participation in income and ownership is an essential foundation for democracy and a real market economy.

We were raised in America to believe that capitalism is synonymous with a market economy, democracy and human liberty. Turns out it isn't true. The term *capitalism* means "rule by capital," which means rule by the owners of capital. It was originally used to refer to an economy in which ownership of the means of production is monopolized by a small financial elite for its exclusive benefit to the exclusion of the interests of the rest of the society. Our current Wall Street–dominated economy is a capitalist economy—and we bear the consequences.

from the editor

Slows BarBQ: Building Restaurants, Community and Hope in Downtown Detroit

No city makes headlines for economic depression more often than Detroit, Michigan. Troubled by the loss of manufacturing jobs, followed by crime and political corruption, downtown Detroit is now littered with vacant lots and condemned buildings. While the Motor City is not the prettiest place today, many entrepreneurs see a city ready to be rebuilt for the New Economy.

After buying a once-prime storefront for pennies on the dollar, Phillip Cooley co-founded Slows BarBQ to start a successful restaurant and help his city because, "If I'm here, and I actually go out and I'm part of the community, I can actually do something and make a difference in Detroit. You don't have a lot of chains choking out smaller stores, so in this city people work together. We're so underserved commercially that small mom n' pops make a lot of sense."[1]

Cooley and his partners cook with fresh, locally sourced ingredients, sell local beer and wine, and frequently volunteer at and donate food for community events. As a result, Slows BarBQ has become a household name, bringing people and hope back into the downtown.

Now Cooley's focus is on rebuilding Roosevelt Park, a plaza that sits in front of the dilapidated Michigan Central Station. Cooley believes that with a little work from community volunteers the park can become a premiere destination for sports, music, and theater. Bringing visitors to the park would encourage the city to redevelop the enormous, vacant train station, opening the doors for thousands more entrepreneurs to follow in Cooley's footsteps.

Photo courtesy Glenn Triest Photographic, www.triestphotographic.com

Slows BarBQ has become a household name, bringing **people and hope** back into the downtown.

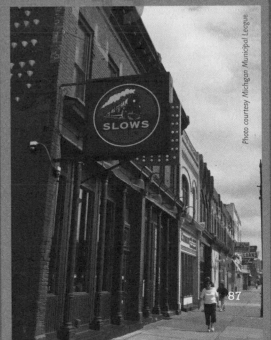

Photo courtesy Michigan Municipal League.

87

In South Carolina, Greenville's Main Street was once lined with numerous vacant buildings, but with the city's long-term commitment to planning and implementation during the past 30 years, Main Street has turned into a magnet of commerce and social activity that is now expanding into neighboring areas.

Transitioning From the Old Economy to a New Economy

The larger change strategy has three primary elements: first, change the cultural stories that frame our understanding of the nature and purpose of the economy and its defining institutions. Second, create a new economic reality from the bottom up through efficiency and self-reliance. And third, change the rules of the game at local, national and global levels to support ecological balance, equitable distribution and living democracy over environmental destruction, wealth concentration and political corruption.

Rather than tweaking Wall Street rules to reduce the fraud and delay the next financial crash, we need to get on with bringing forth the strong, green Main Street living economies that put people to work providing

What is created by human choice can be **changed by human choice.**

their communities with food, shelter, water, education, healthcare, public safety and other basic needs of daily life. The work of economic transformation begins with articulating and spreading a New Economy vision. As a society, we cannot create a future that we cannot see in our collective mind.

The work begins with spreading a vision of a global system of human-scale interconnected Local Living Economies that function in harmony with local ecosystems, meet the basic needs of all people, support just and democratic societies and foster joyful community life. Although, it is an epic, even audacious, undertaking, we now have the knowledge and communication capabilities necessary to achieve it. No single organization is going to achieve such an audaciously ambitious agenda on its own, but fortunately many are contributing to this agenda. From the New Economy Network and the Business Alliance for Local Living Economies (BALLE) to the New Economy Working Group and Business for Shared Prosperity, along with many others, individuals and organizations are making distinctive contributions to the New Economy vision.

Every transformational social movement begins with an idea that spreads through a conversation to challenge a prevailing cultural story and ultimately displace it with a new story of unrealized possibility. The civil rights movement changed the story on race. The environmental movement is changing the story about the human relationship to nature. The women's movement changed the story on gender. The future of humanity lies in the balance, and millions of people the world over are rising to this great challenge. Now is the hour. We have the power. We are the ones we've been waiting for.

. . . . .

David Korten is cofounder and board chair of the Positive Futures Network, which publishes YES! *magazine. His most recent book is* Agenda for a New Economy: From Phantom Wealth to Real Wealth. *His other books include* The Great Turning: From Empire to Earth Community, *the international best seller* When Corporations Rule the World *and* The Post-Corporate World: Life After Capitalism. *Korten has MBA and PhD degrees from the Stanford University Graduate School of Business, served as a Harvard Business School professor and, for 30 years, worked as a development professional in Asia, Africa and Latin America.*

Photo courtesy Ben Fisher/GAVI Alliance

Photo courtesy Royal Family of Bhutan

> There is more to life than money and it's time we focused not just on GDP but on GWB – general wellbeing.

Measuring National Happiness and Well-being

To help guide national policy, the UK government will measure the subjective well-being of its citizens.

"It's time we admitted that there's more to life than money and it's time we focused not just on GDP but on GWB – general wellbeing," said UK Prime Minister Dave Cameron.[1]

The project aims to measure the country's progress in more than national income, which only offers an economic outlook. The British government wants to know how its citizens think and feel about the quality of their lives and the Office of National Statistics will include quality-of-life questions with their regularly scheduled household surveys.[2]

"Wellbeing can't be measured by money or traded in markets. It's about the beauty of our surroundings, the quality of our culture and, above all, the strength of our relationships," said Prime Minister Cameron. "Improving our society's sense of wellbeing is, I believe, the central political challenge of our times."[3]

The UK is not the only country looking beyond GDP. In 2009, French President Nicolas Sarkozy commissioned a report about alternative measures of happiness, which recommended measuring material well-being.[4] In Bhutan, the "Gross National Happiness" indicator is the main indicator of the country's development. Ecuador and Bolivia incorporated *buen vivir* (living well) into their constitutions.[5] In the US, Maryland is experimenting with the Genuine Progress Indicator, which examines 26 different quality of life indicators.[6]

Many examples here in the US show that national income clearly does not measure a nation's welfare. Fortunately, there a few innovative governments and growing awareness for the value of measuring progress that makes life better for its citizens.

from the editor

89

Building a "We" Economy

What do you want out of our economy? A good job? A decent living? Affordable housing? Security in your old age? A "we" economy (versus an "I" economy) would provide these basic economic human rights of stability and fairness.

The gap between the rich and the poor is a better measure of the health of our economy than the S&P 500 or the Dow. Today, the concentration of privately held wealth is at its highest peak since 1929, the year the financial markets crashed and gave rise to the Great Depression of the 1930s.[1] At that time, 25 percent of the population was out of work. Despite the fact that our economy is still recovering from the deepest recession since the 1930s, people in the top 1 percent continue to own as much wealth as all of those in the bottom 90 percent.[2] Fair taxation and good jobs are essential to reversing this trend and constructing a strategy for building a fair and just economy.

Some people say that if we get the economy going again, everyone will do fine. That is, "A rising tide lifts all boats." We've learned, though, that not everyone has a boat. If you don't have a job, a college degree, housing and healthcare you can afford, your feet may be stuck in the mud when the economic waters start to rise. When millions of people are stuck on the bottom without decent jobs or housing,

Mike Prokosch
United for a Fair Economy

Cartoon by Brian Farrington

> **Despite our economy being mired in the deepest recession since the 1930's, people in the top 1% continue to own as much wealth as all of those in the bottom 90% combined.**

we all pay for the extra education and social services they need, the extra police and prisons. It's not much use being the richest country in the world if we "can't afford" those basic economic rights.

Making Every Job a Good Job

Devoted to the principle that people who work full-time should not live in poverty, the living wage movement began in Baltimore in 1994 when the city passed an ordinance requiring businesses to pay employees a living wage while working on city contracts. A living wage is usually defined as the minimum hourly wage required to cover the costs of housing, clothing, food and other essential living expenses. Since then, over 120 communities have followed suit, some setting wage floors more than twice the federal minimum wage, and some requiring various benefits.[3] In fact, a new policy developed by the Obama administration would give companies that pay a living wage an advantage when bidding on government contracts.[4]

Some US employers have voluntarily increased pay rates to a living wage and believe it's also good for business. Borealis Breads, a bakery in Maine, pays its 60 employees a living wage plus benefits. Not only has the company noticed an improvement in recruiting and retention of employees, but it has also been a good marketing tool. Owner Jim Amaral believes that customers are willing to pay a "little bit extra to a socially responsible company." He said, "We're not just selling bread, we're selling the company. Paying living wages, and letting people know that you do it, makes a tremendous amount of sense."[5]

Make Taxes Fair

Over the past third of a century, tax changes have given the very rich more and more of our nation's pie. Statistics from the past few years tell the story. The top-earning 1 percent of the nation's families are getting almost 22 cents out of every dollar in national income.[6] Just 1 percent of the population controls

Photo courtesy Borealis Breads

Workers at Borealis Breads (Wells, Maine) earn a living wage plus benefits.

almost half of the country's wealth. Between 2001 and 2010, the top percent of households received $980 billion in tax cuts introduced by the Bush administration.[7] Tax cuts for the wealthy made little sense when they were passed, and it is unconscionable that they were extended through 2012.[8]

Fair taxation is an excellent way to break up this kind of excessively concentrated wealth and fund programs and services for a "we" economy. Here are a few actions that could have far-reaching consequences:

• **Raise capital gains taxes** (taxes on stock and speculation) and dividends. Right now, most capital gains are taxed at 15 percent, and the Obama administration plans to increase this to 20 percent. That means billionaires are paying the same or lower tax rates than their secretaries. The capital gains rate should be raised at least to the top marginal tax rate—35 percent.

- **Close corporate tax loopholes.** We can start to restore a reasonable level of corporate taxation by closing the overseas tax havens that allow some companies to evade $30 billion in taxes every year.

- **Raise the top marginal income tax rate.** In 1970, the richest people in the country paid 90 percent of their top income (on everything they made over about $400,000) in taxes. Now the top rate is 35 percent. The tax burden was shifted onto the rest of us who can least afford it. The new Fairness in Taxation Act proposes new tax brackets ranging from 45 to 49 percent for incomes starting at $1 million.[9]

- **Set the basic exemption for the federal estate tax at $2 million.** This reform would exempt about 99.7 percent of the households in the US. The estate tax was created so that dynasties of wealth would not take over the country.

Percentage of Federal Budget Paid by Corporations

1940's	Now
40%	10%

This difference allows some companies to evade $30 billion in taxes every year.

It's not just mid- to low-income earners that support these measures. A group of American millionaires is calling for an end to the tax breaks that have benefited them but left the rest of the country with debt and dwindling budgets for education, health and other vital services. These millionaires are among the 700 business leaders and individuals in the top 5 percent of the wealth bracket. They are using their tax breaks to fight for tax policies that benefit all Americans.

In a *New York Times* op-ed entitled "Please Raise My Taxes," Reed Hastings, chief executive of Netflix wrote,

A group of American millionaires is calling for an end to the tax breaks that have benefited them but left the rest of the country with debt and dwindling budgets.

Photo credit: AP Photo/Paul Sakuma

Reed Hastings, chief executive of Netflix giving a keynote address in 2009.

Like my peers, I'm very highly paid. The difference between salaries like mine and those of average Americans creates a lot of tension, and I'd like to offer a suggestion. President Obama should celebrate our success, rather than trying to shame us or cap our pay. But he should also take half of our huge earnings in taxes, instead of the current one-third.[10]

Most Americans agree; 61 percent of people polled said they would like to see taxes for the wealthy increased as the first step to tackling the deficit.[11] Raising the tax rate for the wealthiest Americans could generate more than $78 billion in new revenue annually that could be invested in education, infrastructure and other programs that benefit the public.[12]

Lifting All Boats

What can we do with the money? We can level the playing field and give everyone a fair chance at a decent life by funding programs that benefit everyone, such as

Forty years ago the labor movement, the civil rights movement, the women's and gender freedom movement pushed our country toward a more equitable and fair society.

WOMAN SUFFRAGE HEADQUARTERS.
MEN OF OHIO!
GIVE THE WOMEN A SQUARE DEAL
Vote For Amendment № 23 On September 3 – 1912.

COME IN AND LEARN
WHY WOMEN
OUGHT to Vote.

What will the economic justice movement of our time look like?

universal childcare and free public higher education. Such services are federally funded elsewhere. In Denmark, all state schools from primary through graduate-level are almost completely free,[13] and nearly 45 percent of Danes graduate from a college or university.[14] With universal programs, nobody gets left out. Middle-income families won't have to go into debt to pay for childcare and a college education. Universal programs lift everyone up to the same basic level and give everyone a fair chance to go farther. Universal programs have another advantage: They are really popular. In France, everyone gets childcare, so everyone supports it. That nationwide support makes it hard for any political party to attack childcare or cut down the coverage people are used to.

What Does a "We Economy" Look Like?

Forty years ago, the labor movement, the civil rights movement, the women's and gender freedom movements pushed our country toward a more equitable and fair society. What will the economic justice movement of our time look like?

• It will include coalitions, for example, community organizations and unions getting together and pressuring big corporations for community improvements and better wages.

• People of color will be likely leaders.

• It will be global because the corporations and banks that have the wealth are global.

• Most importantly, we will build solidarity and trust through working together and mutual support.

We dream of nation where prosperity is shared; where there is genuine equality of opportunity; where income, wages and taxes are fair; and where communities are healthy and safe with opportunities for recreation and personal growth. A great nation is one where individuals of varying degrees of wealth come together to work for economic justice to create a "we economy."

.....

Mike Prokosch is a popular economics educator and organizer in Massachusetts. He is currently working on a green jobs-green justice campaign at Community Labor United in Boston and, in his spare time, on the Fund Our Communities—Cut Military Spending 25% campaign nationally. He's also on the board of United for a Fair Economy (www.faireconomy.org).

Closing Tax Loopholes and Funding Key Priorities

Keisty Sample and her daughter Zaria read through a nutrition booklet while attending a nutrition education class at the WIC office in Dallas.

Photo courtesy AP Photo/Tony Gutierrez

There are lots of ideas and conflicting opinions about how to solve the country's budget and deficient woes. Raising taxes or cutting programs are the most commonly proposed solutions.

For example, House Appropriations Committee proposed budget cuts for the Special Supplemental Nutritional Program for Women, Infants and Children (WIC) by $833 million in 2012. The program, which has been in operation for 40 years, provides nutritious foods to low-income pregnant women, new moms, babies and children who have been identified as nutritionally at risk.[1]

These cuts will eliminate assistance to 325,000 to 475,000 eligible mothers, infants and children. However, aside from cutting off assistance to people who need it, such cuts may actually increase other costs. Economists estimate that every $1 invested in WIC saves between $1.77 and $3.13 in healthcare costs in the first 60 days after an infant's birth by reducing the number of low-birth-weight babies and improving child immunization rates. It is estimated that the program has saved more than 200,000 babies from dying at birth.[2]

Instead of slashing funding for programs that help people and raising taxes for working Americans, ending excessive tax breaks and collecting existing taxes could go a long way toward funding valuable programs. For example, the $833 million in proposed WIC cuts equal roughly one week's worth of the Bush administration tax cuts for millionaires.[3] Corporate tax breaks and special interest loopholes are other examples. America's most profitable corporations avoid hundreds of billions of dollars in taxes annually through tax havens, industry-specific provisions and other corporate tax preferences. The IRS estimates that $5 trillion is currently held in tax haven countries, and an independent study found that nearly two-thirds of corporations pay no taxes at all.[4]

TOP 5 Worst Corporate Income Tax Avoiders

Company	2010 Profits	Federal Income Taxes (35% rate)
Exxon Mobile[5]	$30.5 billion	Paid 18%; paid none in 2009
General Electric[6]	$14.2 billion	Paid none; $5.2 billion of profits in US
Chevron[7]	$19 billion	Paid under 8%; paid none in 2009[8]
Boeing[9]	$4.4 billion	Paid .03%; recently received a new $35 billion Pentagon contract
Citigroup[10]	$4 billion	Paid none; received $45 billion in bailout funds in 2008

from the editor

go! green opportunities

> "True sustainability seeks to maximize Triple-Bottom Line benefits, addressing the economy, environment and social justice."

Job Training for the New Green Economy: Green Opportunities

Before becoming involved with Green Opportunities, Demetrius ("D") Wallace had no high school diploma, no job and little direction. Then he, along with eight other unemployed young men and women, climbed mountains, planted gardens, built structures, installed solar panels, captured rainwater, weatherized homes and restored damaged ecosystems. The 15-week program, launched by the nonprofit Green Opportunities designed build skills and confidence, put D and the other participants on a path to a green collar career.[1]

Upon completing the program D's first assignment was with a local solar installation company, FLS Energy. He helped convert an old landfill into a solar farm. Along the way, he learned soldering skills in preparation to become a solar panel installer on massive solar panel installations.[2]

"I got a career, and I never thought I was going have one—[working with GO and FLS Energy] makes you think about the long-term. You recognize what being a man is. You wake up and do it every day. It feels good to belong to something right."[3]

D wasn't the only one to benefit from Green Opportunities's pilot program. Of the eight participants, six completed the full program and all six went on to jobs or paid apprenticeships with local businesses and non-profits. Since its inception, Green Opportunities has provided training for hundreds of Asheville men and women between the ages of 16 and 24. Along the way, participants have weatherized over 50 homes and more than 1,200 public housing units.[4]

Dan Leroy cofounded Green Opportunities in 2007 as a service-based training program, designed to prepare youth for green careers in the context of climate-action projects. "We believe that unless we consciously embrace social justice objectives along with environmental and economic ones, the green economic boom will leave poor, under-served communities behind," said Leroy. "True sustainability seeks to maximize Triple-Bottom Line benefits, addressing the economy, environment and social justice."[5]

Moving the Green Jobs Movement Forward

Phaedra Ellis-Lamkins
Green For All

When it comes to building a thriving economy that creates millions of American jobs and is rooted in environmental stewardship—it's time to stop tinkering. The need for success is greater than ever. Bold action is required. We need to rebuild the pillars of our economy so that it can provide every American with the chance to enjoy a happy and prosperous life. And we can and must do it in a way that heals the planet instead of hurting it. Over the long run, that's the only solution.

With this chance for a renewed economy also comes a chance for a renewed American Dream, a renewed commitment to the loftiest ideals of our country—that everyone deserves a chance to succeed. By creating new waves of investment, new jobs and new sources of wealth, a green economy also creates an opportunity to lift up our most vulnerable communities—those that have too often been locked out, left behind or forgotten.

Signs of Progress: Portland Leads the Way

We are already making progress toward this goal.

Take Portland, Oregon. It has developed a groundbreaking program to provide local residents with energy-efficiency retrofits to their homes. *The Clean Energy Works Portland* program is driving an increase in the demand for these home improvements, which is in turn creating

Portland, OR: Clean Energy Works program

Groundbreaking program developed to provide local residents with energy-efficiency retrofits to their homes.

Creates more business for local contractors and more jobs for local workers, while decreasing C02 emissions.

Program includes wage and benefit standards, local hiring requirements and targeted hiring for disadvantaged workers.

more business for local contractors and more jobs for local workers, all the while decreasing CO2 emissions. Using federal money to build a revolving loan fund, these improvements pay for themselves over time with money saved on energy bills.

More than just a retrofit program, Clean Energy Works includes wage and benefits standards, local hiring requirements, targeted hiring for disadvantaged workers (and contractors) and a screening process for contractors to ensure a solid track record. The goal is not just to put people to work today—but also to put them into careers that can support families. Green jobs need to be sustainable to the planet—and to workers.

The success of this program is serving as a model for different communities across the US, including an expanded initiative in Seattle. It's also the model for a key component in Sacramento's Greenwise Initiative, an effort to transform the region into the nation's next green hub. Riding the wave of innovation that already puts Sacramento on the map as one of the top green cities in the US, the Greenwise Initiative calls for retrofitting 200,000 existing homes—or 25 percent of the region's housing stock—and 60 million square feet of school facilities over the next ten years, while ensuring quality jobs are provided for communities in need.[1]

Zooming Out: The National Picture

Green jobs, despite the economy, are consistently one of the most promising employment sectors in the country. The number of green jobs grew 9.1 percent between 1998 and 2007, two and half times faster than job growth in the economy as a whole.[2] One million green jobs were created and saved by the American Recovery and Reinvestment Act's clean tech investments through 2010.[3] A US Conference of Mayors report

Green jobs, despite the economy, are consistently one of the **most promising employment sectors in the country.**

The number of green jobs grew **9.1%** between 1998 and 2007, **two and a half times** faster than job growth in the economy as a whole.

1 million new jobs **were created and saved** by the American Recovery and Reinvestment Act's clean tech investments through 2010.

One report forecasts that renewable power generation, building retrofitting, and renewable transportation fuels will together generate **1.7** million new jobs by 2018

> **Our success is now transforming the green jobs movement into a movement that looks to green the entire economy, regardless of the industry.**

forecasts that renewable power generation, building retrofitting and renewable transportation fuels will together generate 1.7 million new jobs by 2018.[4]

Large-scale investments in green technologies coupled with policy supports are critical for turning this vision into a reality. The Apollo Alliance proposes an investment of $50 billion per year over ten years to create 5 million jobs in industries such as renewable energy, energy efficiency, transit and transportation, and research development and deployment of clean energy technologies.[5] The Center for American Progress and the Political Economy Research Institute call for spending $100 billion over two years to create 2 million jobs in building retrofitting, expansion of the transit and freight rail grids, construction of a smart electrical grid, wind and solar power.[6]

Investments in clean energy technologies are driving innovation and job creation all over the country. Since 2003, Pennsylvania has invested more than $1 billion in renewable energy projects. As a result of investments and policies, there are now thousands of companies in the green energy industry with more than 350,000 employees. Projects range from a 3.2-megawatt wind project and energy-efficient lighting systems to an 11,000 solar panel installation. Pennsylvania has been recognized as one of the fastest-growing states for wind energy and is expected to be among the top five for solar energy by the end of 2011.[7]

The creation of green jobs was also a key component to former Mayor Richard Daley's plan to transform Chicago into the greenest city in America. A City program, Greencorps Chicago, provides paid nine-month training programs in landscaping, weatherization, environmental remediation, electronics recycling and household hazardous materials processing to individuals with strong barriers to employment and people leaving the prison system. The program is estimated to add 5,000 to 10,000 jobs annually. Additionally, the city has leveraged its purchasing power to attract businesses, ultimately spurring green job creation. When the City committed to purchase solar panels, it attracted two solar power manufacturers to locate their operations in Chicago.[8]

What the Future Can Look Like

Our success is now transforming the Green Jobs Movement into a movement that looks to green the entire economy, regardless of the industry. Key to doing so is cleaning up not only the way we generate electricity, but

Two Greencorps Chicago crew members work in a community garden.

Photo courtesy Greencorps Chicago

99

also the way we fuel our vehicles, manufacture goods and grow our food. The industries and processes involved in those tasks are all still maturing, but promising.

No matter how energy-efficient we make our buildings, we still must generate the electricity we use more cleanly. Renewable energy is beginning to grow but comes nowhere close to providing all of our electricity. As it expands to meet that goal, it will generate jobs and wealth as much as it does power. What's more, this expansion will fuel a similar expansion in America's long-struggling manufacturing sector.

We cannot overestimate the importance of a thriving manufacturing sector to revitalize our economy and ensure it is an inclusive one. An economy that churns out service sector jobs does not create enough demand to reignite our economic engine. Our success requires rebuilding the middle class and replacing low-wage service sector jobs with high-wage manufacturing jobs— typically good high-paying jobs that provide workers health benefits and a living wage. Historically the vehicle into the middle class for a large percentage of workers without a college degree, manufacturing jobs pay 21 percent more in wages and benefits than the entire economy average.[9]

Renewable energy technologies can be an important driver of these types of jobs. Luckily, manufacturers of renewable energy technologies already have operations across the US and are creating jobs. Vestas, a world leader in wind energy, is investing about $600 million at three Colorado locations that together are expected to employ more than 2,000 workers. Solar-World recently opened a $440 million, 480,000-square-foot plant in Hillsboro, Oregon. The plant, said to be the largest solar cell producer in North America, is projected to have a payroll of 1,000 within three years. A wind turbine blade producer has become the largest private employer in Grand Forks, North Dakota, where more than 900 people are employed. The company hopes to create a workforce of comparable size at its operation in Little Rock, Arkansas.[10]

Once this power is cleanly generated, we will need to efficiently deliver it to American buildings. This requires a new, modernized "smart grid." Building this grid will generate a significant number of jobs in every state in the country.

Dirty electricity is certainly not our only significant source of pollution. Vehicles burning petrol-based fuels are massive emitters of the greenhouse gases that cause

Investing in our nation's transportation infrastructure to expand our shared transportation network will not only decrease CO2 emissions and help our environment, but will also put **millions of Americans back to work** in good high-paying construction, manufacturing and operations jobs.

> **We are building new American Dreams for the times we live in, for the new world of the 21st century. We are everyday people with an everyday dream: a safe, healthy, prosperous place for ourselves and our families.**

climate change. The transportation sector currently accounts for 28 percent of greenhouse gas emissions in the US, of which 64 percent are linked to personal vehicle use. Changing this reality will spark a number of American industries. Manufacturing highly efficient automobiles can revive our struggling automotive industry. In fact, the Cash for Clunkers program in 2009, which "provided consumers who traded in their old, gas-guzzling vehicles with vouchers worth up to $4,500 to pay for new, more fuel efficient cars and trucks [...] created or saved over 60,000 American jobs and boosted economic growth by up to $6.8 billion."[11] The need for advanced high-storage batteries will also spur an increase in American manufacturing. Producing clean-burning advanced biofuels will replace dying fossil fuel industries.

Cleaning up our transportation also means expanding shared transportation, specifically public transport and rail. About 50 percent of all Americans do not have access to public transportation.[12] Investing in our nation's transportation infrastructure to expand our shared transportation network will not only decrease CO2 emissions and help our environment but will also put millions of Americans back to work in good high-paying construction, manufacturing and operations jobs. The existing public transit bus, rail vehicle and clean truck supply chains currently support approximately 40,000 US manufacturing jobs. Large-scale investments in the next federal transportation reauthorization legislation could increase these numbers substantially. The Apollo Alliance's proposal to increase federal investments in transit and intercity rail to $40 billion annually could double transit ridership and support 300,000 manufacturing jobs and 3.7 million jobs total.[13] Whether manufacturing clean and efficient buses, building new railway lines or designing and producing the trains of tomorrow, this will also create job, business and investment opportunities.

All told, green sectors remain a vast untapped source for creating American jobs and wealth.

A Dream for a Nation

When I heard the title of this book, I smiled to myself. The first thing that Green For All did as a new organization was organize the first national environmental conference led by low-income people and people of color. We held it on the 40th anniversary of Dr. Martin Luther King's assassination, in Dr. King's honor. And we called it The Dream Reborn.

How fitting, then, to write an essay now about the dream of a green high-road economy for America. As our country's leaders—whether presidents, preachers or prisoners—have from the very beginning, we are building new American Dreams for the times we live in, for the new world of the 21st century. We are everyday people with an everyday dream: a safe, healthy, prosperous place for ourselves and our families.

I know I'm excited about working today to build that tomorrow. I hope you are too.

.....

Phaedra Ellis-Lamkins is the chief executive officer of Green For All (www.greenforall.org). Under her leadership, Green For All has become one of the country's leading advocates for a clean-energy economy, and one of its most important voices on the intersection of economics and environment. Ellis-Lamkins has led Green For All to several groundbreaking policy victories at the federal, state and local levels, and has helped states like Washington and New Mexico pioneer state-level green jobs and energy-efficiency programs. Green For All is redefining the face of environmentalism through partnerships with popular artists to reach new audiences with a message about the benefits and opportunities of going green.

Make It in America

Made in America is more than just a slogan. For over 200 years and millions of Americans, it was a way of life. From the Model-T Ford to the Arsenal of Democracy, production was at the heart of our national identity.

But something has changed in recent years. Today our manufacturing sector is half the size it was in 1960, while our financial sector is twice its size. In 2001, the first full year of the new millennium, 24 factories closed without being replaced every day—a factory loss every hour for the entire year, 24/7/365.[1] First we lost rudimentary industries like textiles, furniture and paper. Next we started to lose core industrial capacity like shipbuilding and machine tools, and now we are losing high-end manufacturing like pharmaceuticals, aerospace and semiconductors. There are over 5 billion mobile phones in use worldwide and virtually none were made in the US.[2] Solar cells were invented in America, but in recent years, we produced only a third as many solar cells as Japan or Germany, and a quarter as many as China.[3]

Eric Lotke
Campaign for America's Future

Photo courtesy Laura Padgett

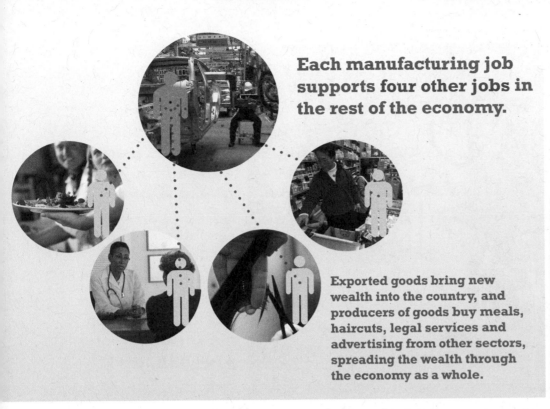

Each manufacturing job supports four other jobs in the rest of the economy.

Exported goods bring new wealth into the country, and producers of goods buy meals, haircuts, legal services and advertising from other sectors, spreading the wealth through the economy as a whole.

Billions of cellphones are in use worldwide.

0

Virtually none were made in America.

This is not natural economic evolution.

Our economy has not simply matured, replacing old industries like manufacturing with new industries in which America has the "comparative advantage"—high-end services like investment banking, software design or telecommunications. This is a loss with nothing in line big enough to replace it.

No matter what happens with top-end services, a country still needs things. Whether it is cars, computers or refrigerators, if we don't make them here, then someone else gets our money. Yes, we ran a $146 billion surplus in services in 2010. But we ran a $645 billion deficit in goods in the same year. Between 2000 and 2010, America imported almost $7 trillion more goods than we exported.[4]

The changes were the result of policy choices that can be made differently.

Our tax code, for example, allows US companies to defer taxes on income earned overseas. This deferral not only reduces US tax revenues, it creates an incentive to move production abroad. In President Obama's own words: "It's a tax code that says you should pay lower taxes if you create a job in Bangalore, India, than if you create one in Buffalo, New York."[5]

Other countries make choices that work to their advantage, like offering subsidies to induce strategic industries to relocate away from America. China started with textiles and consumer electronics but quickly moved up the value chain to aerospace and now semiconductors. In 2007, Intel accepted China's $1 billion subsidy to open its new chip plant in Dalian. China knows that the advanced manufacturing techniques will follow the factory, along with the personal expertise, the R&D and, soon enough, the software design for the computers that use the chips.

Some foreign countries have the advantage of lower costs because of cheaper labor and lower standards for environmental protection or workplace safety. Yet other countries with high wages and high standards are also outperforming us in global markets. Germany generally has higher wages and better benefits than America, and highly advanced production technologies. But Germany ran a trade surplus of $200 billion in 2010, the same year America ran a trade deficit of $500 billion.[6] Germany has simply made a long-term

Solar cells were invented in America. But in recent years we produced only a third as many solar cells as Japan or Germany, and a quarter as many as China.

Countries with high wages and high standards are also outperforming us in global markets.

Germany ran a trade surplus of $246 billion in 2008, the same year America ran a trade deficit of $706 billion.

We need to restore our productive capacity for the next generations of America in the new world economy.

commitment to remaining an industry leader, investing in its research, its machinery and its people.

But even with the losses there is much to preserve. Manufacturing still constitutes 12 percent of US gross domestic product, 60 percent of US exports and 70 percent of private sector research and development.[7] America still exports Ford trucks, Boeing airplanes and Gordon & Smith surfboards. We need to fight for our existing industries and expand into the next generation—solar cells, nanotechnology, titanium surgical tools. We need to restore our productive capacity for the next generations of America in the new world economy.

The American people understand this. A 2010 survey found 66 percent support for the proposition that "manufacturing is a critical part of the American economy and we need a manufacturing base here if this country and our children are to thrive in the future." The finding held across party lines—67 percent among Democrats, 66 percent among Republicans, 64 percent among independents. It had twice the level of support

of a competing proposition that America can leave manufacturing and move into "new areas like high-tech or services."[8]

The path ahead is straightforward. First, we need to rebuild our infrastructure, the backbone of our economy. The US will not thrive in the 21st century unless we lift our economic infrastructure up to 21st century standards, and we can do it with American workers and parts made in America.

Other countries do it this way. When Canada or European Union members buy steel, coal, construction or telecommunications equipment for public purposes, they make every effort to buy it from producers in their own countries, and they negotiate that option into trade agreements.[9] America does not.[10] China exports more than 95 percent of its solar energy products to the US and Europe—but China requires that at least 80 percent of the equipment in its own solar power plants and 70 percent of its wind turbines be made in China.[11]

In some areas, we may need to be patient, as domestic manufacturers are not presently operating at scale or at capacity, and start-up costs may be incurred as they become more competitive. But Americans will be better off if taxpayer-funded projects take a little longer or cost a little more—if more of the money stays at home than disappears overseas.

Other countries make choices that work to their advantage.

China exports more than **95 percent** of its solar energy products to the US and Europe—but China requires that at least **80 percent** of the equipment in its own solar power plants and **70 percent** of its wind turbines be made in China.

A factory worker manufactures photovoltaic cells for solar panels at the Eoplly New Energy Technology Co., Ltd., plant in Nantong city, east China's Jiangsu province.

United Streetcar manufactures modern streetcars in America, with parts made in America, and plans to be a pioneer in this new urban transit option. Employees are seen here with a completed car for Portland, Oregon's new streetcar system,

In some cases, of course, American companies are ready and waiting. United Streetcar, a subsidiary of Oregon Iron Works, Inc., manufactures modern streetcars in America, with parts made in America, and plans to be a pioneer in this new urban transit option. United Streetcar's first customer was the City of Portland, soon followed by the City of Tucson. United Streetcar is betting that Americans will turn to streetcars as a form of urban transit, and that it can compete with the dominant manufacturers in other countries that enjoy advantages of experience, scale and consistent demand.

When Republic Windows closed its factory in Chicago in 2008, workers protested the wrongful denial of severance benefits. The protest caught the attention of Kevin Surace, CEO of Serious Materials of California, who was in the market for a window manufacturing facility. Surace anticipated that the Obama administration would enact an economic stimulus package featuring investments in weatherization and energy efficiency, and he was right.[12] Surace bought the plant, rehired the workers and honored the agreement of the previous owner. Serious Materials is still expanding, fulfilling new market demand for high-performance, thermally efficient windows.

Exxel Outdoors, headquartered in Haleyville, Alabama, makes sleeping bags in America. Exxel produced 1.4 million bags in 2009, 30 percent of the nation's market share. It uses environmentally friendly material and a highly efficient manufacturing process. Add in the cost of shipping from overseas, and Exxel comes out ahead of foreign rivals—even though it pays its workers fair wages with affordable healthcare.

Pittsburgh instituted a whole host of changes all at once. It reinvented itself in the 1990s from a Steel City in decline into a combination economy with high-end services in research and medicine, as well as cutting-edge manufacturing. The change grew from an active collaboration between business and government. Local leaders devised a comprehensive economic strategy that matched Pittsburgh's local strengths with global opportunities. State leadership behind Governor Ed Rendell devised an economic stimulus package focused on infrastructure, transportation and research.

The US will not thrive in the 21st century unless we lift our economic infrastructure up to 21st century standards, and we can do it with American workers and parts made in America.

Committed to American Workers

New Balance is the only athletic shoe manufacturer still making shoes in the US.

to look out for our people like the governments of other countries do. Far too often, our government seems to take the side of multinational corporations that benefit from foreign subsidies and foreign labor rates, but can still sell in America at American prices. Thus the interests of many nominally American businesses diverge from the interests of the American people.

American consumers go last but they are not without power. Next time you see the cheap goods labeled "Made in China," know nearly half of the price advantage comes from currency manipulation, which lowers the cost of imports from China and raises the cost of our exports. Question whether the children's toy has lead-based paint, the pet food has melamine or whether Chinese workers had fair conditions in the plant. Then consider whether there's a differ-

Next time you see something labeled "Made in America," consider using your money to support your people and your vision of a better world.

Pennsylvania enticed Gamesa, a Spanish leader in wind energy production, to open a factory in the Pittsburgh area to anchor a US expansion. Pittsburgh's turnaround shows what can happen when our historical partnerships come back together.

Lastly, we need to stop getting fooled. "Free trade" isn't an international ideology. It is a sales line and a political theory that's entirely optional for every country. We need our government

ent product you can buy with advantages other than price, and whether you can choose differently.

And next time you see something labeled "Made in America," consider using your money to support your people and your vision of a better world. We're all in it together.

. . . . .

Eric Lotke is research fellow at the Campaign for America's Future (www.ourfuture.org), a progressive research institute. He has published on subjects ranging from healthcare to manufacturing to infrastructure investment. Previously, he worked for over a decade in and around the justice system. He managed direct-service programs, litigated individual and class action cases and authored path-breaking research. Lotke has been an adjunct professor at the Georgetown Law Center, the George Washington Law School and the Northern Virginia Community College. He is also author of the novel, 2044: The Problem Isn't Big Brother; It's Big Brother, Inc.

Real World Models
for Creating Stability in the New Economy

Driven by local entrepreneurs and based on relationships and real values, a New Economy is emerging. Today more than 100 local, interdependent networks have emerged in communities across North America, organized by local businesses, farmers and entrepreneurs—the people who grow and distribute our food, build our buildings, provide our power and manufacture many of the goods and services we need. They are supporting each other and addressing the economic, environmental and societal challenges in their own home regions. At the Business Alliance for Local Living Economies (BALLE), our goal is to galvanize an alliance of these local community business networks and to connect them to spread best practices and engage in fair trade.

Michelle Long
Business Alliance for
Local Living Economies

Photo courtesy:
The Bellingham Farmer's Market

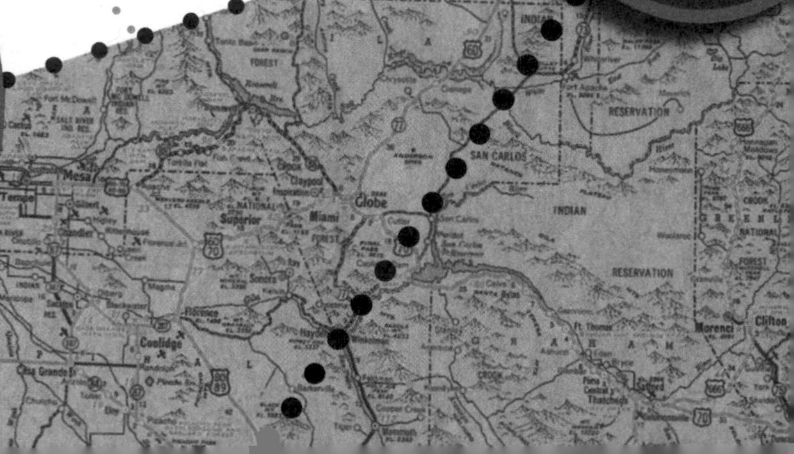

The New Economy is... Built on local ownership

Zingerman's Deli in Ann Arbor, Michigan is a model of local reciprocity and accountability. The Zingerman community of businesses is a $30 million company with 500 employees in a town of fewer than 100,000 residents.

The New Economy Is Built on Local Ownership

Local living economies ensure that economic power resides locally to the greatest extent possible, and that local entrepreneurs have the capacity to produce their communities' basic needs. Abraham Lincoln said, "I like to see a man proud of the place in which he lives. I like to see a man live so that his place is proud of him." This idea of local reciprocity and accountability is crucial to sustaining vibrant, livable communities and healthy local ecosystems.

The New Economy will be made up of businesses like Zingerman's Deli in Ann Arbor, Michigan. The founders started with the goal of creating the world's best delicatessen. When they were ready for a new challenge and a chance to provide development opportunities for staff, they decided to scale up by "growing deep." Rather than franchise nationally and "spend the rest of their lives flying around visiting second-rate versions of their own business," they chose to vertically integrate and bring in new partner-owners with each new business.

Today, 17 co-owners have created a creamery to supply the deli and other local markets, a bakery, a candy company, a farm, a non-profit food bank, a consulting company, a publishing company and a full-service restaurant. Now the Zingerman community of businesses is a $30 million company with 500 employees in a town of fewer than 100,000 residents. Local non-profits erected a billboard thanking Zingerman's for being in their town.

The New Economy Invests in Relationships

Founded in 1905 as an independent community bank, The Mechanics Bank has become one of the largest

> Driven by local entrepreneurs and based on relationships and real values, a New Economy is emerging.

109

> "We firmly believe
> that a community
> bank's activities,
> whether commercial
> or philanthropic,
> **should benefit
> the people in the
> areas we serve.**"
>
> ⇨ Eddie Downer,
> former chairman of
> The Mechanics Bank

The New Economy... Invests in relationships

Eddie Downer (left of center) is the former chairman and third generation member of the founding family of The Mechanics Bank.

banks headquartered in the San Francisco Bay Area. A key tenet is that the bank's money must be spent within the communities it serves. The founder, a former weekly newspaper publisher, postmaster, chairman of the school board for 25 years and a small-town mayor, understood the needs of local communities, and believed a community bank's justification for being was to serve those needs.

"We firmly believe that a community bank's activities, whether commercial or philanthropic, should benefit the people in the areas we serve," said Eddie Downer, former chairman and third-generation member of the founding family. "Being principally family-owned has given us the freedom to do things that large publicly traded companies cannot."

Socially responsible investing (SRI) is another proactive way to manage money. With an SRI approach, investors put their money to work building a more just and sustainable world while earning financial returns. Portfolio 21 Investments has been a pioneer in the field since 1982. This SRI fund only invests in companies that recognize environmental sustainability as a fundamental human challenge and a tremendous business opportunity. Their companies "design ecologically superior products, use renewable energy and develop efficient production methods for prospering in the 21st century."[1] They also are proud to note their independent ownership, which "gives us the autonomy to think for ourselves without the influence of outside shareholders or a parent company."

Where you bank and invest your money makes a difference. Imagine a national bank collaborating with borrowers to decide together on fair interest rates. Uniquely, this is exactly what investors and borrowers do together at RSF Social Finance, a pioneering financial services company offering lending, investing and giving services. They are committed to shifting from "financial

Where you bank and invest your money makes a difference. Imagine a national bank collaborating with borrowers to decide together on fair interest rates. Uniquely, this is exactly what investors and borrowers do together at RSF Social Finance.

transactions that are complex, opaque and anonymous to those that are direct, transparent and personal."

Community banks, credit unions and local financial institutions do more lending to small businesses and family farmers. Non-profit organizations receive 2.5 times more support per employee from small businesses, and most new jobs are created by small businesses.[2] This interdependence means that the vitality of any one is linked to the health of the others.

The New Economy Is Connected

Interconnected networks, because they show rich, deep models of what communities can be, are like Petri dishes or incubators. People say, "Aha! I see how!" and then they share ideas, learn from each other and create huge cultural momentum.

The northwest Washington BALLE network, Sustainable Connections, is one example of this momentum. Founded in 2002 in Bellingham, Sustainable Connections is today a non-profit network of local independently owned businesses that facilitates sustainable economic development by providing education, connections and market development. The network now has 700 member businesses, representing every sector of the local economy, including farmers,

manufacturers, builders, non-profit organizations, service providers and retailers.

Sustainable Connections members are committed to sustainability and thinking local first. Their efforts in green building, renewable energy, sustainable agriculture and local manufacturing have led the National Resources Defense Council (NRDC) to name the community the nation's "number one in progress toward urban sustainability," and American Public Media's Marketplace to call the community the "epicenter of a new economic model."

Business members display the "Think Local, Buy Local, Be Local" logo on their storefronts and include it in articles and newsletters, invoices and advertisements. Businesses now get phone calls from people asking if they are local. Recent studies show that 60 percent of households in Bellingham choose independent retailers and services whenever possible.

In the '70s, '80s and '90s, the county unemployment rate was higher than Washington State and national figures. Since Sustainable Connections' inception, the county has experienced lower unemployment rates than state and nation rates. Plus, purchasing from local farmers is up five times over the rate of growth in other parts of the state, and businesses that start here are more likely to succeed than if they start elsewhere.

The New Economy is... Connected

Photo courtesy of Sustainable Connections

Sustainable Connections hosts a Farm to Table Trade meeting in Northwest Washington, gathering buyers, producers, processors and distributors from multiple counties.

Since Sustainable Connections' inception:

The county has experienced **lower unemployment rates** than the state and nation as a whole.

Purchasing from local farmers is up 5x over the rate of growth in other parts of the state.

Businesses that start here are **more likely to succeed** than if they start other places.

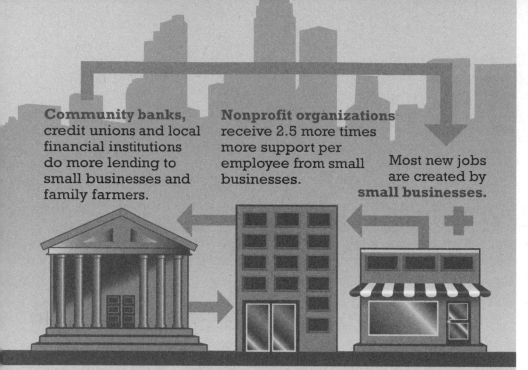

Community banks, credit unions and local financial institutions do more lending to small businesses and family farmers.

Nonprofit organizations receive 2.5 more times more support per employee from small businesses.

Most new jobs are created by small businesses.

This interdependence means that the vitality of any one is linked to the health of others.

The New Economy Is Green

The New Economy is...

Green

In the New Economy, local businesses are connecting the dots between emerging sustainable industries including sustainable agriculture, green building, energy efficiency and renewables, community capital and local zero-waste manufacturing. With a focus on their unique place, they are building innovative and diverse local economies that are community-based, green and fair.

An example of this place-based business model is the Energy Cooperative that started in 1979 when some Philadelphia residents wanted to use the concept of group buying power to get lower prices on heating oil. The Energy Cooperative now provides their members renewable electricity and biodiesel from sources as local as possible. They buy their solar power from the rooftops of their members and buy wind power from wind farms in Pennsylvania and neighboring states. When they were unable to find a source of renewable heating oil, the co-op spun off a new company to produce biofuels from local restaurants' waste grease. Today the co-op's annual sales are about $5 million.

The New Economy Has More Opportunity

In 1965, the ratio between CEO pay and average company pay was 24-to-1 in the US. Since the mid-90s, CEOs of major corporations have been earning more than 200 times the average compensation of workers.[3] Compare that to Japan, a country with one of the lowest pay gaps, where CEOs earn on average 10 times more than the average worker.[4]

The Cleveland Foundation, as part of its Greater University Circle Initiative, is spearheading a new strategy for democratizing wealth creation through the Evergreen Cooperatives. The cooperatives, based on the Mondragon model in Spain, give individuals who would normally be excluded from ownership opportunities the chance both to gain stable employment and to become equity owners in the businesses where they are employed. To date, four new businesses have launched: a commercial green laundry facility, a solar and weatherization installation service, a food production greenhouse and a community newspaper. Within five years, the organization hopes to have ten businesses that provide 500 living-wage jobs.[5]

The worker cooperative and democratic workplace models continue to spread. For example, six worker-owned bakeries in San Francisco employ 125 workers and generate $12 million in sales annually. In the industrial sector, the United Steelworkers, with over a million members, has plans to develop manufacturing cooperatives in the US and Canada.[6]

Shifting to the New Economy

The vision of the New Economy is audacious, but, to become a reality, it must be. Researchers who study complex human organizations and ecosystems have found that once a large complex system becomes corrupted it has almost an impossible time fixing itself. It can play at the edges, the equivalent of "business as usual plus a little recycling," but it simply can't imagine an entirely new way to do things. Instead, researchers have found that what does work is creating a safe space outside the dominant system for something truly new to be created from the ground up. We need Petri dishes. We need to catalyze, connect and strengthen local networks of independent business owners who have the autonomy to re-imagine their industries and who are collaborating in their particular place to create community-based, green, fair economies.

We are now seeing transformational successes led by local BALLE networks of entrepreneurs in small towns, large cities and rural areas, even in regions of high unemployment. There is nowhere we can say it won't work, only that with more resources we could go further, faster.

We are seeing the bright lights of transformation. We need more pinpoints of light coming forward, and we are committed to connecting these lights into a luminous tapestry of national and international action.

The New Economy has... More opportunity

Arizmendi Bakery (below) and the Cheeseboard Pizza Cooperative (above) are two of the six worker-owned bakeries in San Francisco that together employ 125 workers and generate $12 million in sales annually

Photo courtesy kennejima (flickr)

Photo courtesy Ci. Ejon (flickr)

Advancing the **New Economy:**

1 Find a BALLE network near you and patronize the locally owned businesses in your community. www.livingeconomies.org

2 Move your money to a community bank or credit union: www.moveyourmoney.info/find-a-bank

3 If you have money to invest, learn more about socially responsible investing: www.socialinvest.org

.....

Michelle Long, BALLE's first executive director, sat on the board between 2003 and 2009, and is currently once again the executive director of the Business Alliance for Local Living Economies (www.livingeconomies.org). BALLE, an alliance of 80 community business networks comprising 22,000 independent businesses, is the nation's fastest-growing network of socially responsible businesses. Long was the co-founder and executive director of Sustainable Connections in Bellingham, Washington, one of BALLE's oldest networks. She is also the author of Local First: A How-to Guide, *and of the how-to manual,* Building a Community of Businesses.

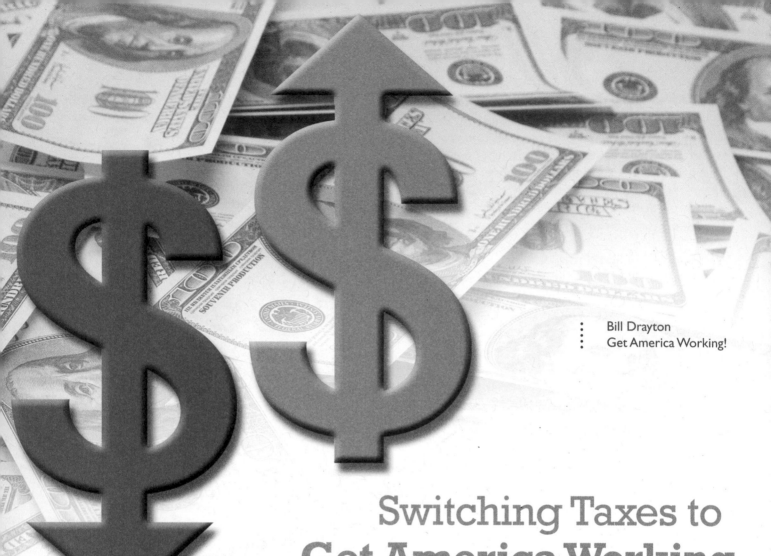

Bill Drayton
Get America Working!

Switching Taxes to
Get America Working

The country is needlessly stuck.

If we stimulate, we risk going over the debt cliff. If we merely stop adding debt, we risk leaving the economy in the ditch and official (i.e., hugely understated) unemployment stuck at destructively high levels.

America's opportunity is to see its situation through a far more realistic framework, to escape a framework as rigid and destructive as the gold standard that did so much to bring on the Great Depression.

If one lowered the price of labor and increased the price of its only substitute, things, we would employ more people and conserve our natural resources. Economics 101.

How could we do that. The simplest way would be (1) to eliminate payroll taxes, which would reduce the cost of hiring by roughly 17 percent, and (2) to keep the government budgets whole by adding equal new revenues by taxing things (materials, energy, land, pollution) roughly 12 to 13 percent.

The result would be a 30 percent change in the relative price of using people vs. things. That is a price signal no one would ignore. Companies would substitute people for energy. Farmers would make more compost and use less chemical fertilizers. Human capital sectors would grow faster and natural resource intensive areas would shrink as a percentage of the economy.

This idea is, in fact, the most powerful way to break out of the old framework. A country can grow and reduce debt if it finds ways to become structurally far more productive. That's a jujitsu move far beyond the ken of business cycle economics.

The most fundamental economic choice every business, indeed every country, makes is what mix of the two key ingredients in production—people versus things (energy, materials, land)—it will put to work.

For decades, governments have put their hands on the scale by taxing employment more and more. Payroll taxes in the US have grown from 1 percent of federal revenues when they were first introduced in 1937 to 40 percent today. (Progressives accepted payroll taxes for valued programs, and powerful interests fought other taxes tooth and nail.) The result has been ever growing, if largely invisible unemployment, and discouraged conservation. Actual unemployment in the US runs eight to ten times the official rate, which does not measure tens of millions[1] who have accepted the unavoidable but who suffer greatly from dependency, less freedom of choice, more illness and less satisfaction. Sixty-eight percent of retirees, for example, think it was a mistake to stop working. But they aren't counted.

The jujitsu is to change the relative price of people versus their only substitute—things. That means reversing the unintended price signal of the last decades by removing payroll taxes and adding compensating taxes on things. The decision-makers have myriad possibilities ranging from familiar options such as a gasoline tax (effective but sensitive) to pollution charges. Get America Working! has identified 22 options that together would at modest rates easily raise more than twice the payroll tax revenue. Consider just two examples:

• Every advanced economy except the US uses a Value Added Tax (VAT) as a major source of revenue. It is collected on the consumption of materials, energy and labor in stages as goods and services are produced and marketed. A non-labor VAT would produce hundreds of billions of dollars annually and send the clearest of messages.

Lowering the Price of Labor, Increasing the Price of "Things":

| Eliminate payroll taxes, reducing the cost of hiring by **17%** | + | Tax things (materials, energy, land, pollution) roughly 12% to **13%** | = | **30%** change in the relative price of using people vs. things |

This is a price signal no one would ignore. This idea is the **most powerful way** to break our of the old framework. A country can grow AND reduce debt if it finds ways to become structurally far more productive.

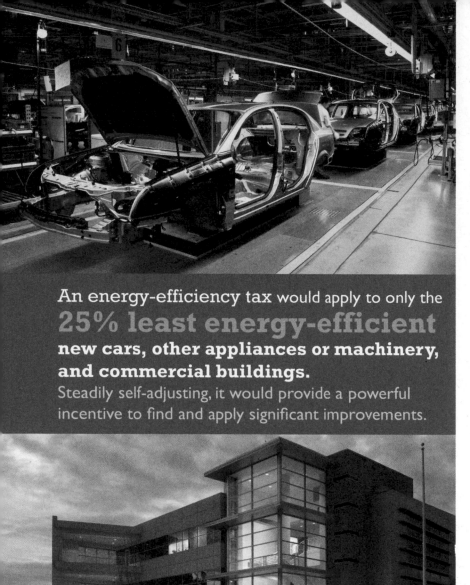

An energy-efficiency tax would apply to only the **25% least energy-efficient new cars, other appliances or machinery, and commercial buildings.** Steadily self-adjusting, it would provide a powerful incentive to find and apply significant improvements.

• An energy-inefficiency tax would apply to only the 25 percent least energy-efficient new cars, other appliances or machinery, and commercial buildings. Steadily self-adjusting, it would provide a powerful incentive to find and apply significant improvements.

This is not a radical idea. Across Europe and, increasingly, now Asia and Latin America, countries are cutting payroll taxes. The International Monetary Fund advises countries to cut payroll taxes to increase employment. Since 2000, more than a dozen European nations have reduced their payroll tax rates. The World Bank recently recommended that Central European nations boost employment by cutting payroll taxes.

In 2007, just before the economic downturn, Get America Working! studied 22 OECD economies and found that countries with payroll taxes below 30 percent have, on average, 11.5 percent more of their population working than countries with payroll taxes over 40 percent.[2] Reducing payroll tax rates by just ten percent could boost employment by ten percent in the long term according to a leading labor economist.[3] Offsetting taxes on things—ranging from energy to materials (e.g., timber and iron)—would roughly double that impact.

For a major new idea to fly, it must pass three tests. (1) It brings major advantages; (2) The tools needed to make it work are both effective and do not offend key actors; and (3) It is a big political win.

This simple idea is very probably the greatest opportunity our economy and society has to break out on the upside. It would mean:

• Roughly 30 to 40 million fulltime equivalent, permanent new jobs over a capital cycle (usually five to 25 years, but likely to be very much faster if the change in relative prices is as substantial as 30 percent).

• A sustainable higher growth rate as we put America's largest unused resource, people and human capital, to work.

• Sharply reduced costs for individuals, families, business and government of paying for people not working.

• Huge reductions in many social costs. (Illness goes up sharply when a person is not contributing. Students who know there is no job ahead are demotivated. Drugs/crime/fear. And much more.)

• No debt incurred.

• The choice to cut taxes and/or invest in solving unaddressed common ills. Growing the economy and tax base at the same time that many public costs fall sharply makes this possible.

This is an idea that can bring America back together because it is about **growing, not dividing the pie.**

The idea works through the simplest, most effective, and most universally accepted tool—a price signal. There is/are no. (1) bureaucracies, (2) choosing of winners and losers, (3) delay, and/or (4) corruption. That is one of the reasons this idea has won support across the otherwise polarized ideological spectrum—from Charles Krauthammer to Paul Krugman and from Robert Reich to Richard Lugar.

The third prerequisite for an idea to fly is politics. Here is the alliance of forces each of which wins big once this idea goes into effect. (1) older people (two-thirds of men over 65 had a job in 1950; now 11 percent do); (2) those with disabilities; (3) many women; (4) young people. (5) those who have ever been institutionalized. (6) minorities; (7) many immigrants; (8) anyone who cares about any of the above; (9) anyone who cares for the environment; (10) workers (it is hard to push up wages with a 40 percent supply overhang in the labor market); and (11) almost all businesses (faster growth, less dependency and social ill costs, a good shot at lower taxes, etc.)

The chief political cost is fear that cutting payroll taxes will weaken Social Security. However, this tax shift (1) replaces a shrinking base (as the ratio of workers to

What is the blockage? This is a new framework. People cannot act on it until they see it. That is where **you can help.**

beneficiaries worsens) with one that is growing (the value of natural resources increases with demand and scarcity), and (2) provides a growing overall economy able to afford a strong safety net. These realities explain why both big parties have advocated payroll tax cuts over the last five years.

As John Gardner (who was an early supporter) said, this is an idea that can bring America back together because it is about growing, not dividing the pie.

So what is the blockage. This is a new framework. People cannot act on it until they see it. That is where you can help.

. . . . .

William Drayton is board chair of Get America Working!, a nonpartisan, fuller employment policy citizen group that framed the payroll tax shifting proposal. Named by US News & World Report as one of America's 25 Best Leaders in 2005, he is a MacArthur Fellow who pioneered social entrepreneurship and founded Ashoka: Innovators for the Public, a citizen movement of social entrepreneurs worldwide. He's currently its CEO. He was previously a management consultant at McKinsey and Company, and faculty member at Stanford and Harvard, and assistant administrator of the Environmental Protection Agency (1977–1981) where he launched emissions trading among other reforms.

A News Media That Informs and Empowers

A look at the numbers...

According to a recent citizen poll, only 8 percent of Americans said **they had a "great deal" of confidence in the national news media...**

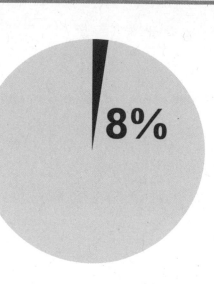

8%

and 18 percent said **they had "no confidence at all."**

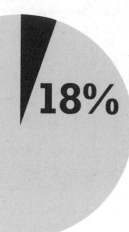

18%

Interviews debating the Iraq War

Of the 393 major network interviews "debating" the Iraq War in the two weeks before the invasion, **just three were with individuals representing anti-war groups.**

VS.

61%

Percentage of Americans before the Iraq War began who thought the US should "wait and give the United Nations and weapons inspectors more time."

Half of states no longer have a single reporter in Washington to keep their representatives accountable.

0

reporters in Washington

30,000

Members of the media laid off since 2008. With this many people, there is no shortage of experienced journalists to hire.

Today, **only 1 in 5 newspapers** are independently owned, which means fewer reporters and more generalized content.

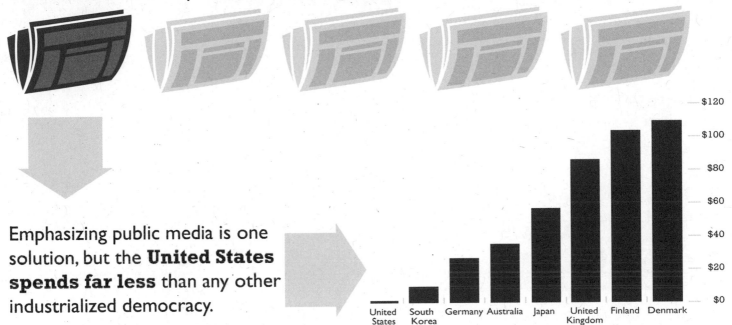

Emphasizing public media is one solution, but the **United States spends far less** than any other industrialized democracy.

CNN.com stories

44%
Entertainment
Scandal
Violence
Crime
Death

CNN.com was chosen for the study because of it's balanced reputation and the good work that they do.

Over a month long period, CNN.com headlined

48 **celebrity news stories**

and **44% of all stories** were categorized as entertainment, scandal, violence, crime or death.

compared to

12%

Percentage of stories categorized as entertainment, scandal, violence, crime or death from the media outlet CommonDreams.org during the same timeframe. They featured zero celebrity headlines.

"Harmony seldom makes a headline."

➤ **Silas Bent**

The news media is a lens through which we perceive the world. But the fact that more than half of the US public believes news organizations undermine our democracy reinforces the need to evaluate the role and responsibility of the news media. The over-saturation of coverage devoted to celebrities, fluff and violence does not contribute to an informed citizenry and does not protect our democracy.

Fortunately there are shining examples of independent and mainstream news organizations that are covering a wider range of topics and focusing on solutions-oriented stories.

A Civic-Minded Media Is...

Affirming that a
strong democracy
requires constructive
journalism

Empowering
people with
information to
shape the future

Serving as a check
and balance to power

Choosing not
to polarize,
sensationalize
and scandalize

Focusing on exploring
root causes to problems
and solutions in addition
to the news of the day

Balancing the
need **to prosper**
with the goal of
contributing to the
greater good

Media: A Tool for Strengthening Democracy

Thomas Jefferson wrote, "Were it left to me to decide whether we should have a government without newspapers or newspapers without a government, I should not hesitate a moment to prefer the latter." Jefferson lived at a time where there was perhaps the appearance of such an option—the US government was in its formative stages, and the free press, from pamphleteers like Thomas Paine to printers like Benjamin Franklin, played important roles.

Amy Goodman
Democracy Now!

IF IT BLEEDS IT LEADS

CELEBRITY GOSSIP

FEAR

24 HR NEWS CYCLE

TRIVIAL STORIES

100% SUGAR

TASTY SOUND BITES

CHOMP CHOMP

NON NEWS

124

There is a reason that a free press is enshrined in the US Constitution: journalists are the check and balance to power. We believe an independent media is an essential part of a functioning democracy.

The Media's Role in Democracy

Now, we are in an age, and in a media environment, that Thomas Jefferson could very likely not have imagined. Yet he saw the importance of a vibrant, independent press. There is a reason that a free press is enshrined in the US Constitution: journalists are the check and balance to power. We believe an independent media is an essential part of a functioning democracy.

While the demise of many newspapers has rightly provoked concerns and discussion about the "crisis in journalism"—as literally tens of thousands of reporters, photographers, editors and support staff are laid off—many have perceived, for decades, a more fundamental crisis in journalism: the lack of independence in news organizations. At a time when newsrooms globally are

These attitudes are typified by recent polls and reports.

In a recent poll:

8% had a "great deal" of confidence in the national news media

18% had a "no confidence at all" in the national news media[4]

87% agree that celebrity scandals receive too much news coverage[5]

63% believe that news stories are often inaccurate[6]

shrinking, or being eliminated entirely, this consistent, daily in-depth coverage of global news is critical.

Fairness and Accuracy in Reporting (FAIR) did a study during the two weeks around then-Secretary of State Colin Powell's speech at the United Nations, making the case for war in Iraq, on February 5, 2003.[1] At the time of the speech, a CBS poll reported 61 percent of television viewers felt the US should "wait and give the United Nations and weapons inspectors more time." In the two-week period, there were 393 interviews conducted about the invasion of Iraq on the four major US nightly newscasts: *ABC World News Tonight, CBS Evening News, NBC Nightly News* and PBS's *NewsHour With Jim Lehrer.* Of those, only three of the nearly 400 interviews were with people who represented anti-war groups.[2]

FAIR also looked at the coverage of the US healthcare debate. In the week leading up to President Obama's March 5, 2009 healthcare summit, according to FAIR, hundreds of stories in major newspapers and on major television network shows mentioned healthcare reform. Of those, only 18 mentioned the single-payer public option, none of which was on television. Most reports and interviews were from critics of single-payer. Only five single-payer advocates were quoted, at a time when polls indicated people in the US favored some form of public health insurance option over a strictly private option by a two-to-one margin.[3]

Media Models that Work

The Internet and increasingly accessible digital technology have vastly leveled the media playing field, with many excellent examples.

Democracy Now! started in 1996 and was the only daily public broadcasting show devoted to covering the presidential election. The program began, in part, because we wanted to investigate why so many people didn't participate and didn't seem to care about politics. What we found were fascinating stories of people engaged in grassroots organizing, building movements and organizations and focused the program around this vibrant world of democratic activity that was not getting any coverage at all from the mainstream media. After the election, the demand for the show remained, so it continued and today is broadcast on more than 850 radio and television stations around the world and online.

Yes! Magazine was founded in 1997 by economist, author and former Harvard professor David Korten as an advertising-free, non-profit print publication that "supports people's active engagement in building a just and sustainable world." Articles emphasize solutions in action that address ecological, social and political problems. Each issue features a series of articles focused on a theme along with coverage of issues such as health, climate change, globalization, media reform, faith, democracy, economy and labor, social and racial justice, and peace-building. Published by the Positive Futures Network, *Yes! Magazine* reaches hundreds of thousands of readers.

The Indypendent is a New York–based free newspaper published 17 times a year by a network of volunteers with a large and growing print and online readership. Since 2000, more than 650 citizen journalists, artists and media activists have participated in this project. *The Indypendent* is "dedicated to empowering people to create a true alternative by encouraging people to produce their own media."[7]

CommonDreams.org is a shining example of web-based news coverage that informs and empowers. The national non-profit, non-partisan citizens' organization was founded in 1997 with the belief that humanity "shares common dreams of peace and security, equal opportunity, and meaningful participation in our society." Published online, the website features breaking news from a progressive perspective and attracts millions of readers each month. Common Dreams also publishes original articles and opinion pieces from a wide range of thought leaders.

There are a number of independent news outlets that are working to shed light on the issues and information that are crucial for creating a positive future.

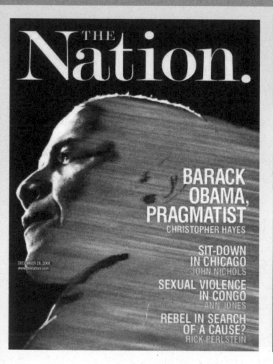

> **It will take continued, concerted, national and global efforts to sustain the practice of independent reporting, to protect journalists in what is among the most dangerous of professions, and, ultimately, to empower people with the information they need to shape the future.**

The Nation is yet another example of a media outlet dedicated to advancing critical thought and societal evolution. The oldest continuously published weekly magazine in the US, *The Nation* was founded in 1865 at the start of the Reconstruction as a supporter of the North in the American Civil War. Coverage is devoted to politics and culture and the publication's weekly circulation is large and growing.

ProPublica is a non-profit, independent newsroom with a staff of 34 journalists dedicated to investigative reporting on stories with significant potential for major impact. Stories are published online and offered exclusively to traditional news organizations, free of charge, for publication or broadcast. Published in the *New York Times Magazine*, "The Deadly Choices at Memorial,"[8] was awarded a Pulitzer Prize for Investigative Reporting. The 13,000-word *ProPublica* report chronicled what happened when Katrina's floodwaters rose, the generators failed and hospitals were cut off from the world.[9]

Independent media outlets work daily to bring the best journalism possible to the widest audience. It will take continued, concerted, national and global efforts, to sustain the practice of independent reporting, to protect journalists in what is among the most dangerous professions, and, ultimately, to empower people with the information they need to shape the future. We need to continue supporting public and independent media

How to get news you can use:

① Subscribe to independent media.
Most independent media rely—solely or in part—on subscriptions and donations from listeners, viewers and readers.

② Encourage mainstream media to do better.
Let them know what you think of their news coverage and what kind of news you want.

sources that strive to strengthen democracy by covering more issues that matter and by empowering people with fair and accurate news coverage.

......

Amy Goodman is the host and executive producer of Democracy Now! *Goodman is the author of four* New York Times *bestsellers including* Breaking the Sound Barrier. *Goodman is a recipient of Right Livelihood Award; Park Center for Independent Media's Izzy Award; the American Women in Radio and Television Gracie Award; James Aronson Award for Social Justice Reporting; thePuffin/Nation Prize for Creative Citizenship; Robert F. Kennedy Prize for International Reporting among others. Democracy Now! is a national, daily, independent, award-winning news program. Pioneering the largest public media collaboration in the US, Democracy Now! is broadcast on Pacifica, NPR, community, and college radio stations; on public access, PBS, satellite television; and on the Internet at www.democracynow.org.*

Making
Coverage Count

Take a drive across the country, and you'll see varied landscapes, stumble across unique landmarks, taste new flavors and hear different accents. But people just about anywhere agree on one thing: their local news must be the worst in the country.

But it's not the worst. It's just the same. If it bleeds, it leads: that means plenty of crimes, fires and accidents. Then there are the healthcare stories, likely framed with frightening graphics and ominous music, celebrity gossip and network tie-ins.

Why We Need the News

TV, radio, movies, books, newspapers and the Internet are our prime sources of news and information, and they shape our values, beliefs and perspectives. When it comes to the news, we need credible, accurate reporters keeping a watchful eye on those in power, attending the meetings and examining the issues we don't have time to follow, translating complex topics and keeping us informed about what's happening in our communities.

A viable self-government is impossible without quality journalism. Democracy requires journalism; but journalism also requires democracy—an engaged citizenry demanding the serious work that holds our leaders accountable.

Often, the media covers the spin instead of cutting through it to get to

Craig Aaron
Free Press

Covering More of What Matters

A Pew poll shows that Americans are hungry for news, spending 70 minutes a day accessing it.[1] Eighty-seven percent of Americans said that there's too much celebrity coverage in the news.[2] They feel environmental coverage should be an average of 18 percent of coverage instead of just 2 percent.

Unfortunately too many news programs ignore important issues and devote too much coverage to sensational and trivial stories. A month-long news headline comparison of a leading and respected corporate news source, CNN.com and a nonprofit news aggregator, Commondreams.org revealed some vast disparities in news coverage. Clearly, less coverage of trivial and celebrity stories will free up more time for covering news that informs and empowers an engaged citizenry.

CNN.com Headline Analysis

44% Trivial, violence, death, crime, celebrity, scandal, entertainment

32% Domestic and International News and Politics

1% Environment

3% Iraq and Afghanistan

(Tracked in September 2010 by SEE Innovation staff)

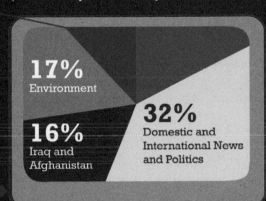

Common Dreams Headline Analysis

12% Trivial, violence, death, crime, celebrity, scandal, entertainment

17% Environment

16% Iraq and Afghanistan

32% Domestic and International News and Politics

the facts. The Pew Project for Excellence in Journalism studied the media's coverage of the 2008 presidential election and found that most outlets covered the election like a sporting event. Pew found "horse race reporting, once again, made up the majority of coverage" and that rather than focus on the issues facing Americans, "53 percent of the coverage focused on political matters, particularly tactics, strategy and polling."[1]

Studies also show a link between access to news and levels of political corruption at the national and state level. One 2008 MIT study found that members of Congress who were covered less by the local press did less work for their local constituents, showed up to fewer hearings and brought less money back to their home districts.[2] Yet according to the Project for Excellence in Journalism, half the states no longer have a newspaper with a reporter covering the US Congress.[3]

What's Missing From the News?

More than 70 percent of Americans get their news from cable and network television,[4] and how these outlets cover the big stories strongly influences who we

A viable self-government is impossible without quality journalism. Democracy requires journalism; but journalism also requires democracy—an engaged citizenry demanding the serious work that holds our leaders accountable.

Ira Glass is the host of National Public Media's This American Life which explores a range of meaningful issues and stories of real people.

> **Larger and larger corporations—in fewer and fewer numbers—have taken control of more and more of our news organizations.**

what news and information is covered, whether important issues are covered accurately, who is hired to report and produce the news, what music and artists get airplay and how women and minorities are portrayed in the media.

Larger and larger corporations—in fewer and fewer numbers—have taken control of more and more of our news organizations. They've merged, consolidated and concentrated into fewer and fewer hands, swallowing up local outlets. Before 1996, for instance, the biggest radio chain owned just a few dozen stations. Now Clear Channel owns nearly 1,000 and only a fifth of newspapers are independently owned. That runaway consolidation has left us with the same cookie-cutter content from coast to coast.

Media and tech companies have spent a billion dollars in the past decade to influence federal policy—even more than the oil and gas industry. Because of their tremendous influence in Washington, media policymaking has been a closed and secretive process, and citizens have been shut out of the debate. So even though we own the airwaves, they decide how media is created, financed and distributed.

elect for public office, how we debate the most pressing issues of the day and when we go to war. Local television is still the number one source for news, but we don't often ask what we get in return for giving broadcasters those free but exclusive licenses to use the public airwaves.

Increasingly, we see the news ignore important issues and devote too much coverage to sensational and trivial stories. A recent study of Los Angeles television news by the University of Southern California found that in a typical half-hour newscast, half of the time was spent on ads and teasers. The remaining 15 minutes were dominated by crime stories, soft features, entertainment news, sports and weather. Just 22 seconds of the typical 30-minute news show was about local government.[5]

Media Ownership Matters

The biggest problem in journalism isn't poorly trained or unethical journalists. The real problem facing our media system is a structural one. Media owners influence

Public Policy for Public Media

What could things look like if policies were made to serve the public? Consider the current state of public broadcasting. National polls conducted in December 2009 and January 2010 found that Americans named PBS the most trusted, least biased, nationally known institution in the US.[6] Yet compared to the rest of the world, we spend peanuts on public media. Americans now spend just a little more than $400 million per year in public money on public media. That works out to just $1.37 per person. By comparison, Canada spends $22 per capita and England spends $80.[7]

If the United States spent the same per capita on public media and journalism subsidies as Norway, which

If we want better media, we need better media policies. If we want better media policies, we need to raise public awareness about these issues and organize for real change.

ranks number one, we would be spending as much as $30 billion a year on public media—which would go a long way toward putting thousands of journalists back to work. Not coincidentally, countries that rank near the top in public media spending are also at the top of *The Economist* magazine's annual Democracy Index, which evaluates nations on the basis of the functioning of government, civic participation and civil liberties. In that same survey, the United States ranks 17th.[8]

At a moment when journalism is in crisis, we could re-imagine our current public broadcasting system and rebuild it as new public media with an overarching commitment to newsgathering and community service. We could put reporters back on their beats and remove commercial pressures from the newsroom. But getting better coverage of our communities starts with new policies and political change.

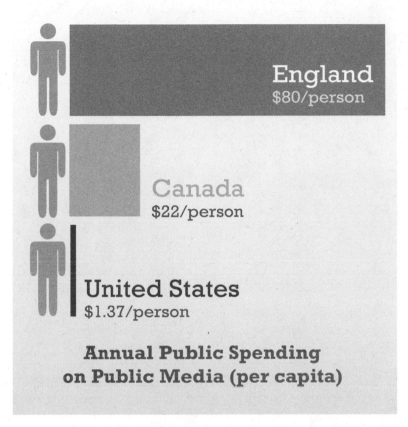

England
$80/person

Canada
$22/person

United States
$1.37/person

Annual Public Spending on Public Media (per capita)

Charting Our Future

Fair and accurate news and information is necessary to guide an informed citizenry, and therefore the media is essential to our democracy. We depend upon media to know what's happening in our communities, to play our part as citizens and to serve as a vital check on government and corporate power.

If we want better media, we need better media policies. If we want better media policies, we need to raise public awareness about these issues and organize for real change. Now more than ever, people across the country need to be engaged in the debates about the future of our media. We need real people to have a seat at the table and a voice in those debates. By holding the media accountable for their content, supporting policies that encourage media diversity and participating in the media reform movement, real people can make coverage count.

. . . . .

Craig Aaron is the president and CEO of Free Press (www.freepress.net), the national media reform group. He is the editor of two books, Appeal to Reason: 25 Years In These Times *and* Changing Media: Public Interest Policies for the Digital Age.

O
ur journalists and politicians know how to talk about problems. Turn on the news, open the paper, and you'll find countless pieces dramatizing the many crises, local and global, that threaten to engulf us. As a result, we know about some of the challenges we face: climate change, unemployment, crime, terrorism, environmental degradation, substandard education and an energy crisis, to name a few. We know much less about potential solutions, however, especially those that go beyond narrow, technical fixes. And the less we know, the less likely we are to act, and the less able we will be to effect the change we need.

In a well-functioning democracy, citizens must have forums in which they can not only identify public problems and air public grievances, but also come together to discuss solutions. On a local level, some such forums still exist: in New England's town meetings, for instance, citizens still gather to compare and debate solutions to municipal problems. And in Britain and other European countries, the government ensures that a certain amount of television airtime is used for public education.[1] But in the US, on a national level, the public conversation is decidedly crisis-focused, with the majority of the media privately owned and profit driven.[2] As media outlets compete for ratings, and as reporters compete for scarce work, only those who can attract attention survive. The it-bleeds-it-leads approach may win ratings, but it contributes to public cynicism and fatigue.

In fact, studies have shown that TV news viewers leave the typical news program feeling anxious and depressed, and are much more likely to catastrophize personal worries.[3] Other studies have found that reading negative newspaper articles can create

Tess Croner,
Solutions
& Ida Kubiszewski,
Solutions and
Institute for Sustainable
Solutions, Portland State
University

> **As media outlets compete for ratings, and as reporters compete for scarce work, only those who can attract attention survive. The it-bleeds-it-leads approach may win ratings, but it contributes to public cynicism and fatigue.**

exaggerated feelings of distrust that extend beyond the content of the story.[4]

But with the massive growth of the blogosphere in recent years, media is changing. The Internet, unlike television, has no major technological or financial barriers to entry, and thus creates a more decentralized and two-directional communication structure. It gives users more control over the distribution of information and allows a message previously overseen by a few media corporations to be shaped by the entire population.

The Internet "allows citizens to gain knowledge about what is done in their name, just as politicians can find out more about those they claim to represent."[5] It does more than just disseminate information; it lets voters talk back. It therefore creates new opportunities for communities to share stories and solutions, ranging from local to global, in ways that were once impossible. WiserEarth, a social networking site that helps people working toward social justice, indigenous rights and environmental stewardship connect, collaborate and share knowledge, has created a solutions directory accessible to all. This directory allows the public to share solutions from within their communities so they can be duplicated elsewhere in the world. The site features over 112,000 civil society organizations in 243 countries and territories.

Similar initiatives have sprung up in recent years. Dowser, a new media organization launched in 2010, reports on social innovation, using case studies and interviews to address the question "Who is solving what and how?"; and the Good News Network posts daily about positive solutions-focused news from around the world. It also encourages authors and readers to collaborate to promote positive change. Says founder Geri Weis, "We need to be informed by a world view that is not dripping with sensationalism and attuned to the police scanner."[6]

Solutions is a hybrid academic journal/popular magazine, launched at the beginning of 2010, that showcases innovative ideas for solving the world's interconnected economic, environmental and political problems. The journal is designed to serve as a starting point for a more constructive and inclusive conversation—a new kind of town meeting in which academics, policy-makers and the informed public can discuss and explore solutions and develop shared visions of the future.

As a brief illustration of this new model of journalism, let's take a look at Appalachia. It's a special place—culturally rich and biologically diverse. But many of us associate it with the problems facing its poorest communities: unemployment, poverty and lagging education. Resource extraction, especially mountaintop removal mining—the practice of using explosives to remove the tops of the region's mountains to more easily reach coal deposits—has devastated both the environment and public health. The rubble is dumped into valleys where it chokes waterways. Native forests are destroyed, and mining wastes are responsible for polluting the groundwater. Tensions are rising between residents who oppose this practice and those whose livelihoods depend on coal mining.

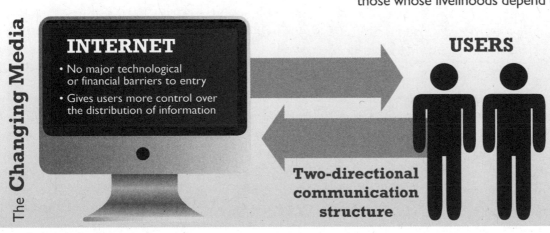

The Changing Media

INTERNET
- No major technological or financial barriers to entry
- Gives users more control over the distribution of information

USERS

Two-directional communication structure

The Internet creates new opportunities for communities **to share stories and solutions,** ranging from local to global, in ways that were once impossible.

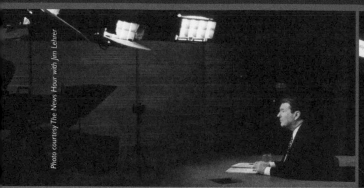

Jim Lehrer on the set of The News Hour *on PBS. Americans named PBS the most trusted, least biased nationally known institution.*

Air Force Chief of Staff Gen. Norton Schwartz answers questions during an interview with Lara Logan from 60 Minutes.

More Good News

For many people, independent media is the go-to place for fair and balanced news reporting. But independent media outlets aren't the only ones getting it right. More and more programs are popping up in the mainstream media that air compelling, useful news that's making a difference.

NBC News Education Nation

"Education Nation" was a weeklong national broadcast event with a focus on improving education in America. Secretary of Education Arne Duncan, New York City Mayor Michael Bloomberg, Harlem Children Zone's CEO Geoffrey Canada, along with other policymakers, educators, members of the business community, and engaged citizens came together for a two-day summit in Rockefeller Plaza to discuss America's education system. For the entire week a variety of NBC programs broadcast stories on the challenges, opportunities and success stories in education in the US with the goal of inspiring "lasting and positive improvements in our educational system."[1]

CBS 60 Minutes

The investigative reporting news magazine program, *60 Minutes* does not simply regurgitate the facts. The program does its own investigations and follows up on investigations done by national newspapers and other sources. Many stories focus on allegations of wrongdoing and corruption on the part of corporations, politicians, and other public officials. The show also features celebrity biographies and profiles of people who have accomplished a heroic action or efforts to improve the world. In addition to informing the public, the program has influenced policy and exposed previously hidden truths.[2]

PBS NewsHour

Aired on public television, there are no commercials in this hour-long news program. After a brief summary of the headline, *PBS NewsHour* dives in to three or four of the headlines events in-depth with 10 to 15 segments on each. The segments include discussions with experts, newsmakers, and/or commentators. Jim Lehrer, co-owner and anchor, created a unique list of 10 guidelines for ethical reporting including, "Cover, write, and present every story with the care I would want if the story were about me" and "Assume personal lives are a private matter until a legitimate turn in the story absolutely mandates otherwise."[3]

This new trend in media is not a quest for cure-alls. Rather, it is an invitation to thoughtful conversation and collaborative consensus-building.

Coverage of the West Virginia mining tragedy only reinforced the region's troubled public image. But there is also a different conversation under way in Appalachia—a conversation that gets much less attention from conventional media. Many groups—private and public, local and regional—are working to create a new, more diverse and more sustainable local economy by reforesting barren mine lands, reclaiming rivers and streams, developing renewable energy industries and supporting the region's many entrepreneurs.

Solutions wanted to expand this conversation, include more voices and give it a wider regional and national audience. Its editors asked academics, activists and nonprofit leaders who have spent their lives working to create solutions for Appalachia to help us imagine coal country's future beyond coal. The result was a special issue with 87 pages of ideas for a more prosperous, more sustainable Appalachia. In essence, it's a playbook for the region: a set of solutions that will focus and motivate future action.

Hearing about solutions can be empowering. And, critically, it can also be contagious: It can start conversations and inspire action. Michael Gleich, founder of the innovative German-based Advanced Journalism Academy, argues for the value, in a time of media sensationalism, of what he calls "constructive journalism." His organization has trained hundreds of journalists in conflicts areas, like Sri Lanka and Rwanda, to find and report on local peacemakers. His success has led him to believe that there is a market for solutions-oriented journalism. Says Gleich, "I became aware that in all conflict areas known only for disaster and death there were intelligent, creative and courageous people working on peace processes. They seemed to be 'unknown heroes' because their stories were hardly covered by mainstream media." He adds, "Constructive journalism is an important additional viewpoint. It completes the picture."[7]

Johan Galtung founded TRANSCEND International, which, through the TRANSCEND media service, explores and supports the field of peace journalism. This field asks journalists to present the root causes of a conflict, give voice to all affected parties and report on ideas for conflict resolution as well as success stories and post-war developments. Galtung compares human conflicts to epidemics. If a disease were to break out in our country, we'd want our journalists to do more than simply tally the death count. We'd want them to offer a diagnosis, explain the causes of the outbreak and, most importantly, report on a cure. Says Galtung, "To say that violence is the only thing that sells is to insult humanity."[8]

Focusing on solutions does not mean ignoring problems or dismissing the obstacles that stand in the way of change. This new trend in media is not a quest for cure-alls. Rather, it is an invitation to thoughtful conversation and collaborative consensus-building. Both are essential steps toward effective action.

. . . . .

Tess Croner is an editor for Solutions, *a non-profit print and online journal that showcases innovative ideas for solving the world's integrated environmental, social and political problems. She graduated in 2009 with honors from Washington University in St. Louis, where she earned a BA in environmental studies with a minor in anthropology. She currently lives in Burlington, Vermont.*

Dr. Ida Kubiszewski is a research assistant professor in the Institute for Sustainable Solutions at Portland State University. She is the Managing Editor of Solutions *and a cofounder and former managing editor of the* Encyclopedia of Earth. *Dr. Kubiszewski is the author or coauthor of over 75 scientific papers and a Junior Fellow at the National Council for Science and the Environment.*

Citizen Empowerment Through Journalism

Sarah van Gelder
YES! Magazine

What can we do as we face a perfect storm of climate crisis, joblessness, growing corporate power, and energy and food constraints? To take on these and the other crises of our times, we need journalism to rise to its fullest potential. High quality coverage of symptoms of the crises by responsible, mainstream journalists is important, but it isn't enough.

We need a new sort of journalism—let's call it constructive journalism. This is journalism that digs deeply and reveals the root causes of our problems. It also explores the emerging ideas and innovations that have the potential to shift our society in more just and sustainable directions. Constructive journalism shows that change is possible and highlights the role each person can play in bringing it about. This sort of journalism opens the door to real empowerment.

Shining the Light on Constructive Solutions

When people are losing their homes to foreclosure, constructive journalism shows that we have an alternative: community land trusts, which are experiencing almost no foreclosures among their modest-income homeowners. A reader of constructive journalism might learn about the Dudley Street Project in Boston, which succeeded in taking over large sections of abandoned inner-city land and transforming it into vibrant business districts and affordable housing.

> **Constructive journalism shows that change is possible and highlights the role each person can play in bringing it about. This sort of journalism opens the door to real empowerment.**

Constructive journalism not only warns of the possible consequences of unchecked global warming; it tells stories of the activists who have prevented dozens of new coal plants from being built. And readers will learn that California voters averted attempts by big-spending out-of-state energy corporations to overturn the state's landmark climate law.

At a time when protracted wars are devastating people's lives, constructive journalism explores ways people are building understanding across divides, helping veterans and civilian victims of war to heal, and countering the powerful military-industrial complex.

Constructive journalism is not only about big issues. In addition to empowering us as citizens—this form of journalism explores ways to live more meaningful, joy-filled lives that don't compromise the well being of the Earth and its other residents.

One writer explores her own choice to live simply in order to have time at home with her children. Another writes of raising bees, and a third describes building a small, simple home to avoid the debt and clutter of living in a sprawling house. These writers are redefining happiness, not allowing their values to be dictated by commercialism.

These examples are just a few of the thousands of stories published in *YES! Magazine*. For 15 years, *YES! Magazine* has pioneered constructive journalism with quarterly themes ranging from local food to alternatives to prison, from DIY education to a new economy. Each issue explores the powerful ideas and practical actions that make change possible.

A Growing Movement

The movement toward constructive journalism has been picking up steam in recent years. This is not surprising given complaints that traditional journalism often leaves readers discouraged and without a way to respond to bad news.

What does constructive journalism do?

■ Digs deep to reveal the root causes of our problems

....

■ Explores ideas and innovations emerging to shift our society in more just and sustainable directions

....

■ Shows that change is possible and highlights the role each individual can play in bringing it about

Photo courtesy Ashoka

Ashoka fellow Michael Gleich trains journalists to produce constructive coverage of social change.

With a background as a reporter, he has focused on the concept of constructive journalism, or news media that focuses on positive social change. That stands in contrast to the truism, "If it bleeds, it leads," or the idea that violence and negative societal problems attract more readership and are easier to report.

Good magazine, founded in 2006, for example, describes itself as serving "the people, businesses, and NGOs moving the world forward." Recent features include people doing polar bear plunges to raise money for the Maryland Special Olympics, and news of California's first stretch of high-speed rail.

Greater Good magazine reports on the science of happiness and altruism, sharing research that improves quality of life and societal well being.

Even *The Nation* now features stories not only on the failings of the corporate-dominated economy, but also on the emergence of a new economy.

Building on the success of the print magazine, *YES!* is stepping up online coverage. New stories can be found daily on the *YES!* website, on the topics of peace and justice, planet, people power, new economy and happiness.

Some commentators mistake constructive journalism for feel-good fluff. But real constructive journalism doesn't shy away from such difficult topics as the US prison system, which locks up more than 2 million Americans, or the mass extinction of species. But instead of stopping there, constructive journalism explores ways to address these tragedies at their roots, and features the people and stories that show the way. As mainstream news continues to evolve and change, we are hopeful that it will incorporate more of the elements of constructive journalism.

Asking the Right Questions & Uncovering Practical Solutions

Instead of accepting without question the key assumptions that dominate popular media, constructive journalism holds them up to scrutiny. For example, most journalists assume that enhancing economic growth should be a principal aim of public policy—they question only how it might be accomplished. Constructive journalism asks whether economic growth can or should continue indefinitely given the resulting degradation of the natural systems on which human civilization depends. And it asks whether economic growth has, to date, enhanced human well being, or whether it's done more to boost the wealth of the already fortunate at the expense of ordinary people.

In addition to empowering us as citizens, this form of journalism explores ways to live more meaningful, joy-filled lives that don't compromise the well being of the Earth and its other residents.

> **"All of us who professionally use the mass media are the shapers of society. We can vulgarize that society. We can brutalize it. Or we can help lift it onto a higher level."**
>
> ⟫ William Bernbach

Constructive journalism isn't afraid to reframe issues, to allow a different story to emerge. Instead of asking how we can maximize economic growth, for example, we ask what policies and practices help ordinary people enjoy a sustainable livelihood that doesn't undercut the Earth's carrying capacity.

Constructive journalism rejects the stale left-right debate. The point isn't to play on fear and anger to win followers by repeating, without fact checking, preposterous claims about "death panels" in the healthcare reform bill or the claims of climate change deniers. Scapegoating the least powerful members of society, or sensationalizing human failings may win audiences. But these practices undercut our ability to build a more just and sustainable society.

Instead of turning to the politicians and experts who have repeatedly failed to address our crises, constructive journalism looks to visionaries with ideas responsive to the deep challenges of our times. Those who are telling new stories about what's possible are featured, along with those doing the hard work of building a new society. Readers meet people like former pro basketball player and corporate executive Will Allen, who runs a thriving urban farm, aquaculture operation and compost facility in Milwaukee, providing fresh food and dignified jobs to people who need both.

Constructive journalism delves into the interrelated and mutually reinforcing systems that threaten economic ruin and ecological collapse, and explores how these systems could be transformed to contribute instead to lasting human and ecological well-being. Local, sustainable food, for example, will probably not be a big story for journalists focused on Wall Street speculation. But in terms of the real economy of people and the planet, it's a winner; it offers more jobs, reduces the distance our food travels, sequesters carbon in the soil, and cuts the massive application of chemicals. It reduces the power of agribusiness, oil, and chemical corporations, and distributes economic and political power instead of concentrating it in a few hands. And it uses less fossil fuel, so it helps extend the life of our current oil supplies.

These sorts of whole-systems solutions are neither liberal nor conservative. They are the way to build a world in which we honor and preserve life.

Constructive journalism goes to the very root of our role as individuals, and as members of families, communities, and cultures. It challenges us to do more than sit back and complain when things go wrong; it asks that each of us consider our own role in fixing our troubled world. Instead of seeing ourselves as the victims of wrongs, we are invited to be agents of history.

Our world is at a turning point. Of thousands of human generations, ours is the one that will determine if future generations will inhabit a livable world. Constructive journalism is one of the tools we can draw on to make change a living reality.

.....

Sarah van Gelder is a co-founder and executive editor of YES! Magazine (*www.yesmagazine.org*), *a national media organization that combines powerful ideas with practical action for a more just and sustainable world.*

Aiming for the Best in Education

five

A look at the numbers...

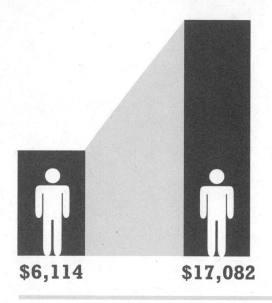

$6,114 $17,082

All school districts are not funded equally. In one state, **per-pupil spending ranges from $6,114 to $17,082** across 500 districts.

22 points

Amount that test scores in poor urban districts of New Jersey have increased after reforming their school funding system.

Estimates suggest that we'll need between:

$100 billion $360 billion

to rebuild the country's **deteriorating school buildings.**

$15 billion

Amount the Obama administration has pledged to rebuild school buildings that are worst-off, but more is needed.

Struggling cities will not be able to rejuvenate without education, yet many organizations estimate that every 26 seconds a student drops out of school in America. **That's more than 1.3 million students per year.**

26 seconds

$900 million

Amount President Obama has promised for the 12% of American schools that produce 50% of dropouts.

$400 – $670 billion

How much higher the GDP would have been in 2008 if the US had narrowed the gap between low-income students and their peers.

~40%

of high school graduates lack the skills necessary to succeed **in college and the 21st century workplace.**

75%

Increase in math and reading proficiency scores in Portland's SUN Community Schools, which coordinate extended learning, service learning, health and social services and parental engagement programs to support their students.

90%

Percentage of graduates from the Harlem Children's Zone (where they are held to the highest expectations) who go on to college.

MEDIAN ANNUAL EARNINGS

High School Dropout

┆┄┄┄┄ **$31,400** ┄┄┄┄┆

College Graduate

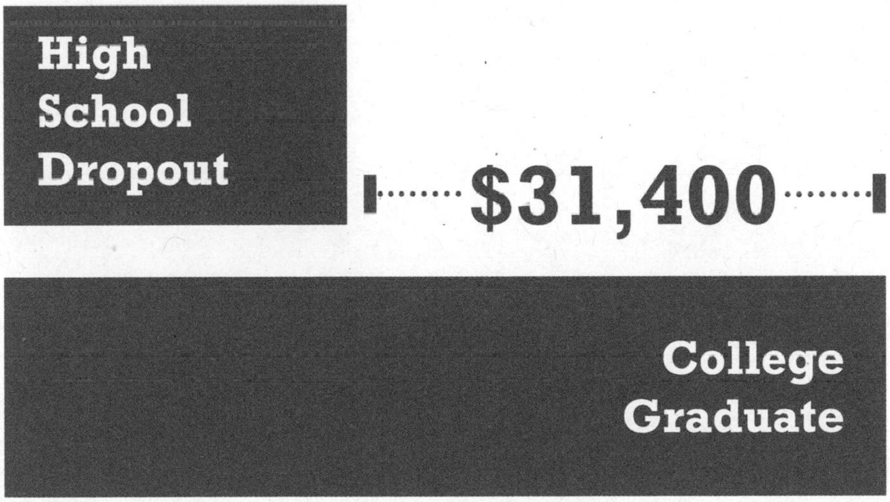

The median annual earnings of **college graduates are $31,400 more** than high school dropouts.

Addressing the achievement gap:

2x

How much more likely low-income students and students of color are to be taught core academics by out-of-field teachers.

Providing low-income students with highly effective teachers **virtually closes the socio-economic achievement gap.**

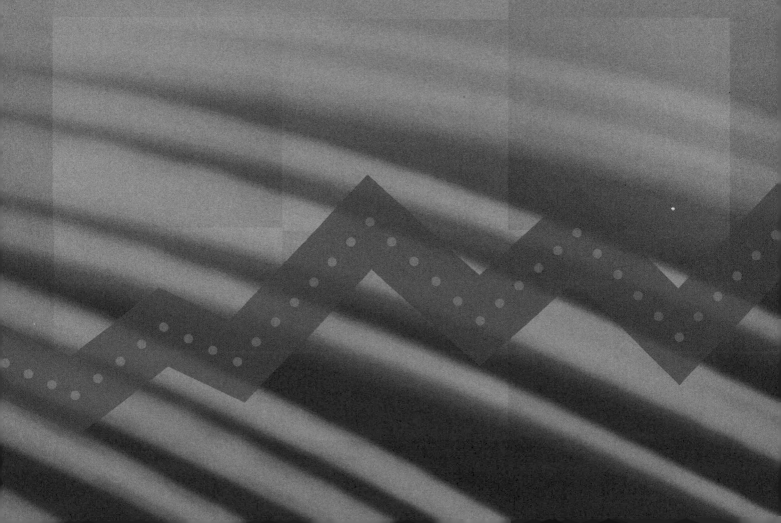

Education is the foundation for success in modern society. The quality of our educational system directly influences the strength of our nation. Educated citizens solve tough problems and contribute to society in meaningful ways. Yet the US is one of only two industrialized countries in which today's young people are less likely than previous generations to complete high school—with nearly one-third of students failing to graduate on time. Among those who do, 40 percent lack the skills to succeed in college and the 21st-century workplace.

Fortunately, there are passionate teachers and administrators, concerned citizens, elected officials and organizations working across the country to create an equitable, effective, high-quality educational system for our students. They are pioneering new models of success that are challenging convention, changing the definition of what education means and catalyzing transformation.

Despite the **big**, tough **challenges** for our public education system, I am **convinced** that we are **at the verge of a transformation.** This is still America—we have unparalleled resources, and "change" is in our DNA. We know the way to fix this, and Americans are awakening to the challenge and finding the will to tackle it.

Geoffrey Canada

Photo Credit: Chester Higgins Jr./The New York Times/Redux

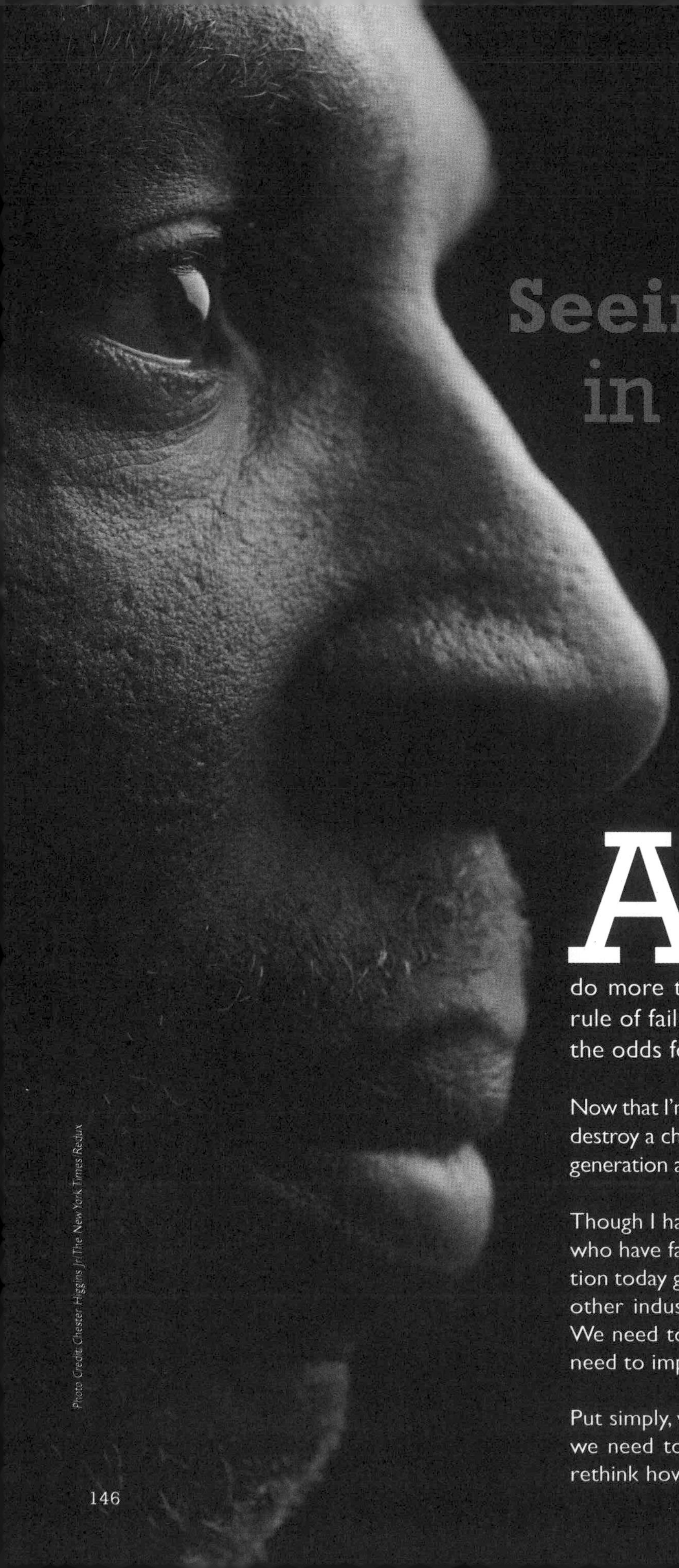

Seeing Education in a New Light

Geoffrey Canada,
Harlem Children's Zone

At a very early age, I knew what I wanted to do with my life: save children who grew up like me—in poor communities, the odds stacked high against them. But I wanted to do more than just help the successful exceptions to the rule of failure in poor neighborhoods: I wanted to change the odds for all the children.

Now that I'm 58, I've seen over and over how a lousy education can destroy a child's chances for a comfortable life. I've seen how failing generation after generation of children can destroy a community.

Though I have concentrated my efforts at helping poor children who have fallen behind, I have also seen that the crisis in education today goes beyond the inner city. America has fallen behind other industrialized countries in educating all of our children. We need to improve our devastated communities, but we also need to improve our entire public education system.

Put simply, we need to place the needs of our children first and we need to look at our education system with new eyes and rethink how schools operate.

We are working to create a tipping point for the neighborhood. We want kids to look around and see peers and older siblings readying themselves for college and the workplace.

Students participate in class at the Harlem Children's Zone's Promise Academy I. More than 8,000 students are part of the Harlem Children's Zone Project.

Strengthen the Community

Education, which is the key to breaking the cycle of generational poverty, has to begin before kindergarten and go beyond the walls of the classroom. As every good parent knows, a child can suddenly stumble off track at any stage of their development, so there is no age when adults can stop being vigilant.

We need to tackle all the various problems that our children are facing. If a child is in a great tutoring program but misses it regularly because of asthma or has to leave it because his or her family is evicted, the program is really of limited value.

From our experience working with families at the Harlem Children's Zone (HCZ), we saw that for children to do well, their families had to do well. From our experience working in a devastated neighborhood, we also knew we had to strengthen the community to support the families.

We have an overall goal of getting children successfully through college so they can enter today's high-skills job market. Toward that end, we try to organize the broadest possible cross-section of community members around these children. To make sure our efforts are on track, we rigorously evaluate how each program is working every step of the way.

Today, the HCZ Project covers 97 blocks and serves more than 8,000 children from birth through college. We are working to create a tipping point for the neighborhood. We want kids to look around and see peers and older siblings readying themselves for college and the workplace. We want college and success to be in the air, a given as it is in middle-class communities.

Programs for Each Stage of Development

The HCZ Promise Academy Charter Schools were created to directly impact the centerpiece of a child's educational life. Since their creation in 2004 and 2005, the Promise Academy schools have done well enough to lead Harvard economist Roland Fryer to conclude that the many of the students had actually closed the black-white achievement gap.[1]

The schools have a longer school day and year, and feature wide-ranging, enriching after-school programs.

"The objective is to create a safety net woven so tightly that children just can't slip through." ⟶ *The New York Times*

All Photos courtesy Marty Lipp and the Harlem's Children Zone

Children receive community support and a high quality education from birth through college.

In 2010, the students at our Promise Academy II had the highest overall scores in the district.

But any teacher in America can tell you a story about a child whose potential was lost because of a problem outside the classroom. That is why we work to remove any barrier to a child's education. The Promise Academy has a great school-based health center that gives the kids free medical, dental and mental-health services, and it has a social work team.

But we also work to support the children at nine public schools in the Zone. We have young men and women from AmeriCorps who we call Peacemakers who work as teaching assistants during the day and then run enriching after-school programs when the school day ends. We make the same promise to these children as we do to our charter school students: we will work with you to get you successfully through college.

We also take a holistic approach at our Beacon Centers, which turn public schools into community centers. In the middle of a block where drug-dealing was once rampant, at the Countee Cullen Beacon Center,

children are now working on computer-based literacy programs after school, earning points for prizes. Where youths once carried, and regularly used, guns and knives, they now prep for the SAT exams, volunteer to help in hospitals and run food drives at our Teen Center. Countee Cullen serves more than 2,200 people annually, from kindergartners to seniors, with a full range of academic, social, recreational and support services.

For years, we informally supported young people once they enrolled in college because we found that many struggled in the new environment. In 2004, we formalized those efforts by establishing the College Success Office. The goal is to give students the resources they need in order to become successful college graduates and active members of their communities. The program now serves more than 640 college students and

The cost of keeping children on track is a fraction of the cost of what happens when young people drop out.

Photo courtesy Marty Lipp and the Harlem's Children Zone

Students are collaborating on a problem in English class at Promise Academy I.

provides year-round academic, administrative, financial and emotional support.

Scaling Up

Hᴄᴢ has been changing the odds for an unprecedented number of children. Communities from across the country who have heard about our work are coming to see what we are doing. We tell them that they don't need to exactly replicate each of our programs, but that they should adhere to the basic principles that keep us on track.

Investing in Children Pays Off

Providing free high-quality services and programs to more than 10,000 children and nearly as many adults in 2010 cost $77 million with an average cost of $3,500 per HCZ participant. Eighty percent of our budget goes to direct program costs.

The cost of keeping children on track is a fraction of the cost of what happens when young people drop out. One recent study found that the median annual earnings of college graduates are $31,400 more than high school dropouts.[2] High school dropouts soon discover how hard it is to make a comfortable living. Many young people who cannot find a job drift into antisocial behavior, which has tremendous costs financially

Scaling Up

1. Work at scale within a specific geographic area where you can meet the needs of a significant number of children and families.

2. Create a pipeline of best-practice programs for children in every age group. Begin working with children as early as possible and stay with them until they graduate from college.

3. Build community among residents, institutions and stakeholders.

4. Evaluate programs rigorously and make sure that the information cycles back to management to help improve programs.

5. Cultivate a culture of passion, accountability, leadership, and teamwork within the organization.

and otherwise. The cost of locking up one young person in the juvenile justice system for a year in New York State can be between $140,000 and $200,000.[3] Prison routinely costs $30,000 or more a year—many times higher than the costs of education or support services—yet incarceration produces almost no benefits.[4]

Despite the big, tough challenges for our public education system, I am convinced that we are at the verge of a transformation. This is still America—we have unparalleled resources, and "change" is in our DNA. We know the way to fix this, and Americans are awakening to the challenge and finding the will to tackle it.

. . . . .

Geoffrey Canada is the president and CEO of the Harlem Children's Zone (www.hcz.org). He was named as one of the most influential people in the world in Time Magazine's 2011 Time 100 list. *HCZ's work has been profiled by* The New York Times Magazine, 60 Minutes, The Wall Street Journal, The Oprah Winfrey Show *and the documentary* Waiting for Superman. *President Barack Obama is seeking to replicate the HCZ Project in 20 cities in his Promise Neighborhoods initiative.*

Fair School Funding and
Equal Opportunities

Many wealthy industrialized countries have built comprehensive social welfare systems that subsidize income, healthcare and housing in order to create more equality among their citizens. In contrast, the US historically has relied on the public school system to be the prime means of improving the lives of the poor and disadvantaged. However, the irony of the American educational system is that low-income children who come to school with the greatest educational needs generally have the fewest resources and least expertise devoted to them—and therefore the least opportunity to improve their futures.

Why Are Some Schools Shortchanged?

Our nation's enormous educational inequities result, in large part, from our tradition of depending on local property taxes for school funding. If a community is poor, it is less able to raise large revenues for its schools. State school funding dollars targeted to poor districts can help to even things out. However, even though state aid formulas often purport to be "equalizing," they rarely are because of the strong political power of affluent districts. For example, in Pennsylvania, per-pupil-spending ranged from $6,114 to $17,082 across 500 school districts.[1] And while the federal government provides additional funding for schools that serve low-income children, it generally amounts to less than 10 percent of school funding nationwide.

Jessica R. Wolff
Campaign for Educational
Equity, Teachers College,
Columbia University

As a result of inequitable local, state and federal funding formulas, many schools in low-income communities lack sufficient funding for basic education essentials.

Per-Pupil Spending

in Pennsylvania

2008
School Year
Ranged from:

$6,114 to $17,082

Across 500 school districts.

That's a difference of

$10,968

The way school districts typically budget for teachers—paying for a number of positions rather than providing a specific amount of money toward teachers' salaries—means that less money is spent on schools that serve low-income students. This is because experienced teachers with higher salaries tend to move to more-affluent schools where working conditions are frequently better. High-poverty schools are then left with higher teacher turnover and many more inexperienced teachers.[2]

A *Washington Post* analysis found that students in DC's poorest neighborhoods are nearly twice as likely to have a new or second-year teacher as those in the wealthiest.[3] Urban districts continue to lack enough effective, diverse teachers who are committed long-term to high-needs schools.

A new model showing promise in Chicago and Boston is Urban Teacher Residencies. The goal of this model is to use best practices in recruitment, preparation, placement, induction and teacher leadership to foster long-term teacher success in urban school districts. Aspiring teachers are selected according to rigorous criteria aligned with district needs. These "residents" integrate their master's-level course work with a full year in the classroom alongside experienced mentor teachers. In their second year, they become teachers with their own classrooms while continuing to receive intensive mentoring.[4]

A *Washington Post* analysis found that students in DC's lowest-income neighborhoods are nearly twice as likely to have a new or second-year teacher as those in the wealthiest.

Photo courtesy Power Design, Inc.

Children in lowest-income schools and districts frequently have to contend with overcrowding. This is in spite of evidence that shows smaller classes are directly correlated with improved student achievement, especially for low-income students.

Nearly 90 percent of the students in the Charlotte-Mecklenburg School District in North Carolina are categorized as economically disadvantaged. In 2008, only 29 percent of the students tested at or above proficient in reading, 44 percent in math and 13 percent in science. The district implemented a Strategic Staffing program, which began with a comprehensive understanding of the needs of the lowest-performing schools, providing appropriate support and taking dramatic action to change staff where needed. As a result, within one year, test scores increased on average 6 to 10 percent.[5]

The Consequences for Our Kids and Our Nation

As a result of inequitable local, state and federal funding formulas, many schools in low-income communities lack sufficient funding for basic education essentials.

Children in the poor schools and districts frequently have to contend with overcrowding.[6] This is in spite of evidence that shows smaller classes are directly correlated with improved student achievement—especially for low-income students. These students are more likely to attend school in dilapidated buildings with insufficient or out-of-date technology and textbooks.[7]

US schools received a D grade on the most recent *Report Card for America's Infrastructure* issued by the American Society of Civil Engineers.[8] The Obama administration recognized that schools are overcrowded, in disrepair and outdated and pledged $15 billion to fix leaky roofs and boilers, install new windows and bring buildings up to a level of acceptable repair and modernize classrooms. While this is a step in the right direction, estimates suggest that between $100 and $360 billion are needed to address the country's school buildings.[9]

On average, low-income students are roughly two years behind in learning compared with financially better-off students of the same age.

High schools in low-income communities often are not able to offer the college preparatory curriculum required for application to universities. Many schools lack science labs, even though students are expected to pass a laboratory science exam to meet state high school graduation requirements.

High school dropouts earn about	The annual price tag of inadequately educating our young people:	In 2008, the GDP in the U.S. could have been:
73 percent	**$250** billion/year	**$400-670** billion higher
of the amount earned by diploma recipients	in health & welfare costs, criminal justice expenses & lost tax revenues	if the U.S. narrowed the gap between low income students and their peers

After-school and summer learning opportunities are limited or non-existent. In spite of steady improvements in the overall caliber of the American public school system and in the educational attainment of the general public, wide achievement gaps exist between low-income students and their peers in more affluent communities.[10] On average, low-income students are roughly two years behind in learning compared with financially better-off students of the same age.[11]

Low academic achievement has a devastating impact on the opportunities available for millions of low-income children. High school dropouts earn about 73 percent of the amount earned by diploma recipients.[12] There are also enormous costs for the nation. The price tag of inadequately educating our young people is staggering, in the realm of $250 billion per year in health and welfare costs, criminal justice expenses and lost tax revenues. The achievement gap also has an effect on the economy. If the US narrowed the gap between low-income students and their peers, GDP would be between $400 billion and $670 billion higher, a 3 to 5 percent increase.[13]

What More Can Be Done? Promising Practices in School Funding Reform

Advocates for low-income children have long sought a fairer system for funding public schools. In many states, parents and advocates have gone to court to fight for these changes. Courts have been asked to decide whether students' rights were being violated as a result of unfair funding. In the majority of cases, the courts held that money matters and additional resources are needed to provide meaningful educational opportunities to poor children. As a result, many courts have ordered changes to state funding formulas.

New Jersey has been in pursuit of a fair funding system the longest of any state and is showing positive results with its targeted population. Thanks to a series of rulings in the landmark *Abbott v. Burke* case, new dollars have enabled urban districts to provide their students with educational programs that are on par with their suburban counterparts. These include smaller class sizes; art, music and technology specialists; student support services; and modern facilities. As a result, more

Money matters and additional resources are needed to provide meaningful educational opportunities to low-income children. As a result, many courts have ordered changes to state funding formulas.

Photo courtesy Baton Rouge Music Studios

Photo courtesy Rio Salado College

A number of states, including New Jersey, Vermont and Kentucky, are developing **effective funding reforms** to provide urban districts with educational programs that are on par with their suburban counterparts.

These include **small class sizes; art, music and technology specialists; student support services and modern facilities.**

Kentucky's Education Reforms:

- Increased funding & improved equity
- A state-funded preschool program
- Extended school services & family support centers
- Higher student outcome goals & a model curriculum
- Improved state oversight of education

= Consistent MODERATE TO LARGE GAINS
in National Assessment of Educational Progress scores

than 80 percent of eligible three- and four-year-olds are enrolled in preschool programs. Additionally, test scores in the Abbott schools, as measured by both state and national assessments, have risen in the fourth grade and eighth grade as much as 22 points, narrowing the performance gap between poor urban and other students in the state.[14]

Court orders have led to promising practices in other states too. Vermont, for example, leads in school funding formula reform. Its school districts are now primarily state funded, and state law requires that dedicated revenues from a number of statewide sources be deposited into a state education fund that is used only to fund schools and to maintain a reserve for times of economic crisis.

Kentucky implemented a thorough set of education reforms, including increased funding and improved equity;

a state-funded preschool program, extended school services and family support centers; higher student outcome goals and a model curriculum; and improved state oversight of education. In the years since then, student achievement in the state has shown consistent moderate-to-large gains in National Assessment of Educational Progress scores.[15]

Providing equal educational opportunities regardless of socio-economic status is vital to our nation's economic well-being as well as to the future of our democracy. All 50 states and the federal government should work to narrow the achievement gap and promote equality in education through fair funding and budgeting practices. For the future of our country and the generations to follow, we can't afford to do less.

.....

The Campaign for Educational Equity at Teachers College, Columbia University, is a non-profit research and policy institute that champions the right of all children to meaningful educational opportunity and works to define and secure the full range of resources, supports and services necessary to provide this opportunity to disadvantaged children.

Jessica R. Wolff is the policy director of the Campaign for Educational Equity at Teachers College, Columbia University, (www.tc.columbia.edu/equitycampaign) and conducts policy research in educational accountability and comprehensive approaches to educational opportunity. She is the executive editor of the Equity Matters research review series, has authored and co-authored numerous articles and two books and directs the campaign's Comprehensive Educational Opportunity Project.

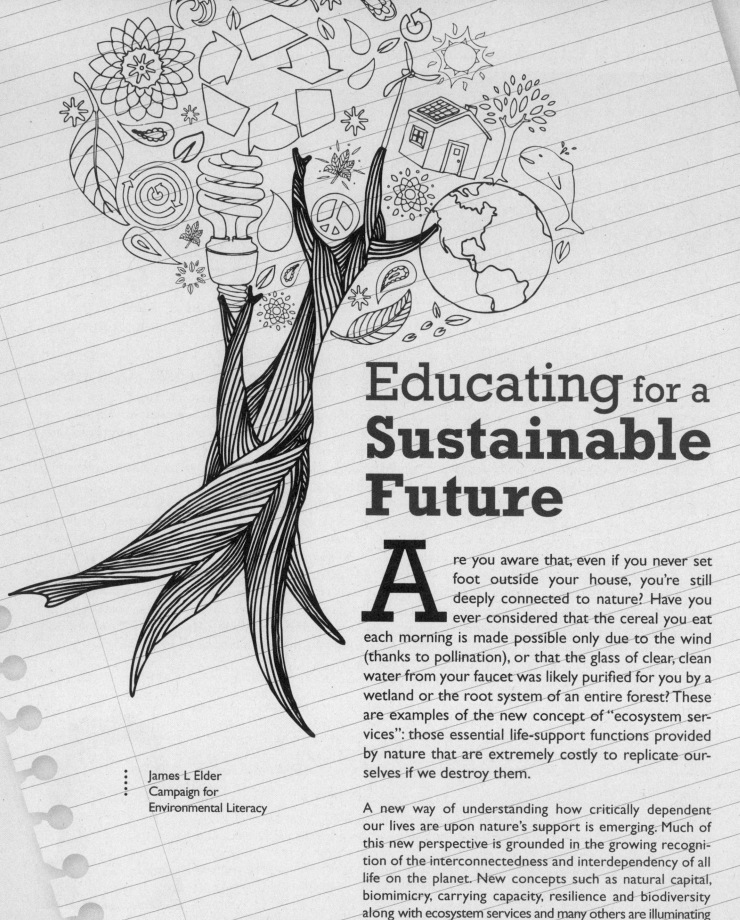

Educating for a Sustainable Future

James L Elder
Campaign for
Environmental Literacy

Are you aware that, even if you never set foot outside your house, you're still deeply connected to nature? Have you ever considered that the cereal you eat each morning is made possible only due to the wind (thanks to pollination), or that the glass of clear, clean water from your faucet was likely purified for you by a wetland or the root system of an entire forest? These are examples of the new concept of "ecosystem services": those essential life-support functions provided by nature that are extremely costly to replicate ourselves if we destroy them.

A new way of understanding how critically dependent our lives are upon nature's support is emerging. Much of this new perspective is grounded in the growing recognition of the interconnectedness and interdependency of all life on the planet. New concepts such as natural capital, biomimicry, carrying capacity, resilience and biodiversity along with ecosystem services and many others are illuminating

Ecosystem Services

Essential life-support functions provided by nature that are extremely costly to replicate ourselves if we destroy them

Natural Capital

The stock of natural assets that yields a flow of valuable goods and services into the future

Biomimicry

A new discipline that studies nature's best ideas and then imitates these designs and processes to solve human problems

Resilience

The ability to cope with ecological surprise in a human dominated world

Biodiversity

The degree of variation in genes, species and ecosystems of a region (greater biodiversity means more resilience and better ecosystem services)

Carrying Capacity

The maximum number of individuals of a species that a given environment can support over the long term

our deep relationship with the natural world, and these concepts are forming a new foundation for the field of environmental literacy.

Environmental literacy has profound implications for how we understand our place on this planet. It grows out of the deep recognition that we humans are part of a larger system that has important limits as well as rules by which we have no choice but to live if the human species is to survive over the long term. It also incorporates "systems thinking"—a way of thinking that emphasizes the qualities of relationships, connectedness and context present in any system, whether an ecosystem or a school system.

This new perspective is emerging not a moment too soon, as we wrestle with finding systemic solutions to the interconnected challenges of mitigating and adapting to climate change; sustaining our nation's lands, waters and other natural resources as well as our economic competitiveness; achieving energy independence and security; creating more livable communities; and transitioning to a green economy.

Successful Models for Teaching Environmental Literacy

Successful models of schools committed to environmental literacy are leading the way. They share a set of embedded values in common that drive all school activity toward helping students become true citizens of the 21st century. The best of these model schools employ a comprehensive "whole school" approach, seeking to both produce environmentally literate graduates as well as to eliminate their negative environmental impact, while using their own built and natural environment as a learning laboratory and a model of best practice for their host communities.

> We humans are part of a larger system that has important limits as well as rules by which we have no choice but to live if the human species is to survive over the long term.

The best of these model schools employ a "whole school" approach, seeking to both produce environmentally literate graduates as well as to minimize or eliminate their environmental footprint.

A teaching garden at the Environmental Charter High School provides hands-on learning that compliments the vigorous in-classroom curriculum.

Photo courtesy Sara Laimon

For example, the Environmental Charter High School in Los Angeles combines "a rigorous college-preparatory curriculum with hands-on learning opportunities in the community." While 80 percent of the students are financially disadvantaged, all students must be admitted to a four-year university in order to graduate. The school's philosophy employs project- and service-based learning as well as an interdisciplinary approach that incorporates environmental science and ecology-inspired activities across all disciplines. In addition to classroom programs, students are required to apply concepts and skills gained in class to problem-solve local civic and environmental issues. Founded by a group of parents, educators, businesses and non-profits in 2000, the school has experienced dramatic improvements in academic results. The school was called "a model of learning" by President Obama,[1] and *US News & World Report* placed it in the top 3 percent of US public high schools.

The Willow School, a small independent K–8 day school in New Jersey, is committed to combining academic excellence, the joy of learning and experiencing the wonder of the natural world. With the help of the Cloud Institute for Sustainability Education, the school faculty has seamlessly embedded the attributes of sustainability education across the curriculum. The buildings and grounds are a laboratory for academic inspiration and sustainability education where students develop a sense of place, become stewards of their environment and learn to appreciate their role in restoring balance to the natural world. For example, students have the opportunity to plant, weed and harvest crops; in social studies, they study cultures and consider the reciprocal relationship between humans and their environment.

Environmental Charter High School · Los Angeles, CA

- Rigorous college-preparatory curriculum
- Hands-on learning opportunities in the community that support real-world applications
- Interdisciplinary approach that incorporates environmental science and ecology-inspired activities

Photo courtesy The Willow School

The school grounds were designed to be integral to all aspects of the curriculum, incorporating natural meadows, butterfly gardens, water harvesting, hedgerows and a constructed wetlands to filter wastewater so it provides clean water to the groundwater system.

Evergreen Community Charter School, a public school in North Carolina, aims to prepare students for successful lifelong learning, environmental responsibility and service. Environmental education and thinking critically about community issues are woven throughout the curriculum, fostering an understanding of ecology and environmental stewardship as well as a sense of respect and wonder for the natural world. Every student is empowered to take action and seek solutions for environmental concerns. Students learn from local experts in many fields, including natural history and conservation, government, business, current events, education and social studies. The school's property is home to many sustainable features such as rooftop solar panels, biodiesel-powered school buses, rain gardens, organic gardens, a greenhouse, bioswales, a natural trail and woods play area and composting systems.

The Need for Systemic Change

Successful model schools offer hope. But with over 100,000 public K–12 schools in the nation, they remain a drop in the bucket. After 30 or more years of environmental education, how environmentally literate are our students? All indications are that we fail as a nation to grasp those essential insights necessary to function on a daily level as proper stewards of both our environment and our children's future. While our awareness of environmental issues appears to be growing, our understanding of these issues is not, and this gap seems to be increasing at the very moment in history when it needs to be rapidly shrinking. For example, a recent study by the Organization for Economic Co-operation and Development (OECD) found that the average US student scores only just above basic proficiency in environmental science, and ranked the US 34th out of 57 countries.[2] While the US ranked above Uruguay and Thailand, we fell below Estonia, Croatia and the Slovak and Czech Republics as well as Canada, Japan, Australia, Russia and the UK.

Photo courtesy Evergreen Community Charter School

In students' knowledge about the environment and environment-related issues, the US ranks:

34th
out of 57 countries

• While the US ranked above Uruguay & Thailand, we fell **below** Estonia, Croatia, the Slovak and Czech Republics, Canada, Japan, Australia, Russia and the U.K.

Photo courtesy gardenproject.wordpress.com

California's Education & Environment Initiative (EEI) curriculum is expected to bring environmental education into the classrooms of 1,000 California school districts serving 6 million students.

Systemic change—changing whole education systems, not just changing individual schools one by one—is clearly needed to move our education system quickly in the right direction. One of the more promising systemic change efforts is California's Education and Environment Initiative (EEI), a $9 million partnership between the State Board of Education, the Office of the Secretary for Education, the State Department of Education and the California Natural Resources Agency. The EEI curriculum, comprising 85 units teaching science and history-social science academic standards, is expected to bring environmental education into the classrooms of 1,000 California school districts serving 6 million students by using the environment as a context for standards-based instruction. The EEI website notes: "Everyone and everything is linked to the environment. California's economic prosperity, the health of its citizens, in fact, our whole future depends on the health of the environment in which we live. Integrating education about the environment into our K-12 school system will make learning relevant to today's world and prepare students to be knowledgeable citizens who can make informed decisions about California's future."[3] Unfortunately, this terrific state-level initiative is the exception rather than the rule.

The Need for Leadership

Systemic change needs to be led from the top as well as the bottom. As acknowledged by President Obama, the transition to a clean, green economy needs to be a top priority—a transition that recognizes and supports the vital connections between climate change, economic stimulus, energy security and job training. Navigating this transition to a green economy will require creating a broad base of environmentally literate citizens who can make well-informed decisions as consumers, workers, business owners, investors and voters. Each year, 3 million graduates enter the workforce armed with the attitudes, skills and knowledge either to advance a green economy and a sustainable future or to continue "business as usual." The impact, good or bad, of each of these 3 million individuals lasts a lifetime.

"**96%** of educators reported that students developed higher-level, critical thinking skills than those of their traditional peers."

Environmental Education Improves Learning and Behavior

Environment-based education is much more than learning about the environment. The natural world is a foundation for acquiring learning skills and creating a wider learning context, all of which are guided by teachers using proven educational practices.

Studies show that environment-based education leads to higher scores on standardized tests. Ninety-six percent of educators from 40 schools reported that students developed higher-level, critical thinking skills than those of their traditional peers. Ninety-eight percent reported increased ability to think creatively. Ninety-seven percent reported greater proficiency in solving problems and thinking strategically and 89 percent saw a better application of systems thinking.[1]

Environmental education improves more than just test scores. Studies also show increased attendance, fewer discipline problems, better behavior and increased enthusiasm for learning.

from the editor

One step in the right direction is the Green Ribbon School Award recently announced by the US Secretary of Education and the EPA Administrator, and originally conceived by the Campaign for Environmental Literacy. The Department of Education will honor with a Green Ribbon those schools which come the closest each year to achieving three interrelated goals: 1) 100 percent of the school's graduates are environmentally literate, 2) the school has a "net zero" environmental impact, and 3) there are no negative health impacts on students or staff from participating in school. More than just another award program, it puts the weight of the US Department of Education behind a comprehensive vision for green schools.

Few doubt that we will leave our children a more problematic and difficult world than the one we inherited from our parents. We are morally bound to provide them with the knowledge, skills and training required for coping with this new world. Parents and local community leaders can encourage their schools to incorporate environmental education and sustainability principles and practices. It just takes a bit of focus and dedication to make it happen. Given the degree to which the environment affects everything from our economy and health to our security and well being, let's do what it takes to get the US to rank first in environmental literacy.

•••••

Dr. James Elder is a prominent environmental/sustainability education policy expert and strategist who founded the School for Field Studies, building it into the nation's leading environmental field program for undergraduates. He subsequently founded the Campaign for Environmental Literacy (CEL: www. FundEE.org), a national advocacy network of stakeholder organizations. With the help of its partners, CEL has restored $200 million in federal environmental/sustainability education funding, passed the Higher Education Sustainability Act and initiated both the No Child Left Inside Act and the Ocean, Coastal and Watershed Education Act.

A School and Community Strategy for the 21st Century

Martin J. Blank
Coalition for Community Schools,
Institute for Educational Leadership

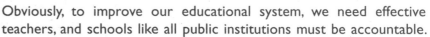

America's schools now enroll the most diverse group of young people in history, and their progress depends on the environment in which they live and learn. Many states are experiencing stagnant high school graduation rates and unacceptably low performance in math and science. Many students are disengaged, and young people are seen as problems rather than as individuals with assets, hopes and dreams. As a nation, we must act collectively to ensure that the youth of today succeed as workers, family members and citizens.

Obviously, to improve our educational system, we need effective teachers, and schools like all public institutions must be accountable. But in order to be successful, young people and their families also need more connections, more support, more opportunities, more learning time and more engaging learning opportunities from the entire community. Schools need to develop and maintain robust relationships with families and other community institutions. At the heart of these efforts must be a commitment for schools and communities to work together to create strong and purposeful partnerships for change and results.

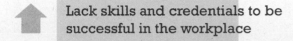

High school dropouts are MORE likely to:

- Lack skills and credentials to be successful in the workplace

- Have lower incomes & be in worse health than high school graduates

- Live in poverty and receive government assistance

- Go to prison

Communities and Schools Move Forward

There are a growing number of communities that are moving this school and community agenda forward. Cincinnati's Board of Education established a policy that all schools built under a major school reconstruction program will be Community Learning Centers. Each school has a different physical and program design that reflects the needs and aspirations of neighborhood residents. The intensive community engagement process that led to these school plans distinguishes Cincinnati's initiative. Networks of community partners focused on extended learning, physical health, mental health, college access and parental engagement, and the partners provide these services at the schools. A full-time resource coordinator, employed by an external partner (i.e., YMCA) integrates the work of community partners in the school, while parents, educators, residents and community partners provide guidance and oversight. School personnel, the YMCA and an independent intermediary provide day-to-day management of the enterprise. The Community Learning Centers are showing improved academic performance, higher attendance rates and greater parent involvement and, moreover, are attracting new families in some neighborhoods.[1]

Multnomah County, in partnership with the city of Portland and six school districts in the county, organized 58 Schools Uniting Neighborhoods (SUN) Community Schools. The initiative provides an array of extended learning, service learning, health and social services and parental engagement support to schools. A Community Coordinating Council led by the county executive and made up of representatives from the city, school districts, non-profit partners and families guides the initiative. Within a decade of their foundation, SUN Community Schools showed a 75 percent increase in reading scores, a 77 percent increase in math scores, an average daily attendance of 95 percent along with student behavior improvements such as increased class participation and homework turned in on time.[2]

Students put on a show after school at one of Multnomah County's SUN Community Schools.

Obviously to improve our educational system, we need effective teachers and schools must be accountable. But in order to be successful, young people and their families also need more connections, more support, and more engaging learning opportunities from the entire community.

Harlem Children's Zone has seen remarkable success both in their students and the greater community because they engage the community in their students' education.

education as well. In 2010, HCZ successes included: 100 percent of third-graders tested at or above grade level on the math exam; 100 percent of high school after-school program participants remained in school; 90 percent of high school seniors were accepted to college.[3] The commitment from the White House to the HCZ vision through the Promise Neighborhoods Initiative is a recognition that our society must target its resources intensively to support our most valuable asset: today's youth.

Strategies that Work

More and more school districts and their communities are moving in this direction. They are positioning schools as centers of community. These are places that have transformed their curriculum and instruction, scheduling, school layout and especially their relationships and responsibilities among school staff, students, families and community partners. They rely on multiple inter-related strategies that combine broad-scale learning along with community involvement to achieve results: They set high expectations for all students, integrate real-world learning, focus on the whole child, and are conduits for engaging people and resources from within the community.

> **Harlem Children's Zone successes include:**
> **100% of third-graders tested at or above grade level on the math exam,**
> **99% of high school after-school participants remained in school, and**
> **90% of high school seniors were accepted to college.**

Harlem Children's Zone (HCZ) represents an intensive effort in Harlem to ensure the success of students and to rebuild the community. Its work reflects many of the principles and values of community schools, including the need for a high-quality academic program, enriched and extended learning opportunities, an array of health and social services as well as engaged families and an engaged community. HCZ also has an intensive focus on early childhood opportunities through its Baby College for young parents and its Harlem Gems preschool program. It extends its efforts to support students who enter post-secondary

Scaling up the Nation's Schools

Moving community schools and initiatives like the Harlem Children's Zone to scale requires significant shifts in how we view pubic schools along with federal and state policy. When introducing the new US Education Secretary Arne Duncan, President Obama agreed, "We need a new vision for a 21st-century education system—one where we aren't just supporting existing schools but spurring innovation; where we're not just investing more money but demanding more reform."[4] This is what it will take to make this happen:

Why Art is Essential in our Public Schools
by Ryan Hurley, Arts @ Large

The arts inspire. The arts challenge. The arts educate. The arts build relationships. The arts provide fresh and creative ways for teachers and young people to interact and learn together.

Studies have shown that involvement in the arts helps kids increase test scores and promotes academic achievement. Kids who are involved in the arts are:

* **4 times more likely to be recognized for academic achievement.**
* **3 times more likely to be elected to class office within their schools.**
* **4 times more likely to participate in a math and science fair.**
* **3 times more likely to win an award for school attendance.**[1]

With so much focus and pressure on standardized testing, little time is left for creative engagement, especially in underserved schools that are so often working impossibly hard to live up to these standards with very limited resources. Most kids are not getting enough art— in or out of school.

At Adams Elementary School in Hamilton, Ohio, Children experience the arts as part of each of their core subjects—math, science, language arts and social studies. They also participate in a class in each of four art disciplines—visual art, music, dance and drama—every week, taught by a certified arts instructor.

Kids at Adams have multiple opportunities to learn and experience a concept. They "don't just learn to tell time, for example, by hearing a description of an abstract concept and watching the teacher move the arrows on a cardboard display. They're taught a dance where they become a clock, with their movements changing to reflect the changing hours. They become time."[2]

Here, art becomes the vehicle for learning and it nurtures the learning process because each child learns differently—some read well, others write well, while others learn by listening and speaking. Programs such as the one at Adams not only offer art for art's sake but also support the learning process in general.

The arts are essential to a child's development and more art education opportunities for children are important. If you are a parent, enjoy the arts with your child together, encourage your child to participate in the arts inside and outside of school, tell your child's school that the arts are an important part of a quality education. Anyone can be an arts advocate by supporting funding for arts education and the local, state and federal levels.

This editor's box was developed with Arts @ Large; a non-profit organization that provides multi-disciplinary arts programming for public schools in Milwaukee. www.artsatlargeinc.org

from the editor

Communitywide Planning and Decision-making:

Youth, parents, community and school leaders should become partners in the planning and oversight of school reform. If the people and places affected by change have a voice, implementation will be most effective.

A New Accountability Framework:

A single standardized test should not be the basis for judging schools or students. "Teaching to the test" doesn't benefit the child's overall education and preparedness for the world. Instead, schools should rely on an accountability model that includes multiple measures of academic achievement as well as measures of engagement, attendance, social, emotional and ethical competencies, physical well-being and family and community involvement.

Learning to Work Together:

Teachers, principals, other school personnel and people in social work, youth development, health and mental health and community development have different experience and academic backgrounds. Some have limited experience working directly with students, families and the average citizen. They need training and support to enable to work more effectively together and in partnership with families and communities.

Increased Funding

Ensuring that disadvantaged students in under-resourced communities have access to an excellent and equitable education has been a cornerstone of the US public school system for more than 40 years. Even as schools work to use resources more efficiently, additional funding is essential for school functions such as early

Communitywide Involvement + A New Accountability Framework + Increased Funding =

More Successful Students and Communities

The graduating class of 2011 are seated for their commencement ceremony.

> John Dewey said that "Education is not preparation for life; education is life itself." This rings true when we reflect upon the potential of a fully functioning educational system that is grounded in the community, serves the whole student and draws the best from each one.

care and education; out-of-school enrichment opportunities; mentoring; preventive health, mental health and family services; family and community engagement; and service, civic, and environmental learning opportunities.

Education Is Life

John Dewey said that "education is not preparation for life; education is life itself."[5] This verity rings true when we reflect upon the potential of a fully functioning educational system that is grounded in community, serves the whole student and draws the best from each one. The strength of our evolving democracy requires our ongoing and renewed commitment to this cause. Those that have blazed the trail of reform and innovation live and breathe to see students succeed. They have developed a recipe for success that is dynamic and needs only to expand through a unified vision, creativity and partnership. Only by intentionally and relentlessly working together across organizational boundaries will our nation get the results we need for the 21st century and beyond.

·····

Martin J. Blank is the president of the Institute for Educational Leadership (IEL) in Washington, DC. He leads IEL in its efforts to build the capacity of people, organizations and systems—in education and related fields—to cross boundaries and work together to attain better results for children and youth. Blank has been associated with IEL since 1985, focusing his work on building bridges between schools and other institutions with assets that can support student success. Blank also serves as the director of the Coalition for Community Schools (www.communityschools.org), which is staffed by the Institute for Educational Leadership. The Coalition is an alliance that brings together leaders and organizations in education, family support, youth development early childhood, community development, government and philanthropy.

For more information on the Coalition for Community Schools, at the Institute for Educational Leadership visit www.communityschools.org or www.iel.org.

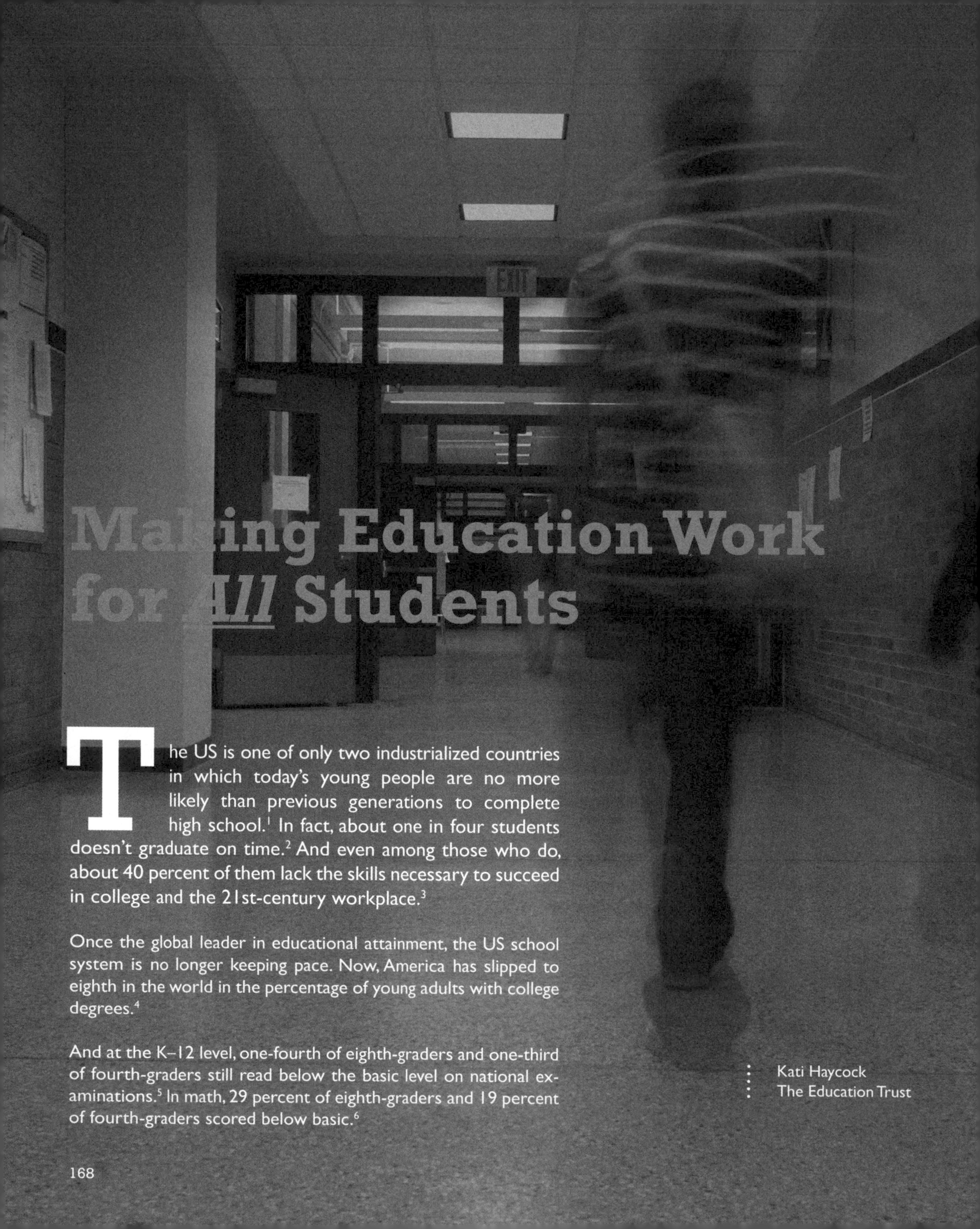

Making Education Work for *All* Students

The US is one of only two industrialized countries in which today's young people are no more likely than previous generations to complete high school.[1] In fact, about one in four students doesn't graduate on time.[2] And even among those who do, about 40 percent of them lack the skills necessary to succeed in college and the 21st-century workplace.[3]

Once the global leader in educational attainment, the US school system is no longer keeping pace. Now, America has slipped to eighth in the world in the percentage of young adults with college degrees.[4]

And at the K–12 level, one-fourth of eighth-graders and one-third of fourth-graders still read below the basic level on national examinations.[5] In math, 29 percent of eighth-graders and 19 percent of fourth-graders scored below basic.[6]

Kati Haycock
The Education Trust

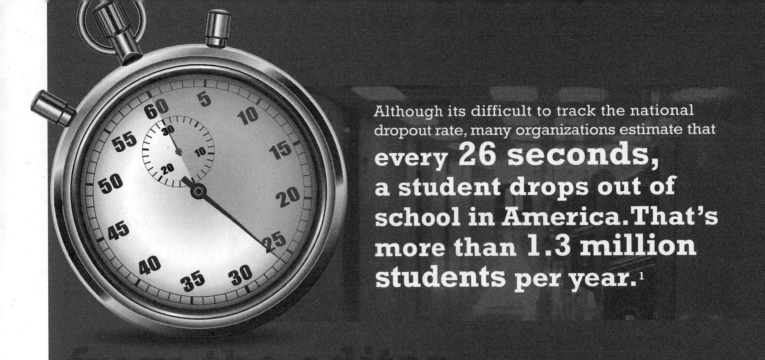

Although its difficult to track the national dropout rate, many organizations estimate that **every 26 seconds, a student drops out of school in America. That's more than 1.3 million students per year.**[1]

To reverse this trend, the way we "do school" in this country has to change. Two steps are crucial: setting higher expectations for all students and hiring and supporting strong teachers.

High Expectations for All Students

Historically, the highest expectations and most resources have typically been set aside for the highest performing students. However, schools with the strongest records of student achievement set high goals; they also leave nothing about teaching and learning to chance. Teachers in these schools work together to ensure that they are all providing the same rigorous content at the same high levels to all students. States like Arkansas, Florida, and New York are making serious progress in closing gaps by adopting robust policies aimed at preparing every student for life beyond high school.

In recent years, Arkansas has ratcheted up expectations by emphasizing instruction across subject areas (for example, ensuring that social studies lessons reinforce reading and math) and by linking assessments and curricula to state standards. State standards are reviewed regularly to ensure appropriate rigor, beginning as early as kindergarten. And as expectations are raised, so too are minimum requirements to be deemed "proficient" on state tests. The result: Achievement is going up for all student groups, and

Decades of research tell us that the single most important factor in a child's education is the quality of their teacher.

gaps between racial and ethnic groups are narrowing on both state and national exams.

On the national exams, Arkansas was the biggest gainer in fourth-grade math achievement from over the past decade, and the second-biggest gainer in eighth grade. Arkansas also ranked among the top states in boosting math achievement in both grades for low-income students. Similarly, the state's improvement in writing was among the biggest in the nation, slashing by nearly half the number of low-income eighth-graders who scored below basic.

This kind of statewide improvement doesn't happen without a lot of local schools and districts pulling in the same direction. Norfork Elementary School is a particularly good example. Located in a rural area known as the methamphetamine capital of the Ozarks, the school enrolls mostly children from low-income families. In recent years, four out of five Norfork sixth-graders met or exceeded Arkansas' math standards. In fact, the school's test scores were so high

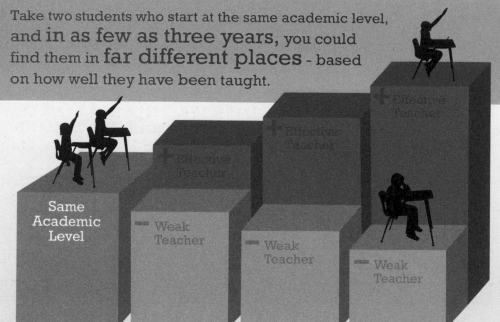

Take two students who start at the same academic level, **and in as few as three years,** you could find them in **far different places** - based on how well they have been taught.

Same Academic Level

Weak Teacher

+ Effective Teacher

Weak Teacher

+ Effective Teacher

Weak Teacher

+ Effective Teacher

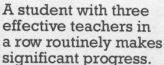

A student with three effective teachers in a row routinely makes significant progress.

Given three weak teachers in a row, another student loses academic ground, and sometimes never recovers.

that the state sent a monitor to the school in 2008 to ensure there was no cheating. That year, Norfork's success continued: its sixth-grade literacy scores were third highest in the state.

A few years earlier, the district had put into place a number of improvements, including raising teacher salaries to compete with nearby districts, expanding communication with parents and families, and improving instruction. But the teachers themselves are adamant that one of the giant steps in the school's improvement was the implementation of Arkansas state standards. The standards allowed teachers to set clearer goals for classroom instruction and to fully align the curriculum so each year's learning provides the foundation for the next.

Reading classes also were increased to 90 minutes, which allows for whole-group instruction, cooperative learning, and independent time to allow teachers to work one-on-one with students. And as their results improved, and the teachers saw their kids could surpass the state standards, they chose to tie the curriculum closely to the even more rigorous national standards developed by the National Council of Teachers of Mathematics.

Hire and Support Strong Teachers

High standards, of course, don't accomplish very much without strong teachers to teach them. And not surprisingly, research tells us that the most important variable in a child's education is his or her teacher.

Take two students who begin second grade at the same academic level. By the end of fourth grade, you could find them at vastly different levels, depending on who teaches them. In fact, a student assigned to three effective teachers in a row will gain ground on peers, while one with three weak teachers in a row will lose ground, regardless of family background.[7] One study found that providing low-income elementary students in Texas with highly effective teachers (rather than merely average ones) would close the achievement gap.[8]

When it comes to strong teaching, content knowledge is critical. On national math exams, eighth-graders taught by math majors scored ten points higher than those assigned to teachers who majored in other subjects. That ten-point difference is equivalent to roughly a year's worth of learning.[9] But tragically, too many students in America are assigned to teachers with inadequate training and skills. And in our middle and high schools, it's even worse for low-income students and students of

> "Teachers should be supported and evaluated based on the quality of their teaching and student results rather than contractual terms."

Re-thinking Teacher Tenure

A teacher's effectiveness has more impact on student learning than any other factor including class size, school size and quality of after-school programs.[1] Many national education reform movement proponents are calling for an end to the tenure systems in an effort to ensure all students have access to effective teachers.

When created early 20th century, the tenure system was designed to protect teachers, who were often fired for reasons unrelated to their work, including race, sex, political views or favoritism. Although it doesn't guarantee lifetime employment, the tenure system makes it difficult to let go of ineffective teachers. New York, Chicago and Los Angeles have each fired fewer than 1 out of 1,000 of their tenured teachers in recent years. Those numbers are not unusual. Reviews of dismissal cases can take years to make their way through the system, costing tens of thousands of dollars each.[2]

Michelle Rhee has been tackling teacher tenure debate since 2007 and it is a cornerstone of her national educational reform organization, StudentsFirst.

"Tenure is the holy grail of teacher unions," Rhee said, "but has no educational value for kids; it only benefits adults. If we can put veteran teachers who have tenure in a position where they don't have it, that would help us to radically increase our teacher quality."[3]

Several state governors are pushing to eliminate tenure and many districts are working to change teacher evaluation practices.[4] Whether or not the tenure system is abolished, the fact is teachers should be supported and evaluated based on the quality of their teaching and student results rather than contractual terms.

from the editor

Math teacher John Squillace teaches a class for students who need extra help before school starts at Elmont Memorial High School.

color: They are about twice as likely as other kids to be taught core academics by out-of-field teachers.[10]

Successful schools are acutely aware of the importance of strong teachers, especially for their most vulnerable students. Take, for example, Elmont (NY) Memorial Junior-Senior High School, where most of the students are African American or Latino and the school's 96 percent graduation rate is almost twice the statewide average for similar students.[11] Early in the school's improvement process, then-principal Diane Scricca made sure all students had access to college-preparatory Advanced Placement (AP) classes, but she knew that some students would need considerable support in order to succeed in them. To teach AP US History, she assigned a dynamic teacher she had recently hired, supplanting a long-standing teacher who objected to working with students thought to not be "ready" for AP-level work.

"Every one of those kids passed [the class]," Scricca said, largely due to the skill, knowledge, and high expectations of the new teacher, John Capozzi. Fittingly, Capozzi is now the principal at Elmont and shares Scricca's passion for ensuring that his neediest students get the best teachers.

Like professionals in other fields, teachers should be paid more if they are especially effective, and effective teachers should be paid more to take on the biggest challenges.

At Elmont, school leaders spend a great deal of time ensuring that every new hire not only has the content knowledge and teaching skill needed to make a rigorous curriculum come to life, but also the "Elmont heart"— a love of kids, high expectations for all, a strong work ethic, and a willingness to spend time outside of the classroom to ensure that struggling students catch up.

Unfortunately, in too few places, teachers aren't supported or evaluated with the kind of single-mindedness employed at Elmont. The performance evaluation systems used in virtually every school system in America fail to differentiate between individual teachers who boost student learning and those who desperately need to improve. As a result of this quality-blind approach,

If we don't start to turn the trends around, to learn from the schools that are getting results, and to refuse to buy into the myths about who can learn & who can't, **we will relegate another generation of young Americans to lives on the margins.**

Not because they couldn't learn, but because we simply didn't bother to teach them.

New Haven Public Schools have implemented a new evaluation system that will help make sure New Haven students get the best teachers possible.

In every part of the country, there are schools that powerfully demonstrate that when you teach all students at high levels and provide them with adequate supports, all students can achieve at those high levels.

the students who need the most from their teachers are far less likely to get those who can help them achieve at high levels—and the teachers who need help to improve are never identified for targeted training and professional development.

But some districts around the country, including the New Haven (Conn.) Public Schools, are beginning to change. In New Haven's recently implemented evaluation system, all teachers will be evaluated on student progress on both statewide and teacher-generated exams, in addition to their instructional practice and professional values. School leaders can then use this information to assist them in teacher assignment, support, and dismissal decisions.

In 2010, after years of negotiation, a groundbreaking collective bargaining agreement was ratified in Washington,

DC, that revises the rules associated with developing and retaining teachers, all with the final goal of ensuring that a strong teacher is working in every city classroom.

No matter how you think about this—through the lens of the children or that of their teachers—more districts need to move in this direction. In communities big and small, all across the country, some schools are powerfully demonstrating that when we focus on high expectations and strong teachers, our children can achieve, even when they live in challenging circumstances.

Unless we stand up for quality schools for all, we will continue to relegate thousands of young Americans to lives on the margins. Not because they couldn't learn, but because we simply didn't bother to teach them.

.....

Kati Haycock is the president of The Education Trust (www.edtrust.org). She is one of the nation's leading advocates in education. She previously served as executive vice president of the Children's Defense Fund, the nation's largest child-advocacy organization. A native Californian, Haycock founded and served as president of the Achievement Council, a statewide organization that helps teachers and principals in predominantly minority schools improve student achievement. Before that, she served as director of the outreach and student affirmative-action programs for the nine-campus University of California system.

Photo courtesy Jason Bache, flickr

Photo courtesy cogdogblog, flickr

Making Higher Education Affordable

A postsecondary credential—whether it's a bachelor's degree, associate degree, apprenticeship, or certificate—is increasingly important for success in today's economy. By 2018, more than six in 10 jobs will require some sort of postsecondary education.[1]

While college enrollment is at an all-time high today, more than half of all students who enter the postsecondary system don't earn a degree or credential within eight years of enrolling.[2]

The number one reason students leave school is due to the stress of going to school and working at the same time. More than half of those who left higher education before completing a degree or a certificate said that the "need to work and make money" while attending classes was the major reason they left.[3]

According to one recent analysis, college costs have risen more than 400 percent in the last 25 years, while the median family income has increased less than 150 percent.[4]

Achieving a postsecondary credential can lift people out of poverty and into the middle class. National statistics show that young people who leave college without a degree are more likely than their peers to come from less privileged backgrounds and to live in more precarious economic circumstances.[5]

Making loans more available and keeping tuition costs in line are important for raising college completion, but the vast majority of young people who left college without a degree said more flexible schedules and help mitigating the challenge of working and going to school at the same time would also make graduation feasible.[6]

One set of solutions might revolve around making part-time attendance more viable by giving those students better access to loans, tuition assistance and healthcare—benefits and services that are frequently available only to full-time students. There may also be implications for employers. Business owners could find ways to help part-time workers to pursue higher education by providing access to health benefits and by offering more predictable or flexible working hours so that students can more easily schedule their classes.[7]

The emphasis on the importance of a higher education credential makes sense given that the country is moving into a more knowledge-intensive-workplace economy. As a society, we need to support secondary education students all the way through graduation.

from the editor

Re-Powering America

A look at the numbers...

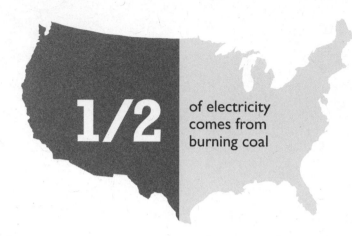

1/2 of electricity comes from burning coal

Almost **half of America's electricity is produced by burning coal-** the country's greatest contributor to global warming.

10x

Amount of electricity wind power could provide compared to what the country requires today, according to a study by the US Department of Energy.

Today in the Appalachian region, more than

450 mountains

(an area estimated to be larger than **800 square miles**)

have been destroyed by mountaintop removal coal mining.

1/2

Amount of all new electricity generation projected to be from solar photovoltaic panels (PVs) by 2025.

1 million

New jobs that could be created by realizing our solar and wind potential in the US.

Today **we waste about the same amount of energy as we use,** so we produce twice the amount that we actually use.

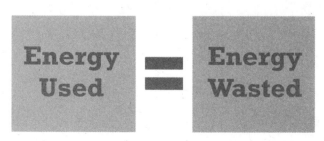

11

Number of power plants worth of electricity that California saved through conservation efforts when faced with energy crunches in the earlier part of the decade.

Exemplifying the power of small acts, 84% of energy saved in California (when faced with an energy crisis) came from **simple behavioral modifications such as:**

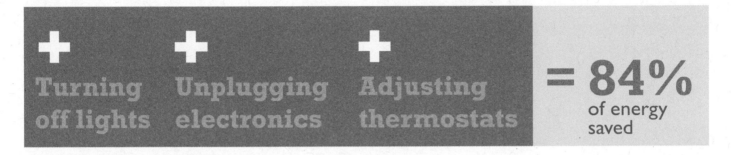

+ Turning off lights   **+ Unplugging electronics**   **+ Adjusting thermostats**   **= 84%** of energy saved

The non-profit Apollo Alliance estimates that a

$10 billion

federal investment in energy-efficient retrofit and conservation programs

would result in more than

100,000
new jobs

&

would reduce energy use in new and existing buildings by

30%

Our driving is a major factor in climate change. **The US transportation sector is responsible for:**

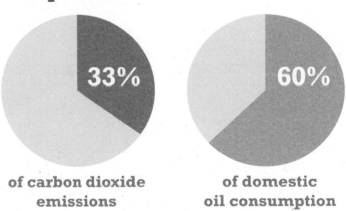

33% of carbon dioxide emissions

60% of domestic oil consumption

10.4 billion

Gallons of gas we would save if every American used public transportation one day a week instead of driving.

100 mpg

Future goal for average US fuel economy. A 100 mpg fleet would eliminate the need to import foreign oil and drop domestic production by 800 million barrels/year, while saving every household $2,700 a year on gas.

Energy. How wisely we use it and how responsibly it is generated will define America for the foreseeable future. Our power lies in charting a new course rather than merely tinkering at the edges. Climate change grabs the headlines. But jobs, economic vitality, global stability, and the preservation of species and cultures are also connected to the energy decisions we make now and in the future.

From conservation initiatives that prevented the need for 11 new power plants in California and a simple light bulb change that could save enough energy to power 3 million homes to fuel efficiency standards that will save nearly a billion tons of greenhouse gases and growth in solar and wind that will create nearly a million new jobs, the possibilities are endless.

Even with steady progress, we still need to think big, invest in the right technologies, challenge status quo interests and make the most of our precious time.

There is no shortage of opportunity to...

Get even more aggressive when it comes to energy efficiency and conservation

Attain 100% carbon-free electricity within 10 years

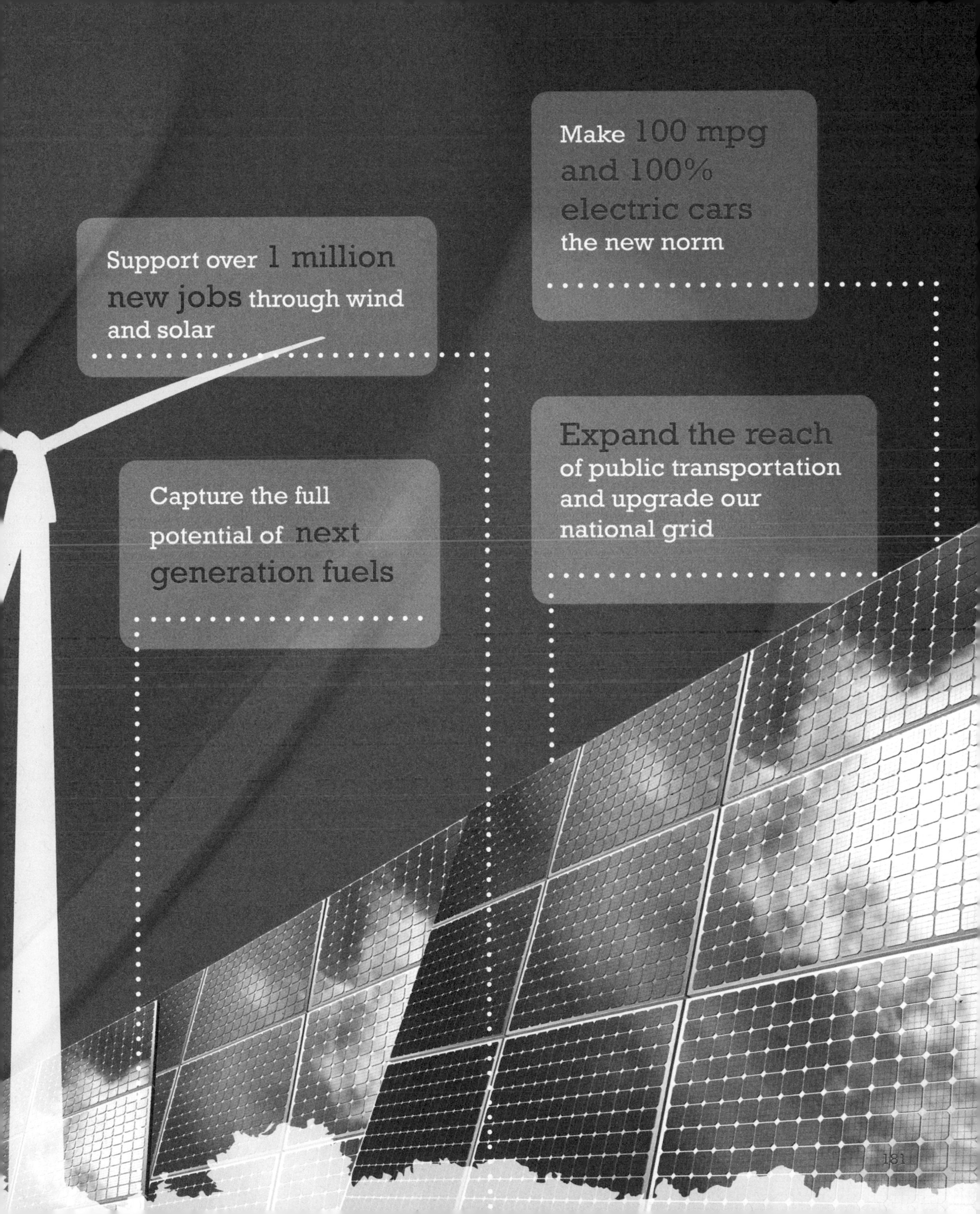

Support over 1 million new jobs through wind and solar

Make 100 mpg and 100% electric cars the new norm

Capture the full potential of next generation fuels

Expand the reach of public transportation and upgrade our national grid

100 Percent Carbon-Free Electricity Within 10 Years

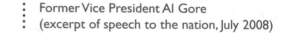

Former Vice President Al Gore
(excerpt of speech to the nation, July 2008)

There are times in the history of our nation when our very way of life depends upon dispelling illusions and awakening to the challenge of a present danger. In such moments, we are called upon to move quickly and boldly to shake off complacency, throw aside old habits and rise, clear-eyed and alert, to the necessity of big changes. Those who, for whatever reason, refuse to do their part must either be persuaded to join the effort or asked to step aside. This is such a moment. The survival of the United States of America as we know it is at risk. And even more—if more should be required—the future of human civilization is at stake...

The answer is to end our reliance on carbon-based fuels.

In my search for genuinely effective answers to the climate crisis, I have held a series of "solutions summits" with engineers, scientists and CEOs. In those discussions, one thing has become abundantly clear: when you connect the dots, it turns out that the real solutions to the climate crisis are the very same measures needed to renew our economy and escape the trap of ever-rising energy prices. Moreover, they are also the very same solutions we need to guarantee our national security without having to go to war in the Persian Gulf.

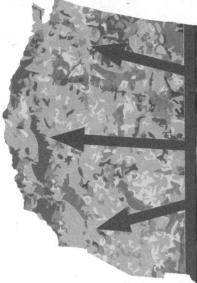

Enough wind power blows through the Midwest corridor every day to meet 100% of US electricity demand.

What if we could use fuels that are not expensive, don't cause pollution and are abundantly available right here at home?

We have such fuels. Scientists have confirmed that enough solar energy falls on the surface of the Earth every 40 minutes to meet 100 percent of the entire world's energy needs for a full year. Tapping just a small portion of this solar energy could provide all of the electricity America uses. And enough wind power blows through the Midwest corridor every day to also meet 100 percent of US electricity demand. Geothermal energy, similarly, is capable of providing enormous supplies of electricity for America.

The quickest, cheapest and best way to start using all this renewable energy is in the production of electricity.... But to make this exciting potential a reality, and truly solve our nation's problems, we need a new start. That's why I'm proposing a strategic initiative designed to free us from the crises that are holding us down and to regain control of our own destiny. It's not the only thing we need to do. But this strategic challenge is the lynchpin of a bold new strategy needed to re-power America.

The Challenge: Setting Our Targets High

I challenge our nation to commit to producing 100 percent of our electricity from renewable energy and truly clean carbon-free sources within 10 years. This goal is achievable, affordable and transformative. It represents a challenge to all Americans, in every walk of life: to our political leaders, entrepreneurs, innovators, engineers and to every citizen.

Enough solar energy falls on the surface of the Earth every 40 minutes to meet 100% of the entire world's energy needs for a full year.

183

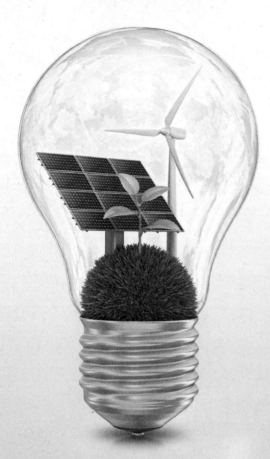

I challenge our nation to commit to producing

100%

of our electricity from renewable energy and truly clean carbon-free sources within 10 years.

This goal is achievable, affordable and transformative. It represents a challenge to all Americans, in every walk of life: to our political leaders, entrepreneurs, innovators, engineers, and to every citizen.

A few years ago, it would not have been possible to issue such a challenge. But here's what's changed: the sharp cost reductions now beginning to take place in solar, wind and geothermal power coupled with the recent dramatic price increases for oil and coal have radically changed the economics of energy....

Sure enough, billions of dollars of new investment are flowing into the development of concentrated solar thermal, photovoltaics, windmills, geothermal plants and a variety of ingenious new ways to improve our efficiency and conserve presently wasted energy. And as the demand for renewable energy grows, the costs will continue to fall....

Defying the Status Quo: Focusing on What's Possible

To those who argue that we do not yet have the technology to accomplish these results with renewable energy: I ask them to come with me to meet the entrepreneurs who will drive this revolution. I've seen what they are doing, and I have no doubt that we can meet this challenge.

To those who say the costs are still too high: I ask them to consider whether the costs of oil and coal will ever stop increasing if we keep relying on quickly depleting energy sources to feed a rapidly growing demand all around the world.

When demand for oil and coal increases, their price goes up. When demand for solar cells increases, the price often comes down. When we send money to

Even those who reap the profits of the carbon age have to recognize the inevitability of its demise. As one OPEC oil minister observed, "The Stone Age didn't end because of a shortage of stones."

foreign countries to buy nearly 70 percent of the oil we use every day, they build new skyscrapers and we lose jobs. When we spend that money building solar arrays and windmills, we build competitive industries and gain jobs here at home.

Of course there are those who will tell us this can't be done. Some of the voices we hear are the defenders of the status quo—the ones with a vested interest in perpetuating the current system, no matter how high a price the rest of us will have to pay. But even those who reap the profits of the carbon age have to recognize the inevitability of its demise. As one OPEC oil minister observed, "The Stone Age didn't end because of a shortage of stones."

To those who say 10 years is not enough time, I respectfully ask them to consider what the world's scientists are telling us about the risks we face if we don't act in 10 years. The leading experts predict that we have less than 10 years to make dramatic changes in our global warming pollution lest we lose our ability to ever recover from this environmental crisis. When the use of oil and coal goes up, pollution goes up. When the use of solar, wind and geothermal increases, pollution comes down.

To those who say the challenge is not politically viable: I suggest they go before the American people and try to defend the status quo. Then bear witness to the people's appetite for change. I for one do not believe our country can withstand 10 more years of the status quo. Our families cannot stand 10 more years of gas price increases. Our workers cannot stand 10 more years of job losses and outsourcing of factories. Our economy cannot stand 10 more years of sending $2 billion every 24 hours to foreign countries for oil. And our soldiers and their families cannot take another 10 years of repeated troop deployments to dangerous regions that just happen to have large oil supplies.

Our families cannot stand 10 more years of gas price increases.

Our workers cannot stand 10 more years of job losses and outsourcing of factories.

Our economy cannot stand 10 more years of sending $2 billion every 24 hours to foreign countries for oil.

Our soldiers and their families cannot take another 10 years of repeated troop deployments to dangerous regions that just happen to have large oil supplies.

Looking Back: Inspiration for Moving Forward

What could we do instead for the next 10 years? What should we do during the next 10 years? Some of our greatest accomplishments as a nation have resulted from commitments to reach a goal that fell well beyond the next election: the Marshall Plan, Social Security, the interstate highway system. But a political promise to do something 40 years from now is universally ignored because everyone knows that it's meaningless. Ten years is about the maximum time that we as a nation can hold a steady aim and hit our target.

When President John F. Kennedy challenged our nation to land a man on the moon and bring him back safely in 10 years, many people doubted we could accomplish that goal. But 8 years and 2 months later, Neil Armstrong and Buzz Aldrin walked on the surface of the moon.

Overcoming the Obstacles and Rising to the Occasion

To be sure, reaching the goal of 100 percent renewable and truly clean electricity within 10 years will require us to overcome many obstacles. At present, for example, we do not have a unified national grid that is sufficiently advanced to link the areas where the sun shines and the wind blows to the cities in the East and the West that need the electricity.

Photo courtesy NASA

> When President John F. Kennedy challenged our nation to land a man on the moon and bring him back safely in 10 years, many people doubted we could accomplish that goal.
>
> **But 8 years and 2 months later, Neil Armstrong and Buzz Aldrin walked on the surface of the moon.**

> **I've begun to hear different voices in this country from people who are not only tired of baby steps and special interest politics, but are hungry for a new, different and bold approach.**

Our national electric grid is critical infrastructure, as vital to the health and security of our economy as our highways and telecommunication networks.

Today, our grids are antiquated, fragile and vulnerable to cascading failure. Power outages and defects in the current grid system cost US businesses more than $120 billion a year. It has to be upgraded anyway. We could further increase the value and efficiency of a Unified National Grid by helping our struggling auto giants switch to the manufacture of plug-in electric cars. An electric vehicle fleet would sharply reduce the cost of driving a car, reduce pollution and increase the flexibility of our electricity grid.

At the same time, of course, we need to greatly improve our commitment to efficiency and conservation. That's the best investment we can make.

America's transition to renewable energy sources must also include adequate provisions to assist those Americans who would unfairly face hardship. For example, we must recognize those who have toiled in dangerous conditions to bring us our present energy supply. We should guarantee good jobs in the fresh air and sunshine for any coal miner displaced by impacts on the coal industry. Every single one of them.

Of course, we could and should speed up this transition by insisting that the price of carbon-based energy include the costs of the environmental damage it causes. I have long supported a sharp reduction in payroll taxes with the difference made up in CO_2 taxes. We should tax what we burn, not what we earn. This is the single most important policy change we can make....

Of course the greatest obstacle to meeting the challenge of 100 percent renewable electricity in 10 years may be the deep dysfunction of our politics and our self-governing system as it exists today. In recent years, our politics has tended toward incremental proposals made up of small policies designed to avoid offending special interests, alternating with occasional baby steps in the right direction....

But I've begun to hear different voices in this country from people who are not only tired of baby steps and special interest politics, but are hungry for a new, different and bold approach....

So I ask you to join with me to accept this challenge: for America to be running on 100 percent zero-carbon electricity in 10 years....We need to act now. This is a generational moment. A moment when we decide our own path and our collective fate.

.....

This contribution is an approved adaptation of Vice President Gore's challenge to the nation on July 17, 2008. Mr. Gore was the 45th vice president of the United States serving from 1993 to 2001. He is a Nobel laureate and global leader who has been engaging in research and coalition building for 30 years to halt the progression of climate change. He is currently the founder and chair of Alliance for Climate Protection, the cofounder and chair of Generation Investment Management, the cofounder and chair of Current TV, a member of the Board of Directors of Apple Inc., and a senior advisor to Google. In addition, Mr. Gore is on the faculty of Middle Tennessee State University as a visiting professor, and was a visiting professor at Columbia University Graduate School of Journalism, Fisk University and the University of California, Los Angeles.

Photo courtesy the pixie, flickr

Photo courtesy 350.org

Photo courtesy NASA

Atmospheric CO2 Concentrations

Prior to the Industrial Revolution of the late 19th and early 20th centuries, the carbon dioxide level was about 280 parts per million. That figure had changed very little over the prior 1,000 years. Today, the CO2 concentration is 391 ppm and rising about 2 ppm each year. The only time in history that we find evidence for carbon dioxide levels that high was 15 to 20 million years ago, when the planet was dramatically different.[1]

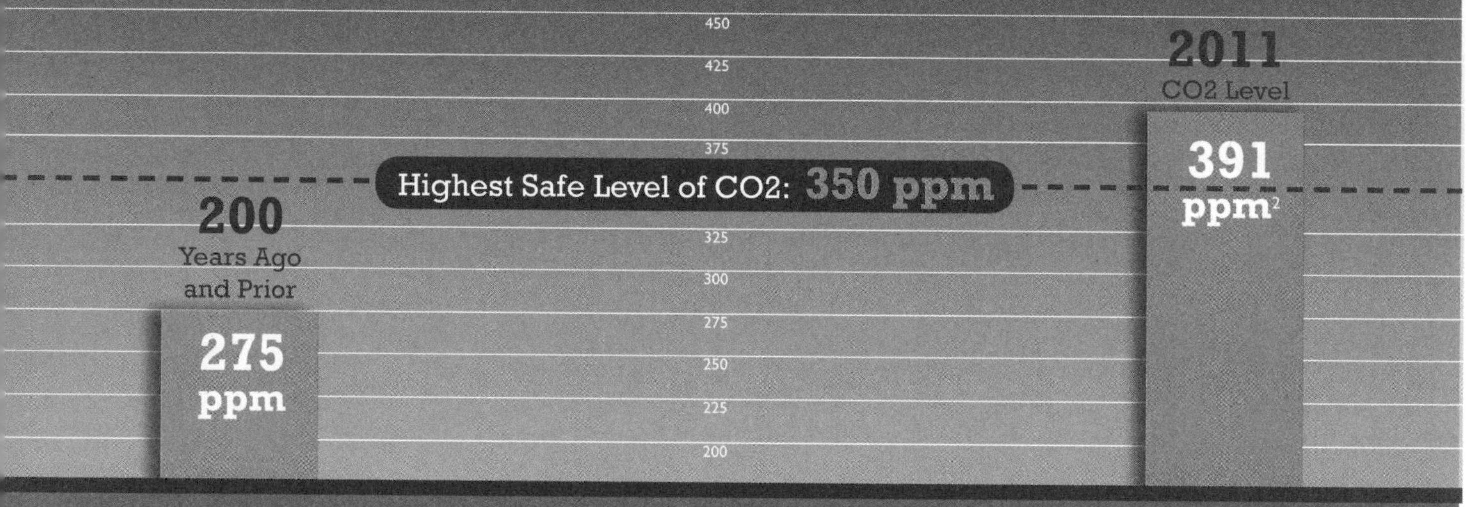

450	**2011**
425	CO2 Level
400	
375	**391**

Highest Safe Level of CO2: **350 ppm**

200
Years Ago
and Prior

391
ppm[2]

325

300

275
ppm

275

250

225

200

Scientists say that the increasing CO2 level is causing sea levels to rise, glaciers to melt, mosquitoes to spread, oceans to acidify and weather to become more severe. Getting back to 350 ppm is possible but will require phasing out fossil fuel use and adopting agricultural and forestry practices that sequester carbon.[3]

Pioneering organizations such as 350.org and the iMatter March are working to build global grass-roots movements to solve the climate crisis through campaigns, organizing and public projects.[4]

from the editor

Youth Activism: Getting Serious About Climate Change

Alec Loorz, a 16-year-old activist is suing the federal government for failure to protect the atmosphere. "The time has now come for young people to stand up and hold our government accountable," said Loorz.[1]

In this landmark case against the government, Loorz along with youth climate activists in all 50 states and the District of Columbia, is asking the government to recognize that the atmosphere is a public trust that needs to be protected for future generations.[2]

"Our addiction to fossil fuels is messing up the perfect balance of nature and threatening the survival of my generation," wrote Loorz. "If we continue to hide in denial and avoid taking action, I and my generation will be forced to grow up in a world where hurricanes as big as Katrina are normal, people die every year because of heat waves, droughts, and floods, and entire species of animals we've come to know disappear right before our eyes."[3]

The lawsuit is backed by NASA climate scientist James Hansen and lawyers say there's precedence for such a case based on the Public Trust Doctrine, which states that common resources like water and air are held in trust by the government for the people and for future generations.[4]

Loorz wants to "let the world know that climate change is not about money, it's not about power, it's not about convenience. It's about our future. It's about the survival of this and every generation to come." He organized the iMatter March, a series of more than 100 marches across planet to empower youth to organize and be heard on the issue of global climate change.[5]

At 16 Loorz is no stranger to activism. At age 12 when his application to be a speaker with Gore's Climate Project was declined because of his age, he founded his own non-profit organization, Kids Against Global Warming, and has since delivered climate change presentations to more than 200,000 youth and adults.[6]

Photo courtesy Alec Loorz and Kids vs Global Warming

> "I'm always impressed with what young people can do before older people tell them it's impossible."
>
> ❧ David Brower,
> *Founder Earth Island Institute*

Photo courtesy Alec Loorz and Kids vs Global Warming

189

Building a
Conservation Nation

What is the real potential of saving energy?

I love electricity. This may come as a surprise to those who have seen my documentary film "Kilowatt Ours." But it's true. Electricity provides a powerful service to me, my family and my work. This medium, as we experience it, is very clean. Its delivery to our light switches and outlets and appliances and electronics and toys is silent, instantaneous, seemingly magical.

The ostensibly clean, silent nature of electricity also contributes to the myth that it is free of negative consequences. So when people learn that mountains are being destroyed in the Appalachian region to generate power or that the 5.4-million-cubic-yard coal ash spill in Tennessee in 2008 was a direct consequence of generating electricity,[1] the usual response is dismay, surprise, shock and concern.

Jeff Barrie
Kilowatt Ours

Coal, Community Impacts and Vanishing Mountains

There are two methods of mining coal: underground and surface mining, more commonly called strip mining. Today, in the Appalachian region, more than 450 mountains, encompassing an area estimated to larger than 800 square miles, have been destroyed by an extreme form of strip mining. More than 7 percent of Appalachian forests have been cut down, and more than 1,200 miles of streams across the region have been buried or polluted. Mountaintop removal mining, if it continues unabated, is projected to destroy more than 1.4 million acres by the end of the decade.[2]

The process of mountaintop removal causes extreme flooding events, air and water pollution, a loss of biodiversity and disruption for impoverished communities in the valleys. The late Julia "Judy" Bonds, coal activist, Goldman Environmental Prize winner and daughter of a coal miner, called her communities of Southern Appalachia "America's sacrifice zone for cheap electricity." She and others have dedicated their life work to ending the destructive practice of mountaintop removal.[3]

America consumes more than one billion tons of coal annually, primarily for electric power.[4] A single train carrying this much coal would stretch across the US from coast to coast and back, then around the world three times.[5] The burning of coal for electricity is linked to acid rain, smog, global warming and toxic heavy metals circulating in the air we breathe.[6] Furthermore, coal-burning power plants are one of the largest users of water worldwide. Water withdrawals to produce electricity make up approximately 48 percent of total water use annually.[7]

Top: An expanse of the Appalachian Mountains untouched by mining companies.
Bottom: The late Julia "Judy" Bonds looks on at a devastated area of the Appalachians.

Photo courtesy James Burling Chase for Majora Carter Group, LLC

Health Impacts of Burning Coal

Respiratory diseases in children and elderly are worsened by the pollution from coal-burning power plants. In recent years, scientists have shown that pollution from power plants is a major cause of asthma attacks, and one in five Americans lives within 10 miles of a coal-fired power plant.[8]

Mercury emissions from coal plants contaminate lakes and rivers. A recent US Environmental Protection Agency study examined fish from more than 200 streams, rivers and lakes nationwide and found 100 percent of the fish were contaminated with mercury and 25 percent

191

showed levels beyond the EPA minimum safety standards.[9] The consumption of fish with high levels of mercury can cause brain damage and developmental disorders in unborn children.[10]

Conserving Energy: The Simple Solution

My definition of "energy conservation" is any act that reduces the amount of conventional energy used to maintain our lifestyles, conveniences and economic well-being. Conservation includes using energy-efficient technologies along with changing our behaviors and choices. I believe conservation is our greatest untapped and readily available domestic energy supply. Today we waste about the same amount of energy as we use, so we produce twice the amount that we actually use.

> **We made small changes. Our upfront investment was less than $300. Our electricity bills dropped by half almost immediately.**

Can power strips, efficient light bulbs and seemingly tiny choices such as turning off a light switch make a difference in solving the great energy challenges of our day? The evidence I found says "absolutely!" Our individual choices make all the difference. In the US, residential and commercial buildings consume about half of all the energy used each day.[11] This is a major source of the problem and, at the same time, a clear starting point for a workable solution. To confirm this, I needed proof. So, I made a documentary film about it.

Conservation in the Home

I started in my home. My wife and I changed all of our light bulbs to energy-saving compact fluorescents. We replaced our 1970s model energy-hogging fridge with a used energy-efficient model we found at a local appliance store. We turned off lights and electronics when not using them. We made small changes. Our upfront investment was less than $300. Our electricity bills dropped by half immediately, begging the question, "What if every home in America were to implement these simple changes?" In my search for the answer, I discovered that I wasn't the only one striving to conserve.

ENERGY CONSERVATION

Any act that reduces the amount of conventional energy used to maintain our lifestyles, conveniences and economic well being.

Conservation includes using energy-efficient technologies along with changing our behaviors and choices.

I believe conservation is our greatest untapped and readily available domestic energy supply.

Energy-Efficient Renovations in Buildings: A Look at Schools

I canvassed our nation to find the true potential of energy conservation. One of the greatest examples I found was Sullivan County School District in rural east Tennessee. Beginning in 2001, school officials spent $24 million to upgrade each of its 24 school and administration buildings with energy-saving measures and technologies. The magic of their program is that the hefty price tag was paid for over time with the savings from reduced operating costs, rather than paying for the project upfront. In other words, instead of paying for wasted energy, Sullivan County is now using that money to pay for its new windows, lighting, boilers and chillers and energy management systems.

Currently Sullivan County School District is realizing a savings of 40 percent on power usage and costs, and nearly half of the up-front investment has been recouped. If one

Photo courtesy NCinDC

Sidwell Friends School in Washington, DC is one of the greenest schools in the US according to the US Green Building Council's Leadership in Energy and Environmental Design (LEED) green building certification system.

Can power strips, efficient light bulbs and seemingly tiny choices such as turning off a light switch make a difference in solving the energy challenges of our day? The evidence I found says "absolutely!"

school district can do this, our entire nation of school buildings could do the same.

In addition to recovering project costs and reduced utility bills, investments in energy efficiency have other benefits as well. The non-profit Apollo Alliance estimates that a $10 billion federal investment in energy-efficient retrofit and conservation programs would result in more than a 100,000 new jobs and reduce energy use in new and existing buildings by 30 percent.[12] Fortunately this investment is part of the American Recovery and Reinvestment Act.

City-wide Conservation

It's one thing to see a small-scale example, but if we are to build a conservation nation, it must work on a large

scale. My search for bigger examples of energy savings took me to Austin, Texas. Instead of building a new $500 million coal-burning plant, the City created a "conservation power plant." Implemented since the 1980s, the energy conservation programs initiated by the City of Austin have eliminated more wasted energy than new demand, helped to create jobs, reduced energy costs, increased comfort in the built environment and kept all that coal in the mountains.

Austin Energy, the City-owned power company, used a portion of the money that was slated for the new coal plant to hire and train teams of inspectors to evaluate energy usage in businesses, schools, apartment units and homes. The energy inspectors found and repaired a wide variety of energy problems, including leaking duct work, inefficient lighting and appliances and poor insulation. Austin Energy provided rebates to its customers who

The city of Austin, instead of building another power plant, used money to improve efficiency of businesses, schools, apartment units and homes.

The resulting savings exceeds the amount of power the new power plant would have produced.

upgraded their inefficient technologies (refrigerators, lighting, etc.). Today, the City of Austin saves more than 700 megawatts of power each day, more than the output of one power plant.[13] This also exceeds the amount of power that the proposed new power plant would have produced (500 megawatts daily at best). They actually built a "conservation power plant!" Imagine if the Austin model were repeated in every city, town and community so that there was a "conservation power plant" worth of energy savings in every American city.

California Averts Energy Crisis with Conservation

In 2001, California faced massive power shortages, the supply of new energy had not kept pace with the demands of a booming population and economy. The state's leaders had a choice: Build new power plants or cut energy usage. The state government chose to conserve its way out of the crisis calling upon all citizens and businesses to do their part to reduce energy use. Through little more than widespread public education and incentives for energy conservation choices and behaviors, the state saved more than 5,500 megawatts of power that summer, or the equivalent of 11 power plants. Exemplifying the power of our small acts, 84 percent of the energy saved in California came from simple behavioral modifications such as turning off lights, unplugging electronics and adjusting thermostats. This offers more proof that conservation is a powerful resource, and abundant. The crisis was avoided without a single new power plant. I believe that a sustained education campaign on a national level can have similar results for America, and our globe, much faster than many would believe possible.

A universal law of action states "in crafting a solution to any problem, the simplest answer of least expense is the best one to adopt first." Conservation ought to be the top priority, and when we've exhausted all energy-saving opportunities, eliminated all the wasted energy

Today, the city of Austin saves more than **700 megawatts** of power each day. This exceeds the original power plant, which would have provided 500 megawatts daily at best.

In 2001, California saved more than **5,500 megawatts** of power, or the equivalent of **11 power plants. Eighty four percent** of the energy saved came from simple behavioral modifications such as turning off lights, unplugging electronics and adjusting thermostats.

we can reach, then and only then, it is time to invest in risky, capital-intensive new power plants. When we all dream, believe, then act, the world can change with the flip of a switch, to a degree greater than many believe is possible in the current reality. My dream is a nation where energy conservation is the centerpiece of our energy policy, all the way down to the individual choices each of us makes. If one household can, then all households can. If one school district can, then all schools can. If one city can, then every city can. If one state can, then so can a nation. Our nation will be strengthened as we become responsible stewards of the abundant energy resources available to us.

.....

TOP 6 steps to conserve

1 Replace the 5 most used lightbulbs with compact fluorescent bulbs SAVE $ .... Lbs coal .... $90/yr .... 662 lbs

2 Plug into power strips and turn them off when not in use .... $95/yr .... 720 lbs

3 Set hot water heater to 120° and use low-flow showerhead .... $40/yr .... 225 lbs

4 Adjust the thermostat to 68° in winter and 78° in summer .... $115/yr .... 864 lbs

5 Weatherize and seal windows, doors, air ducts, etc .... $260/yr .... 1,872 lbs

6 Use a portion of your savings to pay for green power .... $$$$$$ .... 1,800 lbs

Jeff Barrie has been producing independent documentary films since 1993, films that show how we are all part of the solution to environmental challenges. His latest film and non-profit project Kilowatt Ours (www.kilowattours.org) features an award-winning documentary film, a curriculum for K-12 schools and an energy savings workshop series for low-income neighborhoods in partnership with NES (Nashville Electric Service) and Tennessee Valley Authority. Barrie is working on a new film project called Pedaling a Dream which he hopes will motivate more people to become involved in creating the clean, green world of our dreams. Barrie lives in Nashville with his wife and co-star of Kilowatt Ours, Heather, and their daughters Lily and Antonina.

A U-Turn on
Transportation

Americans have unparalleled freedom to go where they want when they want, quickly and directly, thanks to an incomparable highway system built through a century of public investment. They make good use of this freedom. The average American household drives over 58 miles per day, totaling nearly 25,000 miles per year.[1] We are, without question, an automobile society.

But we pay dearly for the convenience of driving. American households spent an average of $9,520 to own and drive a car in 2010.[2] The costs don't stop there. In 2010, US highways were responsible for just under 33,000 deaths,[3] and 2.3 million people went to the emergency room after highway crashes.[4] Pollutants from cars impact health: 36 metropolitan areas, home to a total of 85 million people, still fail to officially meet the national standards for ozone, contributing to a variety of respiratory problems.[5] Our driving is major factor in climate change: The US transportation sector is responsible for more than one-third of carbon dioxide emissions and 60 percent of domestic oil consumption.[6]

Susan Handy
Sustainable Transportation Center
University of California Davis

The average American household drives over 58 miles per day, totaling nearly 25,000 miles per year.

It doesn't have to be this way. Imagine a future in which you can get to work and the store and all the other places you need or want to go to—but spend less time in your car to get there. Imagine a future in which your car, for those times when you still need it, does not pollute our air or hasten global climate change. Such a future is possible, but it will take both technological advances and policies that enable us to drive less.

Technological Advances

Reducing the environmental impacts of driving on a per-mile basis is largely a question of technology. US fuel-economy standards require all new vehicles, for each manufacturer, to average 34.1 miles per gallon (mpg) by 2016, up from 27.5 mpg for cars and 23.5 mpg for trucks. According to the White House, the new standard will reduce oil consumption by 1.8 billion barrels and reduce greenhouse gas emissions by 900 million metric tons.[7] While this is certainly an improvement, it doesn't

yet match European Union and Japan standards, the most stringent in the world, at approximately 45 mpg and 43 mpg respectively.[8]

Reducing the use of petroleum fuels to propel our cars is also important. The next generation of plug-in hybrids and battery-electric vehicles are now coming into the market. Some plug-in hybrids can travel up to 100 miles on a fully charged battery, and new battery-electric cars can go more than 40 miles on a single charge before the gasoline engine takes over.[9] Hydrogen fuel cells, another way to provide electricity, are possible in 10 to 15 years,[10] though it may take a considerable investment of resources[11] before they would have meaningful impact on gasoline consumption and climate change.[12] Use of second-generation biofuels, derived from grasses, biomass waste and other sources like algae, could also be widespread within 10 to 15 years.[13] We don't yet know which technology, or which combination of technologies, will win out in the long run, but we do know that technology is going to change.

Costs of Convenience

- The US transportation sector is responsible for 1/3 of CO2 emission in the US and 60% of domestic oil consumption.

1/3 of carbon dioxide emissions in the US

60% of domestic oil consumption

- American households spent an average of $9,520 to own and drive a car in 2010.

- In 2010, US highways were responsible for about 33,000 deaths & 2.3 million injuries.

A 100 mpg fleet would eliminate the need to import foreign oil and drop domestic production by 800 million barrels/year, while saving every household $2,700 a year on gas.

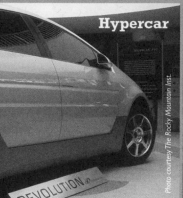

Hypercar

Photo courtesy The Rocky Mountain Inst.

Nissan Leaf

Photo courtesy Boykov

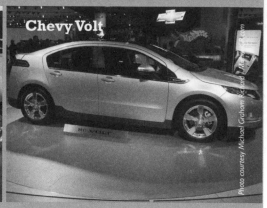

Chevy Volt

Photo courtesy Michael Graham Richard - Mitsu....com

The 100-MPG Car

The Rocky Mountain Institute, a national non-profit, has been working to accelerate electric vehicle technology for about two decades. Conceived of in 1991, the Hypercar vehicle concept combines ultra-light materials, a low-drag design and electric-drive architecture to create an efficient and financially viable vehicle.[1] With help from GM, Bright Automotive is turning the concept into reality with the Idea—a 100-mpg equivalent plug-in hybrid. The Idea will operate in all-electric mode for the first 30 miles before switching to hybrid mode for up to 400 miles.[2]

No longer a far-fetched dream, the all-electric car is a reality. The Nissan Leaf and the CODA sedan are the first two pure electric cars offered in the US. Neither requires gas to run although both use gas as the back up fuel and both claim to have a range of 100 miles from a full charge.[3] Although, it's not a pure electric vehicle, the Chevy Volt was named Car of the Year at the January 2011 Detroit Auto Show.[4] For the first time, consumers have viable options for kicking the oil habit.

from the editor

If every passenger vehicle in the US got 100 miles per gallon, the need to import oil would be eliminated.

Community Change

We must also find ways to reduce the amount of driving we do.[14] It is not easy for Americans to drive less, even when they want to. US communities are designed for driving, not for transit, walking or bicycling, and most Americans thus legitimately feel they need their cars. Reducing this need requires a comprehensive approach to community design and transportation policy that gives people the option to drive less and puts this option on more equal footing with driving.

Europe is much closer to achieving a reduction in driving. For example, Copenhagen has invested in major expansions of on- and off-street bicycle paths coupled with intersection improvements, protected bicycle parking and educational programs, resulting in a 70 percent increase in bicycle trips from 1970 to 2006.[15]

Minneapolis, which recently topped Bicycling magazine's list of the 50 most bike-friendly cities in America, launched the largest bike sharing program in the nation in 2010. It's called Nice Ride Minnesota. This is one of 60 kiosks and 1,000 rental bikes sprouting up in high-traffic locations all around the Twin Cities.

London implemented a congestion charging scheme in 2003 that requires drivers to pay a fee to enter the central area, with revenues used to improve transit service and bicycle infrastructure in the area. The scheme has reduced driving along with greenhouse gas emissions;[16] vehicle traffic in the charging area declined 16 percent in the first year,[17] while bicycle trips have grown by 17 percent per year.[18]

Models of reduced car use can be found outside of Europe as well. In Curitiba, Brazil, implementation of a well-planned bus system and an extensive network of bicycle routes transformed the city, producing a 30 percent reduction in car traffic, despite a doubling of population.[19] Bogota, Columbia, has followed a similar approach. Nearly 217 miles of bicycle lanes plus restrictions on motor vehicles at certain times and places generated an increase in the share of trips by bicycle.[20]

We can look to progress within the US too. Efforts in Portland, Oregon, to reduce auto dependence through expansions of light-rail and other transit service, investments in bicycle facilities and land-use policies that favor central city development over sprawl are paying off. The share of commuters bicycling to work more than tripled from less than 2 percent in 2000 to more than 6 percent in 2008,[21] while transit ridership has shown steady increases. In March 2010, Portland City Council unanimously passed the 2030 Bike Plan. The plan intends to make bicycling a cornerstone of Portland's sustainable transportation system with the ambitious goal of 25 percent of trips in the city by bike in 20 years.[22]

Policies to promote bicycling, walking and transit use will only succeed if land-use policies simultaneously encourage more compact development in which different land uses—residential, retail, offices, schools and so on—are within close proximity of one another. People can only walk and bicycle if their destinations are within walking and bicycling distance; transit works best if both people and destinations are clustered around stations. A number of different planning movements work toward this end: New Urbanism, Transit-Oriented Development and Smart Growth. As a key part of

Carsharing: An Alternative to Owning a Vehicle

The carsharing concept can be traced back to 1948 in Switzerland.[1] The concept began gaining speed in the US in 2000 with the formation of Flexcar, which has since merged with Zipcar. Today small community-based, and even non-profit, carsharing programs are popping up across the US such as Boulder's eGo Carshare, Chicago's I-Go and San Francisco's City Carshare. Peer-to-peer carsharing services like Relay-Rides, Spride Share and WhipCar, which let you rent your car directly to strangers or share a single car among several friends are also becoming increasingly popular.[2] Carsharing works well in locales where public transit, walking, and cycling can be used most of the time and a car is only necessary for out-of-town trips, moving large items or special occasions. Today there are more than one thousand cities in the world where people can carshare.[3]

from the editor

Stapleton's smart design allows for plenty of green space for the community.

An Urban Design Movement that Reduces Vehicle Usage

Developed on the site of Denver's former airport, Stapleton is one of the largest examples of New Urbanist design in the US. With nearly 10,000 residents, 6 schools, 500 acres of open space and 200 shops, restaurants and services, Stapleton is a mixed-use, walkable community with access to public transportation. Apartments and homes are priced for a wide range of incomes and are designed with street-facing front porches to encourage community interaction. The 25 miles of trails and bike paths promote a sense of community along with a reduced dependency on driving for day-to-day errands and activities.[1]

its effort to meet ambitious targets for reductions in greenhouse gas emissions, California is betting on such policies to help reduce driving, both by encouraging alternatives and by reducing distances when residents do drive.

Making it Happen

But how do we make this u-turn? These examples and others point to several possible triggers: federal mandates backed by targeted funding programs, state legislation that pushes change, visionary thinking in the private sector, farsighted leadership at the local level, strong advocacy from grassroots organizations, vocal demand from voters and consumers and individual commitment to action. It may take all of these forces to bring about a full reversal. While the US for the last century has been the model for building a car-dependent society, a model the rest of the world has been too eager to adopt, it can become a model for reversing this course in the century to come.

.....

Drive Less, Save More

If everyone in the US were to:

We could:

- Use public transportation one day per week ....

Save 10.4 billion gallons of gas[1] & reduce CO_2 emissions by 1,040 lbs/person/yr[2]

- Walk 5 miles a week instead of driving ....

Save 2.6 billion gallons of gas/year[3] & cut CO_2 emissions by 240 lbs/yr[4]

- Bike 25 miles a week instead of driving ....

Save 13 billion gallons of gas per year[5] and reduce CO_2 emissions by more than 1,200 lbs/yr[6].

Dr. Susan Handy is a professor in the Department of Environmental Science and Policy and the director of the Sustainable Transportation Center at the University of California Davis (http://stc.ucdavis.edu). Her research on the link between the built environment and travel behavior has produced over 100 academic articles and other publications. Her current studies aim to improve understanding of the factors that influence the choice of bicycling as a mode of transportation. In recent years, she has worked with the Transportation Research Board, the Institute of Medicine, the World Health Organization, the American Planning Association and the Active Living by Design program on the role of city planning in creating communities supportive of walking and bicycling. She and her family have been happily bicycling in Davis, a widely acclaimed bicycle-friendly city, for the last eight years.

A Green Energy Future
Without Expanding Nuclear

After decades of decline, politicians are considering nuclear power as a possible contender in the energy future of the United States. But nuclear power is costly, poses unnecessary safety and environmental risks, is heavily dependent on taxpayer and ratepayer subsidies, and generates deadly radioactive waste. Building new nuclear power plants will not effectively address climate change. Clean, safe, renewable energy sources can reliably generate as much energy as conventional fuels without significant carbon emissions, destructive mining or the production of radioactive waste.

Climate change is a serious problem, and in the past few years, public support for solving the climate change crisis has grown. Increased public understanding of the negative impacts of carbon pollutants has created an opportunity for the dormant nuclear industry to rebrand itself as the "clean" alternative to fossil fuels. Despite the 2011 disaster at the Fukushima Daiichi Nuclear Power Plant in Japan, a new image, combined with 30 years distance from the partial meltdown at Three Mile Island in Pennsylvania, has positioned the nuclear industry for wider public acceptance.

However, myths remain. Nuclear power is not any cleaner or cheaper today than it was in 1973, when construction began on the Watts Barr reactor in Tennessee, the last reactor commissioned.

Tyson Slocum
Public Citizen

Clean, safe, renewable energy sources can reliably generate as much energy as conventional fuels without significant carbon emissions, destructive mining or the production of radioactive waste.

Myth 1: "Too Cheap to Meter"

Despite the promise nuclear proponents made more than 50 years ago that nuclear energy would be "too cheap to meter," the nuclear power industry continues to depend on taxpayer handouts to survive. Since its inception in 1948, the industry has received more than $145 billion in federal subsidies but remains unable to compete economically on its own.[1]

For instance, the industry could not survive without placing all the risk for new reactors on the shoulders of taxpayers via the Price-Anderson Act. An accident at a nuclear reactor could cost more than $600 billion, a financial risk no corporation would be willing to accept. Under this law, an operator's liability is capped at $10.5 billion.[2] Taxpayers would pick up the difference.

There is also the promise of loan guarantees that industry lobbyists secured in the Energy Policy Act of 2005. Under the program, the federal government promises to pay back loans used to build reactors in the event the builder defaults. Although initially designed to back "innovative energy technologies such as renewable wind and solar power," much of the money likely will be used to financially prop up nuclear reactors.

Using taxpayer money to financially back nuclear reactors puts taxpayers at a huge risk. The risk of default on loan guarantees for new nuclear plants is projected to "very high, well above 50 percent"[3]—not good odds for taxpayers. In fact, without the promise of loan guarantees, it's unlikely an energy company could secure a loan to build a new reactor, which can cost upwards of $10 billion.

Even with the subsidies, loan guarantees and limits on liability, some investors recognize that nuclear energy doesn't make financial sense. Early in 2008, financier Warren Buffett ended his pursuit of a nuclear power plant in Idaho after spending $10 million to evaluate the idea. Buffett's company, MidAmerican Energy, decided the numbers didn't add up to make the project viable.

Myth 2: "Environmentally Friendly"

The money Congress is still providing for the industry and the renewed interest in nuclear energy is based on the premise that relying on "low-emission" reactors will somehow address the global warming crisis because nuclear power is "environmentally friendly."

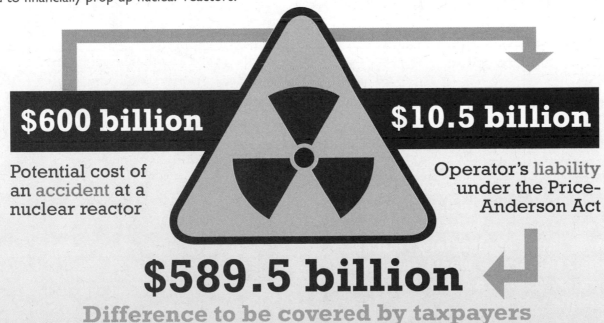

$600 billion
Potential cost of an accident at a nuclear reactor

$10.5 billion
Operator's liability under the Price-Anderson Act

$589.5 billion
Difference to be covered by taxpayers

The nuclear power industry could not survive without placing all the risk for new reactors on the shoulders of taxpayers.

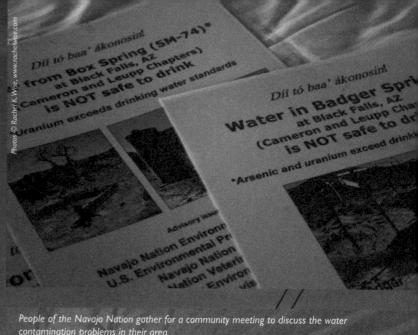

Díí tó baa' ákonosin!
from Box Spring (SM-74)*
at Black Falls, AZ
(Cameron and Leupp Chapters)
is NOT safe to drink
Uranium exceeds drinking water standards

Díí tó baa' ákonosin!
Water in Badger Spri
at Black Falls, AZ
(Cameron and Leupp Cha
is NOT safe to dr
Arsenic and uranium exceed drink

Navajo Nation Environn
U.S. Environmental Pr
Navajo Nation
Nation Veteri
Environ

People of the Navajo Nation gather for a community meeting to discuss the water contamination problems in their area.

CAUTION

ANY AREA WITHIN
THIS FACILITY
MAY CONTAIN
RADIOACTIVE
MATERIAL

The uranium deposit at Crow Butte in Nebraska was discovered in 1980. Now much of the region is contaminated.

During a 30-year period beginning in the 1950s, 3,000 members of the Navajo Nation worked in uranium mines; the consequences were devastating.

Thousands of uranium miners and their relatives lost their lives as a result of radioactive contamination.

Uranium mining on tribal lands continues today and Native communities continue to be exposed to the resulting pollution. Along with existing mines, abandoned and exploratory mines discharge radioactive waste into the groundwater, rivers and streams, that native people rely on.

Residents collect water from their local spring, which is not fit for drinking because of uranium contamination from years of mining run-off.

Conventional uranium mining has caused dust and radon inhalation by workers, resulting in high rates of lung cancer and other diseases, and mining has caused serious contamination of groundwater.

Contrary to what the industry and its lobbyists want you to believe, nuclear power pollutes. Uranium, a finite resource like coal, fuels nuclear power. The process of mining, milling and enriching uranium produces radioactive waste and presents opportunities to contaminate soil, air and water. Uranium is mined by removing uranium ore or by extracting the uranium in a newer process known as in situ leaching. Most uranium mining in the United States takes place in Utah, Colorado, New Mexico, Arizona and Wyoming, and these areas of the

from the editor

Alternative Fuels: Focusing on Smart Solutions

In our search for better, cleaner and more sustainable energy sources, we need to focus on the right solutions. Nearly all energy solutions carry inherent risk if not done correctly. Rather than promoting and subsidizing dangerous options, we need to make an unprecedented commitment to substantially increase energy efficiency in vehicles, homes, and factories and support clean, equitable sources of energy, such as solar and wind power. Here are just a few energy sources currently in use and under consideration.

Fuel	Potential Benefits	Dangers	Implications	Smart Alternatives
Natural Gas	Domestic fuel source Cleaner than other fossil fuels Efficient fuel source	"Fracking" (hydraulic fracturing) is used in 90 percent of drilling Drilling companies are exempt from the Safe Drinking Water Act[1]	Air, ground-water and well pollution Requires hundreds of toxic chemicals Each well uses millions of gallons of water	Regulation that prevents damage to the environment Require the gas industry to be accountable to the Safe Drinking Water Act
Corn-Based Ethanol	Domestic fuel source Renewable resource	Requires as much energy to produce than it generates when burned Soil erosion and water pollution from use of chemical fertilizers and pesticides	Maximum potential is only 12% of current US gasoline usage Expensive: anticipated cost to US tax payers is between $5.5 and $7.3 billion annually[2] Global food insecurity	Other forms of ethanol such as cellusosic which is derived from sugar cane waste, switch grass and other sustainable sources
Biomass	Domestic fuel source	Deforestation Now counted as carbon-neutral but could increase CO2 emissions substantially	Alters biodiversity, regional weather patterns, land use	Use sources that avoid deforestation such as switch grass, salvaged wood waste
Nuclear	Domestic fuel source Cleaner than other fuel sources	Requires uranium Processing results in radioactive waste	Groundwater, soil and air contamination from mining Mining is detrimental to the health of native communities Financially unsustainable: industry is subsidized by US government Radioactive waste leaks and spills	Renewable energy sources

An aerial photo of the former Atlas tailings pile, lower right, next to the Colorado River near Moab, Utah. Tailings are often abandoned above ground and due to the proximity to the river, communities downstream are threatened with contamination.

country are now suffering from its effects. Conventional uranium mining has caused dust and radon inhalation by workers, resulting in high rates of lung cancer and other respiratory diseases, and mining has caused serious contamination of groundwater.

When conventionally mined, uranium metal must be separated from the rock in a process called milling, which forms large radon-contaminated piles of material known as tailings. These tailings are often abandoned aboveground. Twelve million tons of tailings are piled along the Colorado River near Moab, Utah, threatening communities downstream. In the process of in situ leaching, a solution is pumped into the ground to dissolve the uranium. When the mixture is returned to the surface, the uranium is separated and evaporated in slurry pools, and the remaining contaminated water has potential to seep underground and mix with drinking water sources.

Uranium mining has historically threatened the health and safety of tribal communities and continues to do so. A uranium mine in Nebraska has the Oglala Sioux Tribe concerned about the drinking water contamination.

"Geo-chemically changed" contaminated water from the mining process is suspected of flowing into drinking-water aquifers.[4] During a 30-year period beginning in the 1950s, 3,000 members of the Navajo Nation worked in uranium mines, often walking home in ore-covered clothes. The consequences were devastating. Thousands of uranium miners and their relatives lost their lives as a result of radioactive contamination, and many families are still seeking compensation.[5]

In addition to the immediate effects, no country has found a permanent solution for the high- and low-level radioactive waste that nuclear energy creates. Generated throughout all parts of the fuel cycle, this waste poses a serious danger to human health. Currently, more than 2,000 metric tons of high-level radioactive waste and 12 million cubic feet of low-level radioactive waste are produced annually by the 103 operating reactors in the US.[6] This deadly waste, which is so radioactive it can't be moved for years, sits in more than 100 US facilities because there is nowhere to store it safely. Already, more than 54,000 metric tons of irradiated fuel has accumulated at the sites of commercial nuclear reactors in the US.[7]

An aerial view of damage to Sukuiso, Japan, a week after a 9.0 magnitude earthquake and subsequent tsunami devastated the region.

When an earthquake and tsunami caused explosions and nuclear reactor meltdowns at Fukushima Nuclear Power Plant on March 11, 2011, more than 1,600 plant workers were exposed to dangerous levels of radiation. Hundreds of thousands of residents were evacuated and tens of the thousands will never return to their homes. In the months following the incident, high levels of radioactive chemicals were found in food products from the area such as beef, tea, milk, seafood and many vegetables, which have since been recalled. High levels of radiation are suspected at elementary schools dozens of miles of way from the plant. Experts say it could take decades to clean up the area.[1]

Smoke at Fukushima-Daiichi nuclear power plant.

The Yamagata family has to deal with the damage done to their pharmacy along with concerns of radiation contamination after the 9.0 earthquake.

In response to the nuclear crisis in Japan, 250,000 people took to the streets demanding an end to nuclear power in Germany where 17 reactors provide 23 percent of the nation's energy. Under the enormous public pressure, the German government announced that all nuclear power plants would close and be replaced by wind and solar energy by 2022.[2]

Start of the street protest against nuclear power in Essen Germany, April 2, 2011.

> **Trading one dirty energy source for another** is not the only option. We don't have to choose between coal and nuclear.

The Answer

Trading one dirty energy source for another is not the only option. We don't have to choose between coal and nuclear. Renewable energy sources such as wind, solar and geothermal, along with increased energy efficiency, are better alternatives to meeting our energy needs than either coal or nuclear. It is technically and economically feasible to completely meet the energy needs of the US over the coming decades with them.[8]

Researchers at Stanford University recently evaluated the potential of wind power globally. After analyzing wind speeds in various locations around the world, the researchers concluded that wind could generate about one and a half times current annual world energy use.[9]

Existing solar electric technology could also make a significant contribution to energy production. According to a recent study, the US could accommodate about 1 million megawatts of photovoltaic (PV) panels by 2025, which would generate approximately half of current US electricity use.[10] With improvements in panel efficiency, the total long-term technical potential of solar PV in the US could provide more than three times current world energy use, according to a National Renewable Energy Laboratory analysis.[11]

Furthermore, a recent report out of Duke University by John Blackburn, professor emeritus, suggests that nuclear may be overtaking solar energy in its cost per kilowatt hour. The report, *Solar and Nuclear Costs: The Historic Crossover*, examines North Carolina's future energy costs using solar and nuclear sources. Their findings show that, at 16 cents per kilowatt-hour, solar energy becomes more affordable and a better investment. Nuclear plants take years to build, often with great delays. If solar energy can gain the same financial traction currently held by the nuclear industry, it will only become more financially accessible as demand grows.[12]

In addition to renewable technologies, using energy more efficiently is an important part of moving to a clean energy future. Efficiency is the cheapest and easiest way to reduce electricity use and facilitate the transition to renewable technologies.

Renewable energy opponents argue that renewable energy is far too variable and inconsistent to meet our energy needs because of weather conditions and natural cycles of availability. But a recent analysis by the International Energy Agency concluded that intermittency is not a technical barrier to renewable energy. Distributed generation, links across geographic areas, a diverse mix of technologies harnessing different resources and the continued development of storage technologies are potential solutions.[13] Renewable technology growth is steadily increasing its portion of the US energy portfolio. For instance, wind energy contributed up to 39 percent of all new US electric generating capacity in 2009.[14]

When you add up the safety and security risks, financial implications for taxpayers and environmental and community impact potentials, it is clear that nuclear power is not the answer to our future energy needs. It is time for a renewable energy revolution—one that is clean, secure, cost-effective and that will create the jobs and stability that we need.

.....

Tyson Slocum is director of Public Citizen's (www.citizen.org) Energy Program, where he promotes decentralized, sustainable energy and affordable clean-energy solutions. He also works to highlight the significant financial costs and safety risks associated with nuclear power and advocates legislative efforts to address climate change. In addition, Slocum serves on the Commodity Futures Trading Commission's Energy and Environmental Markets Advisory Committee. Prior to joining Public Citizen, Slocum was a policy analyst at the Institute on Taxation and Economic Policy. He received his BA from the University of Texas at Austin and grew up in Newport, Rhode Island.

A Blueprint for a
Clean Energy Economy

Reducing oil dependence. Strengthening energy security. Creating jobs. Tackling global warming. Addressing air pollution. Improving our health. These are just a few of the many reasons for the United States to move to a clean-energy economy, one that does not depend on oil, does not contribute to global warming and invests in technologies that will spur American innovation and entrepreneurship, create jobs and keep the US globally competitive. The transition to a clean-energy economy is under way, but the changes are still too gradual to reduce heat-trapping emissions sufficiently to protect the well being of our citizens and the health of our environment.

Recent analyses by the Union of Concerned Scientists (UCS) and other experts indicate that, even with aggressive action by other nations, the US must reduce its emissions by at least 80 percent below 2005 levels by 2050 to have a reasonable chance of avoiding some of the worst impacts of climate change. UCS has developed a comprehensive blueprint for the way forward. It shows that we can lower US heat-trapping emissions to meet a carbon limit set at 26 percent below 2005 levels in 2020, and 56 percent below 2005 levels in 2030. This would put us on track to meet the 80 percent target by 2050 while saving businesses and consumers money.

The UCS blueprint is made up of many different building blocks. Some of the policies are already in place in some form, but need to be strengthened, others are in active

Kevin Knobloch,
Union of Concerned Scientists

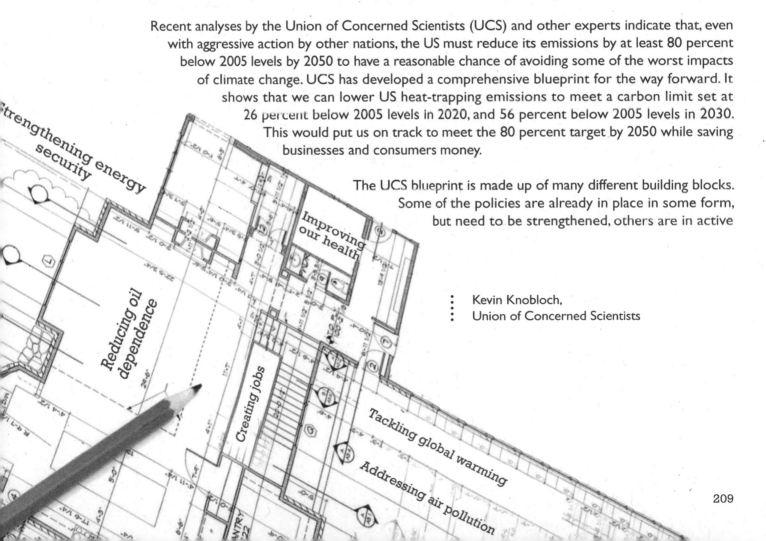

209

discussion, while still others may face large political hurdles, but are nonetheless finding opportunities through state, regional or administrative action. Meeting the blueprint's goals will require continued effort to foster further progress on all fronts. Every year we delay increases the risk of costly climate impacts.

The Blueprint's Building Blocks

Energy efficiency: The energy used to power, heat and cool our homes, businesses and industries is responsible for nearly three-quarters of all US energy consumption and two-thirds of all US carbon emissions. Fortunately, some of the most significant and readily available global warming solutions can be applied in our industries and buildings. If every American home replaced one ordinary light bulb with an efficient one, we would save enough energy to light 3 million homes a year and prevent 9 billion pounds of greenhouse-gas emissions per year.[1] Weatherization programs, which will likely gain popularity with President Obama's "Cash for Caulkers" program, can reduce the average energy consumption of a single-family home by 12 to 23 percent or more.[2]

While installing energy-efficiency measures can reduce emissions and save consumers money, several market barriers are limiting their potential. Barriers include a lack of capital needed for upfront investments in more efficient technologies and a lack of information and expertise for purchasing and installing those technologies. The blueprint shows that increasing energy-efficiency standards for appliances, equipment and buildings and providing incentives for consumers to invest in efficiency are effective policies for overcoming market barriers.

Lower-carbon electricity: Almost half of America's electricity is produced by burning coal, helping to make heat-trapping emissions from power plants the country's greatest contributor to global warming. We can greatly reduce our reliance on fossil fuel–based electricity and create new jobs by shifting to clean, renewable energy sources that are commercially available and ready to be deployed today, such as wind, solar, geothermal and bioenergy. The

from the editor

Dezhou's solar-powered conference center is the centerpiece of China's solar city.

Image from Himin Solar Co. Ltd.

China's Solar Thermal City

In Dezhou, China almost everyone has a solar water heater. Of the city's 5.5 million residents about 90 percent of the homes have solar water heaters. A solar water heater in Dezhou costs about $190 and pays for itself in five and a half years. Solar thermal is much less expensive than gas or electric energy sources. A single-family sized unit can save 660 pounds of coal a year. Multiply that by 200 million families and that's 60 million tons of coal saving 500 million tons of carbon emissions annually, the equivalent of taking 42.5 million vehicles off the road.[1] Not coincidentally, Dezhou is home to the world's largest solar thermal manufacturer, Himin Group. The solar industry is a major employer in the city— about one-third of working-age residents have jobs in the industry— and that figure is only expected to increase. Himin Group company officials project that within 10 years 15 to 20 percent of the China's energy needs will be met by solar thermal energy.[2]

In the US, each Energy Star-certified solar water heater saves about 4,000 pounds of carbon emissions annually. If 40 percent of US homes installed solar thermal water-heating systems, the amount of CO2 saved would be the equivalent of shutting down every power plant in Mexico—about 104 million tons.[3]

Creating a Sustainable Energy Future With a Smart Grid

While much of the talk about our energy future has focused on renewable energy, a quiet revolution has begun that could reimagine our entire energy system. The idea is to marry information, automation and clean technology to create a "smart grid" that moves us toward the cleanest, cheapest and most reliable electricity choices.

In a smart grid world, home thermostats and appliances would adjust automatically depending on the current cost of power, and heating and cooling systems would be powered from the neighbor's rooftop solar panel. Business and facility managers would access a real-time display of energy costs through their cellphones and make adjustments remotely. Utilities would know instantly when the power goes out and would easily shift between conventional power plants and renewable sources.

The US Department of Energy has calculated that smart grids could save about $75 billion and 135 gigawatts of energy over the next 20 years. That's about the same energy output of 170 standard size coal-fired power plants.

Ireland is a leader in smart grid innovation. The country obtains 20 percent of its electricity from wind turbines, and it recently built a smart grid that quickly switches to gas-fired generators when wind power lags.[1]

Plans for a smart grid and other clean energy technologies are underway in the US. The Obama administration's smart grid initiative was designed to speed development of a next-generation electrical network. Under the White House plan, administration will work closely with the nation's power companies as they invest in new power technologies, while a new Energy Department "research hub" will fund smart grid research and development.[2]

from the editor

> **The US Department of Energy has calculated that smart grids could save about $75 billion and 135 gigawatts of energy over the next 20 years.**

Geothermal Map of the US

Heat Flow

25 mW/m² — 150+ mW/m²

mW = milliWatts, m = meters

Hydrothermal sources on land across 13 western states have the potential capacity to produce an estimated **33,000 megawatts** annually, enough to power about **7.5 million homes.**

The Oregon Institute of Technology was the world's first university to be entirely powered from geothermal energy. Geothermal energy was chosen because Klamath Falls sits near a fault line, making it a relatively inexpensive and easily accessible resource.

blueprint shows that a national renewable electricity standard requiring electricity providers to produce at least 40 percent of the nation's power from sources like wind and solar power by 2030 is achievable and affordable for making this shift.

A study by the US Department of Energy found that wind power has the potential to provide more than 10 times the electricity that the country requires today. That study also showed that wind power could be expanded to 20 percent of the total by 2030 without affecting the reliability of the nation's power supply.[3] In fact, that level of wind power would create more than 500,000 new US jobs, displace 50 percent of the natural gas used to produce electricity, reduce coal use by 18 percent, reduce global-warming emissions from power plants by 20 percent and cost only 2 percent more than investing in new coal and natural gas plants (about 50 cents per month per household).

Installing solar photovoltaic panels, which use semiconducting materials to convert sunlight into electricity, on one percent of the nation's land area could potentially generate enough power to meet our entire annual electricity needs.[4] The National Renewable Energy Laboratory estimates that concentrating solar power (CSP) has the potential to generate roughly ten times the nation's entire current electricity capacity.[5] CSP, which works by using sunlight to heat a fluid that drives a turbine to produce electricity, is most often used in large utility-scale plants that are far from urban areas yet connected to the transmission grid. In 2010, the US solar energy industry employed more than 93,500 people—almost 10,000 more people than steel production.[6] One recent study estimates that the industry will create 440,000 permanent jobs and spur $325 billion in investments by 2016.[7]

Geothermal energy—heat from the earth—can be used directly to heat and cool buildings and also to produce electricity in power plants. The US generates more electricity from geothermal power plants than any other country in the world, about two-thirds of it in California, where 43 geothermal plants currently provide nearly 5 percent of the state's electricity.[8] The US Geological Survey estimated that geothermal reservoirs of steam and hot water on private land and accessible public land in 13 western states have the potential capacity to produce an estimated 33,000 megawatts annually, enough to power about 7.5 million homes.[9]

Biomass energy, produced primarily from burning plants and organic residues generated

A study by the US Department of Energy found that wind power has the potential to provide more than 10 times the electricity that the country requires today.

by the agriculture and forest products industries, is the oldest source of renewable energy. The growth of bio-power will depend on the availability of resources, land-use and harvesting practices and the amount of biomass used to make fuel for transportation and other uses. To account for potential land-use conflicts, to ensure sustainable production and to minimize the use of land that now grows food crops, UCS calculated that 367 million tons of biomass would be available to produce both electricity and biofuels, which has the technical potential to produce up to 19 percent of our current electricity needs.

to reduce annual premiums and create an incentive to drive less; and promoting the use of next-generation technologies such as high-speed rail and plug-in hybrid, battery and fuel-cell vehicles powered by renewable sources and lower-carbon electricity.

Each of these solutions will have an important impact, but the biggest savings in the next 20 years will come from more efficient cars and trucks. Recent studies from the US and California governments and UCS show that the average fuel efficiency of new cars and light trucks could reach as much as 60 mpg by 2025—

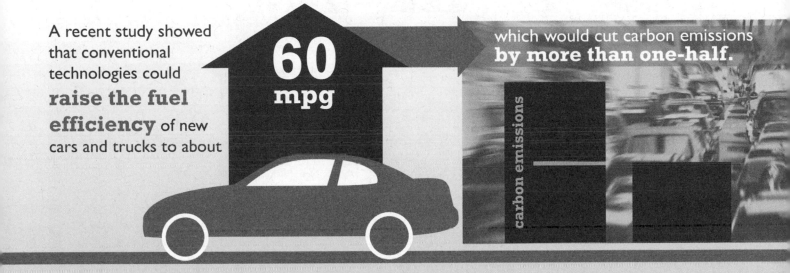

A recent study showed that conventional technologies could **raise the fuel efficiency** of new cars and trucks to about **60 mpg** which would cut carbon emissions **by more than one-half.**

carbon emissions

Cleaner transportation: Transportation—commuting, traveling and shipping goods—produces the second-largest share of US global-warming emissions, increases air pollution and makes our nation dependent on the highly volatile oil market. Creating a more stable transportation system requires three steps: using technology to improve vehicle efficiency, shifting away from oil to cleaner alternatives and reducing the amount of time people spend stuck in traffic alone in their cars.

A broad suite of policies would help break our dependence on oil, including improving fuel economy in cars and trucks of all sizes; requiring the use of low-carbon fuels and supporting the launch of an industry to produce biofuels from grasses, wood waste, and even garbage; encouraging smart growth policies by insisting on more public transit in residential and commercial development; instituting pay-as-you-drive vehicle insurance

an improvement that would more than double today's fuel economy, with most of that boost coming from conventional technology, including hybrids. Cars and trucks would cost about $3,000 more than the typical 34 mpg vehicle that will be required by 2016, but at future fuel prices ranging from about $3.50 to $4.50 per gallon, owners would save $6,000 to $7,000 over the average vehicle's lifetime, even after the initial technology costs are covered.[10] Additional research shows that even a fuel economy boost of about 12 mpg by 2018 would help create more than 200,000 jobs throughout the economy and more than 20,000 new jobs in the auto industry alone.[11] In other words, consumers would save thousands of dollars while cutting carbon emissions, reducing oil use and creating hundreds of thousands of new jobs.

A limit on carbon emissions: A limit on heat-trapping emissions in all sectors of the economy—

Photos courtesy Steve Ryan, flickr

Being Smart About Biomass: Burning Forests Is Far From Clean Energy

As the nation recognizes the need for climate-friendly sources of energy, many options are being explored, including woody biomass—cutting and burning forests for electricity—as a renewable alternative to oil and coal. Proponents claim biomass is carbon-neutral because new tree growth absorbs the same amount of carbon as the old forest released when burned.

However, early experiments with biomass have a poor track record. A study commissioned by the state of Massachusetts found that over a 50 year period biomass and coal-fired power plants have roughly the same carbon footprint.[1] Over a longer period new trees may recapture some of those emissions, making biomass a more climate friendly choice than coal, but biomass will not be carbon-neutral any time soon.

Some critics have pointed out that the Massachusetts study only looks at biomass harvested from natural forests and that larger, industrial "tree farms" would absorb carbon faster. But a large biomass power plant would require turning enormous tracts of land into unproductive, monoculture forests. A single 200MW plant proposed in Ohio is estimated to require 730,000 acres of forest to fuel – an area roughly the size of Rhode Island. And even forests engineered for biomass are still estimated to take 40 years to regrow and absorb their carbon.[2]

Biomass is not all bad. Many smaller plants turn waste products into low-carbon energy, and many rural families run very energy efficient biomass furnaces with low-quality timber culled from local woods. But burning entire forests is neither a solution to climate change nor a smart, efficient use of America's woodlands.

that puts a price on carbon and draws on the power of the marketplace to reduce emissions in a cost-effective and flexible manner – is a critical climate policy. The Blueprint's carbon limits were informed, and designed to be regularly updated, by the latest scientific information to ensure we are on the right track.

A carbon price would encourage companies to find ways to reduce these harmful emissions and would reward innovations in clean technology. We have successfully used this approach to curtail emissions of sulfur dioxide, a major component of acid rain. Those reduction goals were met three years early at a quarter of the anticipated cost and, most importantly, the billions of dollars of public health and environmental benefits outweighed the costs of the program by 40 to 1.[12]

Several states and regions in the country—including ten states in the Northeast and California—have implemented or are in the process of implementing carbon limits. There is strong interest in linking these initiatives to send a powerful, unified market signal favoring a clean and efficient energy system nationwide. The Environmental Protection Agency is also empowered to regulate global warming pollution under the Clean Air Act in order to protect public health and welfare. Beginning on Jan 2, 2011 it will, for the first time, be requiring some large power plants, oil refineries and industrial facilities to purchase permits for their emissions—a step that could prompt important improvements in energy efficiency at these facilities.

Smart Policies Bring Big Results

Taken together, the blueprint policies can help meet our emissions-reduction target in a cost-effective manner. Although they require upfront investment, the economic results are impressive, with consumers and businesses reaping a net annual savings of $255 billion in 2030. Consumers alone would save more than

Thousands of cyclists gathered outside a museum in Melbourne as one of many events around the world to send a message to world leaders in Copenhagen in December, 2009.

Photo courtesy Takver

$126 billion in 2030, about $900 per US household: $320 from lower costs for electricity, natural gas and heating oil and $580 from lower transportation costs.

Addressing climate change will require a concerted effort to show policy-makers and civic and business leaders that our climate and economy are intricately connected and that following the path toward a clean-energy future will not only help ensure a healthy climate for future generations but also encourage long-term economic prosperity. Implementing the approaches outlined in the blueprint is an important step down this path. And as recent climate and economic research shows, the most expensive thing we can do is nothing.

• • • • •

Kevin Knobloch brings 32 years of experience in public policy, government, advocacy and media to his job as leader of Union of Concerned Scientists (www.ucsusa.org), the nation's leading science-based non-profit organization working for a healthy environment and a safer world. Knobloch was named president of UCS in December 2003, after four years as the executive director. In the 1980s, he was the legislative director for US Senator Timothy Wirth and legislative assistant for US Representative Ted Weiss. He began his career as an award-winning newspaper journalist.

215

Improving Health and
Avoiding Alarming Trends

seven

A look at the numbers...

The World Health Organization **ranked the United States 37th out of 191 countries** for overall health system performance

WHO World Ranking

① . . . . 34 35 36 **(37)** 38 (39) 40 191

US

100%

Percentage of French citizens have public health coverage. France is the number-one rated country for healthcare by the World Health Organization.

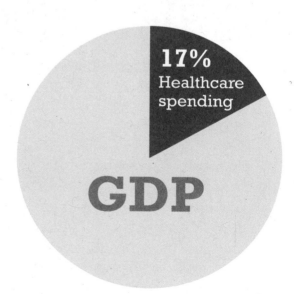

Cuba ranked just two places behind the United States

Healthcare consumes **17% of our gross national product** in the United States.

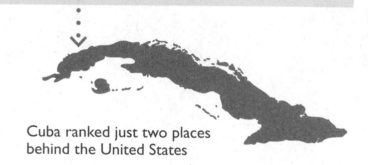

17%
Healthcare spending

GDP

$11.7 billion

Profits of the top five health insurance companies in the United States in 2010, a 51 percent increase from 2008 despite the weak economy.

$10 million

Average compensation of CEOs at major health insurance companies, the highest CEO pay of any industry in the US.

$166,700

Salary of the director of Medicare, considerably less when compared to the above CEOs of top insurance companies.

1 out of every 3 of our children
is now considered overweight or obese.

The American Academy of Pediatrics is now urging doctors to not only screen kids for obesity, but to **write out prescriptions for exercise and healthy eating.** These screenings will be fully covered by insurance.

42
Number of states that have passed regulations that forbid high-calorie and high-sodium items in school vending machines.

1.5 trillion
Calories that food manufacturers have pledged to cut from their products through a "Healthy Weight Commitment."

500
Number of mayors who signed commitments or legislation to tackle obesity in their communities

A study showed that 4 healthy habits:

Eating well

Being physically active

Not smoking

Keeping a healthy weight

slashed the risk of diabetes by 93%
heart attack by 81%
stroke by 50% and
cancer of all types by 36%.

Practicing just one of the healthy behaviors **cut the risk of developing a chronic disease in half.**

1 in 2
Number of American adults who live with at least one chronic illness such as heart disease, stroke, diabetes or cancer. 75% of healthcare costs in the US are due to chronic conditions.

219

When we set our sights on landing on the moon, we imagined reaching the destination first and then worked backward. From this angle, the over-arching framework of success was what guided action and kept the laser-focus on achieving a monumental task. If we can get to the moon, we can no doubt attain success when it comes to health and wellness in America. Other countries have taken excess profits out of the healthcare equation and are ahead of the game when it comes to preventive medicine and reducing exposure to toxic compounds. If they can do it, so can we.

Getting to the destination will require **new ways of thinking** and **different approaches...**

Valuing healthcare as a **right instead of a privilege**

Personal responsibility and **hitting the mark** when it comes to food, lifestyle and exercise

Tackling the elephant in the room—greatly reducing the **excessive profits** in the **healthcare industry**

Learning from other **countries** with universal healthcare, longer life expectancies and affordability

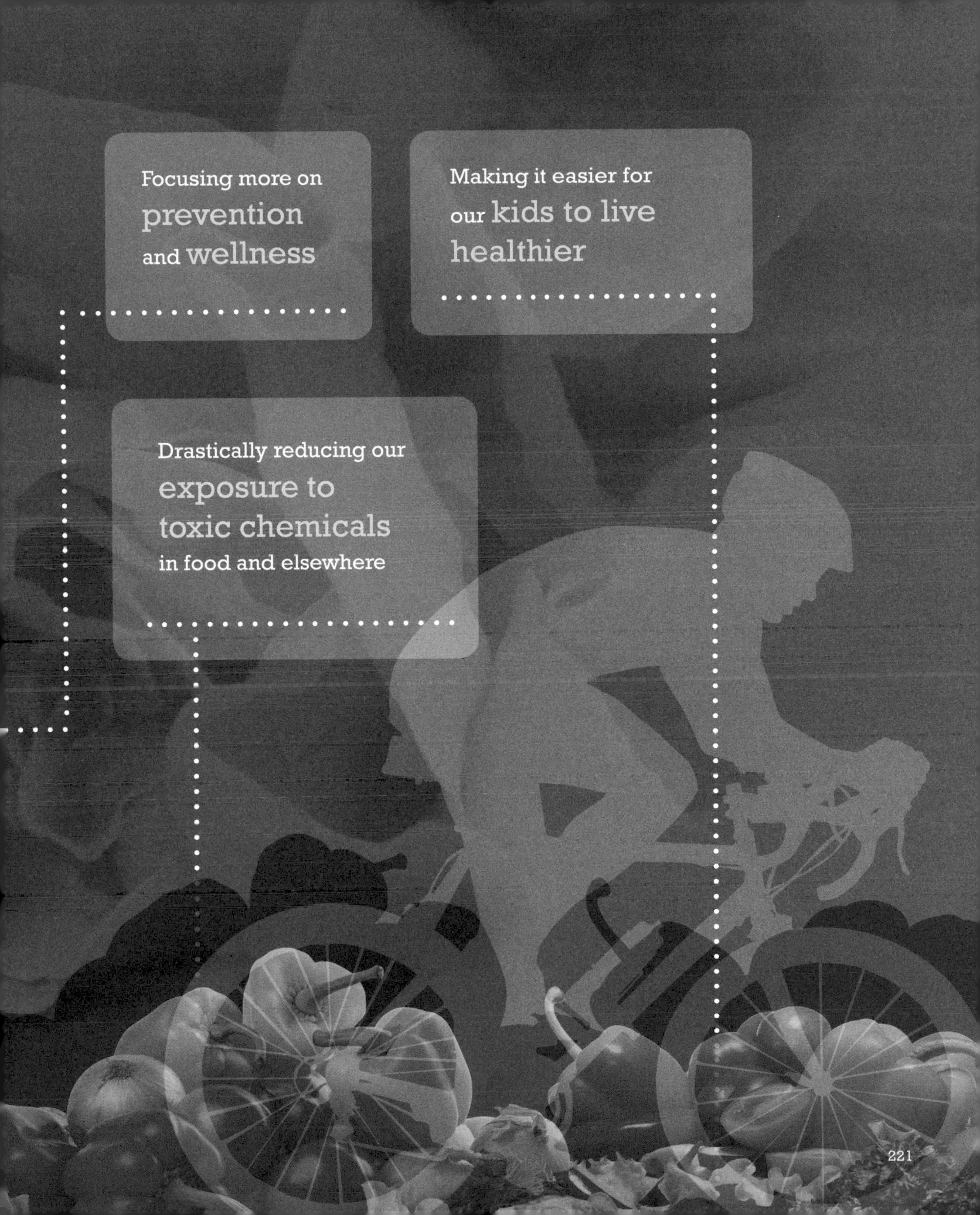

Focusing more on
prevention
and **wellness**

Making it easier for
our **kids to live**
healthier

Drastically reducing our
exposure to
toxic chemicals
in food and elsewhere

Key Steps for a
Healthy Nation

Holly G. Atkinson, MD

As Americans, we are accustomed to thinking of our country as the best in many, if not most, endeavors. We take pride in being the wealthiest nation in the world and the most open of civil societies, with the best educational institutions and the greatest military might on the planet. We delight in exporting our culture: our music, films and fashions. However, when it comes to health, our dream is nowhere near realized. We fall far short.

Our biomedical research and technological capabilities are second to none. But we rank dismally low in most meaningful measurements of well being. For example, according to the most recent data, we ranked 31st among 195 nations in average life expectancy at birth and 29th in infant mortality.[1] We have a healthcare system rife with inefficiencies and built on perverse reimbursement incentives, influencing physicians to over-utilize expensive technologies and downplay powerful preventive strategies.

We also live in a social environment that often sabotages health. Tragically, our food industry, a relentless purveyor of cheap junk food, contributes hugely to the diseases we develop. One out of every three of our children is now considered overweight or obese. These children are increasingly at risk of heart disease, diabetes, stroke and other chronic diseases at

As Michael Pollan, journalist and healthy food advocate, bluntly puts it, "One of the **leading products** of the American food industry has become patients for the American healthcare industry."

The Western Lifestyle Associated with:

Lack of physical activity

High stress levels

Smoking

Unhealthy diet

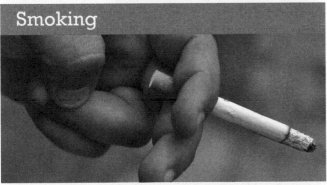

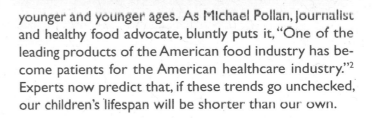

OBESITY

- **1 out of 3** children and **2 out of 3** adults are considered overweight or obese.

CHRONIC DISEASE

- **7 out of 10** Americans who die each year, die from heart disease, stroke, diabetes or cancer.
- * These diseases are among the most costly but most **PREVENTABLE** of all health problems.

younger and younger ages. As Michael Pollan, journalist and healthy food advocate, bluntly puts it, "One of the leading products of the American food industry has become patients for the American healthcare industry."[2] Experts now predict that, if these trends go unchecked, our children's lifespan will be shorter than our own.

In addition, the gap between rich and poor continues to grow, with disease and early death taking an unfair toll on the disadvantaged and disenfranchised. All this in the wealthiest nation in the world. We need a dream of a truly healthy nation.

Disease and Premature Death in America

According to the federal Centers for Disease Control (CDC), seven of every ten Americans who die each year—that's more than 1.7 million people—die from a chronic disease such as heart disease, stroke, diabetes or cancer.[3] What's more, says the CDC, three-quarters of our healthcare dollar goes to treat these chronic diseases, which are among the most costly but most preventable of all health problems. *To reiterate, much of this disease is preventable.* All of these killer diseases have been linked to our Western lifestyle—characterized by a lack of physical activity, high stress levels, smoking and a diet of highly processed foods loaded with sugar and saturated fats.

Influences on our HEALTH

Of these factors, **BEHAVIOR** has the biggest impact on health and well being (or, behavior is the major contributor to an early death).

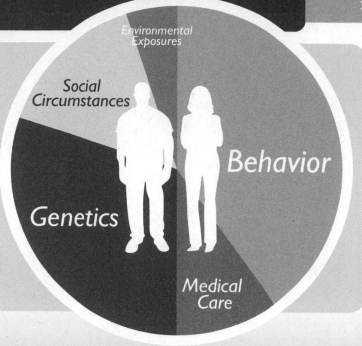

Social Circumstances

Environmental Exposures

Behavior

Genetics

Medical Care

Premature deaths in the US:

40% due to personal behavioral patterns

10% due to a lack of medical care

30% due to genetic influences

15% due to social circumstances

5% due to environmental exposures

Data comes from S.A. Schroeder, "We Can Do Better: Improving the Health of the American People," New England Journal of Medicine, 2007 adapted from J. Michael McGinnis, et. al., "The Case For More Active Policy Attention To Health Promotion," 2002, Health Affairs, 21, no.2, p. 83.

Today, two out of every three American adults are overweight. A 2004 study estimated that almost 30 percent of the increase in healthcare spending from 1987 to 2001 was due to the rise in obesity.[4] Amazingly, in 1980, obesity wasn't even on the list of sources of health spending growth. Now, the medical consequences of obesity account for almost ten cents of every dollar spent on healthcare.[5] And because we're seeing a rise of obesity in our children, we can only expect the chronic diseases that are linked to diet and obesity to continue to soar, along with their costs—both in terms of human suffering and in real dollars. The bottom line: Americans are getting sicker, and we're spending more on expensive treatments that aren't the best approach.

The Real Determinants of Our Health

What supports health? Our health is influenced by five major factors: our personal behaviors, our genes, our social circumstances, our access to good medical care and our environmental exposures. Of these factors, behavior has the biggest impact on health and well-being, or conversely, behavior is the major contributor to an early death. Today, behavioral patterns account for about 40 percent of all premature deaths in the US. Thus, changing our behavior presents the greatest opportunity to reduce chronic disease and prevent an early demise.[6] Medical care, or more accurately the lack of it, plays a surprisingly small part, contributing only about 10 percent to premature deaths in the US. The remaining half of premature deaths is due to genetic influences (30 percent), social circumstances (15 percent) and environmental exposures (5 percent). Thus, the biggest bang for our buck—both literally and figuratively—comes from the lifestyle choices we make every day.

If you look beyond the chronic diseases that now stalk us to the root causes of those diseases, you'll find just three behaviors that cause the greatest harm: smoking, poor diet and lack of physical exercise. The findings of a more recent study reinforce what we already know about the power of healthy behaviors. Among the 23,000 men and women

Americans are getting sicker, and we're spending more on expensive treatments that aren't the best approach.

who participated, those who practiced four healthy habits—eating well, being physically active, not smoking and keeping a healthy weight—slashed their risk of diabetes by 93 percent, heart attack by 81 percent, stroke by 50 percent and cancer of all types by 36 percent! Practicing just one of the four healthy behaviors cut the risk of developing a chronic disease fully *in half*.[7]

The Need for Health Promotion and Disease Prevention

But we all know that following a healthy lifestyle is easier said than done. Knowledge is not necessarily power. For years, experts have been urging Americans to quit smoking, eat well and get moving. And while we've made some progress on giving up cigarettes, smoking remains the leading preventable cause of death worldwide. Embracing a healthy lifestyle continues to be elusive for the vast majority of us. Why? Change is difficult, to be sure. But we also live in a society where it's very difficult to make healthy choices: nicotine is an addictive drug, and as the former FDA commissioner David Kessler has recently documented, the food industry is tireless in its efforts to make its products virtually addictive as well. It is as if each of us is a salmon swimming alone, struggling against a never-ending toxic tide.

We need a much greater focus not only on helping individuals engage in healthy behaviors, but also on creating social and physical environments that promote good health. This two-pronged effort must occur simultaneously, because, according to Healthy People 2010, "the

The Power of **Healthy Behaviors**

Among the 23,000 men and women who participated in a recent study, those who practiced four healthy habits slashed their risk of:

1 Eating well
2 Being physically active
3 Not smoking
4 Keeping a healthy weight

Diabetes .... by **93%**
Heart Attack by **81%**
Stroke by **50%**
Cancer by **36%**

Advancing the Nation's Perspective on Health and Healing

According to Oprah, Dr. Mehmet Oz is "America's doctor." With his own show, Dr. Oz is perhaps the nation's biggest celebrity doctor but he is also quite influential in encouraging the public to adopt healthier lifestyles. *Time* magazine ranked Oz 44th on its list of the 100 Most Influential People in 2008 and *Esquire* magazine placed him on its list of the 75 Most Influential People of the 21st century.

A proponent of integrative health—the practice of combining alternative therapies with conventional medicine—Dr. Oz addresses topics such as anti-aging, cancer prevention, diabetes, fitness, weight loss and other healthy living topics through his television show and his bestselling medical books.

Dr. Oz is not just a television doctor. He is pioneering new ways of thinking about medical care. In treating patients, Dr. Oz doesn't shy away from recommending unconventional therapies such as acupuncture, yoga, hypnosis, music, massage, reflexology, aromatherapy and energy healing. He encourages people to be proactive and experts of their own health and healing.

> Dr Oz's Favorite Healthy Foods:[1]
> - ✓ Almonds
> - ✓ Eggs
> - ✓ Low-fat Greek Yogurt
> - ✓ Dark Chocolate
> - ✓ Broccoli
> - ✓ Oatmeal
> - ✓ Fresh Fruit

"As a child I wanted to be either a pro athlete or a heart surgeon. I failed at the former, so I pursued the latter. In reality, they are scarily similar professions. You have to deliver the goods every day. And no one cares how well you performed yesterday."[2]

Stay vital and engaged. If you do not have an important reason to stay healthy, then you will get sick.[3]

health of the individual is almost inseparable from the health of the larger community."[8] Over the last several decades, we have accumulated irrefutable evidence that underscores the power of public health measures, yet there's been a failure to adequately invest in such transformative initiatives.

To be sure, excellent medical care and disease management must remain top priorities, but we need to spend more on prevention and wellness strategies to save lives and cut costs. For example, we urgently need to reform major aspects of the food industry, including agricultural subsidies and food prices. If we don't address the American way of eating, it will be impossible to prevent the diseases that are major killers of Americans. We also need to address our ever-increasing toxic environment, as we learn more and more about the enormous toll that toxic chemicals are taking on our health.

> **The major challenge will be to bring about the large-scale societal changes necessary to fix the environment that so flagrantly fosters obesity and inactivity and so readily contributes to disease.**

Preventive measures alone won't guarantee healthy lives for everyone, but they would be a giant step toward slowing disease and/or catching it early, rather than making it more profitable to prescribe a drug or send a patient to surgery after disease has taken hold.

Looking Toward the Future

While there are barriers to investing in public health initiatives and preventive health strategies, there are reasons to be optimistic. Change is happening apace. First, individuals are seeking assistance in making healthy lifestyle choices. And employers are stepping up to the plate to help: they continue to institute workplace wellness programs, which are increasingly showing a positive return on investment. Helping employees adopt healthier behaviors is paying off in a number of ways: less sickness and absenteeism, lower healthcare costs and ultimately an increased bottom line.

We also need to create healthier communities that provide better options at every turn, whether it's more nutritious foods in the school cafeteria, neighborhood delis or local restaurants; more sidewalks and parks in our neighborhoods; or more creative local ordinances, such as those that extend smokefree spaces or mandate caloric information on all food items. Pilot projects in schools and communities across the country are showing that changing the environment does make it easier for people to make good choices and avoid bad ones.

Second, physicians, along with other healthcare providers and medical institutions, are beginning to embrace lessons from the field of prevention. For example, since the widespread coverage of the Institute of Medicine's 2006 report, Preventing Medicine Errors, which found that medication errors alone injure 1.5 million people and cost billions of dollars annually in the US, a series of actions throughout the healthcare arena is being taken to prevent these injuries, extending from the use of electronic prescriptions and drug-interaction software programs to improvements in labeling and packaging of medicines.[9]

Third, the Patient Protection and Affordable Health Care Act of 2010 is a major step forward in embracing health promotion and disease prevention. The Act advances a wide array of new initiatives and funding, including coverage of numerous preventive services with no out-of-pocket cost to the individual; Medicare coverage of an annual wellness visit that includes preventive care; the establishment of a Prevention and Public Health Fund to the tune of up to $2 billion dollars by 2015; and a new national prevention, health promotion and public health council to address future activities.[10] Nevertheless, we need to press for even more healthcare reform if we are to realize our dream.

We are moving in the right direction; however, much remains to be done. The major challenge will be to bring about the large-scale societal changes necessary to fix the environment that so flagrantly fosters obesity and inactivity and so readily contributes to disease. This will take bold legislation, industry regulation and targeted taxes, among other determined actions. Resistance will be fierce. Much is at stake. But the dream of a healthy nation is clearly within our grasp.

• • • • •

Holly G. Atkinson, MD (www.drhollyatkinson.com) is assistant professor of medicine and co-director of the Advancing Idealism in Medicine (AIM) Program at Mt. Sinai School of Medicine and is past president of Physicians for Human Rights, an organization that shared in the 1997 Nobel Peace Prize. She is also chief medical officer of HealthiNation.

> *"Let your food be your medicine and your medicine be your food."*
>
> ‹ Hippocrates

Strengthening the **Food & Health Connection**

Baxter Montgomery, MD
Montgomery Heart & Wellness

After many years practicing internal medicine, cardiology and cardiac electrophysiology, I have witnessed amazing advances in medical science. Despite these advances, I have seen more young people than ever before plagued by chronic illnesses. I also noticed over time that I was becoming sicker as well. My LDL cholesterol had risen to 138 by the age of 38. (It should have been less than 100.) As a cardiologist with a genetic predisposition to diabetes and heart disease, I knew this was a significant problem.

I began an intense research effort, looking for alternative ways to achieve optimal health and wellness. I discovered a simple but amazing fact—when it comes to disease reversal and prevention, nutritional excellence is everything.

Federal Government Subsidies

Billions of dollars go to:
Huge Agribusinesses
(Producing feed crops such as corn and soy)

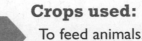

Crops used:

To feed animals

To make high-fructose corn syrup

As a primary ingredient in refined, processed foods

<1% of subsidies go to:
Fruit and Vegetable Farmers

Because of the subsidies, it ends up being the unhealthy, processed, chemical-laden foods that are typically the cheapest.

Through this unequal distribution of funds, the government supports the production of the damaging foods that contribute to our growing rates of obesity and chronic disease.

We need a paradigm shift in our approach to healthcare. Our efforts need to start with removing unnatural foods from our diet, and replacing those foods with ones that are "natural," as a way of reversing illness and facilitating health. This new approach would be a shift away from using medical and surgical interventions as our primary forms of healthcare.

Chronic Disease in America

According to the World Health Organization, the major risk factors influencing mortality today are our patterns of living and consumption. In the United States, chronic diseases—heart disease and stroke, cancer, diabetes, arthritis and obesity—cause seven in ten deaths each year. One in two American adults lives with at least one chronic illness.[1] More than 75 percent of our healthcare costs in this country are due to chronic conditions.[2]

The irony of chronic diseases is that they are the most common and most costly of all health problems in America, while at the same time being the most preventable. Also, many of the most damaging foods are the least expensive and therefore the most accessible to low-income individuals.

Why Does a Salad Cost More Than a Big Mac?

Even though we have the power to choose the food we eat, fresh, healthy, minimally processed foods can be more expensive then unhealthy, processed, chemical-laden foods. This is because the federal government provides billions of dollars in subsidies to huge agribusinesses producing feed crops, such as corn and soy, which are then fed to animals, used to make high-fructose corn syrup, and are a primary ingredient in refined, processed foods. By funding these crops, the government supports the production of the damaging foods that contribute to our growing rates of obesity and chronic disease.

Despite the federal government's historic support of unhealthy foods, there are many opportunities for change: farmers markets, community supported agriculture, local grocery co-ops and farm stands. Schools and workplaces have instituted their own policies aimed at bringing fresh, local foods into their cafeterias.

The irony of chronic diseases is that they are the most common and most costly of all health problems in America, while at the same time being the most preventable.

> **Increasing the price of sugared beverages through taxation would most likely reduce consumption, similar to the reduced usage of tobacco products after the federal government imposed a tax increase.**

I have, as a result of my own careful research and study, developed and then systemically incorporated food prescriptions into my cardiology practice. The results I have seen first-hand from the experiences of hundreds of patients and clients, across a broad spectrum of health conditions, have been astounding.

Developing policies that are more supportive of these initiatives is crucial for truly changing the food system. This is true on all scales, from policies at individual schools and workplaces to city and statewide policies to policies at the national level.

True Health Through Nutrition

Scientific studies have strongly indicated that individuals who live either solely or predominantly on plant-based diets are actually healthier than individuals who live on mostly animal-based diets.[3] Also the over-processing of plant-based foods can be related to disease formation, and therefore, the less processing our foods go through the more valuable they are for ensuring good health.

A whole-foods, plant-based diet can prevent disease states, such as cancer, heart disease, obesity, diabetes, cataracts, macular degeneration, Alzheimer's, cognitive dysfunction, multiple sclerosis and osteoporosis. Furthermore, a plant-based diet can benefit people regardless of their genes, or personal disposition. This makes consuming whole, plant-based foods a superior diet, compared to consumption of animal-based foods, to support prevention of a majority of diseases.[4]

Data compiled from four unrelated studies showed a 26 percent reduction in heart disease and a 30 percent reduction in incidence of stroke in people who consumed no animal products compared to regular meat eaters.[5] A later study performed by Dr. Dean Ornish compared individuals on a plant-based diet with less than 10 percent of calories from fat to individuals consuming 30 percent of calories from fat. The study showed an 82 percent regression of heart disease, a 37 percent decrease in cholesterol and a 91 percent decrease in angina of those on the lower-fat diet after one year.[6]

An estimated 18 million Americans have type 2 diabetes, which is caused by a combination of genetics and poor eating and exercise habits. In one study, researchers randomly assigned people with type 2 diabetes to either a low-fat, low-sugar vegan diet or the standard American Diabetes Association diet. After 22 weeks on the diets, 43 percent of those on the vegan diet were either able to stop taking some of their drugs, such as insulin or glucose-control medications, or lower the doses, compared to 26 percent of those on the standard diet. The vegan dieters lost 14 pounds on average, while the Diabetes Association dieters lost 6.8 pounds. LDL or "bad" cholesterol fell by 21 percent in the vegan group and 10 percent in the standard diet group.[7]

from the editor

Studies indicate that for every **10%** increase in price, consumption decreases by nearly **8%**

IN GOD WE TRUST · LIBERTY · 2006

Encouraging consumers to switch to more healthful beverages would lead to less caloric intake and reduced weight gain.

Tackling Childhood Obesity

In the US, one in three kids are overweight or obese. One-third of all children born in 2000 or later will suffer from diabetes; many others will face chronic obesity-related health problems like heart disease, high blood pressure, cancer and asthma.

First Lady Michelle Obama pledged to end childhood obesity within a generation so that children born today will reach adulthood at a healthy weight. It began with the White House organic garden and evolved into the Let's Move! Campaign, a series of collaborative and community-oriented strategies to address the various factors that lead to childhood obesity.

The Let's Move! Campaign focuses on four areas: empowering parents and caregivers; providing healthy food in schools; improving access to healthy, affordable foods and increasing physical activity. Tips, strategies, meal plans and physical activities are suggested on the Campaign's website and an hour per day of physical activity is recommended for all children.[1] Mrs. Obama said the campaign "has never been about the government telling people what do to."[2]

Launched in tandem with Let's Move!, the new Task Force on Childhood Obesity reviews every program and policy relating to child nutrition and physical activity. The Task Force oversees a national action plan that maximizes federal resources and sets concrete benchmarks toward the First Lady's national goal.

Mrs. Obama also backed the passage of the Healthy, Hunger-Free Kids Act, which aims to improve school lunch nutrition and funding. The bill expands eligibility for school meals programs, establishes nutrition standards for all foods sold in schools and provides a 6-cent increase for each school lunch to help cafeterias serve healthier meals.

Childhood obesity is easier to prevent than to treat and in most cases can be prevented with lifestyle choices. We owe it to future generations to raise healthy kids.

from the editor

Studies show that offering kids healthy foods in school leads to long-term healthier eating habits.

The Healthy, Hunger-Free Kids Act aims to improve school lunch nutrition. This elementary school in Portland, Oregon tested a more nutritious lunch program with great success.

The major benefit of preventing or reversing a chronic illness is the benefit of adding more life to their years, as opposed to more years to their life. Ultimately, the quality of our days is what is most important.

Signs of Progress

As part of the Special Supplemental Nutrition Program for Women, Infants and Children (WIC), the Farmers' Market Nutrition Program provides fresh, unprepared, locally grown fruits and vegetables to WIC participants. Coupons are used to purchase fresh, nutritious, unprepared, locally grown fruits, vegetables and herbs. In 2009, 2.2 million individuals participated in the Farmers' Market Nutrition Program.[8]

In a recent push toward healthier schools, 42 states have passed regulations forbidding the high-calorie and high-sodium items that were marketed in traditional vending machines.[9] Recognizing that these junk foods can lead to obesity, diabetes and coronary artery disease, these forward-thinking schools have replaced unhealthy vending machine snacks with healthier options such as water, juice, yogurt, crackers, fruit and granola bars. While eliminating junk food from school vending machines doesn't guarantee the ideal healthy diet for school-aged kids, it is still progress in the right direction and more schools need to follow suit.

Studies show that offering kids healthy foods in school leads to long-term healthier eating habits. One study showed that fifth graders consumed more fruit and

Steps to a **Healthier** You

① **Focus meals around minimally processed, plant-based foods.**

② **Purchase more of your groceries from farmers' markets, CSAs, local co-ops.**

③ **Interested in nutrition policy?** The Center for Science in the Public Interest is a science-based advocate for nutrition and health, food safety and alcohol policy. www.cspinet.org

Photo courtesy Kirsten Boyer Photography

> Chef Ann is working to create a sustainable model to replace highly processed foods with highly nourishing, whole foods, that are procured regionally and prepared from scratch.

Chef Ann Cooper: Committed to Making School Lunches Healthy

Chef Ann Cooper, celebrated author, chef and educator, is known as "The Renegade Lunch Lady," trumpeting the same simple fact as Dr. Montgomery: When it comes to your health, nutritional excellence is everything. Ann shifted her career from cooking in schools to advocating for a healthier food system after determining that our country could no longer ignore the environmental and health problems with our food production. Working in public K–12 school cafeterias across the nation, Chef Ann is leading the way toward a sustainable model that will replace highly processed foods with highly nourishing, whole foods, that are procured regionally and prepared from scratch. Ann founded the Food Family Farming Foundation, and her current project The Lunch Box (www.thelunchbox.org), provides free and easy to use tools, recipes and community connections to support school food reform. Adamant that a food revolution is in order, Ann foresees a time when being a chef working to feed children healthy food will no longer be considered "renegade."

vegetables when their schools restricted fatty and sugary snacks, even outside of school.[10] Teachers at a high school in Los Angeles reported that students behaved better and are focused in class after the school stocked vending machines with water, juices and healthy snacks. The school also reported a 74 percent reduction in violent suspensions and a 24 percent reduction in all suspensions since before the change in school foods and beverages.[11]

There is a need for revolutionary change in how we address chronic illnesses in this country and around the world. Lifestyle behavior with optimal nutrition will be the central theme. By approaching chronic illness first with nutritional intervention, we will improve overall quality of life for people. We will improve their productivity at work and increase their enjoyment of day-to-day activities. We will help patients avoid costly medications and surgical procedures, allowing them to keep more money in their pockets. All it takes is the realization that true health begins in the produce section of the grocery store, not the pharmacy.

.....

Baxter Montgomery, MD, (www.drbaxtermontgomery.com) is a busy cardiologist in Houston, Texas. As a clinical assistant professor of Medicine in the Division of Cardiology at the University of Texas and a fellow of the American College of Cardiology, he manages heart rhythm problems and coronary disease; performs angiography, heart device implants (defibrillators, pacemakers) and other hospital procedures, and teaches young physicians. Montgomery is also the executive director of the Johnsie and Aubary Montgomery Institute of Medical Education and Research and the author of The Food Prescription for Better Health.

Avoiding the Dangers of
Toxic Exposure

While global warming has grabbed the headlines over the last few years, another phenomenon, global poisoning, has also been making a name for itself. Its effects are less apocalyptic but more intimate. Instead of wildfires and floods, it's the kind of thing that creeps into dinner conversation about a child's problems at school or hovers over the doctor's visit where life-altering news is delivered.

Its cause is unregulated chemicals.

It comes as a surprise to most people that the US does not have a functioning system to regulate the chemicals we use in our homes and workplaces, but it's true. The law that was supposed to do this, the Toxic Substances Control Act (TSCA), passed in 1976 but never got off the ground. There are roughly 84,000 chemicals in use in the United States, up from 62,000 when TSCA passed. The US Environmental Protection Agency (EPA) has required health information on just 200 of the original chemicals and has restricted only 5.[1]

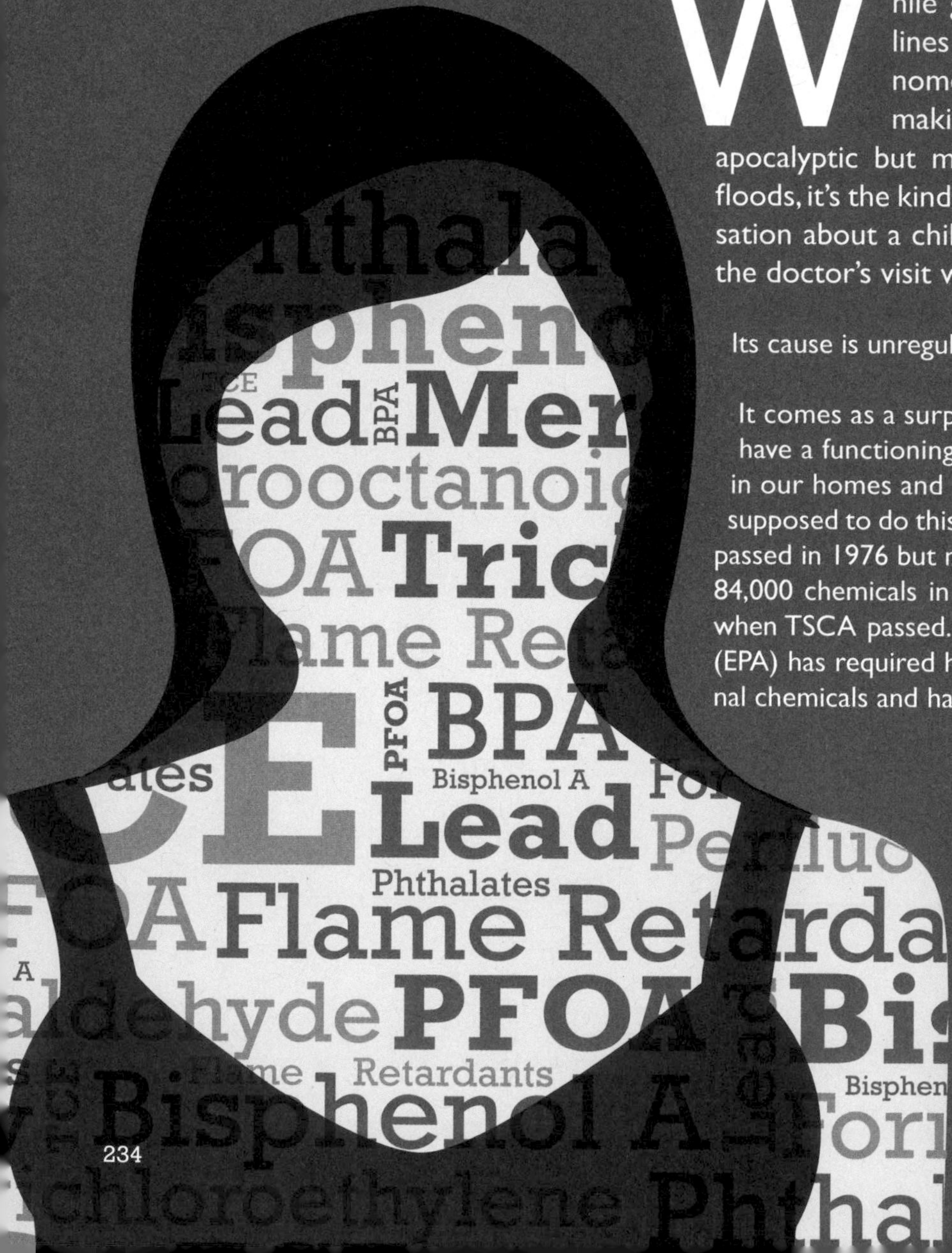

Andy Igrejas
Safer Chemicals, Healthy Families

234

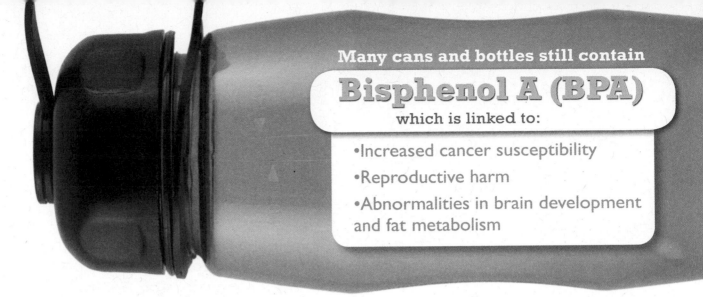

Many cans and bottles still contain

Bisphenol A (BPA)

which is linked to:

- Increased cancer susceptibility
- Reproductive harm
- Abnormalities in brain development and fat metabolism

Body Pollution, Chemical Toxicity

In the mid-90s, scientists began finding that very low doses of some common chemicals were linked to health effects that were also common in the population. The Centers for Disease Control substantially expanded its work in something called "bio-monitoring"—the science of detecting chemicals in human beings. They've found that hundreds of chemicals—including those toxic at small doses—are being carried in the blood, tissue or urine of every man, woman and child in the United States.[2] Only a sliver of this work has made its way into the mainstream press, but it's been enough to grab the public's attention.

The specter of homes and workplaces awash in unregulated chemicals that get into our bodies has revealed common interests that have been hiding in plain sight all along. Until recently, middle-class professionals may have cared about people in industrial neighborhoods, but they didn't see themselves as in the same boat. Increasingly, however, they realize that the same chemicals that go into products in some of these neighborhoods come out of products in your living room or office. The flame retardant in your couch gets out of the fabric and into the household dust that you inhale and absorb through your skin,

much the same way that lead gets into your bloodstream from old paint. Suddenly people have found a common way to relate to chemicals across geographic and socio-economic lines. Unfortunately that shared experience is the burden of chronic illness like cancer, infertility and learning disabilities.

The Environmental Working Group found:

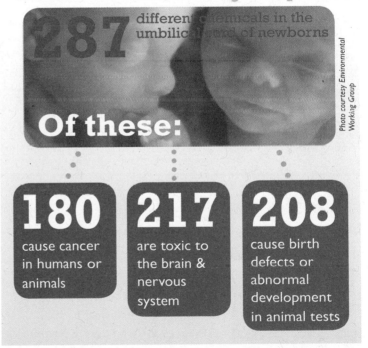

287 different chemicals in the umbilical cord of newborns

Photo courtesy Environmental Working Group

Of these:

180 cause cancer in humans or animals

217 are toxic to the brain & nervous system

208 cause birth defects or abnormal development in animal tests

Out of the 84,000 chemicals in use, the US EPA requires health information on just 200 and restricts only 5. Without fail, each of us is exposed to **toxic chemicals** every day, chemicals that are linked to serious health problems.

+ Get informed. Learn how to avoid exposure to toxic chemicals and understand the potential health effects.

+ Eat organic food, not just produce but meat as well.

+ Know which varieties of fish contain high levels of mercury and replace them with low mercury varieties.

+ Replace toxic cleaners, pesticides and cosmetics with natural, chemical free products.

+ Shop smart: Do your research to seek out nontoxic alternatives for everything from electronics, cookware and clothing to furniture, carpeting and home improvement products.

+ Know your plastics. Be wary of consuming foods or beverage served in polycarbonate plastics. Never heat or microwave food in plastic of any kind. Seek out BPA-free canned foods, sodas and food storage containers.

The punch line of the recent science trends is more chronic disease, earlier in life. More children are getting cancer, younger.[3] Learning disabilities and especially autism are skyrocketing.[4] Fertility problems are on the rise with younger couples.[5] Male reproductive problems and Parkinson's and Alzheimer's are also on the rise.[6] One of the most significant conclusions from recently published studies is that very low doses of some chemicals, very early in life—childhood and even earlier, during pregnancy—appear to contribute to increased disease much later in life.[7]

A New Campaign: The Environmental Health Movement

The link with health problems that touch most American families is what gives the relatively new environmental health movement its power. Research has shown that Americans are greatly concerned about chronic disease, are quick to associate its persistent rise with chemicals, strongly favor increased government regulation of chemicals and completely distrust the chemical industry.

The environmental health movement has already galvanized consumers around several chemicals, like the hormone-mimicking BPA found in plastics, receipt paper and other products. Wal-Mart and Target made headlines when they dropped baby bottles made with BPA from their shelves.[8] Other companies, however, have gone deeper. Healthcare companies like Kaiser Permanente, Catholic Healthcare West and Premier lead the way with comprehensive policies to weed out toxic chemicals from health facilities and the products used in them. The retailer Staples soon followed, as have several manufacturers including Construction Specialties (building materials) and Steelcase (furniture).[9]

Several states have also worked to fill the void in safeguarding health. Washington State was the first with a

> **We should address the legacy of inaction on some of the worst chemicals by naming them and requiring that they be reduced and/or eliminated.**

The EPA needs explicit authority and a new mandate to ensure chemicals are safe for us and our children.

WARNING

PESTICIDE USE

FOR INFORMATION CONTACT
Enviro Master 573-0972
CALL COLLECT
17 Sep 04
DATE POSTED DATE SPRAYED

Chemical	Exposure	Health Advisory	
Perfluorinated Compounds (PFCs)	Grease-resistant packaging, pizza boxes, popcorn bags, stain resistant products for carpets and upholstery, non-stick cookware, shampoo, dental floss	Human carcinogen, liver and kidney damage, reproductive problems, lower birth weigh	
Toxic Flame Retardants (PBDEs)	Consumer electronic plastics, furniture, mattresses, house dust, indoor air	Deficits in learning and memory, altered thyroid levels	
Heavy Metals (Mercury, Arsenic, Lead and Fluoride)	Fluorescent light bulbs, electrical fixtures, medical equipment, dental amalgam fillings, dyes, metals, drinking water	Learning difficulties; reproductive problems; hypothyrodism, brain damage, lung, bone and skin cancer, and a range of other health problems	
Bisphenol A (BPA)	Baby bottles, sippy cups, food and beverage cans, plastic medical devices, adhesives, paints, cash register receipts, dental sealants and tooth coatings	Earlier onset of puberty increased susceptibility to breast and prostate cancer altered brain development; reproductive problems insulin resistance, diabetes heart disease.	
Pesticides	Fruits, vegetables, lawns, gardens, cotton clothing and bedding, bug repellent	Asthma, birth defects, neurological effects, cancer, hormone disruption	

program to identify and restrict chemicals that persist in the environment and build up in the food chain (called persistent, bio-accumulative toxins or PBTs). Maine adopted a policy to identify the "worst of the worst" chemicals and restrict their use in products to which children can be exposed. California is now implementing a Green Chemistry Initiative that may have far-reaching implications. Minnesota, Connecticut, New York and Maryland have passed laws restricting individual chemicals.[10]

One of our largest trading partners, the European Union, is now implementing a relatively new policy called REACH, for Registration, Evaluation and Authorization of Chemicals.[11] Chemical makers will have to provide basic health and safety information for their products under the new law and share the information with companies that use the chemicals. The government is also developing a list of chemicals considered "of high concern," which, once listed, will require authorization before they can be used.

So is all this activity in Europe, several states and some forward-thinking companies enough? No. Most Americans are being exposed to chemicals right now that are having an impact on their health in ways that we are only beginning to understand. While Europe is showing us it can be done, perhaps we can do better,

like back in the days when the United States led the world in protecting public health and set the bar for environmental excellence.

Real reform would restrict the chemicals that are already widely known to be dangerous. It would require the chemical industry to divulge all the health, safety and exposure information it has for chemicals currently on the market—information that is often kept hidden under much-abused loopholes in current law. It would set a new safety standard for chemicals that would protect vulnerable subpopulations and reflect the recent scientific consensus about low doses from certain chemicals and the cumulative effect of multiple exposures.[12]

Most of these ideas were included in legislation introduced in 2011 in the Senate (HR S847). Unfortunately, it has bxeen bottled up under pressure from the American Chemistry Council, the trade association of chemical makers. That leaves plenty of work to implement this vision over the next few years, and plenty of room for this diverse movement—informed by science and committed to reducing the disease burden of our neighbors and loved ones—to grow.

. . . . .

Andy Igrejas is national campaign director of Safer Chemicals, Healthy Families (www.saferchemicals. org). Before SCHF, Igrejas headed the Environmental Health Program at the National Environmental Trust for seven years, and continued in the position when that organization merged with the Pew Charitable Trusts in 2008. In that role, Igrejas helped put chemical policy reform on the national agenda through work on the Kid-Safe Chemical Act. Igrejas also led NET's work on chemical security, right–to-know, food safety and California initiatives like the successful campaign for the Safe Cosmetics Act. Igrejas is a native of Bloomfield, NJ and now lives in Washington, D.C.

Tackling the **Profit Problem** in Healthcare:

What the US Can Learn From Europe

The United States is facing some daunting economic challenges, not the least of which is our broken healthcare system. The US spends nearly twice as much money per capita on healthcare as other developed nations, yet the metrics show that Americans end up with worse care and poorer health. Moreover, American businesses are spending way more on healthcare than their international rivals, making them less competitive in an increasingly global economy. In truth, our hodgepodge healthcare system is going to bankrupt the nation if we don't figure out a better way.

The Obama healthcare plan was a step in the right direction, but only a minor one. By the time it is fully implemented in 2014, it will have increased access to healthcare for millions (though not all) of Americans. But it will have done little to rein in costs. In theory, cost controls should be a goal that Republicans and Democrats can agree on, yet it will be an even bigger political battle than the previous one over access. That's because to rein in costs it will not be possible to tinker around the edges of a broken system, as the 2010 healthcare reform did. It will be necessary to fundamentally overhaul the system in ways that powerful special interests will fight.

Steven Hill
Political Writer

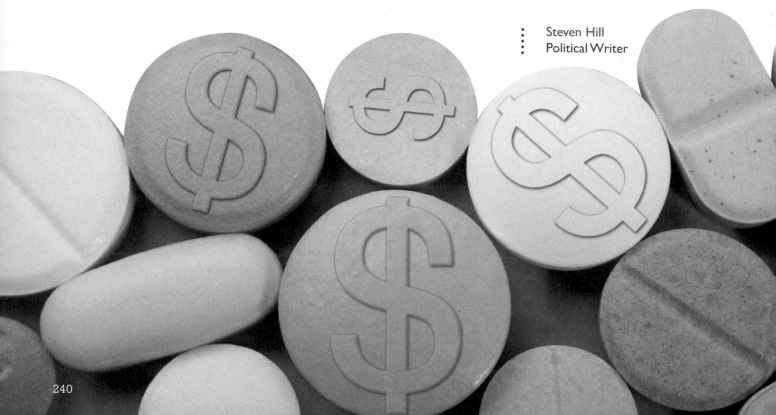

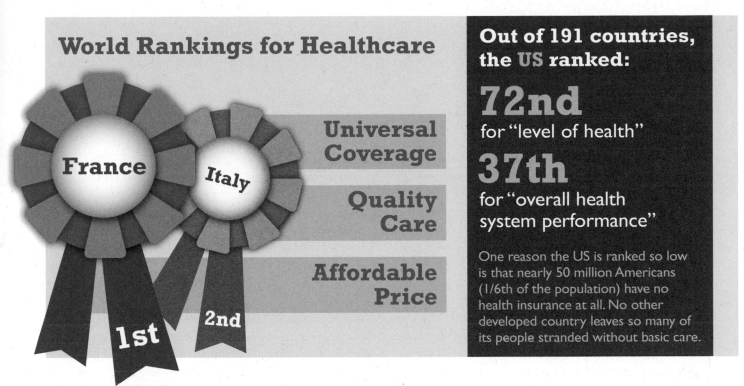

World Rankings for Healthcare

France

Italy

1st

2nd

Universal Coverage

Quality Care

Affordable Price

Out of 191 countries, the US ranked:

72nd
for "level of health"

37th
for "overall health system performance"

One reason the US is ranked so low is that nearly 50 million Americans (1/6th of the population) have no health insurance at all. No other developed country leaves so many of its people stranded without basic care.

At the root of the grotesquely expensive and inefficient US healthcare system is the fact that it is a for-profit system where profit-hungry corporations have incentive to charge premiums as high as they can get away with, while at the same time providing as few patient services as possible. That's the basic formula for how any business maximizes profit—charge more and spend less. Yet those incentives result in perverse outcomes when the goal is providing healthcare for all Americans. In short, the US healthcare system prioritizes profits before people, yet to deliver quality, affordable healthcare it is necessary to do just the opposite.

Healthcare for People, Not Profits

Americans could learn a great deal about how to design an efficient, cost-effective and humane healthcare system by looking across the pond. Europe has substantially achieved what America has yet to figure out—how to enact universal coverage and quality care at an affordable price. And surprisingly, many European nations have accomplished this without using a single-payer system, or "socialized medicine," as it is sometimes called.

To understand the magnitude of what Europe has accomplished, it is necessary to understand how far behind America is on health and healthcare. France and Italy, which have universal coverage for all their residents—even recent immigrants—were ranked first and second in the world rankings for healthcare published by the United Nations' World Health Organization (WHO). Most other European nations also were ranked near the top. The United States meanwhile is ranked 72nd of 191 countries for "level of health" and 37th for "overall health system performance," just behind Costa Rica and Dominica and just ahead of Cuba, all countries with a fraction of America's wealth.[1] One reason the US is ranked so low is that nearly 50 million Americans—one-sixth of the population, including millions of children—have no health insurance at all. No other developed country leaves so many of its people stranded without basic care.

In short, the American healthcare system prioritizes profits before people, yet to deliver quality, affordable healthcare it is necessary to do just the opposite.

The US ranks poorly not only on various health indicators but also when it comes to related metrics such as the number of physicians, hospital beds, medical errors, high out-of-pocket expenses, infant mortality, life expectancy and much more.[2] One commonsense yardstick for measuring the relative merits of different nations' healthcare systems has been called "the heart attack question": If you have a heart attack, are your chances of survival better in the United States than in other countries? The answer is a decided "no." The best place to have a heart attack is Japan if you are a man, France if you are a woman. The United States ranks only twenty-second for men and twenty-third for women among industrialized nations, according to the American Heart Association.[3]

To some extent the quality of healthcare in the American patchwork system depends on one's income level and job situation. If you are the president of the United States or a member of Congress—whose European-level benefits far outpace those of most Americans[4]— or if you work for a profitable corporation, you receive a Cadillac healthcare plan, including access to extremely sophisticated medical technology and procedures. But most Americans don't enjoy such luxurious care, they get the Yugo or jalopy plan, if they have healthcare at all.

Despite the large differences in performance between American and European healthcare systems, somehow Europe manages to spend only a fraction of what the United States spends. According to WHO, the

Healthcare Spending

United States

$7,100
per person

LOW
quality of care

France

$3,500
per person

HIGH
quality of care

Residents of Vermont rally to support healthcare reform at the State House in Montpelier.

US spends nearly 17 percent of our gross domestic product on healthcare, about $7,100 per person, compared to an average 8.6 percent in European countries. France does it for far less, spending just $3,500 per person, even though it has the top-rated healthcare system in the world.[5]

How do the French, Germans, British and other European countries manage to provide better healthcare than most Americans receive for about half the per capita cost? While there are differences from nation to nation, there also are some broad generalities to point to.

La Santé D'abord: "Health Comes First"

The first overriding difference between American and European healthcare systems is one of philosophy. The various European healthcare systems put people and their health before profits—la santé d'abord, "health comes first," as the French are fond of saying. It's no coincidence that as America tries to grapple with soaring healthcare costs and lack of universal coverage, the CEO kingpins of the healthcare industry rake in tens of millions of dollars in individual compensation and bonuses.[6] Healthcare corporations spout platitudes about wanting to provide good service for their customers, but there's no escaping the bottom line reality that the CEOs of giant health corporations ultimately are accountable to one small group—their stockholders. If nothing else, the US healthcare system provides a valuable fable illustrating that corporate profits and affordable, quality universal healthcare are not a viable mix.

The second major difference between American and European healthcare is in the specific institutions and practices that flow from this philosophy of "health comes first." Contrary to stereotype, not every country in Europe employs single-payer, or government-run, "socialized medicine." Unlike single-payer in Britain, Canada or Sweden, other nations like France and Germany have figured out a third way that not only appears to perform better than single-payer, but it also might be a better match for the American culture. This third way is a hybrid that allows private insurance companies and individual choice of doctors (most of whom are in private practice). It is based on the principle of "shared responsibility" between workers, employers and the government, all contributing their fair share to guarantee universal coverage and to hold down costs.

These healthcare plans share some common features with President Obama's 2010 healthcare reform, but with two essential differences. Like the new healthcare reform, participation for individuals is mandatory, not optional, just like it is mandatory to have a driver's license to drive an auto. But a key difference is that in France, Germany and elsewhere, the private insurance companies are non-profits instead of for-profits. The backbone of the German healthcare system, for example, is composed of about 200 private but non-profit insurance companies, all of whom compete against each other for patients. Patients have freedom of choice to go to whichever doctor they wish. Doctors, nurses and healthcare professionals are paid decent salaries but

243

2010 CEO Compensation
of Top Health Insurance Companies

$13.5 million[2]

VS. Director of Medicare salary: **$166,700**[9]

$10.8 million[1]

$8.8 million[3]

$8 million[5]

$6.1 million[4]

$5.9 million[6]

Unitedhealth

Wellpoint Inc.

Aetna

Humana

Healthcare Services

Coventry Corp

It's difficult to fathom why insurance premiums continue to rise and coverage shrinks, while the CEOs take home millions of dollars a year. One glimmer of hope is the announcement by Blue Shield of California, a non-profit and one of the top ten health insurance providers. After public outcries about premiums and executive compensation, the organization promised to refund $167 million to customers and cap future profits.[7]

Other insurance companies will be required to follow suit. The federal healthcare overhaul requires insurers to spend at least 80 percent of their revenue on medical care, leaving 20 percent for administrative costs, including salaries and profits. Insurers that don't meet that target will be required to issue refunds to policyholders. The law also implements government review of individual and small business policy rate increases of 10 percent or more.[8]

from the editor

> **I'm still waiting for the day when Americans decide they want to be number one in healthcare. Wouldn't it be grand to beat the French for a change at something that really matters?**

not as much as their American counterparts, and you don't have healthcare CEOs making tens of millions of dollars. Nor do you have stockholders demanding the highest return for their investment. Generally speaking, the profit motive has been wrung out of the system.

So the most direct way to reduce costs is to introduce a dominant-sized, non-profit sector into the healthcare market, but that's not sufficient. After all, Kaiser and Blue Cross/Blue Shield are US non-profits, but they rake in huge earnings and pay multimillion-dollar CEO salaries. So that's why France and Germany have deployed a second essential element for cost controls—negotiated fees for service. In these "shared responsibility" systems, fees for every healthcare service and product are negotiated between representatives of the healthcare professions, the government, patient-consumer representatives, and the private non-profit insurance companies. Like in the US system for Medicare, together they establish a national agreement for treatment procedures, fee structures and rate ceilings that prevent healthcare costs from spiraling out of control. Contrary to critics' claims about single-payer systems, this has not led to healthcare rationing or long waiting lists for treatment. And this has been good for businesses because it doesn't expose them to the soaring healthcare costs that have plagued American employers.

As just one example of how this affects costs, look at the difference in prices for medical drugs. Because America has nothing like these sorts of negotiated price controls (outside Medicare), some of Europe's drug companies come to the US where they can sell their prescription drugs for a lot more money than they can in their own countries. Europe's pharmaceutical businesses make one-third of their profits in the US market because they can charge five times as much in the US for the same pill made in the same factory.

That combination of non-profit insurance companies and negotiated fees for service prevents costs from spiraling out of control. Now you can see why the for-profit healthcare corporations in the United States, and the politicians who do their bidding, will fight tooth and nail against the only types of reforms that have ever proven successful at reducing costs. But US healthcare costs are so high, and so threatening to the nation's future, that eventually the logic of reform will prevail.

A "Third Way" for Healthcare

The verdict is in, and it's clear that non-profit healthcare is superior to for-profit healthcare. It costs less and it delivers better results. The results speak for themselves, showing the difference between healthcare run mostly as a non-profit venture with the goal of keeping families and workers healthy and productive, or running it as a for-profit commercial enterprise.

Americans love to be number one and win the Gold, whether in Olympic track and field, the Tour de France, the World Series or the Super Bowl. But I'm still waiting for the day when Americans decide they want to be number one in healthcare. Wouldn't it be grand to beat the French for a change at something that really matters?

• • • • •

Steven Hill (www.Steven-Hill.com) is a political writer whose latest books include Europe's Promise: Why the European Way is the Best Hope in an Insecure Age *(www.EuropesPromise.org) and* 10 Steps to Repair American Democracy *(www.10Steps.net). His articles and op-eds have appeared in the* New York Times, Washington Post, Wall Street Journal, International Herald Tribune, Financial Times, Guardian, Los Angeles Times, New York Daily News, The Nation, Washington Monthly, Ms., Salon, International Politik *(Germany),* Hürriyet Daily News *(Turkey),* Courrier Japon, India Times, Egypt Daily News, *and other leading publications. He is a cofounder of FairVote and former political reform director at the New America Foundation.*

Ending Poverty and
Building Common Wealth

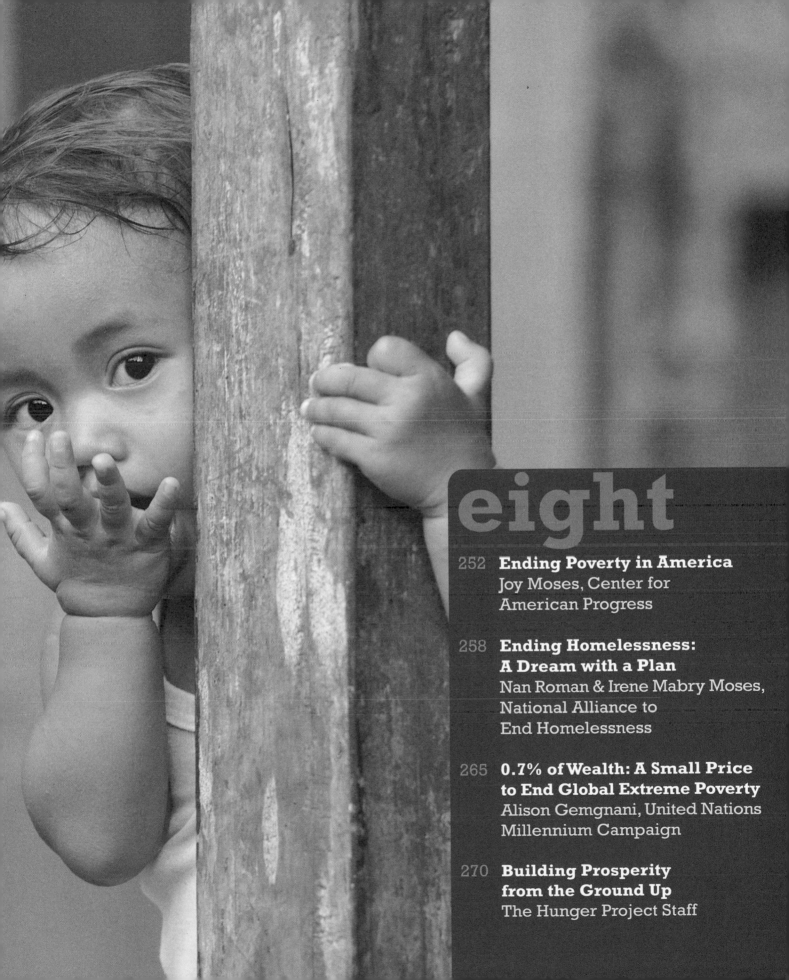

eight

A look at the numbers...

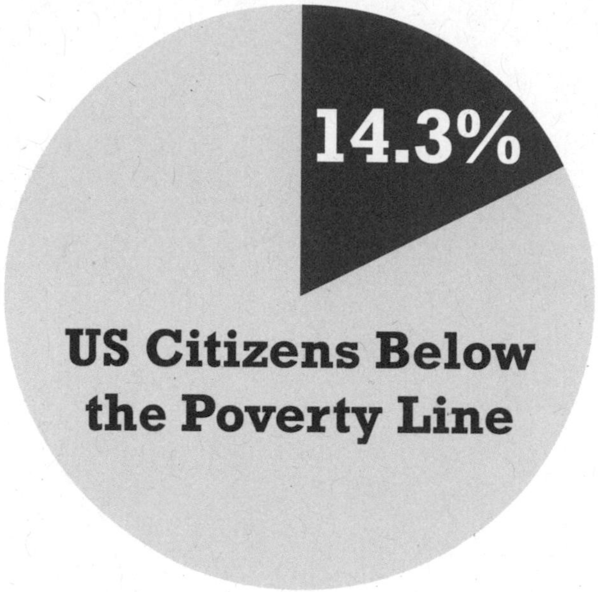

14.3%

US Citizens Below the Poverty Line

14.3% of the US population, **44 million people,** have incomes below the federal poverty line.

4 points

Amount the poverty rate fell during the Clinton administration, proving progress is possible.

12 million

Number of people that would be brought out of poverty by a 4 point reduction today.

Poverty Line:

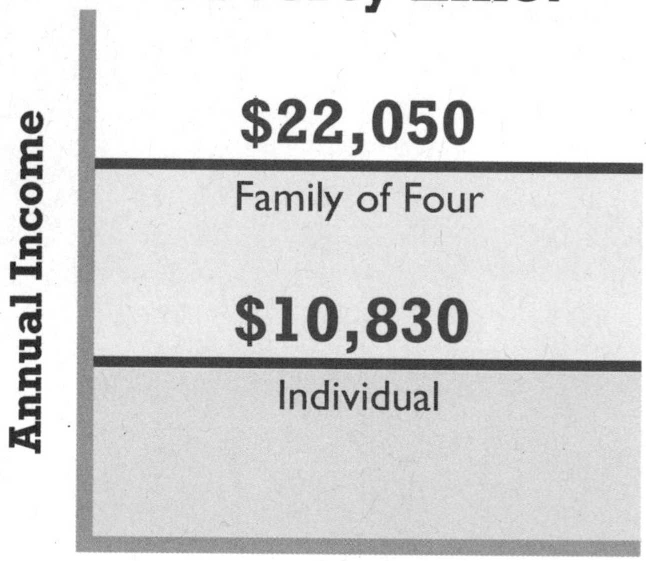

Annual Income

$22,050

Family of Four

$10,830

Individual

14.5 million

Number of children in poverty in America

1 in 5

Of all kids in America.

$22,000

Amount one full-time worker could earn per year if minimum wage were raised 50%.

50%

Amount child poverty was cut in the UK during the '90s by providing tax breaks for families.

At some point during the year, **1.6 million impoverished people will also be homeless.**

$3,500

Amount per individual per year that a community as a whole could save by providing housing for the homeless, avoiding costs in other areas.

$1.4 billion

Amount that could be saved in the economy each year if just one-quarter of the homeless population had housing available.

Worldwide 880 million people **(3 times the US population) are living on less than $1 a day.**

[ +  + ]

0.2%

Percentage of GDP the US gives to help alleviate extreme global poverty.

0.7%

Percentage of GDP many developed nations have pledged to provide.

33,000

Number of Millennium Villages that would be funded by every 0.1% increase in aid.

750 million people

Number of people the United States could provide Millennium Village services for if we met the .7% of GDP commitment.

150 million people

Number of people 33,000 Millenium Villages could provide education, food, water and basic healthcare for.

Poverty is complex, but the solutions to ending it are not.

Nearly 44 million people are living in poverty in the US—over 14 percent of our population. Despite past successes in our country that have moved millions out of poverty, it remains. Empowering people to lift themselves out of poverty requires an investment in each other. It ultimately requires shining a light on what our priorities are and looking at how well we take care of those that are most vulnerable.

On a global scale there are over a billion people living in extreme poverty. Just like in our country, the solutions lie in supporting people to support themselves and for as little as 0.7 percent of wealth it is possible to eradicate extreme poverty in this generation.

In both cases, given the will, the way is clear.

Ending Poverty and Homelessness in the US

Living wages

Affordable housing

Job training
for at-risk youth and others

More access and affordability for all levels of education

Ending Extreme Poverty Globally

Microfinance

Replicating what works
(like the Millennium Villages)

Changing the approach (from food aid) to **empowering communities** with the tools and resources for self-reliance

Empowering women

Ending Poverty in America

Nearly 44 million people are living in poverty in the US, over 14 percent of our population.[1] With governments at all levels struggling to balance budgets, it may seem impossible to fully address the growing need given available resources, but the Center for American Progress and many others are convinced it is possible.

Ending Poverty Is Possible

By way of example, three young men from the impoverished neighborhoods of Newark, New Jersey—Sampson Davis, Rameck Hunt and George Jenkins—mutually supported one another through high school and, given where they were raised, achieved the statistical improbable heights of completing college and medical school. During their junior year, a university recruiter visited their school to talk about a program that groomed underprivileged students for medical careers. After the seminar, Sampson, Rameck and George made a pact to stick together, go to college, graduate and become doctors. These students not only escaped poverty but all three also went on to become doctors. They have since founded the Three Doctors Foundation, which aims "to inspire and motivate youth through education, to achieve leadership and career success

Photo courtesy The Three Doctors Foundation

The Three Doctors, from left: Sampson Davis, Rameck Hunt, and George Jenkins, escaped poverty and formed the Three Doctors Foundation.

Joy Moses
Center for American Progress

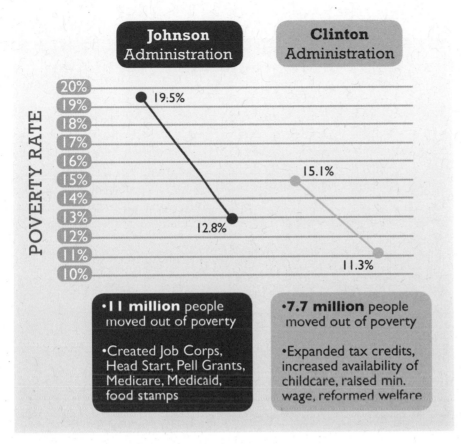

Johnson Administration	Clinton Administration

POVERTY RATE

20% — 19.5%
19%
18%
17%
16%
15% — 15.1%
14%
13%
12% — 12.8%
11% — 11.3%
10%

- **11 million** people moved out of poverty
- Created Job Corps, Head Start, Pell Grants, Medicare, Medicaid, food stamps

- **7.7 million** people moved out of poverty
- Expanded tax credits, increased availability of childcare, raised min. wage, reformed welfare

in their community through the formation of positive peer and mentor relationships."[2]

The Center for American Progress is a part of a larger movement of advocates, faith-based organizations, policy-makers, academics, think tanks and others who believe more stories like that of the three doctors are possible and that we can drastically reduce, and eventually end poverty in America. These groups believe that no problem is too big once the collective will of our nation is behind solving it. That attitude is also based on past successes with drastically reducing poverty here in America and internationally, for example:

•**LBJ's Great Society and the War on Poverty.** Within his very first State of the Union address, President Lyndon Baines Johnson declared a war on poverty. The subsequent joint efforts of Congress and LBJ were comprehensive and multi-faceted, encompassing employment, education, housing, basic needs assistance and national service.[3] Multiple programs were created that still exist today, including Job Corps, Head Start, Pell Grants and federal student loans, Medicare, Medicaid, food stamps and Volunteers in Service to America. During the Johnson administration, the poverty rate

dropped from 19.5 to 12.8 percent, moving 11 million out of poverty. As the programs continued to flourish after Johnson left office, the poverty rate dropped even lower.

•**Clinton-era Reductions in Poverty.** During the 1990s, the economy was strong, and President Clinton and Congress created various government policies that promoted and supported workers. For example, they expanded tax credits for low-income workers, increased the availability of childcare and raised the minimum wage.[4] Significantly, the Clinton years were also defined by large-scale welfare reform that produced some mixed results—many women successfully moved from welfare to work while a significant number (15 to 19 percent) still faced employment barriers coupled with a lack of accesses to federal welfare programs in 2000, leaving them in poverty and possibly worse off.[5] Ultimately, the national poverty rate dropped from 15.1 to 11.3 percent between 1993 and 2000, which equated to 7.7 million people being lifted out of poverty.[6]

•**UK Child Poverty Target.** In 1999, Prime Minister Tony Blair announced a goal to end child poverty within a generation. The country decided to tackle the problem via policies that increased benefits and tax credits for families with children, established a minimum wage and expanded childcare and employment services.[7] Statistics show that child poverty was cut in half within eight years—with 1.7 million fewer children living in poverty.

A Game Plan

Any new movement must be based on an awareness of poverty in America. In 2009, over 43 million people

It is possible to drastically reduce, and eventually end, poverty in America.

In the US, the poverty threshold for a single person under 65 was $10,830, and the threshold for a family group of four, including two children, was $22,050.

lived below the poverty line, representing 14.3 percent of the population. That year the US Census poverty threshold for a single person under 65 was an annual income of $10,830; the threshold for a family group of four, including two children, was $22,050.[8]

Alleviating and eventually ending poverty requires a thoughtful, comprehensive and multi-faceted strategy. A taskforce of well-respected poverty experts from the worlds of academia and advocacy developed an encompassing plan: From Poverty to Prosperity: A National Strategy to Cut Poverty in Half. The plan includes a series of recommendations, such as:

1) **Work Opportunities and Supports.** Work is definitely a key antidote to poverty. However, individuals with limited skills and opportunities may find it difficult to obtain and maintain employment. This is particularly true of the estimated 1.4 to 5 million disconnected youth in their late teens and early twenties who are neither involved in school or work.[9] Thus, the taskforce recommended greater investments in job training, job placement and service programs that help provide such supports, including YouthBuild, AmeriCorps, Service and Conservation Corps and Youth Opportunity Grants.

Additionally, approximately 41 percent of the 2.3 million people incarcerated in the nation's prisons and jails[10] have not completed high school.[11] Once released from prison, they frequently face job discrimination due to their criminal backgrounds.[12] Solutions focused on job training as well as preventing crime and incarceration must be developed at all levels of government.

Finally, childcare improvements and expansions are needed. Parents cannot work at all, or work effectively, if they don't have a safe and nurturing place to leave

AmeriCorps volunteers participate in Habitat for Humanity's 2011 Build-a-Thon, a national event that provides opportunities for youth to share ideas and meet others who are committed to eliminating poverty housing.

Photo courtesy Amanda Capasso

their children during those hours when they are on the job. However, for many low-wage workers, childcare costs are impossibly unaffordable. Forty percent of poor, single working mothers who paid for childcare in 2001 spent at least half of their cash income on childcare.[13] Federal and state governments offer childcare assistance to low-income workers, but current structures and resources are insufficient to truly address the need. It is estimated that only 17 percent of federally eligible children received assistance in 2008.[14] Thus, some restructuring of the system and increased investments are in order.

Participation in preschool and early childhood education programs, such as Head Start, is vital to a child's education and future chances for success.

2) Improving Incomes.
Unfortunately, there are many people in this country who work but are still struggling to get by. In the Department of Labor's most recent study, 10.4 million people were considered a part of the working poor, meaning that they worked for a significant portion of the year, but still fell under the federal poverty line.[15] Thus, the Center for American Progress's Poverty

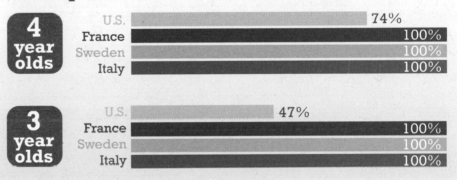

Participation in Pre-School Activities

4 year olds

U.S.	74%
France	100%
Sweden	100%
Italy	100%

3 year olds

U.S.	47%
France	100%
Sweden	100%
Italy	100%

Taskforce recommends that the federal minimum wage be re-established at 50 percent of the average wage (allowing it to automatically increase over time). Fourteen states and the District of Columbia have enacted minimum wage laws that exceed federal requirements,[16] and more states should consider following suit. Income improvements could be further achieved through expanded tax credits for working families and a greater freedom to unionize and collectively bargain for improved wages and benefits.

3) Education.
Education truly opens doors to new opportunities and forms a solid pathway into the middle class. However, in order to be successful, it must work at every level. Thus, children require access to quality early childhood education. Only 74 percent of four-year-olds and 47 percent of three-year-olds par-

ticipate in preschool services,[17] reflecting the need to expand preschool programs such as Head Start, while in Sweden, France and Italy have universal enrollment in preschool.[18]

The Obama administration agrees that continued effort should be placed into improving pre-K–12 education through measures designed to expand learning time, promote high expectations and accountability, improve teacher quality and increase access to valuable programs and services. For example, the Obama administration's Early Learning Challenge Grant proposal challenges states to develop effective, innovative models that promote high standards of quality and a focus on outcomes across early learning settings, and would dedicate $10 billion over ten years toward this effort.[19] "For every $1 we invest in these programs, we get $10 back in

255

> "Chronic unemployment is not a condition anyone **chooses,** nor does it have to be **a fact of life.**"

Cincinnati Works is Finding Answers to Unemployment

"Why don't they just get a job?" It's easy to ask that question when driving through a rundown, inner-city neighborhood. Too often "poor" is associated with "lazy," "dependent" or "unskilled."

When searching for inspiration to enter non-profit work, Dave and Liane Phillips understood that chronic unemployment is not a condition anyone chooses, nor does it have to be a fact of life. There are thousands of skilled and driven people who are unemployed in every major city, and there are also thousands of entry-level positions opening up every year. Dave and Liane realized that the solution to urban poverty is removing the barriers between these two groups.

The couple founded Cincinnati Works to provide anyone who voluntarily comes to their non-profit with the services needed to remove these barriers. Their approach is systematic. All applicants must agree to commit to the Cincinnati Works program with the goal in mind of working towards economic self sufficiency. The next week they must enroll in an individually tailored, 30-hour work-shop to improve their job readiness. Within the next year, they must start developing skills to move beyond entry-level work.

What differentiates Cincinnati Works from other jobs programs is that applicants are not merely referred to a variety of other specialized agencies. Research shows that many individuals raised and living in poverty are depressed or lack confidence, so Cincinnati Works keeps a full-time mental health expert on staff, ready to work with applicants on their first day. Applicants with legal issues work directly with the legal coordinator. Applicants with poor computer skills for example begin to work with staff or a volunteer. The list of quality, free services goes on and on.

Even with all their faith in people, Dave and Liane couldn't have expected their results. New employees from Cincinnati Works have an 80 percent rate of one year, continuous employment retention, compared to a 25 percent average around the nation. Over 90 major employers throughout the city now look to the organization first when filling a job opening. And, most importantly, every year over 400 people are getting employment in jobs that will lead to more stable financial sufficiency.[1]

from the editor

> **A nation that has a sense of purpose, people to accomplish the tasks ahead and policy blueprints that have been proven and refined is able to win the battle against poverty and win for good.**

reduced welfare rolls, fewer healthcare costs and less crime," President Obama said in a 2007 speech in Manchester, New Hampshire.[20]

Finally, higher education should be made more accessible to the poor. The Health Care and Education Reconciliation Act of 2010 made important changes to the Pell Grant program (which provides federal grants or scholarships to low-income students). However, more work lies ahead, including further raising the maximum grant to 70 percent of the average costs of attending a four-year public institution, simplifying the application process and incentivizing institutions to increase completion rates. This would go a long way toward making higher education more accessible.

Additionally states should develop strategies to make post-secondary education affordable for all residents. Georgia, for example, guarantees tuition and fees at any public college for students who graduate with a 3.0 GPA or better. In an effort to revitalize its urban center, the Kalamazoo Promise is a scholarship program that covers the cost of tuition and fees to public universities and community colleges in Michigan for students who graduate from the city's public school system. Many other cities around the nation are looking to adapt the concept.[21]

4) Fixing the Broken Pieces. There are certain elements of our national life, such as housing and the safety net, that have been noticeably broken for a very long time, impacting families of varying income levels—they must be fixed. Many low- and middle-income families pay far too much for housing and/or have been impacted by the recent foreclosure crisis. Appropriately capitalizing the National Housing Trust Fund, which is designed to create affordable housing, and multiplying investments in other programs such as rental subsidies or Housing Choice Vouchers would help in addressing this problem.

Unfortunately, regardless of work and education opportunities, there will be those who experience temporary hardships such as job losses, injuries or health problems that impact their ability to meet their basic needs. For these groups, effective safety net programs such as unemployment insurance, food stamps and energy assistance are a necessity. Yet, these programs need improvement because typically there's only enough funding to serve a small fraction of the people who qualify for services. Many such programs have a host of other problems including burdensome application procedures, bureaucracies and a lack of outreach to potential participants. Congress and administrative officials must continue to address these barriers.

There is definitely much work ahead but there are some signs of hope. A nation that has a sense of purpose, people to accomplish the tasks ahead and policy blueprints that have been proven and refined by its best minds is able to win the battle against poverty and win for good.

.....

Joy Moses is a senior policy analyst at the Center for American Progress (www.americanprogress.org). She produces reports and analyses focused on alleviating, preventing and ending poverty. Her work has covered a broad spectrum of issues including federal safety net programs, access to justice and tax credits. She was previously a staff attorney at the National Law Center on Homelessness & Poverty and the NAACP Legal Defense Fund. Moses currently serves on ABA Commission on Homelessness and Poverty and the board of the Washington Council of Lawyers. She received her JD from Georgetown University Law Center and a BA from Stanford University.

Ending Homelessness: A Dream with a Plan

In our nation tonight, at least 650,000 people will be homeless. Over a third of them will have no shelter at all. While most will be single individuals, 37 percent will be people living in families with children. Nearly a fifth will have serious disabilities and have been homeless for years, even. But for the remaining 80 percent, homelessness will be a relatively brief, one-time-only experience—the result of the nation's chronic shortage of housing that is affordable to low-income people.[1]

Ask a 20-year-old today how homelessness can be ended and chances are you will get a puzzled look in return. In their experience, homelessness has always existed and probably always will. Ending homelessness is a dream.

Except that it is not. Many people are surprised to learn that widespread homelessness is a relatively new phenomenon in the United States. Thirty years ago, we did not have it, and we should not have it now. We should all dream of a nation in which homelessness does not exist. But that dream can be accompanied by a pragmatic, actionable plan for ending it, because ending homelessness is entirely within our grasp.

Nan Roman
Irene Mabry Moses
National Alliance to End Homelessness

Of all the people who are homeless—
650,000 a night; 1,590,000 each year:

The majority will be homeless for only a brief time and never be homeless again.

Only 17% will be homeless for long periods of time
and these are people whose chronic illnesses (mental illness, chronic addictions, and physical ailments) prevent them from getting back on their feet.

Affordable Housing is the Solution

In the course of a year, nearly half of people who become homeless live in families with children; the rest are youth, veterans and single men and women. Most people are homeless because they are poor and cannot afford housing. Of all the people who are homeless—1,590,000 each year—the majority will be homeless for only a brief time and never be homeless again.[2] Only 17 percent will be homeless for long periods of time, and these are people whose chronic illnesses (mental illness, chronic addictions, and physical ailments) prevent them from getting back on their feet.[3]

The major cause of the homelessness crisis is the fact that low-income people can no longer afford housing. Thirty years ago, there were more inexpensive apartments and houses than there were low-income people who needed them. People may have had mental illness, addiction and disabilities—they may have been very poor and living on the edge—but they could afford a place to live. Today, the cost of housing has risen much faster than people's incomes, and there are fewer and fewer inexpensive places to live. The combination of more demand and less supply has led to homelessness. It is like a game of musical chairs: when the music stops, someone is left standing.

Of course, housing is not the only problem. People who are poor have difficulty finding jobs or accessing benefits. They lack medical care and often have untreated illnesses or disabilities. Certainly people who are homeless have unmet service and treatment needs and require more income. But the bottom line is, whatever other problems people may have, if they are housed they are not homeless.

Many people are surprised to learn that widespread homelessness is a relatively new phenomenon in the United States. Thirty years ago, we did not have it, and we should not have it now.

259

> **Often it is less expensive to help someone stay in their existing apartment than to let them become homeless and then find them a new place to live.**

Costs of Serving Homeless Individuals

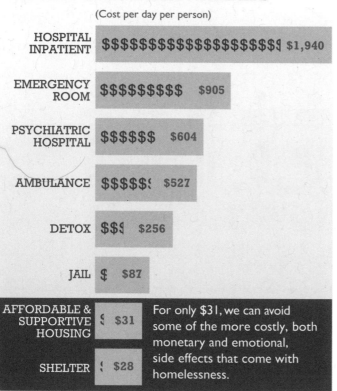

(Cost per day per person)

HOSPITAL INPATIENT	$$$$$$$$$$$$$$$$$$$$$ $1,940
EMERGENCY ROOM	$$$$$$$$$ $905
PSYCHIATRIC HOSPITAL	$$$$$$ $604
AMBULANCE	$$$$$ $527
DETOX	$$$ $256
JAIL	$ $87
AFFORDABLE & SUPPORTIVE HOUSING	$ $31
SHELTER	$ $28

For only $31, we can avoid some of the more costly, both monetary and emotional, side effects that come with homelessness.

(Source: www.usich.gov/PDF/OpeningDoors_2010_FSPPreventEndHomeless.pdf -see p.10)

Plan to End Homelessness

Research has shown us that if people can be helped to quickly return to housing, most are able to get back on their feet, re-establish their lives and move forward: they do not become homeless again. Re-housing ends homelessness and may even cost less than band-aid approaches like shelter. To be sure, people may still be poor, pay too much for housing and lack services. But they are not still homeless.

To help shift our approach to homelessness from shelter to housing, the National Alliance to End Homelessness released *A Plan, Not a Dream: How to End Homelessness in Ten Years*[4] that gives communities a road map to solutions. The step-by-step process begins with a plan and a commitment to ending homelessness completely and implementation of the following programs:

Prevention. After committing to a plan, preventing people from becoming homeless is the first step. Often it is less expensive to help someone stay in their existing apartment than to let them become homeless and then find them a new place to live. It is also the right thing to do: Why put a domestic violence survivor and her children in a shelter when an apartment would be safer and more nurturing?

Besides losing their housing because of poverty or a crisis, many people become homeless after being discharged

In 2010, the Department of Veterans Affairs estimated that there are approximately 76,000 homeless veterans, accounting for 9 percent of the entire homeless population.

from public institutions like foster care, hospitals, mental health facilities, jails or prisons. A more effective, and less costly, approach is to create a support system that helps people transition quickly into housing—the necessary platform for their future employment and stability.

Housing. To get homeless people rapidly back into housing, a whole new set of strategies is being used. More affordable housing must be produced. Communities need a toolbox of housing resources, including rental subsidies, housing locators and landlord negotiators. To house the most vulnerable and challenged street people, permanent supportive housing (housing with services) is necessary. Tens of thousands of such units have been created over the past decade, and they are slowly but surely reducing chronic homelessness.[5]

Big Picture. The final strategy is to make progress on the housing crisis, low incomes and holes in the safety net. This is a huge challenge, especially during difficult economic times. However, a new initiative could help unlock some federal resources in the service of ending homelessness. Released in June 2010, *Opening Doors: Federal Strategic Plan to Prevent and End Homelessness*[6]

> **Communities need a toolbox of housing resources including rental subsidies, housing locators, and landlord negotiators and more.**

sets ambitious five- and ten-year goals. It mobilizes mainstream programs such as housing, veterans' assistance, youth programs, welfare and child welfare to do their parts on the homelessness front. While it will not solve the housing crisis or end poverty, using these federal mainstream resources more strategically can have a major impact on homelessness.

Ending Homelessness is Achievable

More than 240 cities, towns and rural areas across the nation, Congress, several administrations, mayors, governors and legislators have adopted plans to end homelessness and are reducing homelessness nationwide.[7]

Organizations like National Alliance to End Homelessness, EveryOne Home and BOSS are successfully working for solutions to homelessness locally, statewide and nationally.

Janny (yellow shirt) is now a star staff member of the organization that helped her get back on her feet.

"I have survived abuse, addiction and homelessness. My younger years were rough, relationships were hard and I often made decisions that were bad versus what was good for me.

During a 9 year bout with homelessness BOSS gave me the support and time I needed to find subsidized housing and finally to create a stable healthy environment for my children."

EveryOne Home, a project in Alameda County (Oakland, CA), is working to permanently house the 15,000 homeless individuals and families in the county by 2020.[8] To meet this ambitious goal, a hotline has been set up to help prevent homelessness. For those who do become homeless, a centralized intake and screening process assesses needs, and one of eight housing resources centers helps them get back into housing with access to the necessary services. To ensure that there is an adequate supply of affordable and permanent supportive housing, EveryOne Home has adopted housing production goals. To keep everything on track, there is a rigorous evaluation of outcomes and a strong component focused on the development of long-term leadership and political will. EveryOne Home is well on the way to meeting its goal: the county has already reduced family homelessness by 37 percent since 2004.[9]

As long as it's been since I was homeless, the pain is still buried deep inside. When I see a person in that place, I recall that pain.

When my ex-husband returned from Vietnam with a heroin addiction, I made the decision to leave. Even working, I found it hard to maintain my previous life-style and ended up homeless, walking the streets of DC with my two young daughters.

I was soon in a shelter where I stayed for six months. The situation may seem inconceivable to most but I've seen so many people who are just one paycheck away from homelessness.

And the reality of being homeless—without a permanent place of residence—is just one part of the issue. The embarrassment, the self-pity, the stares, the taunting, the rejection—it all compounds the situation. I felt the terror my children did that their schoolmates would find out about us. I felt I couldn't call my parents or friends because I was afraid of what they would think. I know too well the stigma our society assigns to people experiencing homelessness; if you're homeless, people seem to think it must mean you're an addict, disturbed or just lazy.

In my time living in shelter, I met people insincere in their efforts and unable to understand my situation.

But today, that's changed. Today there are more programs, more strategies and more people who are dedicated to helping others move forward. I've seen programs that emphasize rapid re-housing, supportive housing, job opportunities, healthcare and other social services critical to helping vulnerable people move forward with their lives.

As a woman with intimate knowledge of the issue, I am truly blessed to serve on the Board of Directors of the National Alliance to End Homelessness. In this work, and in my personal life as a realtor helping people access housing, I feel that I am returning the blessings that helped me out of homelessness. Words can never express the joy of someone who's experienced home-lessness, stabilized and turned around to lend a helping hand to another in need. It is a joy that I know and embrace wholeheartedly.

an author's story

It's move-in day for a family because of the help of EveryOne Home. The family had been dealing with chronic homelessness for over a year.

Ending homelessness may be a dream for our nation; but with a good plan, it is a dream that we can achieve.

Other cities are also experiencing impressive results as they implement plans to end homelessness. Quincy, Massachusetts cut chronic homelessness by over half. Chicago, Illinois and Fort Worth, Texas reduced overall homelessness by ten percent in just a few years.

Nationally, between the time that homelessness first emerged and the onset of plans to end homelessness, the number of homeless people annually had been increasing, from 550,000 (1987) to 800,000 (1997). Since then, the number has been decreasing (at least until the recession, when it flattened out). Because of a federal focus on ending chronic homelessness with permanent supportive housing, we have done even better in that area: Chronic homelessness has been reduced over 30 percent.[11]

A similar approach has been implemented in Wichita, Kansas. New permanent housing units and services worked to reduce homelessness by 50 percent. An evaluation of the first 12 women housed revealed a 50 percent reduction in emergency room visits and a 90 percent reduction in in-patient hospital stays. These, along with other reductions in public service utilization, have saved the community roughly $41,000 annually for those 12 women alone.[10]

Ending homelessness may be a dream for our nation, but with a good plan, it is a dream that we can achieve. We are not there yet, but we are beginning to see what ending homelessness might look like. While today's 20-year-olds may believe homelessness is inevitable, their children may have to use their imaginations to think of a world where homelessness exists.

. . . . .

Nan Roman, president and CEO of the National Alliance to End Homelessness (endhomelessness.org), is a leading national voice on the issue of homelessness. She developed a pragmatic plan to end homelessness in ten years. To implement this plan, Roman works closely with members of Congress and the administration, as well as with cities and states across the nation. She collaborates with Alliance partners to educate the public about the real nature of homelessness and successful solutions.

Irene Mabry Moses is the founder and CEO of Faith Realty LLC and has served as a board member for the National Alliance to End Homelessness since 2008. The realtor, who once experienced homelessness herself, is an active member of her community, her church and charitable organizations focused on housing and poverty.

(See left for Moses' picture and story.)

Solving the World's Water Supply Crisis

Around the world, nearly 1 billion people lack access to safe drinking water and 3.6 million people die from water-related illnesses each year. Unsafe water and poor sanitation is one of the world's greatest humanitarian crises. And it affects the most vulnerable populations—the world's poor.

Actor Matt Damon co-founded Water.org, a nonprofit that seeks to end the global water supply crisis. Damon is more than the organization's spokesman. He has immersed himself in the issue and is directly involved with the organization's activities.

"I think what resonates with me most is when you see people living without clean water and they're forced to scavenge for water and basically use up all of their time just doing that," said Damon. "You realize that they're in such a crippling cycle of poverty; it's just a death spin that they can't possibly get out of."[1]

Water.org helps communities in Africa, Asia and Central America gain access to safe water and sanitation. The organization helps negotiate loans between microfinance institutions and communities that will be used to building systems to tap into a well. The community helps raise the money, participates in construction and maintenance and as a result is engaged and empowered.[2] "Our vision is clean water and sanitation for everyone, in our lifetime," said Damon.[3]

Since its inception in 1990, the organization has helped hundreds of communities and tens of thousand of individuals gain access to safe water and sanitation. Water.org has been successful in raising money and attracting institutional funders because many believe that its approach and solutions are scalable. Rather than a top-down charity, Water.org's approach is bottom-up sustainability.[4]

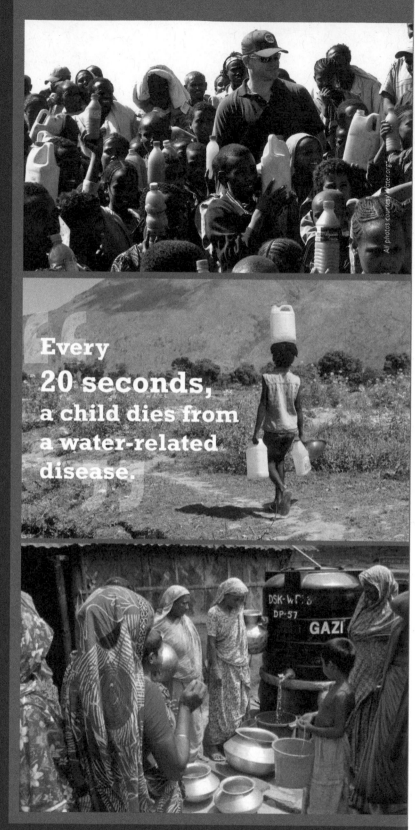

All photos courtesy Water.org

Every **20 seconds,** a child dies from a water-related disease.

0.7% of Wealth:
A Small Price to End Global Extreme Poverty

Alison Gemgnani
United Nations Millennium Campaign

With five years to go to the MDGs [Millennium Development Goals] target date of 2015, the prospect of falling short of the Goals due to lack of commitment is very real. This would be an unacceptable failure, moral and practical. If we fail, the dangers in the world—instability, violence, epidemic diseases, environmental degradation, runaway population growth—will all be multiplied.

⟡ United Nations Secretary, General Ban Ki-moon, Keeping the Promise, February 2010

In the world of development and poverty reduction, statistics are at times the most valuable snapshot for telling us where we are and where we need to be. According to the 2010 UN Millennium Development Goals report, tremendous progress has been made in the fight against poverty. Enrollment in primary school reached 89 percent in the developing world, the under-five mortality rate dropped by 28 percent and rural drinking water coverage increased to 76 percent.[1]

Nevertheless, significant gaps remain, and the road ahead may be more difficult than the one already traveled. Eleven percent of children—a staggering 72 million—are still denied access to primary education. Every year, 8.8 million children die from preventable diseases such as diarrhea and pneumonia. Ensuring that the remaining 24

THE 8 Millennium Development Goals aim to:

1 Eradicate extreme poverty and hunger

2 Achieve universal primary education

3 Promote gender equality and women's empowerment

4 Reduce child mortality

5 Improve maternal health

6 Combat HIV/AIDS, malaria, tuberculosis, and other diseases

7 Ensure environmental sustainability and better access to water and sanitation

8 Create a global partnership for development

responsibility to create a better world. This historic agreement become known as the Millennium Development Goals, more often referred to as the MDGs.

The eight MDGs aim to:
• Eradicate extreme poverty and hunger
• Achieve universal primary education
• Promote gender equality and women's empowerment
• Reduce child mortality
• Improve maternal health
• Combat HIV/AIDS, malaria, tuberculosis and other diseases
• Ensure environmental sustainability and better access to water and sanitation
• Create a global partnership for development

Achieving the Millennium Development Goals

The Goals are achievable; they have timelines and deadlines and are locally defined and measurable. The MDGs have helped transform entire countries and the results are staggering:

• Through a national input subsidy program, Malawi went from a 43 percent national food deficit in 2005 to a 53 percent food surplus in just two years.

• Kenya eliminated school fees and, as a result, enrolled an additional two million children in primary school.

• Due to the government's successful health insurance program, Rwanda is likely to meet—and even surpass—the child and maternal mortality targets by 2015.

• Cambodia has managed to halt and reverse the spread of HIV.

• With an increased investment in water and sanitation resources, Guatemala increased access to improved drinking water for 96 percent of the population and improved sanitation for 84 percent.

percent of rural households gain access to drinking water will require overcoming the current technical, logistical and financial constraints.

When nations gathered at the United Nations Millennium Summit in 2000, they entered an extraordinary promise to work together to rid the world of extreme poverty and its root causes by the year 2015. For the first time, nations recognized that they share an equal

When it comes to the MDGs, in addition to the number of children enrolled in primary school, the number of children dying every year from preventable diseases, or the number of rural households that have gained access to drinking water, one of the most important statistics to achieve the MDGs is the responsibility of rich governments: 0.7 percent.

0.7% represents the percentage of Gross National Income donor countries have committed in Official Development Assistance.

It is believed that 0.7% is vital in **achieving the MDGs and ensuring the end to extreme poverty** within a generation.

5 countries not only reached **but surpassed** the 0.7% target in 2009: } Sweden (1.12%) Norway (1.06%) Luxembourg (1.01%) Denmark (0.88%) The Netherlands (0.82%)

Australia, Canada, Japan, Switzerland and the United States have yet to **commit** to the 0.7% target.

The United States pales in comparison to many other countries with only a 0.2% contribution. } United States (0.2%)

According to development experts, 0.7 percent represents the percentage of Gross National Income (GNI) that donor countries have committed in Official Development Assistance.[2] It is believed that 0.7 percent is vital in achieving the MDGs and ensuring the end to extreme poverty within a generation. First pledged 40 years ago in a 1970 UN General Assembly Resolution, the 0.7 percent target has been reaffirmed in many international agreements over the years.

Even so, the 0.7 aid target alone will not achieve the MDGs. Donor and recipient governments must work in partnership to ensure that aid is used effectively, resources are delivered and allocated properly through transparent channels and countries must practice good governance.

Living Up to Commitments

Five countries not only reached but surpassed the 0.7 percent target in 2009: Sweden (1.12%), Norway (1.06%), Luxembourg (1.01%), Denmark (0.88%) and the Netherlands (0.82%).[3] As of 2005, 16 of the 22 donor countries either have met or agreed to reach the 0.7 percent target by 2015. While reasons may vary among countries for their commitment to the 0.7 percent target, these countries see the value in investment in development and have the political will to ensure that they provide the expected contribution to the MDGs.

Australia, Canada, Japan, Switzerland and the United States have yet to commit to the 0.7 percent target.

> **Together, we can hold our leaders accountable to the promises made to the most vulnerable members in our global community and provide hope for a better future for all.**

The current shortfall is $18 billion (in 2004 dollars) against the 2005 commitments. Despite being the largest donor in terms of volume ($28.7 billion), the United States pales in comparison to many other countries with only a 0.2 percent contribution. If the United States met the targeted 0.7 percent in 2009, the contribution would have been approximately $99.6 billion dollars—a difference of $70.9 billion.

To provide a sense of US Government spending, the Department of Defense's 2010 budget totaled $690 billion, including funding for the wars in Iraq and Afghanistan, whereas the Department of State's 2010 budget, which includes the United States Agency for International Development (USAID), was $54 billion.[4] The State Department and USAID are the lead agencies in charge of US diplomacy and development. Although diplomacy and development spending may never reach the levels of defense spending, leadership within the US government has recognized the need for civilian power to promote stability and economic growth.

President Obama's 2010 National Security Strategy calls development a strategic, economic imperative, and during a September 2010 Conference in Washington, DC, Secretary of Defense Robert Gates argued that "development is a lot cheaper than sending soldiers." Not only is development cheaper, but it also promotes good governance, leads to stability and can help create conditions that no longer require soldiers. Helping others escape poverty is necessary to create a just and stable world. When foreign states malfunction, their societies are likely to experience steeply escalating problems that spill over to the rest of the world, including the United States. Failed states are seedbeds of violence, terrorism, international criminality, mass migration and refugee movements, drug trafficking and disease.

The United States and the Millennium Development Goals: From Rhetoric to Reality

We will support the Millennium Development Goals, and approach next year's summit with a global plan to make them a reality. And we will set our sights on the eradication of extreme poverty in our time.

> ⯈ President Barack Obama, September 2009

In his first appearance before the United Nations General Assembly in New York, President Barack Obama declared that the MDGs are "America's Goals." This declaration set a tone for how the United States would re-engage with the MDGs in the final years before the 2015 deadline. A year later, Obama followed through by pledging to double US foreign assistance to $50 billion by 2012; invested nearly $100 billion dollars in major development initiatives to address the most pressing development issues (global health, food security and climate change;) and announced a Presidential Policy Directive on Global Development—the first of its kind from any administration—demonstrating continued US leadership in global development.

In the US, the Millennium Campaign works with partner organizations and individuals like you to closely monitor US contributions to the MDGs. Together, we can hold our leaders accountable to the promises made to the most vulnerable members in our global community and provide hope for a better future for all.

. . . . .

Alison Gemgnani was formerly the editorial and advocacy consultant for the United Nations Millennium Campaign (www.endpoverty2015.org), North America. In this role, she was responsible for preparing Millennium Development Goals-related outreach materials, including a weekly newsletter. Gemgnani interned with the European Office of the Millennium Campaign in Rome, Italy. Prior to joining the campaign, Gemgnani served as the area coordinator for the State of Illinois for Amnesty International. Gemgnani has a BA in legal studies and psychology from the University of Wisconsin-Madison and a master's in public management with a concentration in international development from Bocconi University School of Management in Milan, Italy.

Ensuring Effective Aid

Author, economist and native Zambian, Dambisa Moyo has a different and emerging view about foreign aid. She is calling for the world to taper off financial assistance to African governments, putting an end to all of it. In her 2009 book, *Dead Aid*, Moyo blames Africa's poverty and corruption on foreign economic assistance. In response to the augments by defenders of aid, Moyo points out the undisputed facts. Dysfunctional regimes have received billions in aid from Europe and the US. Corrupt leaders are the ones that benefit financially, not the impoverished citizens and the continent is saddled inflation and an unsustainable debt burden from huge loans. The final clincher is that most of Africa is poorer now than it was before aid dollars began to increase, a few decades ago.[1]

Moyo does not condemn all aid, only aid to governments large sums of money transferred from government to government. Humanitarian aid, emergency aid and aid given to specific organizations and people on the ground is still necessary. Moyo is advocating for the solutions that have worked in China and India. For Africa, she recommends paths to independence: higher-interest and less lenient, capital market bonds; partnerships with the Chinese who have already done more for Africa's infrastructure and economic growth in the last five years than the US has done the last 50; and more microfinance, efficient banking of savings and remittances. Not everyone is opposed to Moyo's ideas, African government ministers and major charities are listening.[2] Ultimately, Moyo wants what most everyone else wants for Africa: long-term growth and jobs not band-aid responses and temporary solutions.

> **Most of Africa is poorer now than it was before aid dollars began to increase, a few decades ago.**

Photo courtesy Davidgrundy

Building Prosperity
From the Ground Up

Today, more than 925 million people—one-sixth of the world's population—suffer from undernourishment.[1] We have all seen the harrowing images of desperate, grinding poverty in the developing world. We want to take action, but the vastness and depth of global hunger and poverty can make it feel overwhelming and inevitable. It is not inevitable. We can end hunger and poverty, but it will take a groundswell of people to achieve it. With strategic interventions, the women and men of the developing world can end their own hunger and poverty.

Mobilizing People at the Grassroots Level to Build Self-Reliance

When people are chronically hungry, they do not simply lack food. Chronic hunger is often coupled with marginalization, subjugation, disempowerment and resignation. Many impoverished communities in the developing world have watched development initiatives sweep in with abundant goods and services and then depart, leaving the community no better than it started once the goods and services are no longer available. They feel powerless and have little hope for change. They become resigned to thinking that poverty is their fate.

The Hunger Project Staff

Community members help build Zakpota Epicenter in Benin (2007).

All photos courtesy The Hunger Project

> **A mother's social and economic status is one of the best indicators of whether her children will escape poverty and be healthy.**

Simply addressing physiological hunger is not a sustainable solution—it actually perpetuates the cycle. The key is empowering impoverished communities to take action to meet their basic needs. By building capacities, leadership, confidence and sense of community, people living in the conditions of hunger and poverty can be self-reliant, which will ultimately lead to lasting improvement. Using this approach, the cycle of poverty can be broken by the people who are living it every day.

Empowering Women as Key Change Agents

Studies show that when women are supported and empowered, all of society benefits. Their families are healthier, more children go to school, agricultural productivity improves and incomes increase. In short, communities become more resilient. Empowering women to be change agents is an essential element in ending global hunger and poverty. Not only do women comprise almost 60 percent of the world's hungry people;[2] they also bear almost all responsibility for meeting basic needs of the family. They cook and serve food; collect water and fuel; and care for the children, elderly and sick in the community. Women also produce more than 50 percent of all food grown worldwide.[3] Despite their critical role, women are systematically

Rural Bank Manager at Vowogdo Epicenter in Burkina Faso with her child (2010).

denied the resources, information and freedom of action they need to effectively fulfill this responsibility.

Investing in women pays off. Research shows that women are far more likely than men to financially invest in their children's health, education and household needs. For example, when women farmers receive the same inputs as male farmers, output can increase up to 22 percent.[4] A mother's social and economic status is one of the best indicators of whether her children will escape poverty and be healthy.[5]

There are a number of successful microfinance programs that are specifically focused on the economic

> Research shows that women are far more likely than men to **financially invest in their children's health, education and household needs.**

A recent study* showed that **90%** of a woman's income will go back to the family.

*Chris Fortson, "Women's Rights Vital for Developing World," Yale News Daily 2003.

271

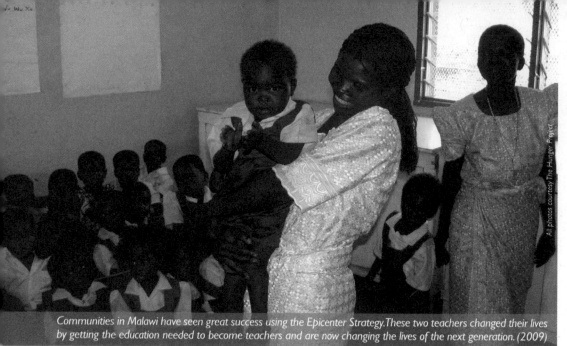

Communities in Malawi have seen great success using the Epicenter Strategy. These two teachers changed their lives by getting the education needed to become teachers and are now changing the lives of the next generation. (2009)

> If we want to end world hunger and abject poverty, it is imperative that we invest in **women.**

and Action Workshop. They create a common vision and commit to take actions, both individually and collectively, to end hunger and poverty in their villages. It is with these collective commitments that a sense of community and accomplishment develops among the villagers.

Another central component of the Epicenter Strategy is the construction of the Epicenter building. Through their own labor, the villagers construct a building that houses a training center, meeting hall, food-processing center, health clinic, library and classrooms. Nurses' quarters, a food bank and demonstration farm, where farmers learn new techniques to improve their crops, are also constructed nearby.

empowerment of women in developing countries. Through access to microfinance, women engage in income-generating activities, increase their incomes and are better able to meet their families' basic needs. Furthermore, women develop self-confidence and assertiveness, and thus gain elevated status in their households and communities. Such programs create a new future where women and men are equal partners in the well being of their families and their community. If we want to end world hunger and abject poverty, it is imperative that we invest in women.

An On-the-Ground Strategy for Success

Fighting hunger and poverty on a global scale hinges on community-led development. In Africa, The Hunger Project (THP) developed an approach called the Epicenter Strategy, which has been successfully used to mobilize clusters of rural villages to create and run programs to achieve sustainable progress in health, food security, education, agriculture and income generation. Through the Epicenter Strategy, communities that were once impoverished become self-reliant in approximately five to eight years.

Initially, people from around 10 to 15 villages voluntarily come together to participate in a Vision, Commitment

After the Epicenter building is in place and the support programs are up and running, the community continues working toward meeting the following goals:

- The empowerment of women
- Increased adult and child literacy
- Improvement in maternal and child health
- Increased food security
- Reduction of diseases such as malaria and HIV/AIDS
- Increased access to credit and creation of income-generating activities
- Environmentally sustainable and appropriate farming practices

As these goals are accomplished, the community's confidence and influence increase, and they are able to successfully make demands of the local government for services and personnel, such as teachers and health professionals. Simply put, the community begins to emerge from the stranglehold of chronic hunger and poverty.

"Power can be taken, but not given. The process of the taking is empowerment in itself." ✈ Gloria Steinem

महिला जनप्रतिनिधि नैतृत्व
फॉलोअप बैठक
दिनांक- ३० नवम्बर एवं 1 दिसम्बर 20
संचालित-शान्ति मैत्री मिशन संस्थान,
सहयोग- दहंगार प्रोजेक्ट, जयपुर

In addition to its work in Africa, THP has other programs around the world to build prosperity from the ground up. In India, THP works with women who have been elected to their village councils. Federation meetings of elected women (top—Jaipur, India) and Women's Leadership Workshops (bottom—Bikaner, India), empower the women to be effective change agents for the end of hunger in their villages (2006).

As the community continues to make progress, a Microfinance Program targeted toward rural women provides a crucial missing link for ending poverty—the economic empowerment of women. With the Microfinance Program, women can expand or start businesses and with their income, improve their farms, purchase food, send their children to school and save for the future. For example, with an initial loan of about $75, Elizabeth Kalimbuka of Malawi started a cattle business. Not only has she since made a profit and repaid her loan, she also has accumulated enough food for her family until the next harvest season (about four months), renovated her home and is able to pay school tuition for her niece and nephew.

The ultimate goal of the program is to gain government recognition and operate as a licensed Rural Bank. Once this is achieved, the Rural Bank provides the entire Epicenter community with sustainable access to savings and credit facilities. Since the inception of the Microfinance Program in 1999, THP has grown the loan portfolio to approximately US$2.4 million across Benin, Burkina Faso, Ethiopia, Ghana, Malawi, Mozambique, Senegal and Uganda.

The Epicenter Strategy is an integrated model of development that can be applied anywhere in the world. It has been implemented in eight countries in Africa, reaching an estimated 1.8 million[6] people, who are proving through their actions that an end to hunger and poverty is possible. To date, 21 Epicenters are deemed self-reliant, meaning they are able to fund their own activities and require little or no financial investment from The Hunger Project. The communities have consistent and reliable access to healthcare, education, food, clean water, safe sanitation, savings and credit.[7] Dozens more communities are well on their way to achieving the same reality.

Our Role as a Developed Nation

The best way for us—as individuals or as a nation—is to partner with and invest our financial resources in the women and men in the developing world.

Both through our government and through charitable non-governmental organizations, Americans spend billions of dollars on aid to the developing world. It is critical that these significant resources constitute more than just a band-aid but a sustainable solution. An example of a band-aid or of intervention that does not promote sustainability or self-reliance is food aid. The United States, in recent years, has provided much of its aid in the form of food, but three-quarters of that food is grown in the US.[8] This US-grown food, when imported to developing countries, leads to destabilization and reduced local market prices, threatening the livelihoods of local producers and traders upon whom long-term food security depends.[9] However, given recent commitments by world leaders, it seems as though the United States and the world is at

3/4 of US foreign aid food **is grown** in the US.

Imported food leads to **destabilization and reduced local market prices**, threatening the livelihoods of local producers upon whom **long-term food security depends.**

All photos courtesy The Hunger Project

This woman was able to greatly improve her and her family's living conditions because of a small loan that allowed her to start her own business selling rice. (2005)

Ultimately, the key to ending hunger and poverty will only be found in the women and men who **live that life** each and every day.

toward building the capacity of rural farmers, particularly women, in the developing world to increase their food production.

In the developed world, in addition to governments, individuals also have an important role to play in the fight against hunger and poverty. A small financial contribution to a non-profit or via a microfinance program that focuses on empowering people, particularly women, at the grassroots level can have a remarkable impact on a family's life. For example, $60 could provide a loan to a rural woman, who in turn starts a small business that will generate income that she uses to send her children to school and provide them with nourishing food.

Ultimately, the key to ending hunger and poverty will only be found in the women and men who live that life each and every day. As governments and individuals in the developed world, it is our responsibility to partner with people and invest in them so they too can lead lives of self-reliance, meet their own basic needs and build better futures for their children. Together—governments and individuals in the developing and developed world—must work to ensure that every woman, man and child has the opportunity to live a dignified life.

. . . . .

the threshold of an extraordinary sea change in how we spend foreign aid and that the focus is shifting to empowering people to become self-reliant. For example, in July 2009, world leaders made an unparalleled financial commitment to end world hunger at the G8 summit. They announced a commitment of $20 billion over three years for a Food Security Initiative that will support rural development in developing countries. This commitment is not only financially significant, but it also represents a shift in how the world is seeking to address the issues of hunger and poverty. Rather than providing short-term food aid, the focus is shifting

The Hunger Project (www.thp.org) is a global, non-profit, strategic organization committed to the sustainable end of world hunger. In Africa, South Asia and Latin America, The Hunger Project seeks to end hunger and poverty by empowering people to lead lives of self-reliance, meet their own basic needs and build better futures for their children.

Re-Imagining Business

A look at the numbers...

The US government has documented the existence of **forced and child labor** in the manufacture of some **122 products** originating from **58 countries**

6,000

Number of Fair Trade-certified products, which are guaranteed to use ethical labor practices, with $4 billion in annual sales.

41 million

Estimated number (19%) of US adults that are considered conscientious consumers and are concerned with supporting social justice and sustainable living with their wallets.

Farmed on 30 million acres and employing some 25 million families worldwide, **coffee is the 2nd largest global commodity after oil** and it has an enormous environmental, social and economic footprint.

30 million acres
25 million families

460 million

Pounds of coffee that were certified by the Rainforest Alliance in 2010, helping to make fair priced, forested and shade grown coffee the norm.

Deforestation currently accounts for 17% of greenhouse gas emissions, as much as all the cars, trucks, trains, planes and boats in the world combined.

DEFORESTATION
=
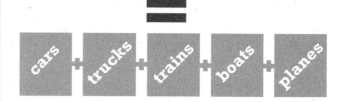
cars | trucks | trains | boats | planes

334 million

Forest acres worldwide (about twice the land area of Texas) that are certified by the Forest Stewardship Council (FSC). FSC maintains the highest standard in forestry by protecting indigenous rights, keeping more trees standing and protecting biodiversity.

Since its inception in 2002, the **1% For the Planet** network has grown to more than **1,400 businesses in 38 countries,** together giving over **$15 million annually** to more than **2,000** social and environmental groups worldwide.

TOMS' one-for-one model has **provided over one million pairs of shoes** (one pair donated for each one sold) to those in need and has also begun to **attract partnerships and spin-offs.**

Newman's Own line of food products gives all of the company's profits to **charitable causes** and has **given more than $300 million to date.**

New Leaf Paper has **saved the equivalent of over 5 million trees and 400 million pounds of greenhouse gases** by developing new and innovative lines of recycled papers.

Impact investing—where an investor proactively seeks to invest in businesses that generate financial returns and have intentional social and/or environmental goals—is growing substantially and it is estimated that the industry could grow from its **present $50 billion to $500 billion** within the next decade.

If we connect the dots between the things we touch every day like paper, electronics, clothes and coffee, to name a few, it might come as a surprise that the way in which "stuff" is made has profound impacts on people and the planet. These impacts can be positive and life-affirming or devastating and destructive.

It all depends on whether the lowest price and the highest profit are the primary forces or whether responsibility and sustainability are in the driver's seat.

The leading forces behind the re-imagination of the market place are ordinary people committed to spending their dollar in a way that is consistent with their values, and visionary business leaders. In this new frontier, the four Ps are all intertwined—**people and planet are just as important as price and profit.**

Emphasizing ethics in the marketplace is critical at this time and has the potential to...

Eliminate the existence
of forced and child labor in the manufacturing of products

Enable millions to create real livelihoods
for their families

Tackle some of our **most pressing** social and environmental challenges

Empower ordinary citizens to use their dollars **to help create the world they want**

281

The Next Frontier of Business

Ask a grade-schooler to draw a picture of the environment, and you'll often see billowing smokestacks and factory drainpipes spewing pollution. Inherently, we see business as the villain, and it is true that the forces driving corporate America have created many of the environmental crises we face today. As our global prosperity has grown, markets have been chewing up the planet because they fail to account for the true costs of pollution.

But what if we could turn that equation on its head and enlist business in a global movement to save our fragile ecosystem? What if we could leverage the profit motive and the human urge for innovation to solve our environmental problems? After all, profit, at its root, comes from smartly anticipating and meeting human wants and needs, which include clean air, clean water and a safe place to live. And innovation is as deeply engrained in the American psyche as the Wright Brothers' "flying machine" and President Kennedy's mission to the moon. Joined and harnessed, these two historic drivers of human enterprise—profit and innovation—can save our planet from catastrophe and pioneering businesses can lead the way.

Gwen Ruta
Environmental Defense Fund

Cartoon sketch by Brian Farrington

> **Innovation is as deeply engrained in the American psyche as the Wright Brothers' "flying machine" and President Kennedy's mission to the moon.**

The Promise of Innovation

Innovation is taking place all over this country every day, from small process improvements on the factory floor to emerging new products that will change the way we work and live. Let's take a look at some examples that illustrate how much there is to build on:

Materials   Building materials that adjust to weather conditions, super-strong but lightweight auto bodies that boost fuel efficiency, clothing that resists stains and repels water—all this and more is in the works. New kinds of materials are being developed every day that can sense and adjust to the world around them and change their properties (like flexibility or electrical conductivity) in an instant. Lightweight, self-healing plastics would make vehicles and aircraft more fuel-efficient and safer.[1] Moreover, it's possible that the next materials revolution will come not from creating new chemicals, but from mining our landfills and using discarded materials. North American landfills contain more aluminum than we can produce by mining, and the same may be true of gold and copper, which are used in the circuit boards of electronics. One ton of trashed computers contains more gold than 17 tons of ore, and there's no shortage of them; Americans toss out 50 million computers annually. Enterprising companies are developing landfill mining technologies such as rotating magnets that pull lightweight metals from the trash heap.[2]

Energy   We're all familiar with wind power and solar energy, but how about ocean energy, which turns wave action into electricity, or geothermal power, which uses the earth's heat to do the same? And what if instead of gasoline from petroleum, we were able to create fuel from yeast, or algae? Algae has the potential to produce ten times the fuel per acre than corn (for ethanol) or soybeans (for biodisesel), and it can be grown in arid land or brackish water—areas that wouldn't compete

One ton of trashed computers contains more gold than 17 tons of ore and there's no shortage of them: Americans toss out 50 million computers annually.

Replacing half of the world's oil with algae-derived fuel could reduce CO2 **emissions by** 25 percent.

A researcher adjusts the nutrient injection ports on an algal tank mixing arm. As part of a project to create alternative sources of energy, researchers at Sandia National Laboratories are cultivating green algae that holds promise as a new supply of biofuel.

with food production. Moreover, algae could have a positive influence on reversing climate change because it consumes CO_2. Replacing half of the world's oil with algae-derived fuel could reduce CO_2 emissions by 25 percent.[3] These advances in energy technology are all in the works today, along with the crucial components that will make them work, like high-efficiency batteries that can store power generated when the wind blows to meet our energy needs in calm weather, or lightweight materials that hold tiny solar cells and act as an energy-generating "skin" around a building. The 2009 Solar Decathlon, a biannual collegiate competition, featured a home that was covered with 250 thin-film solar panels and topped with 11 rooftop panels, producing 200 percent of the energy needed to run the home.[4]

Smart Design Designers of consumer and commercial products are starting to factor environmental impacts into the design process, looking at not just the direct impacts (energy or resource inputs and waste outputs), but also at the full lifecycle from extraction of raw materials to processing intermediaries to manufacturing all the way to use and disposal of the product. One design concept that is catching on is cradle-to-cradle design based on the ecological concept that

> **A new office complex in Zimbabwe stays cool without air conditioning and uses 90% less energy for ventilation than conventional buildings of its size.**

"waste is food." Building on that concept, cradle-to-cradle products are designed to be reused or recycled.

Biomimicry What can termites teach us about architecture? A lot, as it turns out. Researchers have imitated termites' ability to maintain steady temperatures inside their mounds at a new office complex in Zimbabwe. It stays cool without air conditioning and uses 90 percent less energy for ventilation than conventional buildings of its size.[5] This is just one example of biomimicry, a new science that is taking the best ideas of Mother Nature and applying them to help solve society's toughest problems in a sustainable way. After 3.8 billion years of trial and error, animals, plants and microbes have figured out what works. For example, photosynthesis—the process by which plants use chlorophyll to convert sunlight, water and CO_2 into carbohydrates and oxygen—is inspiration for a possible clean fuel solution. Scientists are working to reproduce this process to split water into hydrogen and oxygen, using

People take a first look inside the house of Technische Universität Darmstadt, Germany, on the opening day of the US Department of Energy Solar Decathlon 2009 in Washington, DC. Team Germany's house which integrated thin-film copper indium gallium selenide (CIGS) cells generates 200 percent of the house's energy needs and won overall first place.

BMW showcased its Hydrogen 7 CleanEnergy car, the world's first production-ready hydrogen vehicle.

up excess CO_2 along the way. If commercialized, the process would make hydrogen fuel cells an efficient and inexpensive way to create and store energy.[6]

Hybrid Vehicles Hybrid technology continues to evolve, with new models available for delivery trucks and utility vans, and new ways of storing and managing energy being developed. Foremost among these are so-called hydraulic hybrids, which store energy in the form of pressurized fluid, and plug-in hybrids, where the battery can be charged through an electrical outlet. Because they operate primarily on electricity for the first 20 to 40 miles, plug-in hybrids can achieve 70 to 100 miles per gallon, quadrupling the fuel economy of the average car on the road today.

The federal government calculates that 84 percent of US cars, pickup trucks and SUVs could switch to plug-in hybrid technology without any changes needed to our existing electrical grid. If this happened, we would reduce national gasoline consumption by 6.5 million barrels each day, which is equivalent to over half of US petroleum imports.[7]

A Global Change Engine

Couple innovation with profit—in other words, business innovation—and what have you got? An engine for global change.

That engine is just getting started in the environmental arena, but it has the power to turn our planet's biggest environmental problems into its biggest economic opportunities. As we move from the agricultural revolution of the 18th century to the Industrial Revolution of the 19th century, to the information revolution of the 20th century, can we create a new innovation revolution in the 21st century?

While these innovations are nearly ripe, it will take the right combination of progressive market forces and smart policies to get them from the drawing room table to the factory floor quickly enough to change our planet's environmental trajectory.

Triple Bottom Line: The "3 Ps"

People   **Planet**   **Profit**

• This new way of thinking recognizes that over the long run, a business is not sustainable without healthy, happy employees along with a healthy, productive planet.

Traditional Bottom Line

Profit

• Financial returns are the sole determinant of success.

The innovations discussed earlier are nearly ripe, but it will take the right combination of market forces and smart policies to get them from the drawing table to the factory floor quickly enough to change our planet's environmental trajectory. For example, governments around the world are adopting targets for lowering greenhouse gas emissions and creating carbon markets to help reach those targets. These systems provide a level playing field for entrepreneurs and financiers, opening a tap of investment dollars that will flow to clean vehicles, renewable energy and other green technologies. Some have estimated that the market for trading greenhouse gas emissions could grow to be as large as the stock market in the United States. That would mean tens of billions of dollars invested in new ways to cut energy use and greenhouse gas emissions.

From Orville and Wilbur Wright to Steve Jobs and Bill Gates, America has always been home to great innovators. Today, we look to the next generation to bring business to the forefront of the environmental movement and to launch the inventions that can have profound benefits. There will be a period of trial and error—not every new technology will succeed or be accepted. But some will catch on, and investors and executives will begin to build new businesses and new markets around them.

Competitors will jump on board, and the innovations will spread until eventually they become business as usual[8] and we move on to the next forward revolution. But in the meantime, we just might fundamentally change the relationship between business and our environment, and in the process, change our very future on this earth.

• • • • •

Gwen Ruta, vice president of corporate partnerships, spearheads Environmental Defense Fund's (www. edf.org) work with multinational companies to create innovative solutions to environmental challenges. Ranked number one for effective environmental partnerships by the Financial Times, Ruta's team has kicked off transformations in market sectors from shipping to retail to fleets. Partner companies include Walmart, KKR, FedEx, DuPont and McDonalds. Previously, Ruta held senior positions at Metcalf & Eddy, the US Environmental Protection Agency and Harvard's Kennedy School of Government. She is on advisory boards for Henderson Global Investors, the Environmental League of Massachusetts and the University of Michigan. She holds a M.P.A. from Harvard University and a B.S. from the University of Virginia.

World-Changing Innovations

Examples of individuals, organizations and businesses that are manifesting progressive ideas are highlighted throughout this book. Here are a few more cutting-edge innovations that have potential to solve some of our greatest challenges.

A Mini Power Plant in Box

Photo courtesy Bloom Energy

While developing a technology to produce oxygen for a NASA mission to Mars, former NASA scientist, K.R. Sridhar realized that by reversing the process, he could create an energy source that is cleaner and more efficient than oil, gas or coal and more reliable than wind or solar power. "This technology is fundamentally going to change the world," said Sridhar, cofounder and CEO of Bloom Energy. "It's going to have a disruptive impact on the way energy is produced."[1] Called a Bloom Box, the technology is essentially a fuel cell that generates electricity on site without burning or combustion. The fuel cells work by oxidizing the fuel, which is up to two times more efficient than combustion. In their efforts to reduce their CO2 footprints, Google, Walmart, eBay and other large corporations have installed industrial-sized models. Bloom Energy plans to tap into the residential market with a unit that will power a single-family home using half the fuel and halving carbon footprint of grid-supplied electricity.[2]

Oil-Eating Mushrooms

Photo courtesy Tomorrow Never Knows, flickr

Mycologist and inventor Paul Stamets believes that mushrooms can save the world. One way is through mycoremediation—the clean up of environmental pollution with fungi. "There are dozens of examples of how mushrooms can be used for bioremediation," said Stamets. "Mycelium [the branching, vegetative part of a fungus] of oyster mushrooms can eat petroleum products, denaturing them, and the mycelium converts the hydrocarbons into cellular carbohydrates.[3] One of Stamets' projects introduced oil-eating fungi to a diesel oil-contaminated site. His research showed a 95 percent breakdown of hydrocarbons after eight weeks. As the mushrooms rotted away, gnats moved in to eat the spores. The gnats attracted other insects, which attracted birds, which brought in seeds. Soon the site was teaming with life and well on the way to being ecologically restored. After the Deepwater Horizon spill in April 2010, Stamets submitted a proposal involving oyster mushrooms for the Gulf of Mexico clean up effort.[4]

Magnetic Levitation (Maglev) Wind Power

Combining vertical blades and magnets, a single maglev wind turbine can produce enough energy to power 750,000 homes. The maglev does not need any electricity to operate, there is no energy loss through friction and each unit has a projected life span of 500 years.[5] Conventional utility-scale wind turbines require wind speeds of 13 miles per hour in order to produce energy[6] while the maglev will operate speeds as slow as 5 feet per second. Building a single giant maglev wind turbine would reduce construction and maintenance costs and require much less land than hundreds of conventional turbines.[7] "Unlike any other form of renewable energy, wind energy has the greatest potential for energy independence," said Ed Mazur inventor of a commercial-sized maglev wind turbine.[8]

> **This technology is fundamentally going to change the world.**

> **The 17 most critical services provided by nature were worth between $16 and $54 trillion annually, which averages to about $45 trillion in 2010 after inflation.**

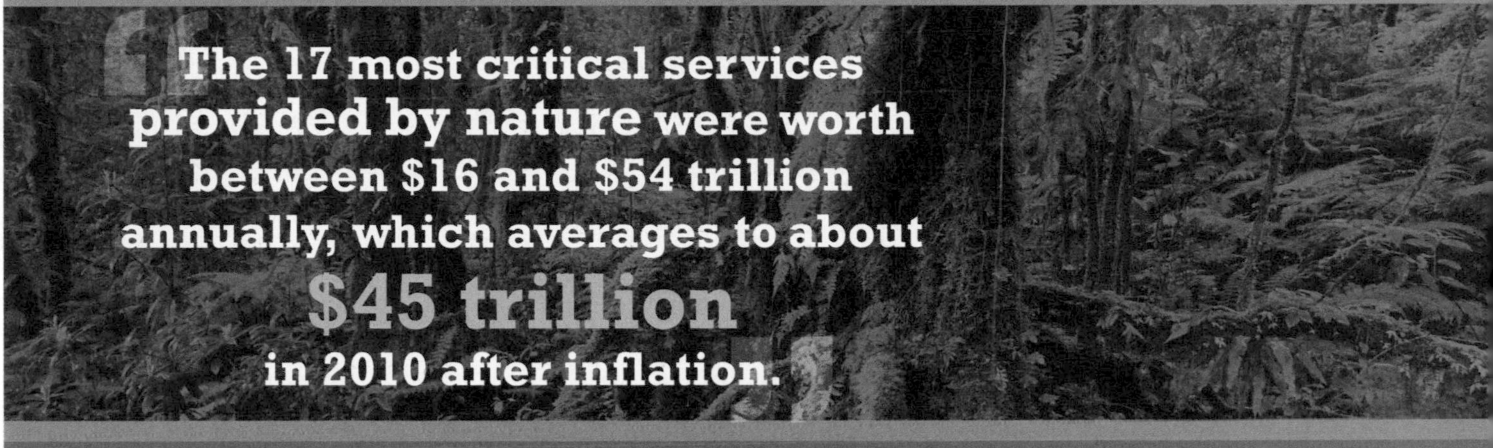

Seeing the Full Value of Ecosystems

In policy, economics and business, decisions are always made with cost-benefit in mind. For years, natural ecosystems were not integrated in this quantitative decision-making process. The environment was not a part of the bottom-line.

But intuitively we all know that ecosystems have value. For example, the shade of a tree eliminates the need to bring an umbrella everywhere. On a larger scale, healthy forests sequester carbon emissions, filter water, and produce oxygen.

Valuing all these services in dollars and cents is a momentous task. In 1997 a group of 13 economists and environmental scientists made the first and only highly-reputed attempt, estimating that the 17 most critical services provided by nature were worth between $16 and $54 trillion annually, which averages to about $45 trillion in 2010 after inflation.[1]

In the years following that landmark study, ecosystems valuations has become far more practical and precise. Faced with the prospect of building an $8 billion water filtration facility to deal with dropping water quality, New York City instead chose to purchase and protect land throughout the Catskills Mountains for $1.5 billion. New Yorkers' water bills might have doubled to pay for the plant—instead they increased just 9 percent.[2] Many traditional economists question the accuracy of dollar values attached to ecosystems, but sometimes the evidence is inarguable. After Hurricane Katrina devastated the Gulf Coast, scientists pointed out that the now fast-disappearing coastal wetlands once buffered the region against storms. Further study prompted by Katrina found that coastal wetlands provide over $23 billion in storm protection services every year.[3] Informed by ecosystems valuations like these, the state of Louisiana decided to reinvest every penny of roughly $200 million of new offshore oil tax revenues into rebuilding its wetlands.[4]

Supplying the Demand for a Livable Planet

Tensie Whelan
Rainforest Alliance

Paper, coffee, chocolate, bananas, beef, cut flowers, fruit—the prices of such everyday products, high as they are, still don't reveal their environmental or social costs. Often, producing these and many other things we consume daily degrades the environment, threatens ecosystems, pollutes drinking water and endangers workers.

It's important we tune into this. How we manage the production, consumption and renewal of natural resources determines the social condition of billions of people, the environmental condition of the planet and our collective future.

Cultivating Conservation on Farms

The principal agent of ecosystem destruction and species extinction is not smokestacks or tailpipes; it's agriculture. Farming has the largest environmental impact of any industry. Occupying 38 percent of the Earth's land area, agriculture uses more fresh water, and affects more of the planet's surface, than any other single human activity.

It occupies

38%

of Earth's land area.

Agriculture uses more fresh water and affects more of the planet's surface **than any other single human activity.**

Agriculture is one of the leading causes of climate change, responsible for **14%** **of greenhouse gas emissions** from soil erosion, poor irrigation practices, uncontrolled use of fertilizers and other agrochemicals, biomass burning and livestock production.

Agriculture is one of the leading causes of climate change, responsible for 14 percent of greenhouse gas (GHG) emissions from soil erosion, poor irrigation practices, the uncontrolled use of fertilizers and other agrochemicals, biomass burning and livestock production.[1] And it's a main driver of clearing forests. When deforestation from farmland expansion and tree plantations is factored into calculations, some 30 percent of global GHG emissions are coming from agriculture today.[2]

But it's not as though we can just stop farming, or do with less of it. We have to find ways to farm sustainably. Sustainability certification is a powerful way to convert global agriculture's negative impacts to positive ones. Rainforest Alliance Certified™, USDA Organic, Sustainable Agriculture Network, Marine Stewardship Council and Forest Stewardship Council are just a few examples of voluntary, independent programs that use the power of markets and certification standards to guide farmers toward sustainable farm management and provide an accountable way to evaluate social and environmental improvements.

It's not as though we can just stop farming, or do with less of it. We have to find ways to farm sustainably.

The agricultural products we use the most—including coffee, bananas, cocoa and many others—tend to be the ones with the largest environmental and social footprints. They also offer some of the largest opportunities for certification programs to turn their impacts into positive ones by converting production to environmentally and socially sustainable practices.

Coffee is a perfect example. In the 1970s, agronomists began promoting a new coffee farming system, where the sheltering forest trees are cleared and coffee bushes are packed in dense hedgerows and doused with agrochemicals. Monoculture farming produces more beans but eliminates wildlife habitats, promotes forest destruction and soil erosion and pollutes streams.

Coffee is the second largest global commodity after oil, and it has an enormous environmental, social and economic footprint. Coffee is farmed on 30 million

Environmental Impacts:

• Monoculture systems clear forests and replace them with densely packed crop plants, doused with agrochemicals.
• Eliminates wildlife habitats; promotes forest destruction, soil erosion, pollution

Opportunity for Sustainability:

• Example: A Rainforest Alliance Certified™ farm where coffee is shade grown can contain diverse wildlife and 100 or more tree species.

Environmental Impacts:

• Use of dangerous pesticides, poor working conditions, water pollution, deforestation
• Agrochemical runoff and erosion kills fish, clogs rivers, and chokes coral reefs.

Opportunity for Sustainability:

• Today, 15% of all the bananas in international trade come from Rainforest Alliance Certified Sources, meaning they exceed standards in terms of environmental protection, social equity and economic viability.

Environmental Impacts:

• Livestock grazing causes 18% of greenhouse gas emissions. Grazing is a major contributor to deforestation and is the single worst driver of land degradation.

Opportunity for Sustainability:

• Certification will require cattle operations to implement practices like sustainable pasture management, animal welfare and carbon-footprint reduction—transforming deforestation, GHG emissions and animal abuse.

coffee

bananas

beef

acres and growing it employs some 25 million families worldwide.[3] Fluctuations in coffee supply and demand, government policies and coffee prices can create unstable financial conditions, not only for the farmers, but also for wildlife. That's because coffee farms can serve as important buffer zones for biodiverse forest habitats.

One coffee cooperative in El Salvador that is Rainforest Alliance Certified holds more than 100 tree species. There, biologists have spotted members of dozens of species of rare birds, wild cats such as ocelots, postcard-size butterflies, technicolor frogs, seldom-seen orchids, monkeys and (once) a giant anteater. There are varying credible certification programs out there and certification is one way to ensure that coffee farms maintain wildlife habitat and other environmental benefits, while also protecting livelihoods and worker rights.

Bananas, the world's most popular fruit, are another example of how specific changes in farming can reduce impacts. Before the 1990s, banana plantations were infamous for environmental and social abuses, which included the use of dangerous pesticides, poor working conditions, water pollution and deforestation. Pesticide-impregnated plastic bags, which protect bananas as they grow, often littered riverbanks and beaches near banana farms, while agrochemical runoff and erosion killed fish, clogged rivers and choked coral reefs.

Today widespread use of certification programs on banana farms is helping protect the environment while also protecting people by fostering farming practices that improve worker health and safety and empower farmers and their communities economically.

Beef, a staple of most American diets, also has significant environmental impacts. More than a quarter of the Earth's terrestrial surface is devoted to livestock grazing, which causes 18 percent of global GHG emissions.[4] Grazing is a major contributor to deforestation and the single worst driver of land degradation.

New sustainable ranching standards developed by the Sustainable Agriculture Network (an international coalition of leading conservation groups) will require certified cattle operations in Latin American, Africa, Asia and Oceania to implement best practices like integrated management systems, sustainable pasture management, animal welfare and carbon-footprint reduction. As farms voluntarily adopt the new standards and get certified, the deforestation, GHG emissions and animal abuse ranching causes now stand to be transformed.

In addition to helping the planet, certification also helps farmers survive economically by encouraging them to operate more efficiently, giving them entrees to consumer markets and often paying them a price premium for what they produce. Programs like Rainforest Alliance Certified, Fair Trade and others can help farmers bear the erratic swings in the global market, so they can remain in business and keep working to adopt more sustainable practices.

These programs are already significant forces in global markets, and are growing fast. In 2010, more than 219,000 metric tons of coffee, 120,000 metric tons of tea and 15 percent of all the bananas in international trade came from Rainforest Alliance Certified farms. But there is plenty of room for further expansion of sustainable markets in all areas of agriculture.

Protecting the World's Remaining Forests

Forests provide food, fuel, fiber, medicine and building materials. They shelter communities and wildlife, prevent erosion, filter water, protect coral reefs, control pests and mitigate climate change by capturing and storing atmospheric carbon. In fact, they contain more carbon than the atmosphere and the world's oil reserves combined. Yet they are also the planet's fastest-disappearing natural resource.

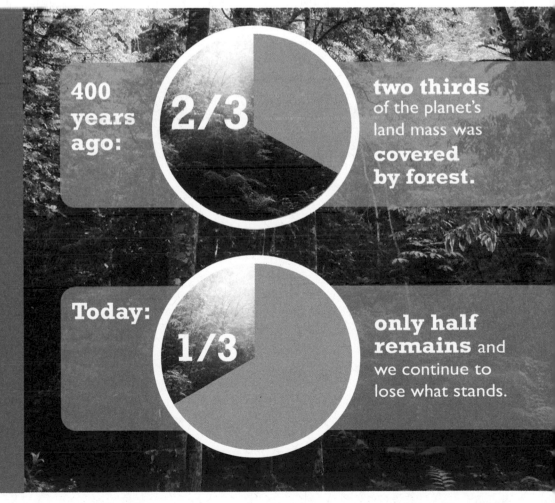

Forests provide food, fuel, fiber, medicine and building materials.

They shelter communities and wildlife, prevent erosion, filter water, protect coral reefs, control pests and mitigate climate change by capturing and storing atmospheric carbon.

They are also the planet's fastest-disappearing natural resource.

400 years ago:

2/3

two thirds of the planet's land mass was **covered by forest.**

Today:

1/3

only half remains and we continue to lose what stands.

Above: A worker holds a package of Rainforest Alliance Certified coffee
Below: Women pluck tea on the Rainforest Alliance Certified tea estates in the Coonoor region of India.

One way to protect them is through global forestry certification programs, such as the Forest Stewardship Council (FSC). FSC is a voluntary, independent certification program acknowledged as the gold standard for sustainable management of working forests. Almost anything made from wood or other forest products is available with the FSC label.

Compared to non-certified forestry, FSC working forests are managed sustainably, harvesting lower volumes of wood with less environmental impact, replanting trees, providing wide conservation areas, preserving sensitive ecosystems and protecting endangered species habitat. Today a total of 334 million forest acres worldwide—about twice the land area of Texas—are FSC certified.

Giving Producers and Consumers a Choice

With substantive, independent certification programs producers have an incentive to make their operations sustainable and beneficial. Operating sustainably has a recognized value, and therefore becomes a viable choice.

Four hundred years ago, two-thirds of the planet's land mass was covered by forest. Today only half remains and we continue to lose what stands. Deforestation currently accounts for some 15 percent of greenhouse gas emissions—as much all the cars, trucks, trains, planes and boats in the world combined.[5] Protecting forests, especially tropical forests, is one of the most cost-effective ways to reduce emissions and preserve biodiversity and support forest-dependent communities.

But less than one-tenth of forests are formally protected. The great majority are subject to logging and other development, and are under pressure from continuing strong demand for wood and wood products. They are also one of the world's most important global carbon stocks. Their soils, trees, wetlands and other ecosystems contain an estimated 205 billion tons of carbon—the equivalent of decades' worth of global emissions from burning fossil fuels.[6]

The same is true for us as consumers, who are the ones choosing to buy the products with credible certified labels. Studies show that given a reasonable choice between products that are sustainably produced and those that aren't, we'll consistently prefer the sustainable product. In fact, demand for environmentally and socially responsible goods is at an all-time high. If we connect the dots between what we buy at the supermarket, and our aspirations for a sustainable future, it opens up all kinds of opportunities for us to be a key part of the solution, and help create positive environmental and social impacts. Our ability to choose, our power as consumers to signal an alignment of economic forces with our aspirations for the future, is the biggest lever we have to create positive global change.

> **Consumers need to recognize the power they have, for good or ill— a power far greater than governments.**

As the market for sustainable goods and services grows, we're rapidly reaching a tipping point beyond which that force will be fully unleashed. When it is, products will carry their "real" prices, with the cost and added value of sustainable production built in. Consumers and businesses will be more aware of the impacts their choices have on workers and the environment, and will demonstrate their support for sustainability through their purchases.

The idea that we can simply shop our way out of looming environmental threats like climate change and mass species extinctions has been justly ridiculed. Buying yet more stuff that happens to be marketed to appeal to the eco-aware won't save the planet. But consumers do need to recognize the purchasing power they have, for good or ill—a power far greater than governments. Gains in the key sectors of farming and forestry would not have happened without consumer demand driving them.

Our choices aren't isolated. They connect with the choices of millions of others and they reverberate, as business people say, across the entire supply chain, from the company boardrooms to the workers who grew the food and the ecosystems that support the farm. Consumers who understand that will continue to drive the sustainable certification movement, which will keep pushing the global economy towards sustainability.

. . . . .

Eco-conscious
choices you can make

. . . .

+ Choose certified products when you shop: Consumers can help drive the evolution of the sustainable economy by choosing products bearing the Rainforest Alliance, FSC seals and other credible certification labels. Find available certified products at: www.rainforest-alliance.org/green-living/marketplace * www.greenerchoices.org/eco-labels * www.ecolabelindex.com/ecolabels

+ Choose sustainable destinations when you travel: Travel and tourism is the world's largest industry, and has enormous environmental and social impacts, for good or ill. Help make it a powerful engine for a sustainable economy by choosing sustainable certified destinations when you travel. Find more information and a searchable database of certified destinations at: SustainableTrip.org

+ Choose positive impacts where you work: Businesses can produce and source goods and services sustainably, which studies show improves their bottom lines as well as their environmental and social impacts. For resources to get started, see www.rainforest-alliance.org and click on "Engage Your Business"

Tensie Whelan serves as the president of the global sustainability non-profit Rainforest Alliance (www.rainforest-alliance.org), which works to conserve biodiversity and ensure sustainable livelihoods by transforming land-use practices, business practices and consumer behavior. She has been involved with the Rainforest Alliance since 1990, first as a board member, then as a consultant, becoming the executive director in 2000. Whelan has been working in the environmental field for more than 25 years, including as the vice president of conservation information at the National Audubon Society and executive director of the New York League of Conservation Voters.

A Look at the Niger River: Understanding the Global Implications of America's Addiction to Oil

Most Americans know the role oil plays in propping up corrupt dictatorships in the Middle East, but American oil consumption has destroyed communities across the globe. Nicaragua, Equatorial Guinea, and Ecuador have all struggled with the "resource curse" of oil. Nowhere are the side effects of American oil consumption more obvious than Nigeria, which exports almost as much oil as Saudi Arabia to the US.[1]

When oil was first discovered in Nigeria in the 1950s, energy extraction was heralded as the industry that would modernize the populous but impoverished African nation. Shell, Chevron, and Exxon-Mobil rushed to develop the oil fields, but never brought their Western quality of life or regulatory standards to the Niger Delta.

Nigeria has the lowest quality of life of any major oil producing nation. Over half of rural communities have no access to clean drinking water—largely because of rampant oil spills—and rural life expectancy is around 40 years. Due to environmental damages, formerly self-sufficient rural communities can no longer fish or farm in the Delta, but also lack the resources needed to enter new industries.[2]

Since oil extraction began, an estimated 12 million barrels of oil have spilled in the Niger Delta by both bandits and the corporations extracting the oil.[3] Americans were outraged at the Exxon Valdez oil spill, but over five decades the rate of leaks, dumping, and spills in Nigeria has equaled one Exxon Valdez every single year.

Even worse is the human cost. Government forces, bandits, private military, and militants intermittently wage open warfare over the corporate oilfields. There are few official records of the hundreds of clashes, but it's estimated that fighting has displaced some 200,000 civilians and killed 14,000 more in the last 10 years.[4] **As we continue to focus our efforts on building a carbon-free society, we stop being complicit in creating a reality that has so often negatively impacted rural and indigenous communities around the world.**

from the editor

Indonesia: Connecting the Dots

The choices we make every day as consumers can have impacts all around the world. Take, for example, Indonesia and its connection to Americans. Indonesia's rainforests provide habitat for an incredibly diverse array of wildlife and are relied upon by some of the earth's most endangered species such as orangutan, Sumatran tigers and rhinoceroses. These rainforests also support the livelihood of more than 30 million forest-dependent peoples.

Indonesia's rainforests also play an important role in global climate change. As a result of rapid deforestation, despite the small size of the country, it is now the third largest contributor of climate changing greenhouse gas emissions after only the United States and China.

While it may not be obvious, many products we use on a daily basis may directly contribute to the destruction of Indonesia's rainforests. Forest and paper products like calendars, notebooks and furniture may be derived from trees harvested in Indonesia's rainforests or from plantations that were established by clearing rainforests. Foods such as french fries, cookies, cereal and ice cream, and personal care products such as cosmetics are often made with palm oil, which is also often sourced from plantations that were established by clearing natural rainforest.

Fortunately, there are a number of things consumers can do to ensure that they are lessening these impacts. Using paper products that contain high levels of recycled and Forest Stewardship Council (FSC) fiber can reduce pressure on endangered forests in Indonesia and throughout the world. When it comes to palm oil, consumers can check ingredient labels and avoid products with palm oil, or support products and companies that use sustainably grown palm oil or alternatives.

The impact American consumers have in Indonesia is just one of many examples how a purchase can have either a positive or negative impact on people, wildlife and forests throughout the world. It shows how much of a difference it can make when we carefully consider the materials, ingredients and source of the products we buy.

The Rise of the Conscientious Consumer

Bama Athreya
International Labor Rights Forum

American consumers have a long history of acting in support of the rights of workers who produce the goods they wear and consume. From combating sweatshop abuses in the US and developing a union label for consumers at the turn of the 20th century, to solidarity boycotts of table grapes in the late 1960s and again in the 1980s that established rights for farm workers, American consumers have time and again demonstrated their commitment to ethical consumerism.

Consumer awareness and activism are more important today than ever, as consumer products ranging from coffee to computers originate not in US factories or farms, but in far reaches of the globe. Rubber for our automobile tires comes from Liberia, where it is has been shown to be produced with child labor.[1] Electronic components for our computers and mobile phones are produced in

Photo courtesy Guldhammer

Product:		Where it comes from:

Rubber
for Automobile Tires

→

LIBERIA
...where it has been shown to
be produced with child labor

Roses & Carnations
to be Sold in the US

→

COLOMBIA
...where women workers are exposed
to pesticides banned in the US

Electric Components
for Computers & Cell Phones

→

CHINA
...where forced labor is alleged
to be used in some factories

Photo courtesy National Labor Committee

China, where forced labor is alleged to be used in some factories.[7] Most of the roses and carnations now sold in the US come from Colombia, where women workers are exposed to pesticides banned in the US and denied their basic rights.[3] The US government has documented the existence of forced and child labor in the manufacture of some 122 products originating from 58 different countries.[4] The conditions these workers and sometimes children find themselves in can be dismal, and the US, as the world's largest consumer, needs to do more to stop this.

In the 1990s, activism and media exposure of sweatshop conditions, such as in Nike shoe factories in Asia,[5] and in Gap[6] and Wal-Mart[7] garment factories in Central America, succeeded in pushing companies to adopt codes of conduct regarding labor and human rights and to develop private, voluntary monitoring systems to supervise these codes. While private, company-directed activities have their role in addressing labor rights abuses, they are not enough because these initiatives are often not verified and regulated by an independent third party. Educated consumers in the US are ready to support ethically produced goods in the marketplace, and it is time for fresh thinking and new approaches to make this the norm.

Consumers Want Ethically Produced Goods

The trend toward ethical consumerism is real, well-documented by the media and supported by academic research. Articles have appeared regularly in the *New York Times*,[8] *Time* magazine[9] and other leading publications highlighting new initiatives directed at ethical consumers. Such initiatives range from eBay's World of Good online marketplace to the socially conscious Edun clothing brand and the Red initiative working to end AIDS globally, both promoted by U2 frontman Bono.[10] Sustainable and ethical initiatives directed at US and European consumers now proliferate, with certification systems in place for wood and wood products,[11] fish and seafood,[12] fresh flowers[13] and a growing number of additional products.

The US government has documented the existence of **forced and child labor** in the manufacture of some 122 products originating from 58 different countries.

Above: A co-op member harvests a cocoa pod.
Below: A cocoa-farming couple in front of their home in the Dominican Republic.

Photos courtesy Fair Trade Foundation © 2003

Based on fair prices, ethical purchasing and sustainability, the Fair Trade certification system appeals to consumers as a powerful way to reduce global poverty through everyday shopping. The Fair Trade label connects consumers directly with small producers and farmers in developing countries to restore ethical trading relationships, stabilize markets and promote justice in conventional trade. By guaranteeing a "fair trade" price for crops, and thus influencing consumer behavior, the system has helped to expand the market for fair trade products in North America exponentially each year. More than 6,000 Fair Trade-certified products are available with an annual value exceeding $3.6 billion.[14]

Organics is another movement-based certification system that has taken hold in North America, stemming from farmers who are dedicated to certain ethical principles of stewardship of the land. Organics has grown into a big business, with an estimated $55 billion in sales globally last year.[15]

Consumer Support of Ethical and Fair Trade

Can this increased consciousness of consumers translate to the issue of workers' rights and the problem with sweatshops? Research from Harvard University suggests that the answer is yes. Based on empirical research in a New York area department store, the study found that consumers would accept price increases of up to 20 percent without any decrease in sales for products they believed to be produced with good labor practices. Over a five-month period, researchers compared the sales of products that were labeled as ethically produced. Using two different product categories—towels and candles—researchers placed comparable items manufactured by different brands side by side with only one brand displaying the label. The study found that sales of labeled items not only increased, but sales of labeled items in both product categories also increased as prices increased.[16]

A Harvard study found that **sales increased** for items labeled as **ethically produced** even as **prices increased** for these items.

SALES

Ethically Produced

Making Ethical Markets a Global Reality: Next Steps

There are a handful of successful experiments in the area of labor rights certification, including the path-blazing GoodWeave program to certify that South Asian carpets are child-labor-free. This program aims to transform the handmade rug industry by certifying child-labor-free rugs and by providing education and opportunities to at-risk children. GoodWeave uses license fees collected from manufacturers to fund educational initiatives.[17] The hand-made carpet industry exploits nearly 250,000 children to weave carpets for American homes, and a reliable certification system is imperative because an independent third party can validate manufacturers' claims and lend credibility in the eyes of consumers.

A few companies in the United States have attempted to pioneer this approach. The Unionwear company applies the old "Look for the Union Label" approach to assure consumers that products are made under fair working conditions.[18] University students have promoted a "Designated Suppliers Program" that would reward suppliers who adhere to codes of conduct with preferential treatment in the university-licensed apparel market.[19] TransFair USA has developed a pilot Fair Trade certification system for apparel and linens that aims to apply standards from cotton through cut-and-sew production.[20] Maggie's Organics recently piloted a "Fair Labor Apparel" system,

GoodWeave helps provide education and opportunities for at-risk children in South Asia. Below, students do homework at a GoodWeave supported school in Nepal.

Photo courtesy ©ROMANO

301

also applying to cotton through cut-and-sew. All of these projects are on a learning curve. However, if any of the pilot programs are able to iron out kinks, and expand globally, then increased consumer consciousness will diminish the demand for sweatshop-produced apparel and linens.

Beyond labeling, the anti-sweatshop movement needs to help consumers sort through the variety of market claims by creating information-sharing platforms. Many have begun to realize that it is just as important to rate certification systems as it is companies. Green America has built a reputation around a credible consumer guide to evaluate the relative claims of companies, and help weed through the multitude of labels on the environmental front. In the area of labor rights, an online initiative called Good Guide has begun work to undertake a similar consumer education platform.[21] Free2Work, a similar platform specific to the issues of forced and child labor, and providing evaluations of certification systems and labels as well as companies, is being launched by ILRF and the Not For Sale campaign.[22] Consumer education is a major pillar of a truly equitable, ethical, and sweat-free market.

Governments also can have a role in ending the confusion over labeling through engagement with market standards. Anti-sweatshop activists successfully pushed for the creation of a new group to evaluate market claims on ending forced labor and child labor in global agriculture. Under the auspices of the US Department of Agriculture, this new stakeholder group is tasked with determining which certification systems in place for agricultural imports can make credible claims to be ending or reducing forced labor and child labor.

Another promising avenue for activism is the focus on government-as-ethical consumer. The North American anti-sweatshop movement has, in recent years, done notable work to promote sweat-free public procurement policies, ensuring that no tax dollars are spent in sweatshops. A coordinating organization, SweatFree Communities, was founded in 2002 by anti-sweatshop organizers who were working separately on local campaigns to achieve sweat-free purchasing policies to prevent businesses from selling apparel made in sweatshops to public institutions. These campaigns have won sweat-free purchasing policies in states, cities and school districts throughout North America.

Members of SweatFree Communities protest the use of tax dollars to support sweatshops.

Photo courtesy Jim West Photography

> **What is encouraging is that the definition of business is changing and the goal is no longer to get the highest profit at the expense of human dignity, worker fairness or environmental impact.**

Pieced together, these initiatives add up to a growing movement—a movement in which consumers have a leading role. As the US public becomes increasingly aware that many daily household products are produced by forced labor, child labor or otherwise exploitative working conditions, increasingly, consumers are asking where to find ethically produced goods. Until an anti-sweatshop or "ethically produced" label is created, consumers need to do their own research. Ask your local retailers to carry ethically made products, look for the Fair Trade label and search for sweatshop-free products online through websites such as SweatFree Communities, Green America, Good Guide and Free-2Work.

Such a movement is poised to grow and catalyze more ethically produced goods. Changes in behavior and consumption will inevitably give rise to new questions and challenges. But one thing is clear: Few individuals want to exploit workers for products even if they are just a bit cheaper, and this message is growing louder. The companies that make the goods we buy need to make profits to survive. But what is encouraging is that the definition of business is changing, and the goal is no longer to get the highest profit at the expense of human dignity, worker fairness or environmental impact.

Commerce needs not be a linear race to the top, but rather designed in a circular manner where community benefit and corporate citizenship play an equal role.

. . . . .

What you can do to be an
Ethical Consumer:

- Ask your local retailers to carry ethically produced products.

- Search for sweat-free products on sites such as: SweatFree Communities, Green America, Good Guide, and Free2Work.

- Ask your state and local government to make sure that your tax dollars are not spent on sweatshop products.

Bama Athreya is a senior fellow and the former executive director for the International Labor Rights Forum (www.laborrights.org), a Washington DC–based non-profit advocacy organization. The ILRF promotes worker rights worldwide through research, publications, public education and advocacy related to trade agreement and corporate accountability. Athreya has published extensively on the issues of corporate accountability and human rights in global supply chains, and has provided public commentary on CNN's Lou Dobbs Tonight, MSNBC, National Public Radio and other major media outlets.

The Role of Business in Tackling Tough Social Problems

Some businesses are changing their business models. They are showing that the purpose of business is to serve. For them, profits are a tool but not the ultimate goal. These businesses are developing products that solve society's most pressing problems, from point-of-use water purifiers, rollable water containers and foot-powered irrigation pumps to sugar cane charcoal, solar ovens and peddle-charged batteries.

Photo courtesy Thirst Relief International

More than 1 billion people around the world lack access to clean drinking water and nearly 2.5 billion lack adequate sanitation. Water-borne diseases cause 80 percent of all illnesses in developing countries and account for an estimated 2 million deaths annually. Life and Water Development Group Cameroon (LWDGC) along with Thirst Relief International USA are working to save lives and improve health by providing clean water to developing areas from two unlikely sources: dirt and bacteria. The filter removes 99 percent of the bacteria in the water. The two organizations have been installing bio sand filters in villages throughout Cameroon, Africa.

Image provided by KickStart International

Realizing that donations are not a long-term solution for impoverished people, social entrepreneurs Nick Moon & Martin Fisher began designing and developing tools to create jobs and wealth for poor people in Africa. Villagers purchase the low-cost tools and establish small businesses. Moon and Fisher's company, Kickstart, creates tools that are profitable, durable, affordable and easy to operate and maintain. Tools such as the micro-irrigation "MoneyMaker" pump and "Mafuta Mali" sunflower and sesame oil press have helped create 35,000 businesses and $35 million annually in profits and wages.

In 2006, American traveler Blake My-coskie befriended children in Argentina and found they had no shoes to protect their feet. Wanting to help, he created TOMS Shoes, a company that would match every pair of shoes purchased with a pair of new shoes given to a child in need. Blake returned to Argentina with a group of family, friends and staff later that year with 10,000 pairs of shoes made possible by TOMS customers. TOMS has given over one million pairs of new shoes to children in need around the world.[1] TOMS' one-for-one mission has also begun to attract partnerships and spins offs Ralph Lauren, Element Skateboards[2] and the SunNight Solar Corp's BoGo flashlight.[3]

Photo courtesy Ariel Waldman

Newman's Own began with salad dressing created for actor Paul Newman's friends and family. The company now manufactures food products such as spaghetti sauce, frozen pizza, lemonade, salsa, cookies, coffee, iced tea, dog food, cat foot and many others. One hundred percent of all profits and royalties are donated to educational and charitable organizations worldwide. The company has given $300 million to charity.[4]

The International Rescue Committee, a Newman's Own Foundation beneficiary, responds to the world's worst humanitarian crises and helps people rebuild their lives.

Photo courtesy Julien Harneis

Clearly, businesses have an important role to play in addressing global social issues and we are seeing a radical positive shift in public interest in social entrepreneurship and the number of businesses working to solve society's toughest problems.

from the editor

Strengthening Communities

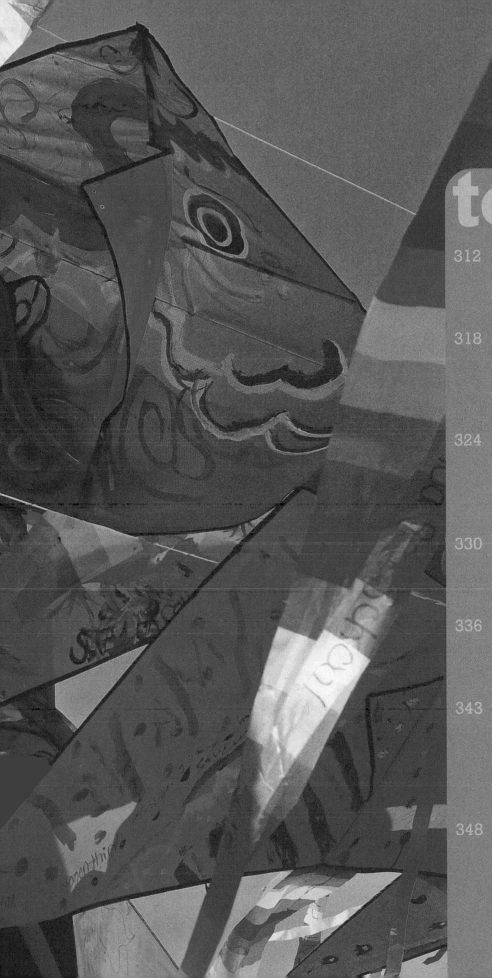

ten

A look at the numbers...

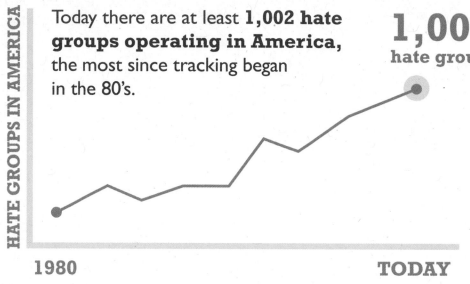

HATE GROUPS IN AMERICA

Today there are at least **1,002 hate groups operating in America,** the most since tracking began in the 80's.

1980 — TODAY

1,002
hate groups

48
Number of "Not in Our Town" campaigns that have been started in cities across America to combat hate groups.

---

11 million undocumented immigrants live and work in America today, most without access to becoming legal US residents.

11 million
undocumented immigrants

$200 billion
Cost to deport all the undocumented immigrants in the United States. In addition, it would take about 30 years.

$66 billion
Tax revenue that would be generated each year by integration of immigrants. **This would more than cover the budget for the State Department and the EPA combined.**

59%
of Fortune 500 companies and 23 states offer equal rights to same sex couples.

Marriage provides over 1,000 benefits that are denied to same-sex couples.

1,000 benefits

x2.3 million

There are currently more than **2.3 million people locked up** in US prisons and jails.

33%

Drop in crime in the 90s after New York began focusing on prevention and rehabilitation, lowering its incarceration rate by 15%

$3 billion

Amount that could be saved annually if 10% of the non-violent prison population were on parole instead of in prison.

Native American reservations have **average incomes roughly one-sixth** the national average.

1/6

Income on Native American reservations compared to the national average

15%

Percentage of the country's electricity that could be provided from wind power on reservation lands.

110,000

Number of jobs that would be supported by that amount of wind power generation on reservation lands

When farmers sell their crops to corporations, most receive just **20 cents of every dollar** of the retail price.

20¢ goes to farmer **80¢** goes to corporations

$10

If every household in America would spend this much on local food per week,

$60 billion

would be invested in their local economies annually.

> "**For a community to be whole** and healthy, it must be based on people's love and concern **for each other.**"
>
> ❯ Millard Fuller

Community is both life sustaining and unifying; it can be as small as a neighborhood and as big as a nation and everything in between. Community is a way of seeing and something concrete that defines and nurtures the human experience. Millard Fuller was the founder of Habitat for Humanity and his simple but powerful words point to a vision for community that is broad, inclusive and timeless. It calls on us to look within and outside of ourselves to build community in a way that is grounded in compassion and is always **aiming for the common good.**

Communities across the land are **growing stronger.**

In hearts and minds,

In inner-cities the seeds of beauty and empowerment are blossoming and need to continue spreading.

In rural areas and on reservations, inspiring stories are unfolding.

the flame of unity and inclusiveness is **growing.**

Transforming Urban Injustice into
Beauty and Empowerment

The story I'm about to share is because of a dog. An abandoned puppy that grew to be a much bigger dog than I'd anticipated. When she came into my life, we in the South Bronx were fighting against a huge waste facility planned for the East River waterfront, despite the fact that our small part of New York City already handled more than 40 percent of the entire city's commercial waste and housed a sewage treatment plant, a sewage sludge pelletizing plant, four power plants, the world's largest food distribution center, as well as other industries that bring more than 60,000 diesel trucks to the area each week.

The neighborhood at that time, not surprisingly, also had one of the lowest ratios of parks-to-people in the city. I've lived in this area all my life, and there was no river access because of all of those facilities. Then, while jogging with my dog one morning, she pulled me into what I thought was just another illegal dump. There were weeds and piles of garbage, but she kept dragging me and, lo and behold, at the end of that lot was the river. I knew that this forgotten little street end, abandoned like the dog that brought me there, was worth saving. And just like my new dog, it was an idea that grew bigger than I had imagined. The project garnered much support along the way, and Hunts Point Riverside Park became the first waterfront park in the South Bronx in more than 60 years.

Majora Carter
MCG Consulting

Photos courtesy Sustainable South Bronx

312

Burdens of the South Bronx

Those of us in communities living without environmental justice are just canaries in the coal mine. We are feeling the consequences of our out-of-balance society now, and have for some time. Environmental justice, for those who aren't familiar with the term, states: No community should be saddled with more environmental burdens and less environmental benefits than any other.

Unfortunately, race and class are extremely reliable indicators as to where one might find the good stuff, like parks and trees, and where one might find the bad stuff, like power plants and waste facilities. As a black person in America, I am twice as likely as a white person to live in an area where air pollution poses the greatest risk to my health. I am five times more likely to live within walking distance of a power plant or chemical facility, which I do. These land-use decisions create the hostile conditions that lead to problems like obesity, diabetes and asthma. Why would someone leave his or her home to go for a brisk walk in a toxic neighborhood? Our neighborhood's 27 percent obesity rate is high compared to the rest of the country, and we know that with obesity comes diabetes.[1] One out of four South Bronx children has asthma. Our asthma hospitalization rate is seven times higher than the national average.

Revitalizing the South Bronx

That small riverside park was the first stage of building a greenway movement in the South Bronx. I wrote a $1.25 million federal transportation grant to design the plan for a waterfront esplanade with dedicated on-street bike paths. Such improvements provide opportunities to be more physically active, as well as encourage local economic development. Think bike shops, juice stands.

Shortly thereafter, I founded Sustainable South Bronx (SSBx), an organization dedicated to greening the local community while providing jobs for residents. We

Green collar workers from Sustainable South Bronx turn a rooftop into a green roof.

Photos courtesy Sustainable South Bronx

Environmental Equality means: No community should be saddled with more environmental burdens and fewer environmental benefits than any other.

secured $20 million to build the first-phase projects—connecting the South Bronx to its waterfront and to the 400-acre Randall's Island Park. And as we nurture the natural environment, its abundance can give us back even more. SSBx created the Bronx Ecological Stewardship Training (BEST), providing job training in ecological restoration, so folks from our community can get the skills to compete for well-paying jobs. Little by little, we're seeding the area with green collar jobs and with people who have both a financial and personal stake in their environment.

This program differed from the popularized "green jobs" images of inner-city youth with solar panels: climate change mitigation jobs in alternative energy go to folks

Unfortunately, race and class are extremely reliable indicators as to where one might find the good stuff, like parks and trees, and where one might find the bad stuff, like power plants and waste facilities.

A black person in America is:

2x as likely as a white person to live in an area where air pollution poses the greatest risk to health

5x more likely to live within walking distance from a power plant or chemical facility

These land-use decisions create the hostile conditions that lead to problems like obesity, diabetes and asthma.

unemployed from other trades with comparable skills. Climate adaptation strategies to combat the urban heat island effect and storm water erosion/flooding costs are new jobs with little organized competition and are both accessible and therapeutic for individuals coming from traumatic experiences like prison and/or combat.

Beyond the Bronx

More than 30 years ago environmental sociologist Robert Bullard identified systematic patterns of injustice in Houston. One hundred percent of the city's garbage dumps were located in black neighborhoods even though only 25 percent of the population was African-American. His book, *Dumping In Dixie*, is widely regarded as the first to articulate the concept of environmental justice.[2] Bullard went on to found the Environmental Justice Resource Center and has since published 12 books on the subject. In a 2008 interview with Smithsonian, Bullard said, "A study 20 years ago found that race—not income, socio-economic status or property values—is the most potent predictor of where these waste facilities are located. In a February 2007 study, we found this still holds true."[3]

Communities around the nation continue to experience environmental injustice, and many are engaged in democratic organizing and solution-based campaigns. In one such example, San Diego–based Environmental Health Coalition (EHC) not only successfully blocked the expansion of a fossil-fuel power plant; they also drafted a detailed energy plan that focused on alternative energy sources. A community-wide protest led to the denial of the permit for the proposed project, which would have been located 1,300 feet from an elementary school and 350 feet from the nearest home. The community provided expert testimony and analysis showing that alternative energy options such as solar and conservation were not only feasible and cost-effective, but they could provide three to four times the energy that proposed plant would provide.[4]

Visionaries in other cities also remind us of greater possibilities, for example Bogotá, Colombia, which is poor, Latino and surrounded by runaway gun violence and drug trafficking with a reputation not unlike that of the South Bronx. However, this city was blessed in the late 1990s with a highly influential mayor named Enrique Penalosa. He looked at the demographics and discovered that few Bogataños own cars, yet a huge portion of the city's resources was dedicated to serving them. As a result, his administration narrowed key municipal thoroughfares from five lanes to three,

> As people began to see that issues reflecting their day-to-day lives were prioritized, incredible things happened. People stopped littering. Crime rates dropped. The streets were **alive**.

(above) Peñalosa transformed this previously decrepit, crime-ridden plaza in Bogotá Colombia into the bustling, thriving city center it is today. (below) Enrique Peñalosa (right, green shirt) reduced vehicular traffic and expanded pedestrian walkways and bike lanes, allowing citizens to travel much more efficiently through Bogotá.

315

Residents of Detroit, MI rally near the city's garbage incinerator to voice their concerns for the health of their community.

outlawed parking on those streets, expanded pedestrian walkways and bike lanes, created public plazas and developed one of the most efficient bus mass-transit systems in the world.

As people began to see that issues reflecting their day-to-day lives were prioritized, incredible things happened. People stopped littering. Crime rates dropped. The streets were alive with people. His administration tackled several typical urban problems at one time, and on a developing country's budget, so we have no excuse in this country. The people-first agenda was not meant to penalize those who could afford cars, but rather to provide opportunities for all Bogataños to participate in the city's resurgence.

A recent report compiled by Alternatives for Community & Environment identified three key principles required for eliminating environmental injustice in our communities (see right).

What's missing from the larger debate is a comprehensive cost-benefit analysis between not fixing an unhealthy, environmentally challenged community, versus incorporating structural, sustainable changes.

3 Principles for building environmental equality in our communities

1. Create cost-benefit analysis of environmental plans vs public health costs

2. Invest in locally relevant green infrastructure and economic development

3. Incentivize small green business development with low barriers to entry

Focused on the Triple Bottom Line, Oakland Green Jobs Corps participants work on solar energy panels at Laney College in Oakland, Ca.

Photo courtesy of the Ella Baker Center

Working Together

I do not expect individuals, corporations or government to make the world a better place because it is right or moral. I know that it's the bottom line—or one's perception of it—that motivates people in the end. It's the triple bottom line generated by sustainable development where community projects have the potential to create positive returns for all concerned. What's missing perhaps from the larger debate is a comprehensive cost-benefit analysis between not fixing an unhealthy, environmentally challenged community, versus incorporating structural, sustainable changes.

This is a nationwide policy agenda, and green is the new black, sustainability is sexy, and now it needs to be a part of dinner and cocktail conversations. I want you to grasp the true value of environmental equality. We need to democratize sustainability by bringing everyone to the table and insisting that comprehensive planning can be addressed everywhere. Our energy, intelligence and hard-earned experience should not be wasted. By working together, we can have the audacity and courage to believe that we can change the world. We might have come from very different stations in life, but we all share one incredibly powerful thing—we have nothing to lose and everything to gain.

.....

From 2001 to 2008 Majora Carter was executive director of the non-profit she founded: Sustainable South Bronx (www.ssbx.org) where she pioneered green collar job training and placement systems in one of the most environmentally and economically challenged parts of the US. This MacArthur "genius" is now president of her own economic consulting firm, and hosts the Peabody Award winning public radio series, The Promised Land (thepromisedland.org).

317

Creating Food Security, Improving Health, Creating Community

Food security is about more than food; it's about social justice and equity. Good food is a human right, and to ensure everyone has access to good food requires healthy food systems. Many individuals and organizations are working toward re-establishing this core value as a foundation for society, a society that is sustainable and high functioning.

Urban Food Security

Surprisingly many urban areas in the nation are food deserts—places limited to convenience stores, fast food and liquor stores that are devoid of grocery stores with healthy food choices. Many times people living in food deserts are food insecure—they do not have access to healthy food or possibly even regular meals.

True food security means all citizens have continuous access to healthy, affordable, sustainably grown and culturally appropriate food and products. To establish these systems, we need to close the loop and create integrated systems. Such systems consider land use and ownership, transportation, health, lowering carbon dependency, creating businesses that are locally owned and operated, education, waste stream management and renewable energy production. These pieces link together to form the apparatuses that create the community food system.

Erika Allen
Growing Power

Photo courtesy, Harvey B. Silikovitz and the Neon Museum, Las Vegas

Creating Urban Food Oases

We cannot have healthy communities without a healthy food system. Everybody, regardless of economic means, should have access to healthy, affordable food. Industrial farming with cross-country supply chains is not a secure food distribution system and doesn't supply the healthiest food. It doesn't create local jobs or support the local economy. Food should be grown where people are. Locally produced food eliminates much of the distribution and transportation costs, providing a bigger return for farmers. In fact, most corporate farmers only receive 20 cents of every food dollar.[1]

In 1993, my father, Will Allen, designed a program that offered teens an opportunity to work at his store and renovate the greenhouse to grow food for their communities. This simple partnership to change the landscape of the north side of Milwaukee blossomed into a national and global commitment to sustainable food systems. With three farms, five satellite educational centers, the Farm-to-City Market Basket Program and farmer's cooperative, Growing Power is now a national touchstone for the community food movement and reaches tens of thousands of community food activists across the country.

Food Security:

The ability to grow, process and consume food locally

To control and operate the food production and distribution systems

The ability to sustain and feed one's population in times of distress (disaster, terrorism, war)

Have access to food that supports the cultural and spiritual traditions of the people

True food security means all citizens have continuous access to "good," healthy, affordable, sustainably grown and culturally appropriate food and products.

Above: Will Allen, founder of Growing Power.
Below: One of the Growing Power greenhouses in Milwaukee, WI.

In 1993, Will Allen designed a program that offered teens an opportunity to grow food for their communities.

With three farms, five satellite educational centers, a Farm-to-City Market Basket Program and farmer's cooperative, **Growing Power is now a national touchstone for the community food movement and reaching tens of thousands of community food activists across the country.**

Jerry Kaufman, a professor at University of Wisconsin-Madison and sometimes called the "father of urban farming," was one of the first to propose using abandoned industrial land back for urban agriculture.[2] Now the urban farm movement is gaining momentum and making lasting change in low-income and food-insecure neighborhoods.

Signs of Progress

Chicago Lights Urban Farm is an urban farm and community garden. This garden, initially a community garden model, has made a transition to an urban farm. A community garden provides space for folks to grow what they like in designated allotment spaces, build relationships and add beauty to the concrete landscape. The urban farm onsite is concerned with production, high-value crops and the ability to provide employment and produce to sell. This transition was enabled by the Youth Corp members from public housing adjacent to the farm seeking living-wage employment in the green jobs sector via urban agriculture. The site will eventually house three greenhouses, a farm-stand and office/classroom space for the community.

The goals of the **Iron Street Urban Farm and Organic Waste Processing Facility**, in Chicago's Bridgeport neighborhood, are two-fold: "growing" healthy soil (via compost) delivered from reputable waste haulers from green restaurants and businesses with sustainability plans and using closed-loop ecological practices to produce local, healthy and sustainable food year-round. The project uses growing and distribution methods that create a carbon neutral footprint with tangible public health benefits for all with a focus on serving the needs of vulnerable populations. The seven-acre site will include 20 hoop houses to grow fresh produce year-round; aquaponics systems, producing healthy mercury-free tilapia; vermicomposting; livestock (chickens, ducks and rabbits); urban apiary; urban orchard and vine fruit production; green roof production and research; and the training and employment of at-risk youth.

Our School at Blair Grocery in New Orleans' Ninth Ward is a resource-rich safe space for youth empowerment and sustainable community development. Founder and former school teacher Nat Turner said, "We must have safe spaces for youth to take risks to transform themselves." The project works to increase students' overall literacy by building skills, abilities and confidence, including their sense of efficacy. It teaches them how access resources that build stronger communities and that they are valued participants in community building efforts.

Operating out of a former grocery store and two empty lots, both flooded by Katrina, Our School is a unique combinatiion of urban farm and youth education. The student-led urban farm produces $2,500 worth of vegetables weekly, and students sell it to popular New Orleans restaurants and at the onsite farmers' market.[3] An after-school activity center, a home-building and construction program and educational classes on topics such as food justice, New Orleans history, urban communities and public health are also offered at Our School.

"We must bring youth to the table with a developed and articulate vision of their own creation to act as agents of social change," said Turner. "We must understand that anyone who is not speaking to the youth in our community is not truly speaking to our community."

Photos courtesy: Our School at Blair Grocery

Our School at Blair Grocery
New Orleans' 9th Ward

Operating out of a former grocery store and two empty lots, flooded by Katrina, Our School is a unique combination of urban farm and youth education. The student-led urban farm produces $2,500 worth of vegetables weekly and students sell it to popular New Orleans restaurants and at the onsite farmer's market.

q&a with Will Allen

Q: What is the Good Food Movement (GFM)?

A movement is something that moves along a continuum. The good food movement is about promoting healthy food to people in all communities. The same type of food that would go to upscale communities, we find ways to get to everyone. That happens along a long continuum that gathers momentum as it moves forward, until it becomes a revolution. That is where we are. The movement started with a few hundred people in the '60s, thousands in the '70s and '80s, continually increasing through the turn of century to where there are now with millions of people involved.

Q: What is the barrier for GFM becoming reality?

I would not call them barriers, and I would call them challenges. First is a lack of healthy soil. We also need to address some of the restrictive policies in place that make getting healthy food to people difficult, particularly in urban and remote rural areas. We have to grow more farmers and producers but educating them takes a long time. Long-term access to land can also be a challenge.

Q: How do we scale up?

For both local and global communities, we need to provide training and resources to grow intensively inside of cities. Because of the high cost of this valuable land and oil, we must maximize space. We have to rethink how we grow—rather than cost per square acre we need to change our mindset to cost per square foot! We want to generate $5 per square foot, on an acre of intensively farmed land that will gross a farmer more than $200,000 per year.

Q: So it's kind of counter-intuitive but scaling up does not mean farming more acres like big agriculture, but maximizing small spaces?

Yes, and scaling up also means creating more jobs, by using small spaces. How do you engage, re-engage communities, who want to be part of it? The key is growing high-nutrient soil, not using chemicals, using natural inputs, closing the loop with our current waste streams. It also means developing relationships with your consumers and CSAs (community supported agriculture) are a good example. Asking the consumer to pay upfront for a share of the farms produce over the season, sharing the risk with the farmer. So when there is a bumper crop, you get more tomatoes than you know what to do with, and when there is a drought, you take the hit with the farmer. This makes the system truly community based.

Q: Hope for the future?

I think one of my hopes for this movement/revolution is that it keeps gaining momentum, that we get thousands of people involved and create a new industry that grows jobs. That is my big thing right now, how do we create more jobs, new strategies? One way is if the regional training centers are able to replicate our work in a culturally appropriate way, we will be able to impact the food system nationally and globally.

Also I would like to see agriculture training back in the schools, re-enchanting our youth and their connection to farming and the earth. I would also like to get more top-down operators involved in supporting community agriculture; this is important too, from all areas and many players need to be involved. The revolution will require hundreds of different job categories to be successful.

> **For sustainable food systems and urban farming to scale up on a national level, not only do we need more farmers; they also need to earn a living wage. Farmers need the support of the community.**

Scaling Up

Expanding the local and sustainable food systems requires farmers, farmers, farmers. Urban agriculture has the potential to generate living wages for farmers who have been trained and know how to grow intensively and market their products.

For sustainable food systems and urban farming to scale up on a national level, not only do we need more farmers; they also need to earn a living wage. Farmers need the support of the community—individuals, business and local government, who see the value in sourcing food locally. Revising city and county zoning policies to legalize commercial urban farms would be the initial step. Local and regional governments could show their support for local farmers by instituting policies that prioritize locally grown products. Consumer education is also important. Consumers will be more likely to seek out locally grown food when they understand the value of supporting the local economy and as well as the likely increase in nutritional value.

Shining examples of success are sprouting up around the country, and it is clear that converting urban areas from food deserts to oases of abundance builds community, creates jobs, improves health and reduces our carbon footprint.

An urban garden, featuring rows of tomatoes and kale, in Chicago, IL.

.....

Erika Allen is projects manager for Growing Power (www.growingpower.org) and is headquartered in Chicago, IL. As the daughter of Will Allen, she has a small-farm agricultural background and experience. She spent her formative years involved in all aspects of farm management, from transplanting seedlings to managing farm stands and farmers' markets. Allen received a BFA from the School of the Art Institute of Chicago and recently received an MA in art therapy from the University of Illinois at Chicago. Growing Power is a national non-profit organization and land trust supporting people from diverse backgrounds, and the environments in which they live, by helping to provide equal access to healthy, high-quality, safe and affordable food for people in all communities.

The Next Generation of Family Farming

Brian DeVore
Land Stewardship Project

The news is full of stories about the demise of family farming in the United States. Indeed, the numbers are sobering—the number of farmers 75 and older has grown by 20 percent since 2002, and the number below the age of 25 has dropped 30 percent.[1] The aging farm population is due to several factors, but a major reason is a simple lack of young people replenishing the ranks.

For much of the 20th century, one could launch a successful farming operation with a little luck and a lot of sweat equity. Today, skyrocketing land values and market prices that often don't cover the cost of putting in a crop or raising livestock have combined with federal farm policies that disproportionately support larger farms to make entry into farming a daunting if not unachievable task.

And once a farmer gets established, she or he is faced with a situation where all aspects of the food chain—from processing to packaging to retailing—are dominated by a few powerful players who can basically call the shots on what prices are paid to farmers, as well as what prices are charged to consumers. Four firms now control at least 83 percent, 66 percent and 55 percent, respectively, of the nation's beef, pork and turkey processing markets, according to the University of Missouri's most recent *Concentration of Agricultural Markets* report.[2] Three firms control 54 percent of flour milling.[3] Based on conventional economic wisdom, when four firms control more than 40 percent of a market, it's no longer

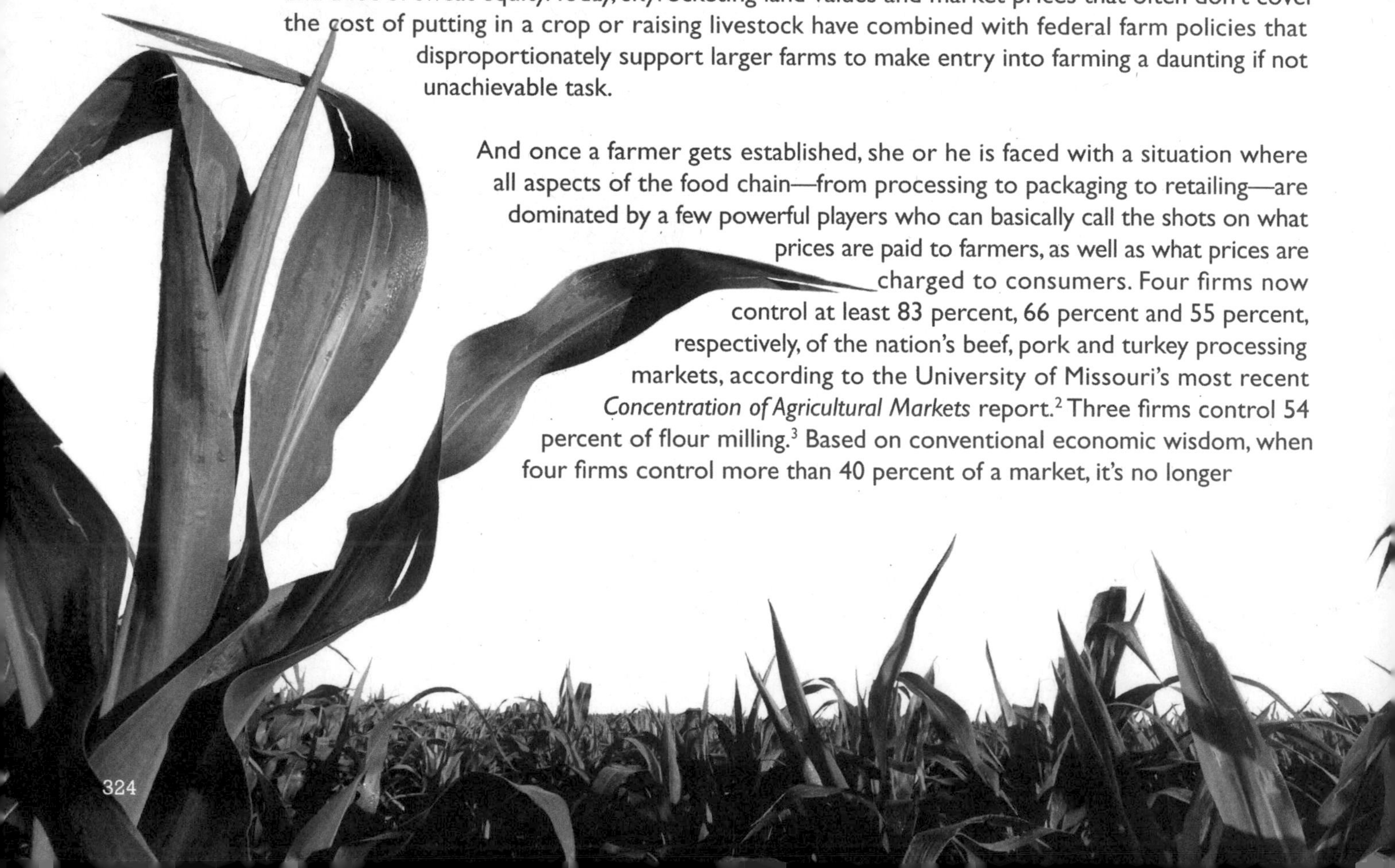

And as large-scale industrialized operations push out diversified family-sized farms, agriculture has become more alienated from its ecological roots. As a result, all those monocrops of corn and lakes of liquid manure are helping make agriculture one of the largest producers of non-point source pollution (polluted surface water runoff) in the US, according to the Environmental Protection Agency.[4]

The US Geological Survey has found that the popular corn herbicide Atrazine, which has been connected to numerous human and animal health problems (like cancer, infertility and heart and liver

This retiring coleseed farmer has no one to pass his farm on to and is having a hard time finding a beginning farmer to buy it.

Based on conventional economic wisdom, when four firms control more than 40 percent of a market, it's no longer a competitive one.

a competitive one, and farmers selling crops and livestock into such a market have little control over their own financial destiny.

Unfortunately, key government policies tend to favor those producing higher volumes of a few targeted commodity crops—mainly corn, soybeans, wheat, rice and cotton. The result of these policies has shuttered Main Streets in rural communities and created a greater reliance on food controlled by a handful of mega-firms.

problems) was present in streams in agricultural areas about 75 percent of the time, and in groundwater in agricultural areas about 40 percent of the time.[5] Water contamination levels of nitrogen, a keystone fertilizer for corn production that causes, among other things "blue baby syndrome" in human infants as well as the Gulf of Mexico's dead zone, are going up.[6] Seven to 20 percent of all wells in states like Iowa, Minnesota and Wisconsin contain levels of nitrate-nitrogen that exceed health standards.[7]

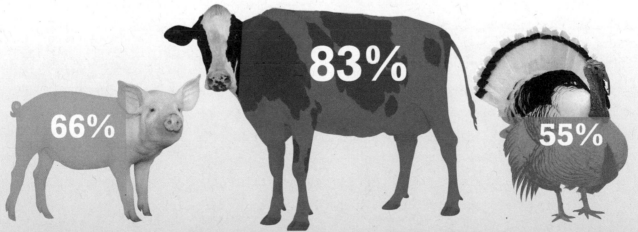

66%   83%   55%

Four firms now control at least 66 percent, 83 percent, and 55 percent, respectively, of the nation's pork, beef and turkey processing markets.

Consumers, environmentalists and communities are calling for a more sustainable agriculture, one that is reliant on good management and an intimate knowledge of the land.

This kind of farming requires more, not fewer farmers.

But there are real opportunities and a great need for a new way to work with the land. It seems that all of the problems associated with industrialized agriculture—the emptying communities, pollution and concerns about food safety—have created a backlash. Consumers, environmentalists and communities are calling for a more sustainable agriculture, one that is reliant on good management and an intimate knowledge of the land. This kind of farming requires more, not fewer farmers.

Within the past decade, there's been an explosion in demand for local food raised using environmentally sustainable methods. Direct food sales—a direct transfer from the farmer to the consumer via such avenues as Community Supported Agriculture (CSA) operations, farm stands, farmers' markets, the Internet, etc.—skyrocketed from $812 million to $1.2 billion in just 5 years—a 49 percent increase, according to the latest Census of Agriculture. The Organic Trade Association has more good news: sales of organic foods in the US more than tripled from $8.6 billion in 2002 to $26.7 billion in 2010.[8] By the end of 2010, there were 6,132 farmers' markets in the US, which is around 5,000 more than there were two decades ago, according to the USDA.[9]

Another positive trend has been the explosion in the development of farming systems that are low-cost, profitable and environmentally sustainable, and that produce food products that consumers are willing to pay more to buy such as grass-fed beef; grass-fed dairy; and organic grains, fruits and vegetables. But farming methods that rely on alternative production and marketing models take a lot of management skills. Studies show that a major barrier to adopting sustainable farming methods is lack of information and firsthand

In the past decade there's been an explosion in demand for local food, raised using environmentally sustainable methods.

$1.2 billion +49%

$812 million

2002   2007

CSA Sales

$26.7 billion

$8.6 billion +310%

2002   2010

Organic Food Sales

6,132 farmers' markets in 2010

+5,000

Approximately 1,000 farmers' markets in 1988

Farmers' Markets

knowledge related to such systems. Farmers adopting alternative production methods are more likely to be successful if they are part of some sort of formal or informal network of like-minded farmers.

Farm Beginnings

That's why, when Roger and Michelle Benrud decided to launch a grass-based dairy farming enterprise, they enrolled in the Land Stewardship Project's Farm Beginnings course on sustainable farm management. Courses like this provide firsthand training in low-cost, sustainable methods of farming. The Benruds learned business planning and goal setting, as well as marketing methods that help farmers capture the most value for their production. Perhaps most importantly, through the class they were introduced to farmers who were already running profitable operations of their own. The opportunity to visit established farms and see firsthand farm management systems successfully put into action is priceless. And through this interaction, an informal farmer network is created.

Studies show that a major barrier to adopting sustainable farming methods is lack of information and firsthand knowledge related to such systems.

A lesson at Farm Beginnings in sustainable farming techniques

An Iowa State study found that **if just 25 percent** of the fruits and vegetables consumed in the state **were grown** by local farmers, the statewide economic impact would be **nearly $140 million in output**; over $54 **million** in labor income alone would be **paid to roughly 2,000 jobholders.**

After learning crucial management skills, the Benruds gradually built up a successful dairy operation. Their milk is sold through the organic market and has been sold through a specialty butter and cheese cooperative, which has racked up numerous national awards for its excellent butter. This means the Benruds receive a premium price from health-conscious consumers who also appreciate the environmental benefits of pasture-based dairying.

Sixty-six percent of graduates of sustainable farming courses in Minnesota who are farming say their annual net farm income has increased on average $12,500 since taking the course.[10] Over 20 states have initiatives that help beginning farmers get started, and many are using a community-based approach. Since the majority of the new farmers coming out of these programs are pursuing enterprises centered around local, sustainably raised foods, the economic development potential is tremendous. Counties with organic farms have stronger farm economies and contribute more to local economies, according to a University of Georgia economic analysis. An Iowa State study found that if just 25 percent of the fruits and vegetables consumed in the state were grown by local farmers, the statewide economic impact would be nearly $140 million in output; over $54 million in labor income alone would be paid to roughly 2,000 jobholders.[11]

Community Building

This movement is not just about creating the next generation of livestock producers, CSA farmers and specialty crop growers. It's also about revitalizing rural communities and creating active members of society. With the network in place and a business focused on community, it's not a far leap for these farmers to take on bigger roles in their communities by serving on boards, volunteering and getting involved with local decision-making institutions like townships.

This is developing a solid constituency of citizens who can educate lawmakers about the bright future for family farming. Graduates of these programs hosted lawmakers during the debate over the 2008 Farm Bill and talked about their own farms, and the expanding market for their regionally and sustainably produced meat, dairy and vegetable products. They shared their vision for the renewal of a family farm system of agriculture that supports vibrant rural communities and a healthy landscape. And they zeroed in on the public policy that was needed to help more people like them get started. They were living proof that there are many opportunities in agriculture that go beyond bolstering the bottom lines of the Cargills and ADMs of the world.

As a result of such efforts, when it was signed into law, the 2008 Farm Bill provided financial and administrative support for the Beginning Farmer and Rancher Development Program (BFRDP). BFRDP is a precedent-setting attempt by the federal government to support community-based programs that conduct beginning farmer education, training and mentoring.

Supporting the Next Generation of Farmers

Enlightened government agriculture policy will help clear the way for revitalizing family farms, but even more exciting is that anyone who eats has a chance to play a role in reinventing our food and farming system. The benefits of buying locally grown food from your nearest farmers' market or CSA operation go far beyond simply benefiting the farmer. The health and environmental benefits that come with local, fresh, sustainable food are worthy of support in their own right, but then also consider the economic and community perks that can result. If residents of just one Iowa county,

The outdoor market in Madison, WI is the largest outdoor farmers' market in the US, and is a signature weekly event for Wisconsin's capitol.

With an ever-expanding community of family farms, we have a chance to **reinvent the agriculture industry,** revitalize rural communities and improve the land through an expanded transition to more sustainable farming practices.

Black Hawk, spent $10 of their weekly grocery bill on locally grown food, that would amount to $2 million every month invested in local people, local farms and independent local businesses, according to the University of Northern Iowa Local Food Project. Try replacing or augmenting your produce from the big chain grocery store with a CSA membership next summer. Make an effort to replace your meat with locally grown grass-fed varieties at least once a week.

Buying local, sustainable food shows government decision-makers and the business community that there is a demand for these kinds of products. But it also provides a critical morale boost to the hardworking farmers themselves. Whenever we make a food-buying choice, we are sending a tremendously powerful message back to rural America about what sort of farming is valued.

. . . . .

Brian DeVore is a staff member of the Minnesota-based Land Stewardship Project (www.landstewardshipproject.org), which, among things, coordinates the Farm Beginnings program. Since 1997, Farm Beginnings has trained hundreds of farmers in sustainable management techniques. Farm Beginnings-licensed courses are now being taught in six states.

Supporting a Green Future in Native American Communities

Ojibwe prophecies speak of a time during the seventh fire when our people will have a choice between two paths. The first path is well-worn and scorched. The second path is new and green. It is our choice as communities and as individuals how we will proceed.

The economy of the future is the green path, and we are keenly interested in having our communities at the center of this transition. With reservation unemployment rates at between 15 to 80 percent and per capita annual incomes roughly one-sixth the national average, the well-worn and scorched path is not the solution. A path with food security, clean energy solutions and a green jobs initiative is a part of our prophecies and is, for our Mother Earth, essential.[1]

Winona LaDuke
Honor the Earth

The Challenges We Are Facing

Two generations ago, most of the tribal communities in the north produced our food locally. Today, we buy food shipped from far away, whether by Wal-Mart, Food Services of America or SYSCO. The average meal moves between 1,200 and 2,500 miles from farm to table.[2] And because we also rely so heavily on petroleum to grow our food, some scientists suggest that we are using between 10 to 15 calories of fossil fuels to create one calorie of food.[3] This means that our food security is now tied to industrial food systems and oil. We are feeling the consequences of that relationship. Food prices are skyrocketing as the cost of oil rises. Food is costing more and more, not just in dollars but also environmentally and in terms of our physical and cultural health.

Nationally, tribes spend tens of millions of dollars on fuel assistance each year to support our low-income tribal members. That is a lot of *zhooniyaa*. As electricity and fuel prices continue to rise, the dollars we spend on energy will increasingly outpace all subsidies. We need to create long-term, sustainable solutions to poverty by creating a renewable, energy-efficient future. In today's climate-challenged world, food sovereignty and energy sovereignty are the keys to creating green economies on tribal lands. Not only will these strategies be viable for tribal self-determination, but they will also lead to independence, jobs and sources of export revenues.

Approximately 50% of a tribal economy's money is spent outside the reservation on food and energy, the largest drain on tribal wealth.

Food Security   Approximately 50 percent of a tribal economy's money is spent outside the reservation on food and energy, the largest drains on tribal wealth. Native peoples often live in food deserts, meaning we have very few places we can easily get to that sell healthy foods. However, many of our traditional foods are drought- and frost-resistant, making them less susceptible to food production problems associated with climate change. Traditional food restoration through organic farming is a means of restoring our food security but it can also help mitigate climate change by limiting and even absorbing carbon emissions.

Many tribes are implementing traditional food programs such as local food production, seed saving, educational workshops and ecological restoration work for wild rice, buffalo and other culturally essential foods. The Tohono O'odham Nation in Arizona received a Native Communities Grant from Honor the Earth, and the funds are being used for programs that encourage traditional foods in school lunch programs. The tribe also conducts traditional food educational presentations at community events and hosts two farms that grow traditional foods,

Students pick apples for their school's Traditional Foods program.

Photo courtesy of Honor the Earth

covery Project, working with the White Earth Band of Ojibwe and local utilities, is working on weatherization renovations and alternative heating sources for the 700 homes that qualify for fuel assistance. The program is set to expand with a proposed local training program in both energy audits and weatherization and additional solar heating panel installations. Program staff also worked in collaboration with Honor the Earth, Little Earth of United Tribes, the Rural Renewable Energy Alliance and Fresh Energy to install two solar heating panels on Little Earth's Elders Housing Unit in Minneapolis. Replicating this type of work in all reservations will save our people millions of dollars in utility costs and create thousands of meaningful jobs.

Renewable Energy

Like energy efficiency, renewable energy has excellent potential to create living-wage, dignified jobs. Tribal lands are incredibly rich in energy resources, with an estimated 10 percent of the country's energy resources,[5] which holds promise to create valuable job opportunities. It is estimated that renewable energy and energy efficiency were responsible for $970 billion in industry revenues and 8.5 million jobs.[6] Wind and solar energy generate 40 percent more jobs per dollar invested than coal mining.[7]

one of which is being transitioned into a learning center. In addition to food security, returning to a traditional diet has the potential to undo much of the illness and harm processed foods have caused in our communities because traditional foods are healthier.

Energy Efficiency

Our current homes and buildings waste a great deal of energy. In fact, 30 percent of the energy we pay for in our homes and buildings is wasted because of inefficient construction and appliances.[4] Energy efficiency and conservation are the simplest ways to save money and the first step toward creating a clean energy economy.

Weatherization and energy-efficiency retrofits are also the first steps in energy sovereignty. The White Earth Land Re-

In order for the US economy to stabilize carbon emissions, we will need to produce around 185,000 megawatts of new power over the next decade. The ten-year total projection for wind energy, according to the Renewable Energy Policy Project, entails the creation of 125,000 megawatts of power. This means up to 400,000 domestic manufacturing jobs in wind power alone.[8] The new jobs of the green economy can and should include investment and progress in Native communities. both urban and reservation.

Tribal lands are incredibly rich in energy resources, holding an estimated **10 percent** of the country's energy resources, which lends well to valuable job opportunities.

Photo courtesy Windustry © 2010

Reservation communities are among the windiest sites in the country, with studies indicating that reservations could produce from one-fourth to one-third of present installed electrical demand.

Young People Affirming a Prosperous, Green Future for the Navajo Nation

During the summer of 2008, about 50 young people dressed in green gathered outside the Navajo Nation Council. As the Council deliberated over funding a program to provide loans to small-scale sustainable businesses, the young demonstrators marched into the session cheering and waving green flags to show their support. Behind the group's vocal support, the Council passed the program by a vote of 62 to 1.

Many of those activists went on to form Navajo Green Jobs, which continues their grassroots campaign to strengthen the economy of the Navajo Nation with sustainable business and industry. The group still marches in their trademark green shirts to raise environmental awareness throughout the Southwest, and they have also started programs to map the progress of green initiatives within the Nation and provide community members with the tools and support needed to start their own sustainable businesses.

And according to activist Nikki Alex, Navajo Green Jobs has a mission that extends off the tribal lands, "The indigenous people have an answer, yet we're the least heard people here. We're just trying to get the word out that we indigenous people live with very small carbon footprints, we live sustainably, we do have answers."[1]

from the editor

Tribal Wind Energy   Nationally, tribal wind-power potential is tremendous. Reservation communities are among the windiest sites in the country, with studies indicating that reservations could produce nearly 15 percent of the nation's electricity.[9] Wind energy represents an excellent opportunity for reservation-based employment and also represents a fuel source with economic predictability and security into the future. Many reservations in the Dakotas and Montana have class-six or class-seven wind, which is the best you can have.

In Minnesota, White Earth, Red Lake and several Dakota reservations have class-four wind, which represents good potential for commercial-scale projects and the export of energy. The Shakopee Mdewakanton Dakota Community has installed a 1.5-megawatt wind turbine, solar hot water panels and a green roof. The community also partially owns a biofuels plant. The White Earth reservation hosts a 20-kilowatt wind turbine and is looking to install 250-kilowatt and 750-kilowatt wind turbines over the next three years.

The Campo Reservation in Southern California partnered with the local utility to build California's second-largest wind-power project in the mountains east of San Diego. At peak capacity, the 160-megawatt wind farm will produce enough power for 104,000 homes. The tribe has an equity stake and hopes to eventually own the project.[10]

There is great potential for some of the ongoing demand for electricity generation to be met by tribal installations and tribal power. Actualizing this potential will require resources and investment, training and a national strategy that incorporates Native peoples.

Tribal Solar Energy   Solar also has vast potential for self-sufficiency, revenue and jobs for First Nations. Tribal lands could produce an estimated 17 trillion kilowatt hours of solar electricity annually, over four times total US annual electrical generation.[11]

The US Department of Energy's Tribal Energy Program, which provides financial, technical and educational assistance, has funded several solar projects, both feasibility studies and installations, on tribal lands.[12] The Jemez Pueblo tribe, in New Mexico, has taken it a step further and is building the first utility-scale solar plant. The project is slated to include 14,850 solar panels on 30 acres. It is estimated at $22 million and will be financed through government loans, grants and tax credits.[13] With a transmission line already available at the site, and an average of 310 sunny days a year, the 4-megawatt solar project is expected to generate $25 million in revenue over the next 25 years for the tribe through the sale of the electricity.[14] As well, there is interest in putting a solar power

Green jobs advocates celebrate the success of their campaign to bring green jobs to the Navajo Nation after the Navajo Nation Council voted to create a green jobs policy and establish a commission to pursue grants and opportunities for green color job development.

> **Tribal lands are incredibly rich in energy resources, holding an estimated 10 percent of the country's energy resources, which lends well to valuable job opportunities.**

project of at least 200 megawatts on the former Black Mesa coal strip mine, which has the potential to create a good energy source out of an ecologically bad history.

Clean Energy, Local Food, Green Jobs: Bright Future

Tribes across the country are proving that it's possible to take control of our future by looking to clean energy, food security and the promises of the growing green economy. For example, on the Dinetah-Navajo Nation in Arizona, the first green jobs bill among First Nations was passed to create the Navajo Green Economy Commission. Committed to zero or minimal C02 emissions and other pollution, the Commission will focus on sustainable green manufacturing, local and self-sufficient business ventures and traditional agriculture projects.[15]

In recognizing the links between food, health, fuel poverty and energy, we can address the global challenge of climate change and peak oil and the economic and health challenges afflicting our communities. By investing in energy efficiency, renewable energy and local food systems, Native communities can help secure a place in the developing green economy and ensure a sustainable future. Native nations, the federal government and private enterprise are helping to make this a reality, but the pace of change and financial support need to be greatly scaled up.

In the end, we as Indigenous peoples need to control our own destinies by exercising food and energy sovereignty. Our future generations are counting on us.

. . . . .

Winona LaDuke (Anishinaabe) is an internationally renowned activist working on issues of sustainable development, renewable energy and food systems (www.honorearth.org). She lives and works on the White Earth reservation in northern Minnesota, and is a two-time vice presidential candidate with Ralph Nader for the Green Party.

Envisioning an
Inclusive World

The Importance of the Gay Civil Rights Movement

"Constitutional amendments should be used to expand freedom, not restrict it. Gay and lesbian people have families, and their families should have legal protection, whether by marriage or civil union. A constitutional amendment banning same-sex marriages is a form of gay bashing and it would do nothing at all to protect traditional marriages."

> ✥ Coretta Scott King[1]

In a world defined by difference, our strength depends on our common humanity. As a country, we've made great progress in improving equality for women and minorities, but there's still room for improvement in recognizing our common humanity. Our nation was built on the ideals of fairness and equality for all, but all do not experience those values. Gay Americans still face discrimination on many levels, in the workplace and in places of worship, to name a few. Same-sex couples do not experience the same safeguards and legal rights as opposite-sex couples, such as Social Security, health insurance and unquestioned hospital visitation.

Donna Payne
Human Rights Campaign

In a world defined by difference, our strength depends on our common humanity. As a country, we've made great progress in improving equality for women and minorities but there's still **room for improvement** in recognizing our common humanity.

Black Civil Rights Movement and Gay Civil Rights Movement

I cannot separate the African-American part of me and the lesbian part of me. They make up my whole being. However, there are concerns around equalizing the hardship that the black civil rights movement faced with that of the gay civil rights movement. There are differences between the struggles my ancestors faced during slavery and the civil rights movement, and the modern LGBT civil rights movement. However, there are shared basic inequalities that cannot be overlooked, such as housing and workplace discrimination. But civil rights are really about the way that we treat people. Discrimination shows through our behavior toward each other.

The NAACP recognizes the need for civil rights for the gay community as well. At a historic event in New York City in September 2010, Benjamin Jealous, the President of the NAACP, visited the New York Lesbian, Gay, Bisexual, and Transgendered Center and spoke to a large audience about working together. It was the first such public appearance by a sitting NAACP president openly stating that gay rights are civil rights.[2]

Bringing Fairness Into Focus

Fairness in the workplace has been recognized as a fundamental right protected under federal law. In the US, we are legally protected against employment discrimination on the basis of race, gender, religion, national origin or disability. However, working Americans are not legally protected against sexual orientation or gender identity and gender expression discrimination. Currently, there is no federal law that consistently protects lesbian, gay, bisexual and transgender (LGBT) individuals.

In recent years, businesses have implemented policies aimed at creating safe and productive workplaces for gay and lesbian employees. The majority of Fortune 500 companies have prohibited discrimination based on sexual orientation since 1995 and have offered partner benefits since 2006. The number of companies that receive top ratings from the Human Rights Campaign Foundation's Corporate Equity Index rose from only 13 in 2002[3] to 337 in 2011.[4] However, more work needs to be done to translate inclusive policies into an inclusive climate as more than half of LGBT employees hide their LBGT identity at work.[5]

SIGNS OF PROGRESS:
NUMBER of COMPANIES to receive top ratings from HRC's Corporate Equality Index:

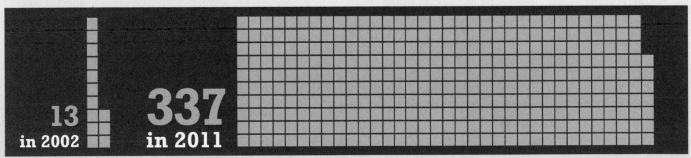

13 in 2002   337 in 2011

HOWEVER... More work needs to be done to translate inclusive policies into an inclusive climate, as **more than half** of LGBT employees hide their LGBT identity at work.

All families deserve the ability to protect themselves with basic legal rights and safeguards.

There are over

1,049
benefits

that come with marriage that make day-to-day family life manageable.

Those rights include:

Hospital visitation, Social Security benefits, immigration, health insurance, estate taxes, family leave, nursing homes, home protection & pensions

None of these benefits are available to same-sex couples because they can't get married.

Civil unions and domestic partnerships only grant

1/4 of marriage protections

Marriage and Relationship Recognition

At its core, the push for marriage equality is simply about making the day-to-day lives of same-sex couples and their families secure. All families deserve the ability to protect themselves with basic legal rights and safeguards. There are 1,049 benefits that come with marriage. Those rights include hospital visitation, Social Security benefits, immigration, health insurance, estate taxes, family leave, nursing homes, home protection and pensions. None of these benefits are available to same-sex couples because they can't get married! Many argue that civil unions and domestic partnership laws can offer this protection, but they only grant one-quarter of marriage protections.

The Domestic Partnership Benefits and Obligations Act (DPBO) would provide domestic partnership benefits to all federal civilian employees on the same basis as spousal benefits. These benefits, available for both same- and opposite-sex domestic partners of federal employees, would include participation in applicable retirement programs, compensation for work injuries and life and health insurance benefits. DPBO would bring employment practices in the federal government in line with those of America's largest and most successful corporations. In addition, 59 percent of Fortune 500 companies, 23 states, the District of Columbia and over 150 local governments make benefits available to public employees and their same-sex partners. This is great progress, but we need to be working toward equal rights and benefits for both opposite- and same-sex couples.

Currently, only marriage can provide families with true equality, due to the federal legal rights associated with marriage. Vermont, New Jersey and New Hampshire offer civil unions, which are, like domestic partnership recognition, a form of relationship acknowledgment that grants same-sex couples access to state-level marriage rights but not federal-level rights. In the US, same-sex marriage is legal in six states: New York, Massachusetts, Connecticut, Iowa, New Hampshire and Vermont, as well as in Washington, DC. Equality-seeking groups across the country have created marriage campaign initiatives in other states.

At its core, the push for marriage equality is simply about making the **day-to-day lives** of same-sex couples and their families secure.

59% of Fortune 500 Companies provide domestic partner benefits to their employees.

In addition,

23 states + the District of Columbia + over

150 local governments make benefits available to public employees and their same-sex partners.

This is great progress but we need to be working toward equal rights and benefits for **both opposite and same-sex couples.**

In the US, same-sex marriage is legal in five states:

Massachusetts, Connecticut, Iowa, New Hampshire, Vermont, New York and Washington, DC.

Our liberties we Prize and our Rights
We Will Maintain
—IOWA STATE MOTTO

Photo courtesy Alan Light

Participants in an Iowa City rally celebrate after the Supreme Court legalized same-sex marriage in Iowa. The poster in the center reads, "Our liberties we prize and our rights we will maintain," Iowa's state motto.

> **Several countries have joined the ranks of showing support to same-sex couples and their families. The list is growing and reflects the equality that is possible.**

Seeing Equality Throughout the World

Since the gay civil rights movement started, there has been progress around the world to secure protections for individuals, their relationships and families. Several countries have joined the ranks of showing support to same-sex couples and their families. The list is growing, and they reflect the equality that is possible.

• **South Africa** was the first country in the world (in 1996) to include a section in their constitution on LGBT rights, which declares, "The state may not unfairly discriminate directly or indirectly against anyone on one or more grounds, including sexual orientation." Adoption rights and marriage recognition followed in 2005.

• **The Netherlands** was the first country to legalize marriage in 2001 and became the beaming light in the world that gave us all a glimpse of possibility for the future.

• **Canada** followed with marriage recognition, adoption and the banning of all discrimination including gender identity in 2003.

We are now surrounded by a path that shows us how things should be for everyone. For the past four years, more countries have recognized same-sex marriage, adoption and openness in the military and banned all discrimination against gay and lesbian individuals and families, including Norway, Sweden, Spain, Belgium, Iceland and Argentina.

Gaining Fairness in America

Nothing smells better than progress! We're seeing it around the world and in the US. Don't Ask, Don't Tell, a policy that was put in place to restrict US military officials from efforts to reveal the sexuality of a service member was repealed in 2010. This policy also kept the military from adding to their ranks if a person was openly gay, lesbian or bisexual. Removal of this federally mandated law was preceded by military research showing that its repeal would not harm military effectiveness.

Another step in the right direction is the Matthew Shepard and James Byrd, Jr. Hate Crimes Prevention Act.

President Obama signs the repeal of Don't Ask, Don't Tell in 2010.

Public domain photo courtesy Chuck Kennedy, White House photographer

Conceived as a response to the bias-motivated murders of Shepard and Byrd, the act gives the Department of Justice the power to investigate and prosecute bias-motivated violence by providing them with jurisdiction over crimes of violence where a perpetrator has selected a victim because of the person's actual or perceived race, color, religion, national origin, gender, sexual orientation, gender identity or disability.

Progress is also being made in terms of relationship recognition. New federal regulations regarding patients' hospital visitation rights have gone into effect nationally. These new regulations require all hospitals participating in Medicaid and Medicare programs, which is almost every hospital in the country, to permit patients to designate visitors of their choosing and prohibit discrimination in visitation based on a number of factors, including sexual orientation and gender identity. That's equality!

America was founded on the ideals of liberty and justice for all. We have come a long way in strengthening civil rights for US citizens; however, progress toward fundamental fairness and equity for gay and lesbian individuals and families is still possible. At the Human Rights Campaign, our dream is of an America where lesbian, gay, bisexual and transgender people are ensured equality and embraced as full members of the American family at home, at work and in every community.

. . . . .

Support Fairness in America

① **State your support for full marriage equality.**

② **Patronize businesses that support equality and encourage others to implement non-discrimination policies.**

③ **Become informed of initiatives in your area, locate local LGBT advocacy groups and support their work.**

④ **Vote for candidates that support LGBT civil rights.**

As one of the Human Rights Campaign's (www.hrc.org) key representatives, Donna Payne works closely with our civil rights organizations and leaders across the country to increase inclusiveness of lesbian, gay, bisexual and transgender communities of color. Her work includes leading HRC's Historically Black Colleges and Universities program. In 2009, she was chosen by TheRoot.com as one of 100 established Black Americans who are making exceptional contributions in their professions and communities. Payne is also a founding board member of the National Black Justice Coalition. She graduated from the University of Tennessee, Knoxville, in political science.

"Our goal is to create a **beloved community** and this will require a qualitative change in our souls as well as a quantitative change in our lives."

❧ Dr. Martin Luther King Jr.

from the editor

Immigrants in America:
Common Values, Common Dreams

America's success has always been driven by a unique combination of core values, clear-eyed pragmatism and unity of purpose. It's a fusion that has carried us through war and recession, through disaster and recovery and onward toward the quest of a more perfect union.

When it comes to the increasingly heated debate over immigration, however, we seem to have forgotten our national formula for success. Where we should be lifting up our core values of fairness and accountability, our policy discourse is spiteful and arbitrary. Where we should be seeking realistic solutions based on evidence, we are opting for shrill gestures and political theater. And where we should be working together as a nation, we are mired in division.

Alan Jenkins
The Opportunity Agenda

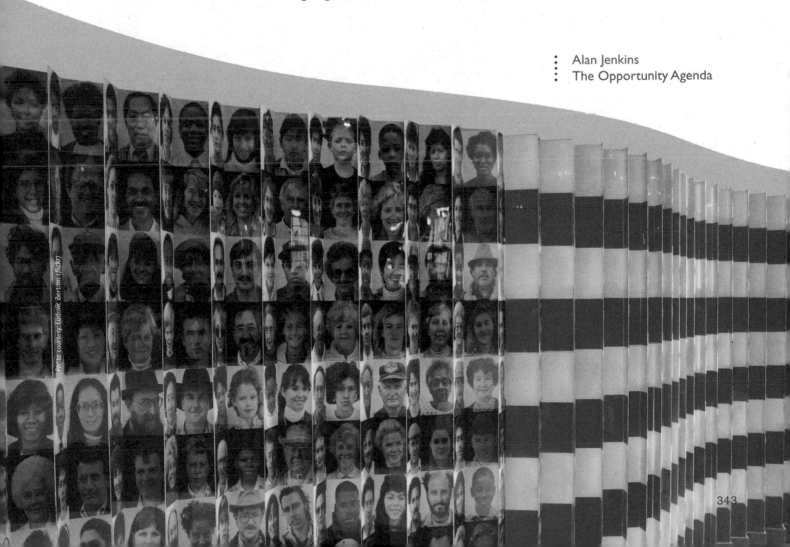

Photo courtesy: Ludovic Bertron (flickr)

343

> **The system for legal immigration is shockingly outdated and inadequate for the needs of American industry in agriculture and many other sectors.**

This is not the first time that America has lost its footing on an important national issue. But neither is it too late to turn things around. When it comes to immigration, it's time for practical solutions that uphold our nation's values and move us forward together.

First, the Facts

Americans are understandably frustrated by a badly broken immigration system. Yet there is inadequate discussion of precisely how it is broken. There is simply no way for the 11 million undocumented immigrants in our country to become legal residents or begin a path toward citizenship. The system for legal immigration is shockingly outdated and inadequate for the needs of American industry in agriculture and many other sectors, and the backlogs of immigrants with close family ties in the United States have made that process unworkable.

Though they have no way of legalizing their status, those immigrants are a part of our nation's economic engine and of the social fabric of many communities around the country. They are caregivers, mechanics,

Though they have no way of legalizing their status, those immigrants are a part of our nation's economic engine and of the social fabric of many, many communities around the country.

They are caregivers, mechanics, laborers, professionals & college students.

They are a part of us.

laborers, professionals and college students. They are a part of us.

Immigrants can also be a vital part of our nation's future, including our much-needed economic recovery. Even before we were a nation, those who chose to journey to the New World were people who wanted to rewrite their destinies, who wanted their stations in life to be determined by their own efforts rather than by the circumstances into which they were born. With them came an entrepreneurial spirit that time and again has led to innovation and progress.

In the 21st century, that innovation has often translated to job creation and a boon to the economy. In 2010, for example, approximately 340 out of every 100,000 Americans created a new business each month; the rate for foreign-born Americans that year was 620 out of 100,000—more than double the average.[1]

"Immigrants not only help fuel the Nation's economic growth," wrote Edward P. Lazear, chairman of the Council of Economic Advisors to President George W. Bush in 2007, "but also have an overall positive effect on the income of native-born workers."[2] A study authored by the Council went on to state that immigrants have lower crime rates than natives and improve the solvency of entitlement programs such as Social Security and Medicare. The dairy industry estimates that half of US farms rely on immigrant labor to put produce and dairy products in our grocery stores.[3]

Returning to Our National Values

Yet these new Americans' full contribution has not yet been tapped, due to our broken system. To avoid the threat of deportation, they are forced to live underground. Unscrupulous employers can and frequently do take advantage of this situation, opting to pay sweatshop wages—or not pay at all—because they know these workers have no recourse under the law.

While attempts to right this situation have fallen victim to partisan bickering and ideological arguments, we have too often witnessed the ills brought by misguided efforts to enforce the laws under our current broken system. In May 2008, federal officials conducted the largest immigration raid in US history at a meat-packing plant in Postville, Iowa. Nearly 400 workers—more than a third of the plant's employees and almost ten percent of the town's population—were taken into custody. The aftermath was akin to that of a natural disaster. Businesses were shuttered, including the meat-packing plant. Churches were empty. Half of the school system's 600 students were absent. And families were torn apart.

Policies that allow such actions are unnecessarily harsh and do not live up to our national values. Neither do laws like Arizona's S.B. 1070 and similar copycats, which single people out based on ethnic stereotyping and put cities and police departments at risk of significant and costly lawsuits. These efforts violate our cherished civil liberties and illustrate the America we *don't* want to become.

Protesters in Minneapolis, MN march on International Worker's Day, against immigration raids, deportation policies and the Arizona S.B. 1070 law.

Photos courtesy Fibonacci Blue (flickr)

345

Three generations of Mexican-American citizens stand together at a rally for immigration policy reform in the nation's capitol.

The Bigger Picture

While the frustration felt by many in Arizona and other states is understandable, a patchwork of draconian solutions will not solve our national problem. Those who focus on deportation and border fences are missing the bigger picture. Nearly 50 percent of undocumented individuals currently living in the United States came into the country legally, through a guarded port of entry, then overstayed their visas.[4] Yet between 1993 and 2005, US spending on border security tripled—and some legislators are calling for more.[5]

Likewise, mass deportation is not a realistic option. In 2010, a record 392,000 people were deported from the United States.[6] Even if that rate were maintained year after year, deporting 11 million undocumented immigrants would take nearly 30 years and cost over $200 billion.[7] More importantly, it would tear our nation and communities apart. These are people who work in American farms and factories, people who buy clothes and food for their families. In many cases, they are also people who have taxes deducted from each paycheck,

though they have no way to access that money later or get the full benefits of being taxpaying citizens. Removing them from the economy would reduce the US GDP by an estimated $2.6 trillion over just the next ten years.[8] And the human impact on families and neighborhoods would be staggering.

Our immigration system is broken, and Americans are hungry for solutions—workable, comprehensive solutions that address the entire problem. Above all, Americans value fairness. When asked, the majority of those polled said they would favor a solution in which undocumented individuals are put on a path to citizenship if they agree to learn English, pay a fine and pay back any taxes they owe the US government.[9] That's a solution that works.

And in addition to reflecting our values, integration of the existing 11 million undocumented immigrants would bring in an additional $66 billion of revenue from income and payroll taxes as well as various administrative fees.[10] If there were ever a time for actions that

In 2010, a record

392,000 people were deported from the United States

Even if this rate were maintained **year after year,**

deporting

11 million

undocumented immigrants

would take

28 years

and cost over

$200 billion

bolster the US economy, that time is now. Continuing to sacrifice America's values and economic opportunities, solely for the sake of partisan bickering and ideological posturing, benefits no one but the politicians.

Though fixing our broken immigration system at the federal level would be the most efficient approach, there are a number of proactive steps that state legislatures can take to integrate immigrants living in their communities. Affordable courses for English-language learners typically have long waiting lists and are in need of funding. Wage and hour laws should be enforced for all workers, not just those with documentation. And implementing policies that limit police inquiry into immigration status, especially when working with a victim or witness to a crime, improves public safety for all.

Despite the negative rhetoric that has controlled the debate around immigration and held us back from national progress, there are civic and political leaders who understand the benefit of recognizing the reality of immigration, as well as the many contributions immigrants make and the value of integrating them into the fabric of society. Those who want to see positive change in our country must make their voices heard. Only when Washington hears a chorus of Americans demanding real, effective, values-based solutions will the bickering end and the action begin. We cannot afford to wait any longer.

. . . . .

Alan Jenkins is executive director of The Opportunity Agenda (http://opportunityagenda.org), a communications, research and policy organization dedicated to building the national will to expand opportunity for all. His previous positions have included director of human rights at the Ford Foundation, assistant to the Solicitor General at the US Department of Justice and associate counsel to the NAACP Legal Defense and Educational Fund, Inc. Jenkins has also taught law at Brooklyn Law School and clerked for Supreme Court Justice Harry A. Blackmun and US District Court Judge Robert L. Carter. He holds a JD from Harvard Law School, an M.A. in Media Studies from New School University and a B.A. in psychology and social relations from Harvard College.

Reforming Prisons
Saving Billions
Creating Opportunity

Nastassia Walsh
and Tracy Velázquez
Justice Policy Institute

Sadly, "the land of the free" has become the land of the imprisoned for millions of Americans. The United States has by far the highest incarceration rate in the world.[1] While we have just 5 percent of the world's population, the United States holds 25 percent of the world's prisoners. There are currently more than 2.3 million people locked up in US prisons and jails, and the numbers continue to increase. The number of people in US prisons has increased 275 percent over the last 25 years.[2] It will take dramatic change in the way the US reacts to crime and social problems in order to turn around our current state. We as a nation need to come to terms with our national impulse to try to solve our social problems with more and more iron bars.

There are several reasons for the dramatic increase in the number of people imprisoned over the last 25 years, but one area that cannot be convincingly attributed to growing prison populations is crime. Prison populations grow when crime is up, and they grow when crime is down. Bruce Western at Harvard University recently found that only 10 percent of the crime decline in the 1990s was due to increased use of incarceration.[3] Some states lowered their incarceration rates and still experienced a drop in crime.[4] New York, for example, lowered its incarceration rate by 15 percent while experiencing a 33 percent drop in crime. And Maryland's crime rate fell 5 percent at a time when they lowered their incarceration rate by 24 percent. Such uneven results do not support continued over-reliance on incarceration.

New York lowered its incarceration rate by 15% while experiencing a 33% drop in crime, and Maryland's crime rate fell 5% at a time when they lowered their incarceration rate by 24%.

The poor and communities of color are the most severely impacted by US incarceration policies. African-American adults are 4 times as likely as whites and nearly 2.5 times as likely as Hispanics to be under correctional control.[5] One out of every nine young black men is currently behind bars.[6] Disparate policing practices, access to council, treatment before the courts and availability of drug treatment are some of the factors that contribute to this disproportionality.[7] Incarceration breaks up families and disrupts communities, creating a cycle that is reinforced by an unequal allocation of resources that create meaningful employment and educational opportunities.

In addition to the lack of proportional public safety benefits from increased incarceration, this burgeoning correctional system costs taxpayers over $74 billion per year. Some states, like California, are spending more on their corrections systems than they spend on higher education.[8] California now spends over $10 billion on its corrections system and provides only $1.6 billion to its public university system.[9] While there was a time when rehabilitation and services were part of the correctional system, many states have all but done away with these programs due to shifts in philosophy and budget cuts. Without these programs, fewer people are able to be successful after serving time in prison: in fact, two

in three people released from state prison will be rearrested for a new offense within three years.[10]

With 95 percent of the people in prison returning to the community someday,[11] it is to the benefit of individuals, families and public safety to ensure that they make a successful transition.

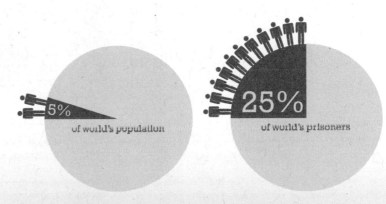

5% of world's population

25% of world's prisoners

While we have just 5 percent of the world's population, the United States holds 25 percent of the world's prisoners.

There are now more than

2.3 million

people locked up in US prisons and jails

2010

2000

1990

1980

The number of people in prisons has increased

275%

over the past 25 years.

The correctional system costs Americans over **$74 billion** per year

Some states are spending more on their corrections systems than they spend on higher education. California now spends over $10 billion on its corrections system and provides only $1.6 billion to its public university system.

Providing Treatment and Services in the Community Can Improve Public Safety

With the "war on drugs," society has moved from a largely public health approach for treatment of substance abuse to one of law enforcement. Individuals with substance abuse problems have become a significant percentage of the prison population. Police have more resources to proactively seek out people involved with illegal substances. These factors have led to a dramatic increase in the prison population over the last 30 years. Now, more than a quarter of prisoners are incarcerated for drug offenses alone.

Numerous studies have shown that providing substance abuse and mental health treatment, employment and education in the community are more effective at improving public safety and life outcomes for individuals than incarceration. The Washington State Institute for Public Policy estimates that for every dollar spent on drug treatment in the community the state receives more than $18 in benefits in terms of reduced crime—more than three times the benefits of providing treatment inside prison.[12] Yet states continue to put the lion's share of this type of funding into systems of corrections that have not been shown to be the most effective way to improve public safety.

Reforming Parole Can Improve Safety and Save Money

There is an enormous benefit to allowing people to live in the community, contribute to that community and participate in family life,[13] but fewer people now are being released to parole than are being admitted to prison. Increased utilization of parole for individuals who are no longer deemed a risk to public safety is a readily available way to reduce prison populations quickly and safely. However, as the current system operates, most parole systems are in the business of supervision, not providing services and resources necessary to help people succeed as they are leaving prison. For this reason, 27 percent of people released on parole will be returned to prison on a technical violation—that is, something that isn't a new crime but violates their conditions of parole, such as missing appointments or not paying fees.[14]

Ideally, parole should be a way to provide resources and support for people who are returning from prison and trying to be productive members of their community. Reducing the number of people returned to prison on technical violations could save states millions of dollars annually. At an annual average cost of around $23,000 per person,[15] prison is a costly endeavor compared to a

---

The Washington State Institute for Public Policy estimates that for every dollar spent on drug treatment in the community, the state receives more than $18 in benefits in terms of reduced crime—more than **three times the benefits** of providing treatment inside prison.

maximum of about $4,000 for people on parole.[16] Reforming the agenda of parole systems to one of support and services could save states millions by keeping people in the community, while improving public safety and individual life outcomes.

Doing it Better in Maryland

One example of such reform is Maryland's Proactive Community Supervision (PCS) program, a pilot program with quantifiable results that is being brought up to scale statewide. With the PCS program, parole agents are in a more cooperative, service-oriented role, rather than merely a role of supervision. A case plan is developed for each person on parole, which identifies potential triggers for participation in illegal behavior. A risk assessment instrument is used to determine appropriate levels of supervision and support and helps identify ways in which to best support people who might be at higher risk of rearrest. Visits with people on parole are based on the performance of the person on parole, rather than an arbitrary or preset level of supervision or number of visits. People on parole who participated in this program were less

likely to be arrested for a new offense (32 percent vs 41 percent) and less likely to violate their parole (20 percent vs 29 percent). The services that PCS provides decrease the chances that a person will return to prison, but also reconnect people during the often difficult transition back into the community.

Reducing the Need for More Prisons in Kansas

In 2007, Kansas approved criminal justice legislation with the potential to significantly reduce the projected need for additional prison beds. This legislation included the creation of a performance-based grant program for community corrections to reduce parole revocations by 20 percent and restore earned good-time credits for good behavior for individuals incarcerated for non-violent offenses, so that more people will be released on parole.[17] This change in the parole system is projected to save $80 million over the next five years in reduced capital and operating expenses, about $7 million of which will be reinvested in community corrections and substance abuse and vocational training programs.

Individuals preparing to be released from prison attend a graduation ceremony after completing a technical education apprenticeship program.

Photo courtesy California Department of Corrections and Rehabilitation

351

States with the highest percentage of high school graduates have the lowest crime rates.

Minnesota and Utah have the highest percentages of high school graduates and have violent crime rates **nearly half** the US average.

States like Connecticut and Illinois, which increased their higher education spending by over 30%, saw a **15% drop** in the violent crime rate over a five year period.

Making an Early Investment Can Save Money in the Long Term

Making smart investments in communities and social institutions is the most effective way of improving public safety and supporting communities. Research shows that states that spend more on education have lower crime rates than states that spend less.[18] States with higher levels of education attainment, where the largest percentage of their population has at least a high school diploma, have the lowest violent crime rates. Minnesota and Utah have the highest percentages of high school graduates in the country and have violent crime rates nearly half the US average. In addition, states like Connecticut and Illinois, which in-

money saved on prisons, states could put more money into education and employment skills, while also funding community-based services for both youth and adults that have been proven to be effective.

While there is no single answer for solving states' public safety challenges, it is clear that attempting to spend our way to public safety via more "cops, courts and corrections" is not the type of comprehensive strategy that is needed to protect public safety. This strategy will only continue to bloat US prisons and perpetuate the racial disparities now associated with the criminal justice system. We should instead seek effective alternative methods to dealing with social problems that promote public safety, strengthen com-

> The Alliance for Excellent Education reported that a 5 percent increase in male high school graduation rates would produce an **annual savings of almost $5 billion in crime-related expenses.**

creased their higher education spending by over 30 percent, saw dramatic reductions in their crime rates: a 15 percent drop in their violent crime rate over five years.[19] The Alliance for Excellent Education reported that a 5 percent increase in male high school graduation rates would produce an annual savings of almost $5 billion in crime-related expenses.[20] With the

munities through prevention and educational services and improve the way we support people returning to the community. This more comprehensive strategy is good for people, good for communities and good for the overall well being and safety of our country.

. . . . .

Tracy Velázquez is JPI's executive director. A passionate advocate and committed progressive, she was recently a senior program associate at the Vera Institute of Justice's Center on Sentencing and Corrections. She holds a bachelor of arts degree from Harvard University and a master's of public administration degree from Montana State University.

Nastassia Walsh is JPI's research manager. In her five years at JPI, she has worked on a number of criminal and juvenile justice issues and advocated for reform at the local, state and federal level. She began working at JPI after earning her master's degree in forensic psychology from Marymount University and her bachelor of science in psychology and justice studies at Arizona State University.

Waging Peace

eleven

A look at the numbers...

The US accounts for **43% of total global military expenditures** annually, which is more than 7 times what China spends, the next biggest spender.

Global Military Expenditures

US 43%

50%

Percentage less Britain and France spend per capita than the US on their military budgets, while still maintaining robust and able military forces with the most modern equipment.

$1 trillion

Amount that could be saved over 10 years by implementing the Sustainable Defense Task Force's recommended spending cuts.

The US maintains over 800 military bases and outposts around the world, **with a total price tag of $102 billion annually.**

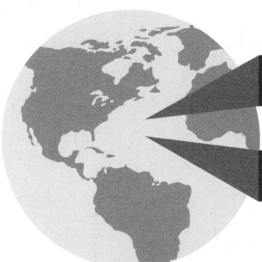

Worldwide, the US has:

800 military bases and outposts

Costing over:

$102 billion annually

392

Number of US bases and outposts located in Japan and Germany, countries with their own modern militaries.

200–300

Number of military bases that Donald Rumsfeld acknowledged that could easily be closed, saving at least $12 billion annually.

The **unemployment rate for veterans aged 18 to 24 is 21.1%,** compared to 16.6% for that age group as a whole.

21.1%   **Unemployment Rate for VETERANS aged 18–24**

16.6%   **Unemployment Rate for ALL 18–24 year olds**

The federal government is starting to help... **25%** Percentage of new hires in 2010 that were veterans. 8% of new hires were disabled veterans.

Between 2001 and 2010, there were more than **7,000 US military fatalities** and an estimated **150,000 civilians were killed** in Iraq and Afghanistan.

Iraq and Afghanistan Fatalities
Between 2001 and 2010

7,000
US Military

150,000
Civilians

76 years

Length of time that the concept of a federal Department of Peace has been considered, with more than 90 pieces of legislation introduced during that time.

71

Current members of the US House of Representatives who support the creation of a Department of Peace.

During his farewell speech to the nation, Republican President and Five-star General Dwight Eisenhower spoke sobering words warning the public of the "unwarranted influence, whether sought or unsought, by the military-industrial complex." He saw the horrors of war, its effects on soldiers and innocent people, and he knew the tradeoffs that exist when we build up our military war chest at the expense of priorities like education and taking care of those in need. Although spoken over 50 years ago, his words ring true today as the United States maintains nearly 800 military bases around the globe and account for over 40 percent of global military expenditures (even though we represent 5 percent of the global population).

Albert Einstein said that peace cannot be kept by force; it can only be acheived through understanding. His words paint a picture of possibility that can inspire us to...

Come to terms with and change our societal acceptance of war

Create a military budget that is **in line** with those of other developed nations

Re-allocate resources to provide more opportunity for veterans and invest in **critical domestic priorities**

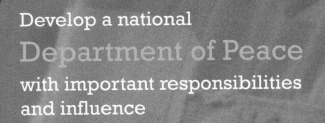

Develop a national **Department of Peace** with important responsibilities and influence

Expand peaceful approaches to conflict in schools, communities and international relations

Do what it takes to lead the world in eliminating all nuclear weapons within years, not decades

War and **Ending It**

I always knew I would join the military. It was simply a matter of choosing the Marines or the Army. Growing up in the shadow of Fort Bragg and Fort Lee, in North Carolina and Virginia, I was highly influenced by the presence of the soldiers. I saw them everyday. Not just your regular run-of-the mill soldiers, Bragg is home of the Green Berets—the real John Waynes. In my mother's house we were taught God, Family and Country. These beliefs guided me to crave and need to serve. I still have the need to serve, but now I see that there is no place for war and I serve to bring humanity to a peaceful coexistence.

As military service goes, mine was relatively uneventful. I spent time in the Army Reserve as an enlisted man and, after Reserve Officer Training Corps (ROTC), as an active duty officer. I served in combat during what many know as the 1st Gulf War; Operations Desert Shield and Desert Storm in the 3rd of the 41st Artillery Battalion of the 24th Mechanized Infantry Division. But I was blessed not

Michael T. McPhearson
Veterans For Peace

"There is no way to peace; peace is the way."
→ A.J. Muste

360

to have experienced the true horrors of war. I did not kill first-hand. I did not see the aftermath of a firefight, or the consequences of my battalion's artillery shells. I contributed to the deaths of tens of thousands of Iraqis, some in a more direct manner than others. But it was from a distance and impersonal. For every US combat solider on the ground, there is a system of troops providing a host of services working together to destroy and kill. That is war; stark and naked violence.

Why Do We Walk the Road to War?

Of course there are the practical reasons why wars happen, to gain access to resources and to protect one's homeland. There are the base motivations of power and greed that drive what many call "the ruling class" who lead us to war. There is the belief that the patriarchal system is the fundamental building block for the social and political forces driving us to war. But none of these explain in full what allows humans to gather in large groups and attempt to kill each other.

I believe humans have a natural aversion to killing each other that must be overcome to participate in war. There is a process that conditions us to accept war. This process plays on a number of our basic instincts and uses our complex social and political systems to help us agree to war. There are three components to this process: the warrior myth, the creation of an encompassing identity myth and dehumanization of "the other." One can take this process and overlay it on most any conflict between groups and see it at work, but let us look at the US to see why we walk the road to war.

The Creation of the Warrior

The creation of the warrior begins when we are children. Boys are taught that combat is the ultimate test of manhood. The female inclusive version teaches us that war

tests our mettle; our mental toughness and our ability to succeed. "Be All You Can Be," "An Army of One" and, today, "Army Strong" are self-esteem-building catch phrases that convey this message. With this in mind, we are given the toys to practice war; the slingshot, the plastic sword, the bow and arrow, the repeating cap guns and machine guns with authentic sound. We are taught to play the role of the warrior with miniature replicas of combatants; a hundred green men to a bag or the multi-colored cowboys and Indians. The GI Joes, Transformers and various video simulations make the act of war possibly fun, exciting and tempting.

Still this is not enough to build a warrior. It takes more than toys and the TV screen. I believe a basic instinct of the human mind is to have a sense of meaning. Our

The US was born in a struggle for liberation, thus creating a national character of a people who hold in the highest regard the ideal of freedom, and war is accepted as a means to attain it.

Photo courtesy Jez Coulson

361

Since the American Revolutionary War, the US has been involved in nearly **two dozen wars** that have resulted in millions of casualties.

society reinforces the acts we learn at play by giving the function of a warrior meaning. The purpose of the warrior is to serve. It is the opportunity to commit the most altruistic act; to make the ultimate sacrifice. The soldier is prepared to give one's life for family, tribe or country. This is the base of the ideal warrior. Called to serve and prepared to give all for little or nothing in return.

War as Part of Our Identity

The warrior's purpose is to protect the larger group. However, warriors do not go to war alone. A nation goes to war. The warrior must see the larger group or the protection of it worth the service and possible ultimate sacrifice. The group must believe itself worth the possible death of the warrior so that it will send its sons and daughters to the horrors of war. This meaning is provided by the identity myth. Every nation develops a narrative that provides an identity to its people. This identity binds the group members together and, on whole, demands a subservience to the will of the group for the glory of the group. The United States was

born in a struggle for liberation thus creating a national character of a people who hold in the highest regard the ideal of freedom and the acceptance of war as a means to attain it. Because this is so engrained in our national fabric, those that question the road to war are branded unpatriotic.

Dehumanization and the Creation of "the Other"

War is the ultimate example of dehumanization. In the rhetoric espoused before wars, the enemy is juxtaposed with the image and values of this myth and is always found wanting, alien and evil. Evil places the enemy beyond salvation and allows for easier dismissal of the killing of both the enemy combatants and innocent civilians. The deaths of millions are worth the sacrifice of ensuring that our manifest destiny is fulfilled. In my estimation, the creation and dehumanization of "the other" is the heart of why people are able to participate in war: "I, the warrior, must defend my group, my myth against you, the evil other. You are not

While it is true that there are millions of armed soldiers ready to do battle across the planet, **there are also hundreds of thousands of organizations around the world with millions of people diligently working to bring about a vision of human cooperation.**

Photo courtesy World March for Peace and Nonviolence

Our most basic task as peacemakers and justice seekers is to cut through the politics of the moment with the undeniable truth of our common humanity.

Photo courtesy Christy Dow-Briggs

like me. You never will be and if there is a possibility of change it must be through violent redemption."

The Path of Peace

I believe that to travel the path of peace our efforts must work to accomplish many things, but the first is to end the use of war as a means to solve conflicts. I believe this task, which is also the mission of Veterans For Peace, is most central to achieving peace. The absence of war does not constitute peace. However, while I am not sure what peace looks like, I know there cannot be peace in the presence of war.

There is a growing world consciousness via religion, science and philosophy recognizing the unity of humanity. Herein lays a portion of a strategic framework to build a world free of war. We must clear away the artificial walls that lead to hate, indifference and greed. We must do this work both in domestic and international settings. Most crucial, we must do this work in our personal lives and spheres of influence. We need to engage in activities that connect people in efforts to help us to accept differences and highlight our common humanity. These actions also build a sense of a collective destiny, therefore undermining the human tendency to wage war. These challenge individual societal identity myths and replace them with the truth of our human identity. Peace requires fundamental transformations. In how we see ourselves and others and peace, as an ideal, needs to be elevated and integrated into every facet of society and strategically planned for and resourced.

While it is true that there are millions of armed soldiers ready to do battle across the planet, there are also hundreds of thousands of organizations around the world with millions of people diligently working to bring about a vision of human cooperation. Most soldiers, just like most people, at their core want this too. Our most basic task as peacemakers and justice seekers is to cut through the politics of the moment with the undeniable truth of our common humanity so that over time a majority can see that it is in our universal interest as humans to live in a world free of war. Then we will begin to see what peace really looks like.

......

Michael T. McPhearson is the former executive director of Veterans For Peace (www.veteransforpeace. org) and is co-convenor of United For Peace and Justice (www.unitedforpeace.org). He is a native of Fayetteville, North Carolina and was a field artillery officer in the 24th Mechanized Infantry Division during Desert Shield / Desert Storm, also known as Gulf War I. McPhearson joined the Army Reserve in 1981 as an enlisted soldier at the age of 17 and attended basic training the summer between his junior and senior high school years. He is a ROTC graduate of Campbell University in Buies Creek, North Carolina with a BS degree in sociology. His military career includes six years of reserve and five years active duty service. He separated from active duty in 1992 as a captain. During his time in the Army he held numerous positions, attended Airborne School and received several awards.

Reallocating Military Spending, **Taking Care of Soldiers,** & Increasing National Security

T he saying goes, "Rome was not built in a day." It did not fall in one day either. An economic, cultural and military powerhouse, the Roman Empire once seemed unassailable, permanent and omnipotent. Confident in their enduring supremacy, emperors pushed expansion, putting more gold into spears, fleets and cavalries while neglecting the day-to-day needs of their subjects, which led to the fall of the Roman Empire according to historians.

Today the US is the world's sole superpower, enjoying huge economic and cultural sway, with interests and influence in every corner of the globe. Our military might is unparalleled. However, as history shows, in time a rising nation becomes preoccupied with national security, diverting profit into war and preparations for war. Economic strength wanes, industrial capacity atrophies and the great power falls. George Washington once said, "Overgrown military establishments are, under any form of government, inauspicious to liberty, and are to be regarded as particularly hostile to republican liberty." Our own "liberty" is in danger, and we must learn from history, instead of repeating mistakes of the past. This begins with acknowledging the imbalance of resources invested in the military, broadening the definition of "security" and reallocating some of these resources to better support the strength of our nation.

Frida Berrigan
New America Foundation

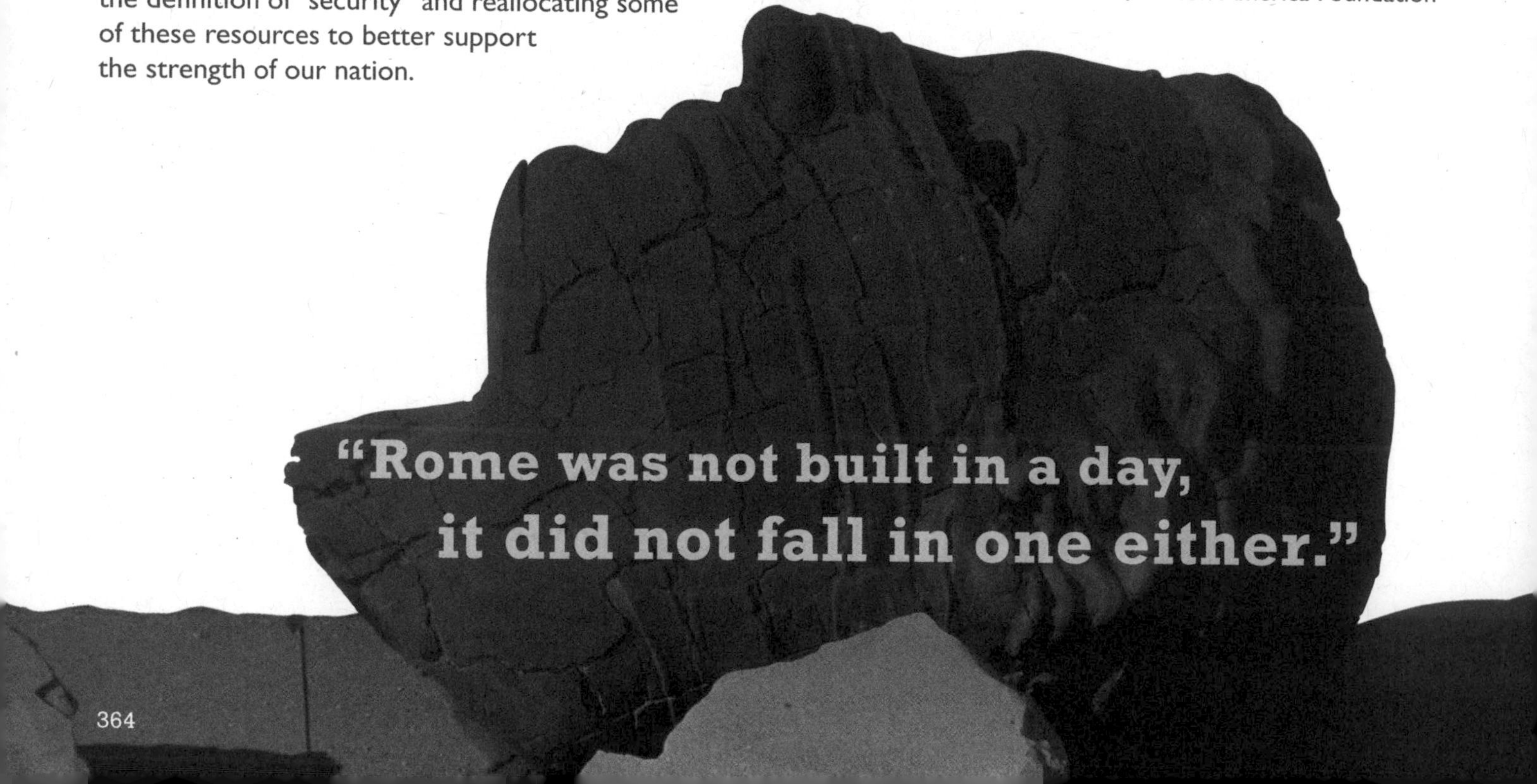

"Rome was not built in a day, it did not fall in one either."

Out of Step: US Military Budget

The US' 2010 military budget was over $690 billion, including funding for military personnel, research and development, new weapons procurement, as well as operations and maintenance. Also included in this figure is $128 billion for military operations in Iraq, Afghanistan and elsewhere. Of the $690 billion military budget, 87 percent of it goes to defense spending while only 8 percent for Homeland Security and 5 percent for preventative measures. For comparison, in 2010 the federal government spent $108 billion on services for veterans, $93 billion on education, $23 billion on community and regional development and $19 billion on foreign aid.[1]

To understand these huge numbers, it is helpful to look at the US military budget within the context of the rest of the world. The US outspends China, the next biggest military power, almost seven times over. According to the Stockholm International Peace Research Institute, global military expenditures passed $1.6 trillion in 2010. When the costs of US military operations were added to the defense budget, US spending was nearly half of the global total.[2]

Many individuals and organizations are advocating for spending reductions, including the Sustainable Defense Task Force, a newly formed ad hoc advisory panel. Commissioned by a bipartisan group of five congressional representatives, the Task Force outlines nearly $1 trillion in cuts to defense spending through 2020. The 16-member panel of individuals from non-profits, non-governmental organizations, think tanks and a private college identified measures that remove inefficiencies and redundancies within the Pentagon's budget. The strategy is intended to convince Congress and the deficit reduction commission to include a reduction in military spending among the solutions for the nation's rising budget deficit and debt.[3]

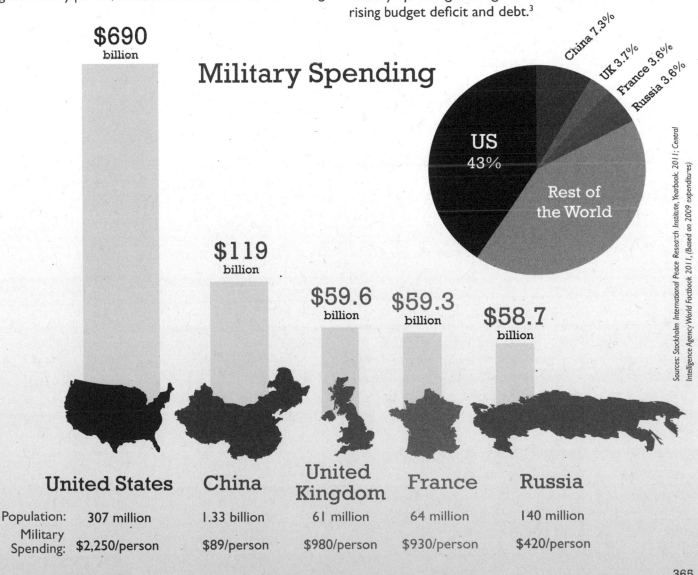

Military Spending

$690 billion

$119 billion

$59.6 billion

$59.3 billion

$58.7 billion

China 7.3%
UK 3.7%
France 3.6%
Russia 3.6%

US 43%

Rest of the World

Sources: Stockholm International Peace Research Institute, Yearbook 2011; Central Intelligence Agency World Factbook 2011, (Based on 2009 expenditures)

	United States	China	United Kingdom	France	Russia
Population:	307 million	1.33 billion	61 million	64 million	140 million
Military Spending:	$2,250/person	$89/person	$980/person	$930/person	$420/person

Two Military Budgets in One: The Legacy of the Military Industrial Complex

The US military budget is two military budgets rolled into one: one for national security, the other for industry. Despite the fact that the Cold War ended in 1991, tens of billions of dollars in outdated, irrelevant and expensive systems—ballistic missile defense, trident submarines and ships such as the Zumwalt class destroyers ($3.9 billion per ship)—remain barnacled in the budget, bloating it to such an extent that it eclipses a host of other priorities that are central to the notion of security.[4]

The DDG-1000 Zumwalt Class Destroyer, a $3.5 billion ship conceived during the Cold War, isn't relevant to our national security strategy any longer.

plenty of money left over for a strong social safety net, generous pensions, enviable health care and a modern infrastructure. The US spends over $2,200 per man, woman and child on the military while budgets for education, housing, health and infrastructure repair barely keep up with the rate of inflation.

Reallocating the US military budget could make us more secure as a nation. If half of the military budget was reallocated to provide more benefits to veterans and to pay for other domestic needs, for example, the US would still have the largest military budget in the world three times over. But, we would also have the funds to invest in the education and even better services and opportunities for veterans, infrastructure and building a green and sustainable energy platform, which would ultimately create hundreds of thousands of well-paying jobs to power prosperity and ingenuity into the 21st century.

How do we get there from here? There are concrete ways to revise the size and mission of the US military that will make us more stable and secure as a nation and, at the same time, add new resources to invest in national revitalization.

Reduce US Military Operations Abroad:

Between 2001 and 2010, the US

> **These Cold War–era systems endure not because they are critical to national security but because of the influence from the weapons industry.**

These Cold War–era systems endure not because they are critical to national security but because of the influence from the weapons industry. This warning was offered to the nation by two-term President and Five-star General, Dwight Eisenhower. In his 1961 farewell address, he stated, "In the councils of government, we must guard against the acquisition of unwarranted influence, whether sought or unsought, by the military-industrial complex. The potential for the disastrous rise of misplaced power exists and will persist."[5]

Reallocate the Military Budget to Increase National Security

Britain and France both spend about $1,000 per person on their military budgets, have robust and able military forces with the most modern equipment and

spent more than $1 trillion on military operations for the occupation of Iraq and Afghanistan. Looking forward through 2019, additional costs for continuing these wars could total as much as $867 billion.[6] These military operations have emptied the US treasury and resulted in thousands of war casualties, while the resulting increase in national security is questionable at best. Despite stabilization progress, remaining troops must be withdrawn, occupation ended and real reconstruction commenced in order to restore America's place in the world and ensure lasting peace.

Cut Back on Bases:

The US maintains military bases and outposts in more than 800 locations around the world, and the Pentagon spends about $102 billion a year to run these overseas bases (not including the facilities in Iraq or Afghanistan). More than half a century

The US' 2010 budget was $690 billion in military spending, over 7 times that of China, the next highest military spender.

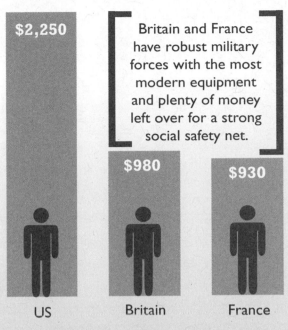

Britain and France have robust military forces with the most modern equipment and plenty of money left over for a strong social safety net.

$2,250

$980

$930

US   Britain   France

Military Spending per Person

after World War II and the Korean War, we still have 268 bases in Germany, 124 in Japan and 87 in South Korea.[7] Are they really necessary today? In 2004, Defense Secretary Donald Rumsfeld suggested shuttering about one-third of US overseas bases; a move he estimated would save $12 billion.

Nuclear Disarmament:
The US possesses about 5,200 nuclear warheads, and an estimated 1,000 of those are ready to launch at a moment's notice.[8] President Barak Obama presented his vision of nuclear disarmament to the world, saying, "I state clearly and with conviction America's commitment to seek the peace and security of a world without nuclear weapons." Since then, his administration has ratified important arms control treaties and engaged Russia in nuclear reductions.

As the Obama administration pursues this commitment to disarmament, billions of dollars will be available for building real security in the form of programs for jobs, education and opportunities for veterans and all citizens. In a Carnegie Endowment report, analysts estimated that nuclear weapons activities throughout the federal budget totaled at least $52 billion annually. Of this, only about $14 billion was for non-proliferation, waste clean-up and nuclear incident response.[9]

Eliminate Waste:
In a recent report on Pentagon weapons acquisition, the Government Accountability

The US spends over $2,200 per man, woman and child on the military while budgets for education, housing and health barely keep up with the rate of inflation.

Office identified $295 billion of cost overruns on 95 major weapons systems.[10] Some of which had doubled or tripled original cost estimates and were years behind schedule. Because of the way contracts are written, the Pentagon is still obligated to award billions of dollars' worth of performance bonuses to private contractors regardless of the results of their work. The Pentagon's procurement budget is about $100 billion annually, much of this going to weapons systems for the last or the next war, rather than systems relevant to today's security environment. Renovating this system so that it only purchases what it needs from manufacturers able to deliver a product on time and at budget is a huge undertaking—but without significant change, the Pentagon's purchasing will remain a form of socialized support for a military-industrial complex that has far too much influence.

The V-22 Osprey is a telling example. Although the program is being phased out, nearly two decades ago, then-Secretary of Defense Dick Cheney called the V-22

If we didn't waste **$295 billion** on weapons systems overruns we could:

Provide healthcare for the 42 million the 46 million Americans with no healthcare coverage.[1]

OR

Increase the average $40,500 salary of the 4,180,000 teachers in the US by 25%, and do so for approximately seven years.[2]

OR

Build enough wind turbines to power 52 million homes, which accounts for 40% of the country's home energy needs.[3]

And this is **not cutting a dime** from the military budget; it's simply sticking to the (already enormous) budget.

from the editor

"a program I don't need," and cited it as one example of how Congress "forces me to spend money on weapons that don't fill a vital need in these times of tight budgets and new requirements."[11] An estimated $54 billion has been spent on the program since its inception even though the aircraft was reported to be unsafe, overpriced and completely inadequate.[12]

What's Our Mission? Redefining National Security:

Currently the US has a very broad and encompassing definition of what constitutes a threat to national security, but that must be scaled back so that US territory and significant interests can be robustly protected. Just because the US can project power to any corner of the globe, at any moment in time, should it do so? Carl Conetta of the Project for Defense Alternatives suggests that a more narrow and sustainable role for the US's armed forces would focus on "containing, deterring and defending against actual threats of violence to critical national interests."[13]

A New Blueprint: The Path Forward

These are just a few of the steps that we need to take to halve the US military budget and increase national security. But that is only part of the work. If the US military is smaller and has a more limited mission, what is the role of military personnel—especially given the fact that economic necessity and job scarcity have driven many men and women into the military?

The other part of charting a new path forward is caring for our veterans and building a stronger and more sustainable US economy. There are about 440,000 US military personnel stationed or deployed overseas right now. Of that number, almost half are engaged in combat operations and more than 30,000 have been wounded in action. As these men and women return from battlefields and bases around the world, they will need long-term care and services, and they will require jobs and stability.

The annual budget in 2010 for the Veterans Administrations (VA) was close to $108 billion. While that might sound like a lot of money, it equates to only about $4,700 per veteran—for health care, education, pension programs and job training.[14] Making an unequivocal commitment to veterans and their families by augmenting the budget and improving services is nothing more than fair compensation for their service.

Then there is the question of jobs for veterans. The unemployment rate for veterans aged 18 to 24 is almost 5 percent higher than for that age group as a whole. In addition to the recession, veterans groups attribute the high jobless rate to a lack of education, job experience and job training in the years before entering the service.[15]

Vocational training for veterans should focus on emerging industries that have the potential for well-paying jobs. For example, there are about 3,400 companies in the solar energy sector in the US, employing 60,000 people. The Solar Energy Industries Association is bullish about growth, estimating 110,000 direct solar jobs by 2016.[16] Policies supporting both renewable energy and jobs for veterans are in the very early stages,

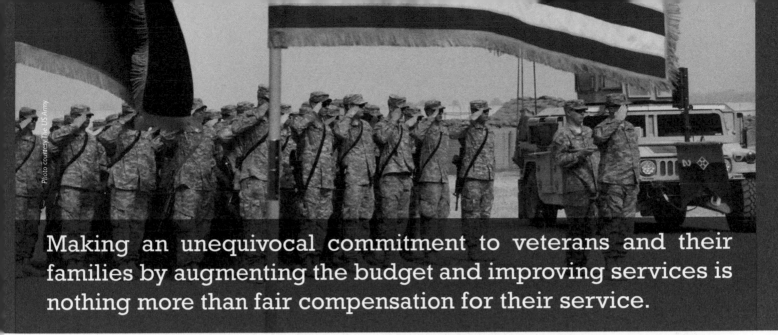

Making an unequivocal commitment to veterans and their families by augmenting the budget and improving services is nothing more than fair compensation for their service.

and the expansion of them could lead to more employment opportunities for veterans and a sustainable economy creating a new kind of national security, one with clean energy and good jobs.

The potential for jobs is vast, and Congress seems to agree. The new Energy Jobs for Veterans Act calls for the establishment of a pilot program to encourage the employment of eligible veterans in energy-related positions. Under the Veterans Energy-Related Employment Program, the Department of Labor will award competitive grants to three states for the establishment and administration of a state program to reward energy employers who employ eligible veterans.[17] Instituting this and other similar programs in every state in the nation would go a long way towards offering more opportunities for veterans in all areas of the US while benefiting the national economy.

In an effort to increase sustainable development and reduce our dependency on foreign oil, the Apollo Alliance proposes $10 billion in investments to develop and expand public transit systems and fund infrastructure repair on those systems, creating a total of 172,500 jobs in construction and repair work.[18] Retraining returning soldiers and Marines for jobs in public transit would offer union representation, a steady paycheck, job security and a visible and respectable job for men and women accustomed to collaborative work that is of service.

These are just a few ways in which money reallocated from the Pentagon can be invested with confidence for a high-yield gain. Clearly some progress is being made; through existing and new programs. A comprehensive strategy to reallocate money from the military budget will go a long way toward bolstering needs in education, foreign aid, infrastructure, healthcare and a range of other national priorities.

We know where we will end up if we follow the trajectory set by the military industrial complex of ever-rising military budgets and ever-new enemies: we will fall as Rome fell, as all great powers fall. But, we are also learning that there are new paths forward. With foresight and thrift, diplomacy and cooperation, the US can be a great and powerful nation, a strong and secure nation, an enduring and exemplary nation.

· · · · ·

Frida Berrigan is a consultant with the Arms and Security Initiative at the New America Foundation (www.newamerica.net). She is the author of reports on arms trade and human rights, US nuclear weapons policy and the domestic politics of US missile defense and space weapons policies.

Creating a World
Without Nuclear Weapons

David Krieger
Nuclear Age Peace Foundation

We are in the seventh decade of the Nuclear Age. With the capacity to destroy civilization and end life on the planet, more than 20,000 nuclear weapons remain in the arsenals of nine nuclear weapon states.

The United States and Russia head the list of countries with nuclear weapons, and together have more than 95 percent of the total on the planet. These two countries still maintain over 2,000 nuclear weapons on hairtrigger alert, ready to be fired within moments, raising concerns for accidental launches. The UK, France, China, Israel, India, Pakistan and North Korea hold the remaining 5 percent of nuclear weapons.

Nuclear weapons endanger the future of our species along with all other forms of life. The only safe and stable number of nuclear weapons on the planet is zero. Achieving zero will require political will, which in turn will require strong public support. It will also require an effective means to verify honesty. As Ronald Reagan, a nuclear abolitionist, said, "Trust, but verify."

Every year, on the anniversary of the Hiroshima atomic bombing there are memorials like this one seen at the A-Bomb Dome, the site of the bombing. They serve as a remembrance of the victims of Hiroshima and Nagasaki, and a reminder of what these very powerful weapons can do.

France
China
Israel
India
Pakistan
North Korea
United Kingdom

5%

95% US & Russia

Possession of Nuclear Weapons on Earth

The Limits of Deterrence

Weapons of mass annihilation have been used throughout the Nuclear Age to threaten retaliation. But the threat of retaliation, known as deterrence, is not defense. Nuclear deterrence is meaningless when it comes to terrorist groups, which, without territory, cannot be subject to retaliation. No matter how powerful a country's nuclear arsenal, it cannot deter a determined extremist group in possession of a nuclear weapon.

For deterrence to work, the country's leaders must believe in the intent, as well as the opponent's capacity, to retaliate. Without that belief, such a threat may be doubted or dismissed, rendering the deterrence effort useless. Deterrence also relies upon rationality, and history proves that all political leaders do not act rationally at all times.

> **The more countries that have nuclear weapons, the greater the danger that these weapons will be used by accident, miscalculation or design.**

Weapons of the Weak

Nuclear weapons may provide *perceived* security for a weaker country in relation to a stronger one. Iraq, Iran and North Korea were branded as an "axis of evil" in the early days of the Bush administration. The US then proceeded to attack Iraq on the false charge that it had a nuclear weapons program, overthrow its leadership and occupy the country. With North Korea, a country suspected of having a small arsenal of nuclear weapons, the US was much more cautious and engaged in negotiations. This sent the message to Iran that they would be more secure with a nuclear arsenal, which is surely not the message that the US wishes to send to the world.

Thought of as "military equalizers," nuclear weapons may make a country think twice about attacking. But this is a dangerous game of Russian roulette. And the more countries that have nuclear weapons, the greater the danger that these weapons will be used by accident, miscalculation or design.

Today's nuclear weapons, many times more powerful than those that obliterated Hiroshima and Nagasaki, have the capacity to destroy cities, countries, civilization, the human species and most life on our planet. As Mikhail Gorbachev has said, "It is my firm belief that

TSAR BOMBA (USSR)
50,000 Kilotons of TNT
(50 million tons)

Castle Bravo (USA)
15,000 Kilotons of TNT
(15 million tons)

Ivy Mike (USA)
10,400 Kilotons of TNT
(10.4 million tons)

Nagasaki: Fat Man
20-22 Kilotons of TNT
(20-22,000 tons)

Hiroshima: Little Boy
12-15 Kilotons of TNT
(12-15,000 tons)

**Today's nuclear weapons, many times more powerful
than those that obliterated Hiroshima and Nagasaki,
have the capacity to destroy cities, countries, civilizations,
the human species and most life on our planet.**

the infinite and uncontrollable fury of nuclear weapons should never be held in the hands of any mere mortal ever again, for any reason." Nuclear weapons could cause irreversible damage, not only to humanity and to the human future, but also to all life.

The Nuclear Non-Proliferation Treaty

The Nuclear Non-Proliferation Treaty (NPT) was signed in 1968 and entered into force in 1970. The NPT requires the nuclear weapon states that are parties to the treaty—the US, Russia (formerly Soviet Union), UK, France and China—to engage in good-faith negotiations for nuclear disarmament in return for other countries agreeing not to acquire nuclear weapons. Obviously, this agreement has not been kept. The number of nuclear weapons in the world grew from some 39,000 in 1968 to a high of over 70,000 in 1986, before coming down to some 20,000 today, still enough to destroy civilization many times over.

Many world leaders believe that the United States has been the principal obstacle to nuclear disarmament. Under the leadership of President Obama, the United States has been playing a more constructive role and

negotiated a new Strategic Arms Reductions Treaty (New START) with Russia. Under the treaty, which entered into force on February 5, 2011, each side must reduce the number of its deployed strategic warheads to 1,550 and the number of its deployed delivery vehicles to 700 by the year 2017. In actuality, due to counting rules and past reductions, neither side would have to eliminate large numbers of weapons to meet the new limits. But the treaty re-establishes a lapsed inspection regime and could be a foundation for deeper reductions later.[1]

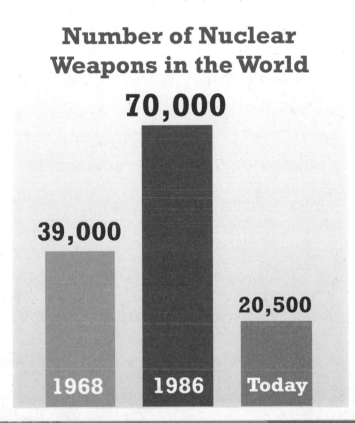

Number of Nuclear Weapons in the World

	70,000	
39,000		
		20,500
1968	1986	Today

President Barack Obama attends a New START meeting hosted by Vice President Joe Biden in the Roosevelt Room of the White House, Nov. 18, 2010.

> **Nuclear weapons are immoral weapons.... They are the enemy of humanity and the future, and we must rise up and make our voices heard for the total elimination of these weapons.**

Although it's not a pledge to zero, it is a small step in the right direction. However, the Nuclear Non-Proliferation Treaty refers to the peaceful uses of nuclear energy as an "inalienable right." This moves the world in the wrong direction in terms of nuclear proliferation and nuclear waste. Nuclear energy provides a pretext for the creation of fissile materials for nuclear weapons through uranium enrichment and plutonium reprocessing technologies. Once commerce is established in such bomb materials, the prospects of nuclear proliferation, even to terrorists, increase dramatically. In addition, there is still no good answer to the problem of nuclear waste, which will remain dangerous to human health and the environment for many times longer than human civilization has existed.

Changing Our Thinking

We need to shift our thinking if we are to confront the serious dangers to the human future posed by nuclear weapons. As Albert Einstein warned early in the Nuclear Age, "The unleashed power of the atom has changed everything save our modes of thinking, and thus we drift toward unparalleled catastrophe." The needed changes in thinking will require a major shift in our orientation toward nuclear weapons, in our willingness to imagine possible alternative futures and in our empathy for others.

Nuclear weapons are immoral weapons; they are not just another, albeit more powerful, weapon of war. They

Forty-seven heads of state gathered for the Nuclear Security Summit to discuss a plan for locking down nuclear materials.

Public domain photo courtesy Chuck Kennedy/White House Photographer

are the enemy of humanity and the future, and we must rise up and make our voices heard for the total elimination of these weapons. Countries with nuclear weapons must stop basing their security on the threat to annihilate vast numbers of innocent people.

The Need for Greater US Leadership

The United States, as the world's most powerful country, must lead in achieving a world free of nuclear weapons. In his speech in Prague on April 5, 2009, President Obama said, "...as a nuclear power—as the only nuclear power to have used a nuclear weapon—the United States has a moral responsibility to act. We cannot succeed in this endeavor alone, but we can lead it."[2]

To get to zero nuclear weapons in this lifetime, the leaders of the world's nations, particularly the leaders of nuclear weapon states, need to agree upon the phased elimination of all nuclear weapons, with provisions for effective verification and enforcement.

On the 60th anniversary of the atomic bombing of Hiroshima, rallies and demonstrations around the world encouraged the ban of nuclear weapons and a peaceful way forward together.

To get to zero nuclear weapons, the leaders of nuclear weapon states need to agree upon the phased elimination of all nuclear weapons, with provisions for effective verification & enforcement.

Each generation has a responsibility to pass the world on intact to the next generation. Those of us alive today are challenged as never before to accomplish this. Technological achievement does not necessarily make us stronger. It may simply make us more vulnerable, and our old ways of thinking may seal our fate. The alternative to waiting for another nuclear catastrophe to occur is to join with others who are committed to assuring a human future, and act to rid the world of this most menacing of all human inventions. It is the power of ordinary people working in concert that has the potential to move political leaders to effective action. It is this power that must be mobilized on behalf of ridding the world of nuclear weapons.

. . . . .

David Krieger is a founder of the Nuclear Age Peace Foundation (www.wagingpeace.org) and has served as its president since 1982. He is a leader in the global effort to abolish nuclear weapons. Among the books he has written or edited are Nuclear Weapons *and the* World Court *(with Ved Nanda),* At the Nuclear Precipice: Catastrophe or Transformation? *(with Richard Falk) and* The Challenge of Abolishing Nuclear Weapons.

Establishing a
US Department of Peace

Matthew Albracht
The Peace Alliance

"**I** cannot tell you with what weapons mankind would fight WW3, but I can assure you that WW4 would be fought with sticks and stones."

⟩ Albert Einstein

At the center of the human spirit there is a great longing for peace. During this moment in our history, it is becoming imperative that we invest and prioritize in the work that can help bring about more of the peace we all desire. The possibilities of manifesting it, in contrast to the consequences of continuing down the current course of rampant violence, are both enormous. Thankfully, the heroic work and practices of the growing field of peacebuilding offer a prescription for our times, one that could make the great dream a reality.

> The creation of a Department of Peace will augment our current problem-solving options, providing **practical, nonviolent solutions** to the problems of domestic and international conflict.

The Challenge We Face

From the personal to the collective, violence, in all its forms, has been the greatest and most devastating struggle we have ever faced. Current levels of violence in our nation and around the world are fiscally, environmentally and ethically unsustainable. There are a myriad of great challenges around the issue of violence in our homes, communities and world.

From the growing rate of domestic incarceration, to the crippling problems of community, school and gang violence, to conflict in our homes, relationships and at work, to the ravages of international conflict and war there is much to be addressed. Consider just a few sobering statistics:

• A World Health Organization report estimates the cost of interpersonal violence in the US at $300 billion per year, excluding war-related costs.[1]

• US youth homicide and suicide rates are more than ten times that of other leading industrial nations. Homicide is the second leading cause of death for youth ages 12 to 24, and the number one cause for African American youth.[2]

• During the 20th century, more than 100 million people lost their lives to war—most were non-combatants.[3]

We can longer continue down this unsustainable path.

The Possibility

Hope is not only on the horizon, it's here now. Over the last few decades, we have begun to see the field and work of peacebuilding more strongly materialize. Its impact is helping to foster more peaceful solutions in many arenas of challenge we face. We are seeing a sophisticated, pragmatic, proven-effective, economically sustainable set of practices and models emerge that already are and can more greatly make a profound difference toward a more sustainable peace.

And yet the gap between what is possible and what is actually our collective priority is wide. We need to am-

What would the Department of Peace do?

Domestically:

Develop policies and allocate resources to reduce the levels of domestic and gang violence, child abuse and various other forms of societal discord.

Internationally:

Advise the president and Congress on the most sophisticated ideas and techniques regarding peace-creation among nations.

A memorial to John Lennon from Yoko Ono, the Imagine Peace Tower is a beam of light projected from stone structure bearing the words "imagine peace" in 24 languages. Located near Reykjavik, Iceland, the tower shines for two months every year—October 9 through December 8, the dates of John Lennon's birth and death.

plify the already growing choir that is leading the charge to make this work a national and international priority. We must make solutions to violence a part of our collective everyday understanding and to help take programs to scale. If this burgeoning field of peacebuilding is to become what it needs to be, we must help catalyze and galvanize a movement behind it and create much stronger systems and infrastructure to support it.

Federal Infrastructure:
Department of Peace

We currently do not have within the US government structures or priorities to make the kind of impact we desire. As a country, we have yet to place institutional heft behind efforts to address the underlying issues of violence, diminishing their psychological force before they erupt into material conflict.

One solution to addressing the challenges we face would be through the establishment of the US Department of Peace. Whether it is a federal department, or other large-scale structure that will work to organize and prioritize the work of peacebuilding, we must seriously invest in peace infrastructure if we are to make the changes necessary to turn the tide. Along with reinforcing nonviolence as an ongoing value in our society, the creation of a Department of Peace would augment our current problem-solving options, providing practical, nonviolent solutions to the problems of domestic and international conflict.

Photo courtesy Seeds of Peace, flickr

"By avoiding the contentious politics of official international cooperation, private citizens can often accomplish more than diplomats."

Citizen Diplomacy: Everyday People are Building Peace Across Borders

Foreign diplomacy has long been among the most elaborate, formal and inaccessible functions of government.

In an increasingly globalized world, however, politically active citizens are throwing this historical model of international relations out the window, often with full approval of the Departments of State and Defense. By avoiding the contentious politics of official international cooperation, private citizens can often accomplish more than diplomats.

Journalist John Wallach gathered together 45 Israeli, Palestinian and Egyptian teenagers in 1993 and sent them to a youth leadership camp in Maine. Away from the conflict and constantly interacting with their peers, the young people quickly came to make friends with "the enemy." Wallach named the camp Seeds for Peace, and his project made headlines when all the campers attended the signing of the Oslo Accords later that same year. Today Seeds of Peace has empowered over 4000 more young people from the Balkans, Cyprus, Afghanistan and numerous other conflict zones to lead the reconciliation process in their home countries.

Others go straight to the conflict zones themselves. In 2003, California dentist James Rolfe traveled to Afghanistan to provide a rural village with care. But Afghanistan had just 137 trained dentists in a population of 27 million, and Rolfe quickly discovered that peoples' needs far outpaced the amount of care he could provide. Shocked by this inadequacy, Rolfe started the Afghanistan Dental Relief Project, which has provided the Afghani people with over 120,000 pounds of dental supplies and a mobile training center to build capacity in rural villages.

The Fellowship of Reconciliation has used this approach since the 1920s, sending delegations to Europe in WWII to rescue Jews fleeing Nazism, to China, Vietnam, and the former Soviet Union during the Cold War, and to the Middle East today. Currently the Fellowship is focused on protecting protestors and non-violent revolutionaries in Iran. With small delegations of American citizens in the crowd, the Iranian military will be less likely to suppress peaceful protests with violence.

Most importantly citizen diplomacy promotes a global understanding that people around the world may have different values and ways of life, but will happily cooperate to build a better world when political tensions are pushed to the side.

from the editor

Peace Is a Strategy

Domestically, the Department of Peace will develop policies and allocate resources to reduce the levels of domestic and gang violence, child abuse and various other forms of societal discord. Internationally, the Department will advise the president and Congress on the most sophisticated ideas and techniques regarding peace-creation among nations.

A Department of Peace will be led by a secretary of peace, who will advise the president on peacebuilding needs, strategies and tactics for use domestically and internationally. The Department will create and expand upon proven domestic peacebuilding programs in our communities, such as nonviolent communication programs in public schools and mediation training for police, firefighters and other emergency services personnel. In partnership with our military service academies, the Department will train a faculty of peacebuilding experts who will analyze peacebuilding strategies, advise government and facilitate the training of peacebuilding for domestic and international service.

If we can avoid one war, end any war even one month sooner or reduce our need for criminal adjudication, investing in a Department of Peace or other large-scale infrastructure, will ultimately save the nation and the taxpayers money. A study by the Institute for Economics and Peace estimates that if the US had the same levels of peacefulness as Canada, then over 2.7 million additional jobs could be created while reducing state and federal government expenditures. This improved state of peacefulness would have a positive economic effect of around $361 billion per year.[4] Additionally programs that reduce juvenile delinquency and prison recidivism rates are expected to save us more than the entire Department will cost. Much greater investment in the work of prevention and intervention is an economic stimulus and a taxpayer savings measure.

The sole focus of a US Department of Peace will be to reduce and prevent violence. Thus it will augment and support other efforts such as the US Institute of Peace (USIP) by working proactively to provide nonviolent strategies and solutions to the many complex issues we face.

The USIP is doing powerful work internationally to expand the effective application of nonviolent conflict resolution. Unlike the plan for a Department of Peace, USIP has no mandate to do violence prevention work domestically. Although funded by the government, it operates much like any other nongovernmental organization and thus has no voice in policy creation. For the US to truly master nonviolent alternatives to dealing with conflict and crises, we need structures directly within our government's highest offices and agencies, as well as independent bodies, all working together to make peace a priority.

People gather in Maryland to show their support for the establishment of a Department of Peace.

> "It isn't enough to talk about peace. One must believe in it. And it isn't enough to believe in it. **One must work at it.**"
>
> ⟩ **Eleanor Roosevelt**

The idea for a cabinet-level Department of Peace is not a new one. Carrie Chapman Catt, the founder of the League of Women Voters, first publically suggested it in 1925. Senator Matthew M. Neely (D-West Virginia) introduced the first official legislation in 1935. Since then, legislation proposing the creation of a US Department of peace has been introduced nearly 100 times.

The ongoing movement is supported by several members of Congress, the late former *CBS Evening News* anchor Walter Cronkite and author Marianne Williamson. This movement has a list of bipartisan endorsements from city councils in California, Florida, Georgia, Illinois, Michigan, New Mexico and Ohio.

Internationally, campaigns for peace-oriented government departments are underway in 32 countries, including the United States, but only Costa Rica, Nepal and the Solomon Islands have been successful.[5]

Costa Rica's tradition of peace dates back to 1877, when the president abolished the death penalty. In 1948, Costa Rica became the first country to formally abolish its armed forces; its constitution still forbids a standing military. By law, peace education is offered in every school and the legal system encourages peaceful conflict resolution, such as mediation.[6]

Conflict Is Inevitable, Violence Is Not

Violence is one way to respond to conflict, and like virtually all behavior, is learned. Just as we learn to be violent, we are equally able to learn to use nonviolent tools and techniques. We do not lack the ability, but the systems and structures to teach those tools. A Department of Peace will help fill this void. Over the last decade we have spent trillions in developing our capacity to fight by developing new weapons and the strategic plans for using them. It is time for us to invest attention and resources to cultivate a Department of Peace, save lives and reduce human suffering at every level of society.

While addressing the federal government's responsibility to adequately meet our national security needs in today's world, Defense Secretary Robert Gates said, "[n]ew institutions are needed for the 21st century, new organizations with a 21st century mind-set." A Department of Peace is part of this new mind-set.

Peace is far from a utopian ideal. It is a possibility that becomes ever more likely as we invest time, energy and resources into its strategic use. Experts consider "peace" a concrete strategy that provides measurable results rather than an unattainable ideal.

We have no illusion that having a Department of Peace, or something of its stature, will be the panacea that brings forth a violence-free society. What is certain is that if we don't try, we will never even get close.

It isn't enough to talk about peace. One must believe in it. And it isn't enough to believe in it. One must work at it.

⟩ Eleanor Roosevelt

.....

Matthew Albracht is on the board and staff of The Peace Alliance. (www.thepeacealliance.org) The Peace Alliance empowers civic engagement toward a culture of peace. We are an alliance of organizers and advocates throughout the United States taking the work of peace-building from the margins of society into the centers of national discourse and policy priorities. Our network includes volunteer grassroots teams in hundreds of cities, towns, colleges and high school campuses.

A Nation That Shines

"Dreaming the future can create the future,,

Everything has a weight to it. Even the smallest molecule is defined by the balance of weight of its component parts. So, what is the weight of a nation that is fully realizing its highest potential? Of a nation that has reached a critical mass and is wholeheartedly dedicated to peace, equality and stewardship?

The principles of liberty, opportunity, peace and justice are **rooted into the fabric of our identity** as a country. In many ways, we are indeed a bright light when it comes to these virtues. But we also fall short—sometimes stuck in the muck of greed, indifference and closed-mindedness.

Kenny Ausubel, one of the authors in this chapter, plainly states that "dreaming the future can create the future." Indeed the dream of this nation is not some far off ideal. It is a dream that has been unfolding for over 230 years and **is unfolding right now.** It is unfolding in the hearts and minds of women, men and children across the land.

Gandhi said, "Be the change you want to see in the world." There is great power in the simplicity of this truth. **It calls us, whoever we are, to be a part of the creative process.** To be active participants. To get informed, to build hope, to paint beauty, to serve. To dream.

The luminaries who share their voices in this closing chapter echo the message that is found in the pages throughout this book. Their words weave a vision for the present and the future that reminds us to **remember our purpose and our potential.**

Dreaming the Future Can Create the Future

Kenny Ausubel
Bioneers

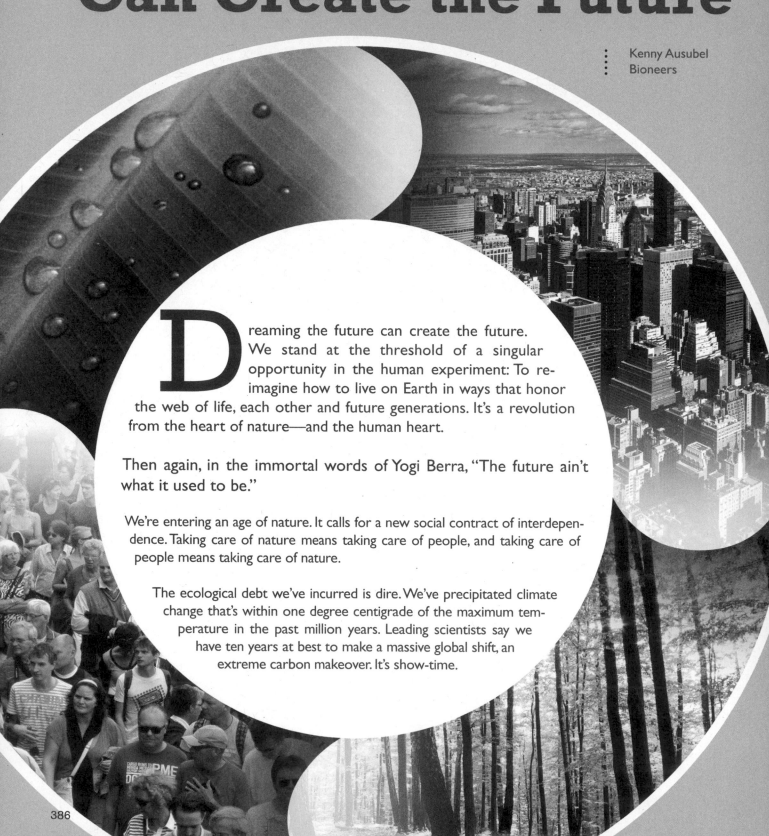

Dreaming the future can create the future. We stand at the threshold of a singular opportunity in the human experiment: To re-imagine how to live on Earth in ways that honor the web of life, each other and future generations. It's a revolution from the heart of nature—and the human heart.

Then again, in the immortal words of Yogi Berra, "The future ain't what it used to be."

We're entering an age of nature. It calls for a new social contract of interdependence. Taking care of nature means taking care of people, and taking care of people means taking care of nature.

The ecological debt we've incurred is dire. We've precipitated climate change that's within one degree centigrade of the maximum temperature in the past million years. Leading scientists say we have ten years at best to make a massive global shift, an extreme carbon makeover. It's show-time.

We're entering a drastic period of creative destruction. We've already begun to trigger what some ecologists call "regime shift," irreversible tipping points. Global warming is getting all the ink, but other intimately interdependent issues equal its magnitude: the mass extinction of 30 to 50 percent of Earth's biological and cultural diversity—freshwater shortages that will lead to wars, the universal poisoning of the biosphere, and the greatest extremes of inequality in modern history, a world that's 77 percent poor.

We're going to be busier than a cat in a room full of rocking chairs.

Periods of creative destruction also present transformative opportunities to make the world anew. These tectonic shocks are evolutionary exclamation points. They release vast amounts of energy and resources for renewal and reorganization. Novelty emerges, and small changes can have big influences. It's a time of creativity, innovation, freedom and transformation.

The grail is resilience—strengthening the capacity of natural and human systems to rebound—or to transform when the regime shifts. As Charles Darwin said, "It is not the strongest of the species that survive, nor the most intelligent, but the ones most responsive to change."

The driving force behind this unprecedented globalized collapse is financial. Author, economist and futurist Hazel Henderson has characterized conventional economics as "a form of brain damage." We're experiencing its devastating effects right now. It rationalizes the insatiable predation of nature and people, while disappearing environmental and social costs from the balance sheet. It concentrates wealth and distributes poverty. It exalts greed and self-interest. It conflates free markets with democracy. It merges corporations and the state. Its foreign policy is empire. It has been a catastrophic success.

Leading scientists say we have ten years at best to make a massive global shift, an extreme carbon make-over. It's show-time.

We've begun to trigger IRREVERSIBLE tipping points...

Global warming is getting all the ink, but other intimately interdependent issues equal its magnitude:

The mass extinction of 30–50% of Earth's biological and cultural diversity *

FRESHWATER SHORTAGES that will cause wars

The universal POISONING of the biosphere

The greatest extremes of inequality in modern history, a world that's 77% POOR

We're going to be busier than a cat in a room full of rocking chairs.

*Photo courtesy Dave Kimble **Photo courtesy Pierre Holtz, UNICEF

Every major empire over the past several hundred years has undergone a depressingly **predictable cycle of collapse,** usually **within 10 to 20 years** of its peak power.

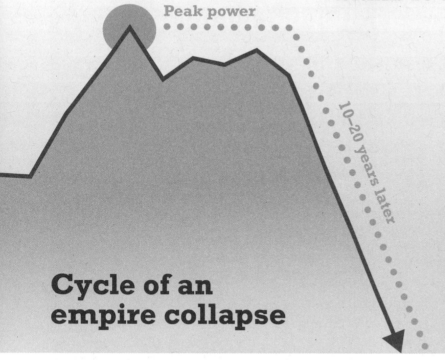

Peak power

10–20 years later

Cycle of an empire collapse

The hallmarks are always the same:

• The financialization of the economy, moving from manufacturing to speculation

• Very high levels of debt

• Extreme economic inequality

• Costly military overreaching

The Dutch, Spanish and British empires followed this pattern. **The US is repeating it.**

As political commentator Kevin Phillips has chronicled, every major empire over the past several hundred years has undergone a depressingly predictable cycle of collapse, usually within 10 to 20 years of its peak power.

The hallmarks are always the same:
  • the financialization of the economy, moving from manufacturing to speculation;
  • very high levels of debt;
  • extreme economic inequality; and
  • costly military overreaching.

The Dutch, Spanish and British empires followed this pattern. The US is repeating it. But as J. Paul Getty said, "Every time history repeats itself, the price goes up."

Yet there's an even deeper story behind empire crash.

Energy is a nation's master resource. Each empire has had an idiosyncratic ability to exploit a particular energy source that propelled its rise to economic power. The Dutch learned how to tap wood, wind and water. The British Empire fueled its ascendancy on coal. The American empire has dominated with oil.

The cautionary tale is this: No empire has been able to manage the transition to the next energy source. The joker in the deck this time around is the climate imperative to transition off fossil fuels worldwide. It requires the most complex and fiercely urgent passage in the history of human civilization. Nothing like it has ever been done.

Just as economics is driving the destruction, it needs to power the restoration. The charge is to transform the global economy from a vicious cycle to a virtuous cycle.

Real wealth creation is based on replenishing natural systems and restoring the built environment, especially our infrastructure and cities. It's based on investing in our communities and workforce. It's been shown to work best when done all at once. Restoration is an estimated $100 trillion market. There's plenty of work to do, plenty of people to do it and abundant financial incentive. And every dollar we spend on pre-disaster risk management will prevent seven dollars in later losses.

The question is: Will we change our old bad habits fast enough to beat forbidding odds?

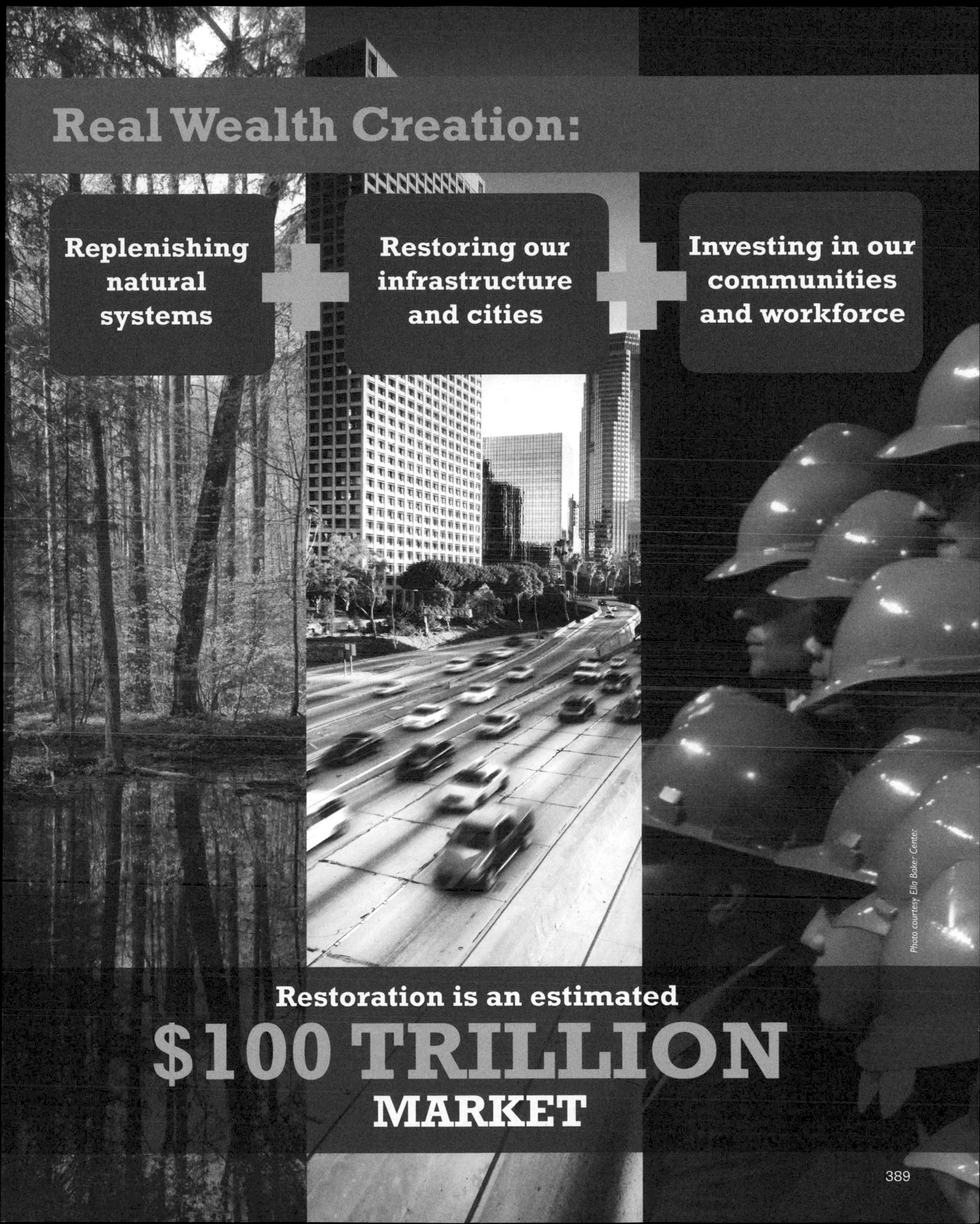

Real Wealth Creation:
Replenishing natural systems
+
Restoring our infrastructure and cities
+
Investing in our communities and workforce
Restoration is an estimated
$100 TRILLION
MARKET
Photo courtesy Ella Baker Center

Many of the solutions are already present. Where we don't know what to do, we have a good idea what directions to head in. Game-changing technological and social innovations are surfacing constantly.

A big bang of brilliant, effective work is meeting with unprecedented receptivity. Yet still the pace of destruction outstrips our response. Real success will require a giant leap across the abyss on visionary currents of bold action. It will take skillful means. It will take a big heart. And in times like these, as Albert Einstein said, "Imagination is more important than knowledge."

Many of the solutions are already present. Where we don't know what to do, we have a good idea what directions to head in. Game-changing technological and social innovations are surfacing constantly. Global digital media can spread them at the speed of text messaging.

At the forefront is biomimicry, the art and science of mimicking nature's design genius. As Janine Benyus observes, nature has already done everything we want to do, without mining the past or mortgaging the future. There's nothing like having four billion years of R&D at your back.

A riptide of capital is mainstreaming biomimicry and clean tech, now the third-largest domain of venture capital investment. In Silicon Valley, the "watt-com" era has dawned. Compared with hundreds of billions for the entire Internet market, the worldwide energy market is $6 trillion. Google just put forth a $4.4 trillion Clean Energy plan. By 2030, it proposes to slash fossil fuel use by 88 percent and CO2 emissions by 95 percent.

The smart money is hot on the trail of the next industrial revolution. There's mounting pressure on Uncle Sam because government policies make or break markets.

But for now, the real action is happening at local and regional levels.

Real success will require a giant leap across the abyss on visionary currents of bold action.
It will take skillful means.
It will take a big heart.
And in times like these, as Albert Einstein said:

"Imagination is more important than **knowledge."**

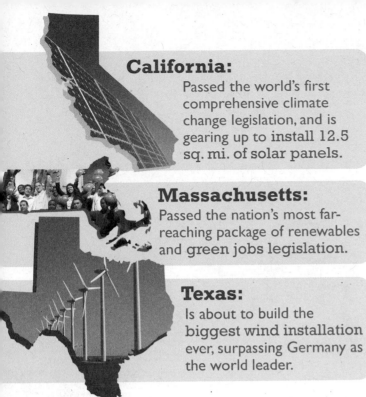

California:
Passed the world's first comprehensive climate change legislation, and is gearing up to install 12.5 sq. mi. of solar panels.

Massachusetts:
Passed the nation's most far-reaching package of renewables and green jobs legislation.

Texas:
Is about to build the biggest wind installation ever, surpassing Germany as the world leader.

California, the world's sixth-largest economy, passed the world's first comprehensive climate change legislation and is gearing up to install 12.5 square miles of solar panels—12 times the previous largest.[1] In 2008, Massachusetts passed the nation's most far-reaching package of renewables and green jobs legislation.[2] Texas just finished building the biggest wind installation ever,[3] surpassing Germany as the world leader, and California already has plans to build an installation double its capacity.[4]

Breakthrough technological innovations have to spread rapidly, as do the government policies that drive these markets. Of equal importance are social innovations and political regime change.

Michael Kinsley of Rocky Mountain Institute has said, "We've got to go from success stories to systemic change." It's going to take epic cooperation among business, government and civil society, and among nations. We need to play big and aim high. It begins with a dream. In the words of Janine Benyus, "The criterion of success is that you keep yourself alive, and you keep your offspring alive. But it's not your offspring—it's your offspring's offsprings' offspring ten thousand years from now. Because you can't be there to take care of that offspring, the only thing you can do is to take care of the place that takes care of your offspring."

I'd like to close with the words of David Oates from an essay called "Imagine" in *High Country News.*[5]

A vision predicates an imaginative leap: that we are—after all—fundamentally connected to each other—that my fate and happiness are not private matters only, but a shared project. A tax cut takes no imagination: It's a few more bucks in your pocket. But seeing one's ownership in a community, one's own face in someone else's child, that takes imagination.

Imagine—combining our resources to relieve suffering and to open up dead-ends of poverty and hopelessness. Imagine knowing that our fate is each other.

Imagine: knowing that our fate also swims with the salmon and grows with the trees.

Imagine living beyond yourself—finding the thing you're good at and in love with, even if it doesn't pay so well. That would be like coming back to life, wouldn't it? It would be like grace.

Imagine.

.....

Kenny Ausubel is an award-winning social entrepreneur, author, journalist and filmmaker. For 25 years, his work has been at the forefront of environmental, health and progressive social-change movements. Ausubel is co-CEO and founder of Bioneers (www.bioneers.org), a globally acclaimed non-profit that highlights breakthrough solutions for restoring people and planet. Ausubel co-founded the biodiversity organic company Seeds of Change in 1989 and served as CEO until 1994. His films include Hoxsey: When Healing Becomes a Crime (Best Censored Stories journalistic award), which played in theaters and on HBO and international TV, and helped influence national policy. He wrote the acclaimed companion book When Healing Becomes a Crime.

Everyone a **Changemaker**

Diana Wells
Roshan Paul
Ashoka

Mark Hanis grew up as the grandchild of four Holocaust survivors. Living and working in Ecuador, Sierra Leone and New York City, he came to acutely experience how we so often "otherize" and alienate those who are not like us. He also saw how the lessons of the Holocaust had not been learned—we've allowed genocide to happen again and again despite the world's "Never Again" pledge after World War II.

As a senior at Swarthmore College, he was disturbed that there weren't any events planned to mark the tenth year of the Rwandan genocide. So Mark went about organizing a commemoration event, which turned out to be a success. From that modest beginning, Mark, along with his colleagues, has gone on to build one of the foremost and most innovative anti-genocide organizations in the world, the Genocide Intervention Network (GI-NET). One of the cornerstones of GI-NET's approach has been the realization that the world's failure to stop genocide was due not to lack of awareness so much as to lack of political will. The best way to galvanize this was to ensure there were effective ways for citizens to take political action. So GI-NET created effective new techniques for enabling citizens to communicate their opposition to genocide. For instance, they came up with the first-ever anti-genocide hotline that connects callers directly to their elected officials for free, provides talking

Mark Hanis has built one of the foremost and most innovative anti-genocide organizations in the world: the Genocide Intervention Network (GI-NET). He is 28 years old.

What is a
Social Entrepreneur?

- An individual with **innovative solutions** to society's most pressing social problems.

- Ambitious and persistent, **endlessly creative** in coming up with solutions to daily obstacles and frustrations

- Possessed by an idea that they are convinced can **change the world.** Determined to work on making this idea successful for as long as it takes.

Members of the Ashoka Globalizer community are focused on spreading social impact.

points related to current legislation, suggests other actions elected officials can take to help end genocide and even enables citizens to listen to genocide discussions taking place in Congress. GI-NET also leverages the idealism, energy and tech savviness of youth; there are over 800 anti-genocide chapters in high schools and colleges across America. Mark will soon be transitioning out of a full-time staff role and onto the board of the organization in search of his next big idea. He is 28 years old.

What makes Mark a social entrepreneur? Of all the grandchildren of Holocaust survivors who went to college in America, why was it he that went on to become president of the world's largest organization dedicated to preventing genocide a mere six years after graduating? At Ashoka, we've elected nearly 3,000 such people as Fellows from over 65 countries, and we see the same qualities shine brightly within each of them. They are possessed by an idea they are convinced can change the world, they are determined to work on making this idea successful for as long as it takes, they are endlessly creative in coming up with solutions to daily

obstacles and frustrations, and they possess a strong ethical streak that makes people, society, instinctively trust them. These leaders, or social entrepreneurs, are changing the world.

But alone, even they are not enough. We live in a world where problems seem to be breeding faster than we can count them. Our economy is being transformed, painfully so for millions of Americans. Climate change continues to loom over our heads. The gap between the richest and the poor widens every year. The House and Senate seem to be caught in a perpetual cycle of implacable hostility between both major parties. What is the solution to this juggernaut of multiplying problems?

We need a world where every individual is a changemaker.

We need to create a world that multiplies changemakers who can attack these problems, or prevent them from happening in the first place. By this, we don't mean that everyone should turn off their lights when they leave a room, though that is of course important, and we should.

They are endlessly creative in coming up with solutions to daily obstacles and frustrations, and they possess a strong ethical streak that make people, society, instinctively trust them. These leaders, or social entrepreneurs as we call them, are changing the world.

> **We need to enable individuals to feel like they have the confidence, creativity, and empathy to address the problems they see around them.**

The Ashoka Changemaker Campus Fellows.

By this, we mean that we need to enable individuals to feel like they have the confidence, creativity and empathy to address the problems they see around them, whether it is to create a conflict resolution process in the family or a neighborhood recycling program or prevent the sale of toxic mortgages.

And here's the good news: The world will conspire to let you be a changemaker. If you are a young person, there have never been as many opportunities or resources to help you come up with a plan to solve a problem and walk you through implementing this plan. If you are a college student, look around you: Is your campus joining the Changemaker Campus movement? If you are a business owner, you should know that the levels of collaboration between companies and citizen groups have never been as high as they are today (and are only getting higher). Companies are partnering with citizen sector organizations to extend their reach to underserved populations with products that are essential and affordable. If you are a budding social entrepreneur, there is a plethora of start-up funding organizations waiting to help you.

We could go on. But we'd rather show you some more people who are walking this path. At Ashoka, we work with many of America's best social entrepreneurs: Wendy Kopp who founded Teach for America, Jimmy Wales who founded Wikipedia, J.B. Schramm of College Summit and over a hundred more. Yet, to truly illustrate the point that everyone can be a changemaker, let us tell you two stories of youth who are transforming the world we live in.

First, let's meet Heather Wilder, 17 years old, from Las Vegas. She is a passionate advocate for the rights of foster care children in the United States, with a clarity of conviction that can only come from having lived the experience herself. Heather was removed from an abusive situation as a young child. After several years in the foster care system, she was adopted into a loving and supportive family at age 12. To help foster kids who are still in the system, Heather wrote a series of booklets that address issues faced by foster children on a daily basis, like moving homes frequently, not being adopted or dealing with previous and sometimes ongoing abusive situations. Today, social workers give Heather's booklets to children as they come into the foster care system. She acknowledges that it can be difficult to speak up about the abuse she endured, but she's driven by her determination to be a voice for other children who haven't left the system: "Being brave helps me feel better, because I pretend that I am being brave for someone else who can't share their stories yet."

And now let's meet Talia. Fifteen years old, Talia is the CEO and a founder of RandomKid, a nonprofit organization that leverages the power of youth to solve real problems in the world. To date she has leveraged the power of 12 million youth from 20 countries to bring aid on four continents, ranking the giving power of youth with the top US corporations. Talia is the winner of numerous national and international awards for her philanthropic work—including World of Children's Founder Youth Award, which is considered to be the Nobel prize for efforts that serve the world's children. Nicholas Kristof wrote of Talia in his column in the *New*

Fifteen years old, Talia is the CEO and a founder of RandomKid:

A non-profit organization that leverages the power of **12 million youth** from **20 countries** to bring aid on **four continents,** ranking the giving power of youth with the top US corporations.

Photo courtesy Talia Leman, RandomKid

York Times: "If your image of a philanthropist is a stout, gray geezer, then meet Talia Leman, an eighth grader in Iowa who loves soccer and swimming, and whose favorite subject is science. I'm supporting her for president in 2044."[1] Talia travels across the world speaking about "The Power of ANYone."

This is what a world in which everyone is a changemaker can look like. A world where people who grew up with the memories of the Holocaust can design solutions for those affected by other genocides in far-away lands because we pledged that this would never happen again, where children who have had disturbed childhoods come up with concrete solutions so that those that follow them don't have to suffer the same experiences, and where someone with a bright idea can have a global impact before her 15th birthday.

President Obama's creation of the Office of Social Innovation and Civic Participation is an important, proactive step. It is an attempt to harness the power of innovation and entrepreneurship to drive systems-changing solutions to our nation's most pressing problems. This shows that the administration recognizes something that many do not. It is not simply about building institutions, but more important, it is about creating an enabling environment—one that surfaces a variety of innovative solutions and helps them spread. With the ever-increasing rate of change around us, it is now more critical than ever to ensure more individuals are mastering the skills of empathy, teamwork and leadership to be effective changemakers. The only answer to more problems is more problem-solvers. For this reason, we believe the only answer is to build a world where all citizens are playing roles to solve the world's most pressing needs—an *Everyone a Changemaker* world.

When you see the front page of the newspaper or switch on cable news, this world may seem a very long way away. And it is. We do have a long way to go. But every day there are events unfolding that are reshaping the very contours of our world. We know so many other Marks and Talias and Heathers, and together they prove, incontrovertibly and emphatically, the power of the individual to change the world. We're excited about our future.

.....

Diana Wells first joined Ashoka (www.ashoka.org) in the 1980s after graduating from Brown University. She completed a PhD in anthropology from New York University as a Fulbright and Woodrow Wilson scholar. Post-PhD, Wells returned to Ashoka to provide leadership for Ashoka's process of finding and supporting the world's leading social entrepreneurs, including managing Ashoka's geographic and portfolio growth. Wells was named president of Ashoka in November of 2005. She is on the advisory board for Center for the Advancement of Social Entrepreneurship (CASE) at Duke's Fuqua School of Business, and has taught anthropology and development at Georgetown University.

Roshan Paul has been involved in creating several new Ashoka programs, most recently Ashoka Peace (launching entrepreneurs in conflict zones) and Ashoka Globalizer (helping social entrepreneurs accelerate their impact globally). He has also managed Ashoka's Fellow Security and Senior Fellows programs. In an earlier stint, he co-launched Ashoka's Youth Venture program in India. Paul has degrees from Davidson College and the Harvard Kennedy School, and currently serves on the advisory boards of Lifting Voices, TechChange and Peace Direct US. He juggles passions for social entrepreneurship in conflict-stricken areas, and for the use of storytelling as a critical leadership skill.

Realizing Our Roots and the **Power of Interconnectedness**

I embrace you as "beautiful relatives of the world." This is the Hopi way of greeting those from other nations with an open hand to show that I come in peace. As an indigenous person, I come from a culture that has been on this continent for thousands of years, surviving and thriving despite many hardships and challenges. Over the ages, simple and fundamental truths have supported our survival that I think are relevant for society at large today more than ever. The principles of interconnectedness, humility and making decisions with the consideration of seven generations might seem basic and easy to take for granted. But it is precisely these principles that need to be integrated into our lives, institutions and our structures of government in a deeper way.

Mona Polacca
Native American Elder

> **In my upbringing, I was taught that everyone is my relative. That we are all relatives. My parents and grandparents instilled this value since I was a child and I notice that, without question, it helps me to see the value in each person and living thing.**

An Inter-Connected Family

In my upbringing, I was taught that everyone is my relative, that we are all relatives. My parents and grandparents instilled this value since I was a child, and I notice that, without question, it helps to me to see the value in each person and living thing. Looking back at Earth from 200 miles up in space, divisions don't exist, and it is abundantly clear that we are one family on one Earth. But, in our political dealings, in our relationship with our Mother Earth, in the media world and in our relationships with those inside and outside our country, how often do we remember that we are all related? That we are all one family? This simple realization, as basic as it is, has profound implications. If we recognize that all people, plants, animals and even the forests and fish are our relations, then we are guided to act in a way that is life-sustaining and our worldview is more open and inclusive. We listen more and have greater patience, finding solutions more readily instead of keeping the fight alive. The fact of the matter is that we don't exist independently. The honor of one is the honor of all, and the hurt of one is the hurt of all.

Humility

Corn is vitally important for our people. It has been a source of sustenance for thousands of years and also carries a much deeper meaning representing our connection to the forces of nature and the unseen world. There is a story that, long ago, our people were given a choice regarding which seeds of corn to choose. We chose the humblest seeds, those that produce small stalks and ears of corn. But even though these kernels are small and humble, they are hearty, capable of growing in the desert, in extreme temperatures with little water. The humble nature of these seeds is also their strength. Humility is a key ingredient in life. There are

If we recognize that all people, plants, animals, and even the forests and fish are our relations, then we are guided to act in a way that is life-sustaining and our world view is more open and inclusive.

A cultural philosophy from my ancestry is the concept of thinking and acting in the present with the awareness of children seven generations in the future.

I believe this unique culturally based practice is important for all peoples in these times. It places value on community, cultural survival, selflessness, and on taking care of each other and our Mother Earth.

certain challenges that we all face, and these challenges are a teaching of humility. No doubt, we are facing many challenges as a country. But it is important to acknowledge that whatever we are presented with is like a gift. How are our current struggles causing us to take pause, to reorganize, to commit to new and different priorities? To cast away old and habitual ways of being that don't serve us? How are our current challenges actually opportunities for renewal if we face them with a spirit of collaboration and creativity?

Seven Generations Ahead

A cultural philosophy from my ancestry and of many indigenous peoples in North America and across the world is the concept of thinking and acting in the present with the awareness of children seven generations in the future. I believe this unique culturally based practice is important for all peoples in these times. It places value on community, cultural survival, selflessness and taking care of each other and our Mother Earth. Its beauty and truth is in its simplicity and calls us to find common ground and work to leave the world a better place.

This principle plays out in many different ways. If we are thinking and acting with sensitivity to our future descendants seven generations ahead, how does this inform our decisions now? Do we start to prioritize differently as a country? Perhaps in the coming generations we will turn the tables so that we spend eight times more on education than on our military instead of the other way around. Perhaps in the next generation, it will become a reality that every home will be powered by the sun and wind? Thinking ahead, perhaps we begin to measure our richness in terms of happiness and equality instead of Gross Domestic Product? This way of thinking is taking root more and more across this land and across the world. It is good to see, and it needs to keep growing.

The Grandmothers' Council

Looking at my grandchildren gives me hope. To have hope is to realize that there is going to be something more coming, like looking at the dawn before the sunrise. Being a member of the International Council of 13 Indigenous Grandmothers also gives me hope. We represent indigenous peoples and traditions from all over the world and have come together in unity to further education and healing for our Mother Earth, all Her inhabitants and for the next seven generations to come. We come together in prayer and ceremony to imagine a different vision for our future and serve as spokespeople on a wide range of social justice and environmental issues.

The International Council of Thirteen Indigenous Grandmothers represents indigenous people and traditions from all over the world that come together in unity to further education and healing for our Mother Earth and all Her inhabitants. Here, the Grandmothers gather in New York.

In Italy, the International Council of Thirteen Indigenous Grandmothers fulfill a long-held intention to preform prayer ceremonies at the Vatican.

Mona Polacca offers prayers during an International Council of Thirteen Indigenous Grandmothers gathering in the Southwest US.

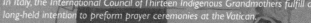

By stepping forward between and within cultures and languages we can overcome boundaries.

We can cross borders not only geographically but also psychologically and spiritually.

> **As the great Lakota leader, Sitting Bull said, "Let us put our minds together and see what life we can make for our children," let us chart a course of peace and harmony.**

In a sense, the Council is a microcosm for a way of being and working in partnership that is growing on a global scale. One of my sisters in the Council, Agnes Baker Pilgrim, is fond of saying, "The greatest distance in the world is the 14 inches from our minds to our hearts." Facing a world in crisis, we believe solutions will come as people and institutions continue to come together in partnership, from a place of heart and compassion.

Indigenous people have come through a time of great struggle, a time of darkness. The way I look at it is like the nature of a butterfly. In the cocoon, a place of darkness, the creature breaks down into a fluid, and then a change, a transformation, takes place. When it is ready and in its own time, it begins to move and develop a form that stretches and breaks away from this cocoon and emerges into this world, into life, as a beautiful creature. We grandmothers, we have emerged from that darkness, see this beauty, see each other and reach out to the world with open arms, with love, hope, compassion, faith and charity. Finding strength and purpose in each other is a beautiful thing.

A Future Vision

We find ourselves in transition, in a place of uncertainty where all is not resolved, where there are great questions and concerns, but also hopes. This state of transformation, movement and becoming is not final; it is not perfect. The key is to know and acknowledge that within us all exist the conditions for creativity and the conditions for grace to descend. We are living in a time of definitions and decisions. We are the generation with the responsibility and option to choose the path with a life for our children. Now is the time of awakening, where we become more aware of our connections and our fundamental relation to each other. Aware of our existence in this world. What it means to be human.

By stepping forward between and within cultures and languages, we can overcome boundaries. We can cross borders not only geographically but also psychologically and spiritually. This means that one is never finished, that one is always journeying onward. It is time to make a commitment to encourage the development of a new history and partnership among us. As the great Lakota leader Sitting Bull said, "Let us put our minds together and see what life we can make for our children," let us chart a course of peace and harmony. Let us have the courage, strength, the will and the wisdom to do this for the next seven generations.

.....

Mona Polacca, M.S.W., is a Havasupai, Hopi and Tewa Native American whose tribal affiliation is of the Colorado River Indian Tribes of Parker, Arizona, where she has served as the treasurer and tribal council member. Today she is a self-employed human services consultant to tribal communities. She is committed to supporting initiatives that involve developing effective strategies and sensitive approaches and action towards addressing indigenous human rights and works towards improving the quality of life of global indigenous peoples. Currently, she is a member of a working group planning the Indigenous World Forum on Water and Peace. Polacca, a founding member of the International Council of 13 Indigenous Grandmothers (www.grandmotherscouncil.org), is featured in a collection of teachings and stories compiled in the Grandmothers' book, Grandmothers Counsel the World: Women Elders Offer Their Vision for Our Planet, *and their documentary film,* For the Next 7 Generations. *She lives in Arizona and has a son, two daughters and nine grandchildren.*

Painting Hope
in the World

Lily Yeh
Barefoot Artists

I was born in China and grew up in Taiwan. My parents nurtured me with firm guidance and support, and I came to the States in the '60s to study art at the University of Pennsylvania. Upon receiving my MFA, I began teaching and started a family, traveled, raised my son, exhibited my work and took care of my father when he got Alzheimer's. Although I faced my share of struggles, my life was sweet and blessed.

Yet I felt that I was looking for something that I could not quite name, something that would anchor me and make my life more authentic. I searched for it far and wide, in books, places, my work and relationships. It was in the broken land of North Philadelphia that I stepped into the purpose of my life.

> **Making art in a distressed community ravaged by violence, poverty and drugs, is like making a fire in the darkness of a winter's night.**

A Simple Summer's Art Project

In the summer of 1986, I received an invitation from Arthur Hall, a tremendously talented African-American dancer and choreographer, who also headed the Ile-Ife Black Humanitarian Center in inner-city North Philadelphia. He asked me to create an art park on the abandoned lot next to his center. Everyone—friends, family, colleagues—advised me "No. Do not go into the badland. You are an outsider. Kids will destroy everything you build." I was scared and wanted to withdraw from the project. But I summoned my courage and ventured into North Philadelphia.

Art alone cannot rebuild a community. But making art in a distressed community ravaged by violence, poverty and drugs is like making a fire in the darkness of a winter's night. Giving out light and warmth, it attracts people both from near and far. That was what happened on the vacant lot at the corner of Tenth Street and Germantown Avenue. Sensing new ideas and energy, children responded first. Joseph "JoJo" Williams who lived right next to the lot became my assistant and foreman of the park building project. Through Jojo and the children, the project became rooted in the community.

Working in a dilapidated neighborhood with a disenfranchised community impacted me so deeply that I eventually left my tenured professorship and threw myself whole-heartedly into my life's journey to find purpose and meaning.

The Village of Arts and Humanities (VAH)

During the first three summers, Jojo and I worked mainly with children. It was through them that we gained the trust of the adults in the neighborhood, who gradually joined us in restoring the neighborhood. Our effort also attracted professionals from the fields of construction, the arts, law and education. In 1989,

The first park was named after Arthur Hall's Ile Ife Black Humanitarian Center. It is located at Germantown Avenue and 10th Street in North Philadelphia. Arthur Hall, the late renowned dancer and choreographer, invited Lily Yeh to build an art park on the abandoned lot next to his building in 1986. Drawn to their activities, many children from the area participated in their park building project.

with the help of Stephen Sayer, lawyer/writer/builder, the summer park building project became a non-profit organization, which, as cofounders, we named the Village of Arts and Humanities. The mission of the Village is to "build community through its innovative arts, educational, social and construction programs." In all that we do, we aim to do justice to the people we serve.

Working together with residents, Sayer renovated a three-story warehouse into our headquarters where we could hold classes and community meetings. From then on, the Village evolved into a complex entity that included programs and activities for the entire community. From 1986 to 2004, we created 17 art parks and gardens in the Village neighborhood and converted 200 abandoned lots into green spaces including the establishment of a two-acre tree farm.

Concurrently, we ran an extensive building program through which we renovated six dilapidated buildings into office spaces, studios and an apartment. We completed six new three-story homes for first-time low-income homebuyers from the neighborhood. Collaborating with schools and public housing agencies in North Philadelphia, the Village on the Move program impacted neighborhoods and communities within the 260-square-block areas in North Philadelphia.

The heart of all our activities laid with our year-round after-school and Saturday programs for children and youth in visual and performing arts, computer skills, spoken word, summer work, nutrition/health and homework help. The Village hosted a youth theater that produced an original play each year, which was performed in Philadelphia and other cities in the States.

Every year in early fall, we celebrated our talent and accomplishments through an art festival in which we paraded through our neighborhood, blessing the land, families and all our children. The pivotal event of the festival was the Rites of Passage designed to help our youth to root in the community. We passed on to them the torches of light, symbols of their own inner light and talent with encouragement and blessings.

From 1986 to 2004, we created 17 art parks and gardens in the Village neighborhood, converted 200 abandoned lots into green spaces including the establishment of a 2-acre tree farm.

Formerly abandoned lots in north Philadelphia are now works of art and community gathering areas.

Through imagination and daring actions, we can create new spaces, into which people can enter on equal footing, each bringing his or her inspiration, talent, and voice.

This abandoned land once contained six dilapidated homes that eventually were demolished by the city and buried underground. It gradually became a dumping site for trash, debris and human waste. So when we succeeded in constructing a garden on this site, we named it Magical Garden because the transformation of the place felt truly magical and momentous.

Lily Yeh, Joseph Habineza (Rwandan Minister of Sport and Culture) and two local dignitaries attend the dedication of the new Rugerero Genocide Memorial.

This is how a simple summer art project evolved into a complex organization that has been impacting the lives of tens and thousands of people on different levels and became a celebratory model nationwide of successful community building through the arts.

Success demands its own price. The fast expansion of the Village gradually burdened me with more responsibility in fundraising and staff management. I felt the need to return to my original role as an artist to work directly with people. I understood that my canvas lay in the dilapidated places; my pigments are people's talent and stories. My mission is to bring the transformative power of art to

> **My mission is to bring the transformative power of art to broken communities to create something that would express our shared quest for freedom, equality, justice & compassion.**

broken communities to create with residents something that would honor their sensitivity and cultural heritage, something that would express our shared quest for freedom, equality, justice and compassion.

Barefoot Artists, Inc.

In 2004, I left the Village of Arts and Humanities and became the lead artist and founding director of Barefoot Artists, Inc. Inspired by the model of barefoot doctors in China during the 1950s, the goal of Barefoot Artists is simple: Go to places in need, practice one's art of healing and community building; jump-start projects through art making; pass on methodology in self-empowerment and innovative solutions; move on to other places in need.

Under the auspices of Barefoot Artists, I've been able to launch several projects in China and Africa. Working with and learning from the communities working to rebuild after genocide in West Rwanda has been profound and confirms that the journey of my life is still unfolding.

> **Whatever our talent & expertise, they are tools for action. When our action serves the public, it has the power to transform. Mother Theresa said, "We can do no great things, only small things with great love."**

Painting the Colors of Unity, Renewal and Hope

Sometimes the problems we are facing in the world seem so overwhelming because of the conflicting situations, vast scale and complexity. Twenty-four years of working with communities overwrought in negativity, poverty and hopelessness taught me that, through imagination and daring actions, we can create new spaces into which people can enter on equal footing, each bringing his/her inspiration, talent and voice. Through these long years of practices emerged a kind of living social art that was created for the people at the beginning, then with the people and by the people along the way and then, at the end, belonged to the people. This kind of art has no commercial value, yet it is valueless in its transformative impact on individual, family and communal life.

Because I am an artist, my vehicle is art. I define art not only by its literary, performing and visual expressions, but also and more importantly as creativity in thinking, methodology and implementation. Whatever our talent and expertise, they are our tools for action. When our action serves the public, it has the power to transform. Mother Teresa said, "We can do no great things, only small things with great love."

In my quest for authenticity, my life's journey has unfolded in ways that I never could have dreamed. In

Yeh and children in Accra, Ghana. This project took place in an impoverished neighborhood in Jamestown, located in the old section of the city. The undertaking engaged hundreds of children and adults in transforming a bleak courtyard into a public space full of patterns and colors.

addition to making art, being an artist to me is a way of life, a life dedicated to the realization of one's vision, sharing one's talent and doing the right thing without sparing oneself.

We all are blessed with the innate illumination of creativity and imagination. When guided by our vision for a more compassionate, just and sustainable future, we have the power to imagine, create and take action together that will drive away the darkness of ignorance, neglect, bigotry and greed. I believe that here lies the hope for our future.

· · · · ·

Lily Yeh is an internationally celebrated artist whose work has taken her to communities throughout the world. As founder and executive director of the Village of Arts and Humanities in North Philadelphia from 1986 to 2004, she helped create a national model of community building through the arts. In 2004, Yeh pursued her work internationally, founding Barefoot Artists, Inc. (www.barefootartists.org) to bring the transformative power of art to impoverished communities around the globe through participatory, multifaceted projects that foster community empowerment, improve the physical environment, promote economic development and preserve indigenous art and culture.

We are the Ones
We Have Been Waiting For...

It was the best of times, it was the worst of times...

Alice Walker

It helps tremendously that these words have been spoken before and thanks to Charles Dickens, written at the beginning of *A Tale of Two Cities*. Perhaps they have been spoken, written, thought, an endless number of times throughout human history. It is the worst of times because it feels as though the very Earth is being stolen from us, by us: the land and air poisoned, the water polluted, the animals disappeared, humans degraded and misguided. War is everywhere.

It is the best of times because there are passionate people and institutions committed to making the world better. Actively working to create more equality, to preserve, to educate, and to heal. It is the best of times because we have entered a period, if we can bring ourselves to pay attention, of great clarity as to cause and effect. A blessing when we consider how much suffering human beings have endured, in previous millennia, without a clue to its cause. Because we can now see into every crevice of the globe and because we are free to explore previously unexplored crevices in our own hearts and minds, it is inevitable that everything we have needed to comprehend in order to survive, everything we have needed to understand in the most basic of ways, will be illuminated now. We have only to open our eyes, and awaken to our predicament.

We see that we are, alas, a huge part of our problem. However, we live in a time of global enlightenment. This alone should make us shout for joy.

It is as if ancient graves, hidden deep in the shadows of the psyche and the earth, are breaking open of their own accord. Unwilling to be silent any longer. Incapable of silence. No leader or people of any country will be safe from these upheavals that lead to exposure, no matter how much the news is managed or how long people's grievances have been kept quiet. We will know at least a bit of the truth about what is going on, and that will set us free. It is an awesome era in which to live.

It was the poet June Jordan who wrote "We are the ones we have been waiting for." Sweet Honey in the Rock turned those words into a song. Hearing this song, I have witnessed thousands of people rise to their feet in joyful recognition and affirmation. We are the ones we've been waiting for because we are able to see what is happening with a much greater awareness than our parents or grandparents, our ancestors, could see. This does not mean we believe, having seen the greater truth of how all oppression is connected, how pervasive and unrelenting, that we can "fix" things. But some of us are not content to have a gap in opportunity and income that drives a wedge between rich and poor. Not willing to ignore starving and brutalized children. Not willing to let women be stoned or mutilated without protest. Not willing to stand quietly by as farmers are destroyed by people who have never farmed, and plants are engineered to self-destruct. Not willing to disappear. We have wanted all our lives to know that Earth, who has somehow obtained human beings as her custodians, was also capable of creating humans who could minister to her needs, and the needs of her creation. We are the ones.

The happiness that guides this understanding is like an inner light, a compass we might steer by as we set out across the lengthening darkness. It comes from the simple belief and understanding that what one is feeling and doing is right. That it is right to protect rather than terrorize others; right to feed people rather that withhold food and medicine; right to want the freedom and joyful existence of all humankind. Right to want this freedom and joy for all creatures that exist already or that might come into existence. Existence, we are now learning is not finished! It is a happiness that comes from honoring the peace or the possibility of peace that lives within one's own heart. A deep knowing that we are the Earth—our separation from Earth is perhaps our greatest illusion—and that we stand, with gratitude and love, by our planetary Self.

It is to our dreams that we must turn for guidance; it is to the art inside us that hungers to be born. It is to the literature of writers who love humanity. It is to the wisdom teachings that have come down to us from those who would ease our suffering. We are an ancient, ancient people who need to be more connected to the source of our greatest strength: an accurate knowledge of who we are. This nature that is nonviolent, this nature that is creative and kind and yearns to see joy unfold in the hearts of many, this nature that is celebratory and people and animal loving, this nature, is indeed our birthright, literally.

To bless means to help.

HELPED are those who find something in
Creation to admire each and every hour.
Their days will overflow with beauty and the
darkest dungeon will offer gifts.

HELPED are those who receive only to give;
always in their house will be the circular energy
of generosity; and in their hearts a beginning of a
new age on Earth: when no keys will be needed to
unlock the heart and no locks will be needed on the doors

HELPED are those whose every act is a prayer
for peace; on them depends the future of the world

HELPED are those who find the courage to do
at least one small thing each day to help the existence
of another—plant, animal, river or human being.

The world is as beautiful as it ever was. It is changing, but then it always has been. This is a good time to change, and remain beautiful, with it.

We are the ones we have been waiting for.

This passage is drawn in large part from the book We Are the Ones We Have Been Waiting For. Alice Walker is a poet, author and activist. In 1982 Walker published The Color Purple, which was awarded the Pulitzer Prize for Fiction and the National Book Award. Walker has written many other novels, short stories and poems. Her writings have been translated into more than two dozen languages, and her books have sold more than 15 million copies. During the summer of 2011, Walker was part of Gaza Freedom Flotilla which attempted to deliver supplies to Gaza in response to Israel's siege of the Gaza strip.

So, what's next?

Go to www.dreamofanation.org
to be a part of a growing community and open a door
to a world of more information and inspiration.

Acknowledgments

It has been an honor and a privilege to have been a part of this book coming to life. *Dream of a Nation* is a true collective effort and I want to express my deep appreciation to the authors of each and every contribution who saw the potential of this project and dedicated time and capacity to contribute something meaningful. Beyond your written piece, I also wish to acknowledge your important work in the world. A special thank you goes to Paul Hawken and Alice Walker—thank you for your decades of dedication and for being a part of this book. And thanks to Ryan Hurley and Arts @ Large, and to Neosha Hampton. Your words are inspiring and I look forward to reading your poetry for years to come.

It is with deep appreciation that I thank the core team members that have been so vital to this project. Kelly Spitzner—as design director, your dedication, creativity, and enthusiasm shines brightly through each of the pages of this book. You found ways to bring the material to life with authenticity and you stayed up many a night to meet the deadlines. You are amazing and I thank you for all that you contributed. Gretel Hakanson—as a project editor and writer, you brilliantly found ways to make the essays come to life through your research, writing, and editorial skills. The content that you developed for editor's boxes was also top-notch and your project management capabilities were also invaluable and really helped to keep things on track. Allen Law—as researcher, you so aptly completed invaluable research; double checking hundreds of pieces of data, calculating "what-if" possibilities and authoring content for editor's boxes. Casey Bass—as design associate, your talents and creativity also shine on every page. Your contributions were immeasurable and how lucky we are that the timing all worked out. This small but dedicated team has pulled something valuable together and it wouldn't be what it is without your unique contribution. Thank you.

There are others who also have my sincere gratitude. The following foundations believed in this project and took a risk on a small organization and a big idea and we are so thankful for your support:

Shumaker Family Foundation, Park Foundation, Herb Block Foundation, Foundation for Sustainability and Innovation—this book and project simply would not have come to light without your belief and support. There are so many wonderful initiatives and organizations out there and we thank you for believing in ours. My sincere gratitude also goes to Judy Wright for your invaluable time, guidance and encouragement. Thank you also to Megan Shumaker, Bill Bondurant, and Marcela Brane for having faith in this project.

To my wife and boys, Kathie, Ayden and Kyle—thank you for believing in this work and for putting up with me throughout the process and helping to balance out the work with fun. To my parents Jeff Miller and Nicolee McMahon and my sister Dana Cuffari and grandmothers Grace and Eileen and to Shirley and Phil Gach and Wendy Ramstad and all the other members of my family and network of friends, thank you for your support and encouragement.

Additional appreciation goes to Margo Baldwin of Chelsea Green and Martin Rowe of Lantern Books for your words of wisdom and for seeing the potential of this project; and to Jason McMahon for your research help and to Tom Pope for your editorial guidance. It is also with gratitude that I thank the range of reviewers (some mentioned previously) for your input and want to give a shout out to Jeff Barrie, Cassidy Pope, Todd Pollak, Erin Johnson, Shannon Binns, Anne Ulizio and Joshua Martin. And to the members of the team that are helping to bring *Dream* out into the world, including Jessica Wallner, Ilana Bercovitz, Lauren Tenant and others.

And to the collective spirit and the people that have gone before, are working hard now and in the future to nurture the dream.

Thank you.

one

Numbers Pages Notes

1. 'Cares what people think' CBS, NYTimes poll, 2010, www.cbsnews.com/htdocs/pdf/poll_Obama_Congress_021110.pdf, accessed September 1, 2010.
2. 'Do what is right' Pew Charitable Trusts poll, 2009, http://people-press.org/report/?pageid=1523, accessed September 1, 2010.
3. 'Military spending' Stockholm International Peace Research Institute, "Military Expenditure Data, 2001-2010," 2011, http://www.sipri.org/yearbook/2011/04/04A, accessed June 21, 2011.
4. 'Federal Education & Natural Resources and Environment Spending' Office of Management and Budget, "Outlays by Function and Subfunction," http://www.whitehouse.gov/omb/budget/Historicals/, accessed June 21, 2011.
5. '$5 billion / $600,000 an hour' CommonCause, "Business Leaders for Fair Elections ad in Roll Call," 2009, http://www.commoncause.org/site/pp.asp?c=dkLNK1MQIwG&b=5346571, accessed July 7, 2011.
6. 'Canada $300 million spending' Chief Electoral Officer of Canada, "Report of the Chief Electoral Officer of Canada on the 40th General Election of October 14, 2008," 2009, http://www.elections.ca/content.aspx?section=res&dir=rep/off/sta_2008&document=p2&lang=e#p2_11, accessed July 1, 2011.
7. 'Puerto Alegre' Environmentally and Socially Sustainable Development Network, www.sasanet.org/documents/Case%20Studies/Participatory%20Approaches%20in%20Budgeting%20-%20Brazil.pdf, accessed September 1, 2010.
8. 'New Orleans' see AmericaSpeaks, Citizens Strengthening Democracy, p. 27
9. 'New Leaders' – Harvard Kennedy School, www.innovations.harvard.edu/awards.html?id=909886, accessed October 13, 2010.
10. 'Hocking High School' see Frances Moore Lappe, Toward a Living Democracy, p. 13
11. 'Healthcare lobbying' OpenSecrets, "Diagnosis: Reform," 2009, www.opensecrets.org/news/2009/06/diagnosis-reform.html, accessed July 1, 2011.
12. 'Fair Elections / Connecticut' see Common Cause, Getting Money out of Politics, p. 23–24.

Essay Notes

Frances Moore Lappe:

1. Also known as, "Clean Money," "Voter-Owned Elections," or "Fair Elections."
2. "From Poverty to Prosperity: A National Strategy to Cut Poverty in Half," Center for American Progress, Washington, DC, April, 2007, 8-9.
3. "Participatory Budgeting Project," www.participatorybudgeting.org/, accessed April 28, 2010.
4. Econimic Policy Institute, www.stateofworkingamerica.org/charts/view/17, accessed May 27, 2011.
5. Seventh Generation, Our Compensation, Principles and Beliefs. www.seventhgeneration.com/learn/inspiredprotagonist/our-compensation-principles-beliefs. August 15, 2009.
6. "Local Living Wage Ordinances and Coverage," National Employment Law Center, December 6, 2010, www.nelp.org/page/-/Justice/2011/LocalLivingWageOrdinancesandCoverage.pdf?nocdn=1, accessed May 25, 2011.
7. Personal communication with author, Dr. George Wood, August 15, 2005.
8. Erich Fromm, The Heart of Man, New York: Harper & Row, 1964, 26-27.

National Priorities Project:

1. Stockholm International Peace Research Institute, "Military Expenditure Data, 2001-2010," 2011, http://www.sipri.org/yearbook/2011/04/04A, accessed June 21, 2011.
2. Albeit more slowly than originally projected by Obama Administration officials.
3. Jackie Calmes, "Obama to Seek Spending Freeze to Trim Deficits," New York Times, January 26, 2010, available at www.nytimes.com/2010/01/26/us/politics/26budget.html?scp=1&sq=discretionary%20spending&st=cse, accessed October 4, 2010.
4. Office of Management and Budget, "Outlays by Function and Subfunction," http://www.whitehouse.gov/omb/budget/Historicals/, accessed June 21, 2011.
5. Task Force on a Unified Security Budget, A Unified Security Budget for the United States, FY2011, Introduction, Foreign Policy in Focus, Institute for Policy Studies, August, 2010, available at www.ips-dc.org/reports/USB_fy_2011, accessed October 4, 2010.
6. Task Force on a Unified Security Budget, p. 3.
7. US Census Bureau, "Number in Poverty and Poverty Rate: 1959 to 2008," http://upload.wikimedia.org/wikipedia/commons/b/b7/US_poverty_rate_timeline.gif, accessed October 14, 2010.
8. US Census Bureau, Income, Poverty, and Health Insurance Coverage in the US: 2008, US Department of Commerce, September, 2009, p. 99, www.census.gov/prod/2008pubs/p60-235.pdf, p. 12, accessed October 4, 2010.
9. US Census Bureau, American Factfinder, August, 2008, Table GCT1704, available at: factfinder.census.gov, accessed October 4, 2010.
10. Harry J Holzer, Diane Schwarzenback, Greg Duncan and Jens Ludwig, The Economic Costs of Poverty in the US: Subsequent Effects of Children Growing Up Poor, Center for American Progress, Washington, DC, January, 2007, p. 1, available at www.americanprogress.org/issues/2007/01/pdf/poverty_report.pdf, accessed October 4, 2010.
11. Libby Quaid, Study Laments Drop Out Rates, Associated Press, in The Springfield Republican, October 24, 2008, p. A7.
12. Marguerite Rosa, "What If We Closed the Title 1 Comparability Loophole?", in Ensuring Equal Opportunity in Public Education, Center for American Progress, June 2008, pp. 63-67, 74-75, available at: http://zedc3test.techprogress.org/issues/2008/06/pdf/comparability_part3.pdf, accessed October 4, 2010.
13. American Society of Civil Engineers, www.asce.org/reportcard/2010, accessed June 21, 2011.
14. American Federation of Teachers, Building Minds, Minding Buildings: Turning Crumbling Schools into Environments for Learning, Washington DC, www.aft.org/topics/building-conditions/downloads/minding-bldgs.pdf, accessed October 4, 2010.
15. National Priorities Project, The Hidden Costs of Petroleum, October 2008, p. 1, www.nationalpriorities.org/auxiliary/energy_security/petroleum_fact_sheets/petroleum_US.pdf, accessed October 4, 2010.
16. National Priorities Project, Priorities for Energy, October, 2008, p. 1, www.nationalpriorities.org/auxiliary/energy_security/energy_fact_sheets/energy_US.pdf, accessed October 4, 2010.
17. United Nations Development Programme, Human Development Reports, 2009, http://hdrstats.undp/indicators.html, accessed October 4, 2010.
18. Stockholm International Peace Research Institute (SIPRI), World Military Expenditures Database, www.sipri.org/result.php4, accessed October 4, 2010.
19. Human Development Reports, ibid.
20. Task Force on a Unified Security Budget, chapter 4.
21. Based on American Federation of Teachers estimate of $234 billion total cost to repair all public schools. See American Federation of Teachers, Building Minds, Minding Buildings: Turning Crumbling Schools into Environments for Learning, Washington DC, www.aft.org/topics/building-conditions/downloads/minding-bldgs.pdf, accessed October 4, 2010; $75 billion is 32% of $234 billion.
22. The funding request for the federal Department of Education budget for fiscal year 2010 was $64 billion. National Priorities Project, The President's Budget: Fiscal Year 2011, February 9, 2010, available at www.nationalpriorities.org/Presidents_Budget_FY2011, accessed October 4, 2010.
23. The cost of a full Pell grant is $5,500, www.nationalpriorities.org/tradeoffs?location_type=1&state=888&program=707&tradeoff_item_item=999&submit_tradeoffs=Get+Trade+Off). According to the federal government, there were 13,245,000 full-time undergraduate college students and 5,387,000 undergraduate part-time college students in the US in 2008, www.census.gov/population/www/socdemo/school/cps.2008.html, table 5. The cost of providing all full-time students with the $5,500 grant, and all part-time students with $2,750, or half the grant, would be $87.6 billion; $75 billion is 85% of the full cost.
24. Congressional Budget Office, "The Budgetary Effects of Selected Policy Alternatives Not Included in CBO's Baseline," www.cbo.gov/ftpdocs/100xx/doc10014/BudEffects.pdf, accessed June 14, 2010.
25. Task Force on a Unified Security Budget, based on data in category entitled "Preventive," Table 3, p. 9.
26. www.cnn.com/SPECIALS/war.casualties/index.html, accessed June 6, 2011.
27. John Bohannon, "Counting the Dead in Afghanistan," March 11, 2011, Science Magazine, www.sciencemag.org/content/331/6022/1256.full, accessed June 6, 2011.
28. Andrea Shalal-Esa, "Task Force See Pentagon Cuts Key to U.S. Budget Fix," Reuters, June 11, 2010, available at: www.reuters.com/article/idUSN1117080020100611, accessed July 5, 2010. Full report at www.comw.org/pda/fulltext/1006SDTFreport.pdf, accessed July 9, 2010.
29. President Eisenhower's Farewell Address to the Nation, Washington, DC, January 17, 1961.

Common Cause:

1. www.opensecrets.org/overview/DonorDemographics.php, accessed February 8, 2011.
2. www.opensecrets.org/news/2009/06/diagnosis-reform.html, accessed October 19, 2010.
3. www.opensecrets.org/lobby/billsum.php?id=107281, accessed October 19, 2010.
4. www.cfinst.org/pdf/federal/PostElec2010_Table3_.pdf, accessed February 10, 2011.

AmericaSpeaks:

1. CBS, NYTimes poll, 2010, www.cbsnews.com/htdocs/pdf/poll_Obama_Congress_021110.pdf, accessed September 1, 2010.
2. Pew Charitable Trusts poll, 2009, http://people-press.org/report/?pageid=1523, accessed September 1, 2010.
3. www.sasanet.org/documents/Case%20Studies/Participatory%20Approaches%20in%20Budgeting%20-%20Brazil.pdf, accessed September 1, 2010.

Alliance for Innovation:

1. www.ecitygov.net/about/default.aspx, accessed October 27, 2010.
2. Bridgette Meinhold, "Greensburg Kansas Rebuilds Better and Greener After Tornado," May 24, 2010, http://inhabitat.com/2010/05/24/greensburg-kansas-rebuilds-better-stronger-and-greener/, accessed October 8, 2010.
3. www.appsfordemocracy.org/about, accessed October 8, 2010.
4. Russell Nichols, July 11, 2010, "Do Apps for Democracy and Other Contests Create Sustainable Applications?" Government Technology, http://www.govtech.com/e-government/Do-Apps-for-Democracy-and-Other.html, accessed October 8, 2010.
5. http://sfwater.org/Files/Reports/GoSolarSF_StatReport_SEP_2009.pdf, accessed October 8, 2010.
6. http://sfwater.org/detail.cfm/MC_ID/12/MSC_ID/139/MTO_ID/361/C_ID/4428/ListID/1, accessed October 8, 2010.
7. www.nyc.gov/html/doh/html/cardio/cardio-transfat.shtml, accessed October 11, 2010.
8. Kim Severson, 2006, "New York Gets Ready to Count Calories," New York Times, December 13, www.nytimes.com/2006/12/13/dining/13calo.html, accessed October 11, 2010.
9. William Neuman, 2010, "Citing Hazard, New York Says Hold the Salt," New York Times, January 10, www.nytimes.com/2010/01/11/business/11salt.html?_r=1, accessed October 11, 2010.
10. www.innovations.harvard.edu/awards.html?id=909886, accessed October 13, 2010.

Bipartisan Bridge:

1. Except the budget and departmental appropriations.

two

Numbers Pages Notes

1. '8 billion hours' Susan Kinzie, "Number of volunteers has grown despite recession, study says," Washington Post, June 15, accessed March 7, 2011.
2. '$300 billion' www.charitynavigator.org/index.cfm?bay=content.view&cpid=42, accessed March 7, 2011.
3. 'Bottled water' Ariel Schwartz, "Annie Leonard's 'Story of Bottle Water' Should Make Fiji Nervous," Fast Company, March 22, 2010, www.fastcompany.com/1593405/annie-leonards-story-of-bottled-water-should-make-fiji-nervous, accessed April 14, 2010.
4. '5 planets' Global Footprint Network, "Ecological Footprint Atlas 2010," http://www.footprintnetwork.org/images/uploads/Ecological%20Footprint%20Atlas%202010.pdf, accessed May 27, 2011.
5. 'Junk mail' Center for a New American Dream, www.newdream.org/junkmail/facts.php, accessed September 2, 2010.
6. 'CO2 footprints' Encyclopedia of Earth, www.eoearth.org/article/Carbon_footprint, accessed March 7, 2011.
7. '1,100 lbs' Green Energy Council, "Home Tips," http://www.greenenergycouncil.com/pdfs/home_tips.pdf, accessed July 1, 2011.
8. '2,500 lbs' Energy Star, www.energystar.gov/index.cfm?fuseaction=find_a_product.showProductGroup&pgw_code=RF, accessed July 1, 2011.
9. '1,040 lbs' American Public Transportation Association, www.publictransportation.org/facts/, accessed March 11, 2010.

Essay Notes

Global Footprint Network:

1. WWF, "Living Planet Report," 2010, www.footprintnetwork.org/press/LPR2010.pdf, accessed May 27, 2011.
2. Richard Heinberg, Peak Everything: Waking Up to the Century of Declines (Gabriola Island: New Society Publishers, 2007)
3. Global Footprint Network, "Ecological Footprint Atlas 2010," www.footprintnetwork.org/images/uploads/Ecological%20Footprint%20Atlas%202010.pdf, accessed May 27, 2011.

Center for a New American Dream:

1. New American Dream Survey Report, September 2004, web2.newdream.org/about/pdfs/Finalpollreport.pdf, accessed September 2, 2010.
2. www.simpleliving.net/, accessed April 13, 2010.
3. Ellen Goodman, womenshistory.about.com/od/quotes/a/ellen_goodman.htm, accessed September 2, 2010.
4. Sarah W. Caron, "Frugal ways to keep your family warm at home," www.sheknows.com/articles/806732/frugal-ways-to-keep-your-family-warm-at-home, accessed October 19, 2010.
5. Energy Star Refrigerators: www.energystar.gov/index.cfm?fuseaction=find_a_product.showProductGroup&pgw_code=RF
6. www.eartheasy.com/live_energyeff_lighting.htm, accessed April 9, 2010.
7. Brian Halweil, "Home Grown: The Case for Local Food in a Global Market," 2002, www.worldwatch.org/node/827, accessed October 19, 2010.
8. Calculation of impact of one ton of 100% recycled copy paper vs. one ton of virgin copy paper from www.edf.org/papercalculator/index.cfm?tagID=20848, accessed September 2, 2010.
9. Calculated from www.epa.gov/oms/climate/420f05004.htm, accessed September 2, 2010.
10. www.publictransportation.org/facts/, accessed March 11, 2010.
11. www.wrppn.org/Custodial/Be%20Healthy%200.pdf, accessed September 2, 2010.
12. The Responsible Purchasing Guide to Cleaners, available at www.responsible-purchasing.org/purchasing_guides/cleaners/purchasing_guide.pdf, accessed September 2, 2010.
13. Jerry Yudelson, Dry Run: Preventing the Next Urban Water Crisis, Gabriola Island, BC: New Society Publishers, 2010, pp 2, 15, 26, 82.
14. Ariel Schwartz, "Annie Leonard's 'Story of Bottle Water' Should Make Fiji Nervous," Fast Company, March 22, 2010, www.fastcompany.com/1593405/annie-leonards-story-of-bottled-water-should-make-fiji-nervous, accessed April 14, 2010.
15. www.newdream.org/junkmail/facts.php, accessed September 2, 2010.

Citizen Effect:

1. United Nations, 2010, Factsheet on Water and Sanitation, http://www.un.org/waterforlifedecade/factsheet.html, accessed October 27, 2010.
2. Samiha Khanna, "Brother Ray," Indy Week, November 25, 2009, available at: www.indyweek.com/indyweek/brother-ray/Content?oid=1298972, accessed November 19, 2010.
3. www.nationalservice.gov/about/spiritofservice/2010.asp, accessed November 19, 2010.
4. www.ashoka.org/fellows/paul_rieckhoff, accessed October 27, 2010.
5. www.barronprize.org/2009, accessed October 27, 2010.

Girls Helping Girls:

1. Raymond, et al., "Sex Trafficking of Women in the United States: International and Domestic Trends," National Criminal Justice Reference Service, 2001, http://www.ncjrs.gov/pdffiles1/nij/grants/187774.pdf.
2. "Human Rights Facts and Figures," Women's Learning Partnership, 2000, http://www.learningpartnership.org/resources/facts/humanrights.
3. "HIV/AIDS Programs with Youth," Pathfinder International, 2004, http://www.pathfind.org/site/DocServer/PF.Fact_Sheets.HIV.Youth.pdf?docID=6299.

Editor's Boxes Notes

No Impact Man

1. http://noimpactman.typepad.com/blog/waste_not_want_not/page/5/, accessed June 14, 2011.
2. http://noimpactman.typepad.com/blog/about-colin-beavan.html, accessed June 14, 2011.
3. http://noimpactman.typepad.com/blog/2008/04/lv-grn-42-ways.html, accessed June 14, 2011.
4. http://noimpactman.typepad.com/blog/2007/02/the_no_impact_m.html, accessed June 14, 2011.
5. http://noimpactman.typepad.com/blog/waste_not_want_not/page/4/, accessed June 14, 2011.

three

Numbers Pages Notes

1. 'Richest 1%' Working Group on Extreme Inequality, http://extremeinequality. org/?page_id=8, accessed August 30, 2010.
2. '$980 billion tax cuts' United for a Fair Economy, "Take Action to End the Bush Tax Cuts," http://www.faireconomy.org/enews/bush_tax_cuts_action_letter_to_editor, accessed July 6, 2011.
3. 'One-half of work-ready adults' www.businessinsider.com/real-employment-rate-47-percent-2011-1, accessed August 8, 2011.
4. '1.7 million' US Mayors' Conference, www.usmayors.org/pressreleases/uploads/GreenJobsReport.pdf, accessed January 26, 2011.
5. '30 million' see Bill Drayton, *Switching Taxes to Get America Working*, p. 116
6. 'Locally owned businesses' Local First Arizona, www.localfirstaz.com/studies/index.php, accessed March 4, 2011.
7 'Population of 770,000' Local First Grand Rapids, http://www.localfirstaz.com/studies/local-works/index.php, accessed July 1, 2011 (if we want to go with U.S. population, then note would read: "Based on a study of a population of 770,000, …".

Essay Notes

David Korten:
1. www.happyplanetindex.org/.

United for a Fair Economy:
1. Emmanuel Saez, "Striking it Richer: Evolution of Top Incomes in the United States," August 5, 2009. Available at: http://elsa.berkeley.edu/~saez/saez-UStopincomes-2007.pdf, accessed August 30, 2010.
2. Working Group on Extreme Inequality, http://extremeinequality.org/?page_id=8, accessed August 30, 2010.
3. Jeff Chapman & Jeff Thompson, "The economic impact of local living wages," Economic Policy Institute, Available at: www.epi.org/publications/entry/bp170/, accessed April 20, 2010.
4. Sam Hananel, "'Living Wage' Could Be Factor in Govt Contracts," ABC News, February 26, 2010. Available at: http://abcnews.go.com/Business/wireStory?id=9950908, accessed April 21, 2010.
5. Chris Pentilla, "Who's Paying?" Entrepreneur, December 2001. Available at: www.entrepreneur.com/magazine/entrepreneur/2001/december/46346.html, accessed April 21, 2010.
6. Gerald Prante, "Summary of Latest Federal Individual Income Tax Data, Tax Foundation, July 30, 2009. Available at: www.taxfoundation.org/news/show/250.html, accessed August 30, 2010.
7. Tax Fairness Pledge, www.faireconomy.org/taxpledge, accessed August 30, 2010.
8. David M. Herszenhorn and Carl Hulse, "Bush Tax-Cut Deal with Jobless Aid Said to Be Near," New York Times, December 5, 2010, www.nytimes.com/2010/12/06/us/politics/06cong.html, accessed February 3, 2011.
9. Lucia Graves, "Jan Schakowsky Introduces Bill to Raise Taxes for Wealthiest Americans, March 16, 2011, The Huffington Post, com/2011/03/16/jan-schakowsky-income-tax_n_836624.html, accessed June 21, 2011.
10. Reed Hastings, "Please Raise My Taxes," *New York Times*, February 5, 2009. Available at: www.nytimes.com/2009/02/06/opinion/06hastings.html, accessed April 21, 2010.
11. "Most Americans Say Tax Rich to Balance Budget," Reuters, January 4, 2011, www.commondreams.org/headline/2011/01/04-8, accessed February 3, 2011.
12. Lucia Graves, "Jan Schakowsky Introduces Bill to Raise Taxes for Wealthiest Americans, March 16, 2011, The Huffington Post, wwwhuffingtonpostcom/2011/03/16/jan-schakowsky-income-tax_n_836624.html, accessed June 21, 2011.
13. Undervisnings Ministeriet, http://eng.uvm.dk/Aktuelt/News/Eng/090618%20Danes%20keen%20on%20learning%20throughout%20life.aspx, accessed April 28, 2010.
14. Tertiary education graduation rates, OECD Library, www.oecdilibrary.org/oecd/sites/20755120-2009-table1/index.html;jsessionid=1erlfdv5aey9w.delta?contentType=/ns/KeyTable,/ns/StatisticalPublication&itemId=/content/table/20755120-table1&containerItemId=/content/table/20755120-table1&accessItemIds=&mimeType=text/html, accessed April 28, 2010.

Campaign for America's Future:
1. The total loss was 8,928, an average loss of one factory per hour over the year. "Establishment and Employment Changes from Births, Deaths, Expansions, and Contractions," www.census.gov/econ/susb/data/susb2002.html, accessed October 13, 2010.
2. BBC News, "Over 5 billion mobile phone connections worldwide," http://www.bbc.co.uk/news/10569081, accessed June 14, 2011.

3. Earth Policy Institute and Worldwatch Institute, "Annual Solar Photovoltaics Production by Country 1995-2008," www.earth-policy.org/datacenter/xls/book_pb4_ch4-5_16.xls, accessed October 13, 2010.
4. Private Services Transactions, the Bureau of Economic Analysis, http://www.bea.gov/international/index.htm#trade, accessed June 14, 2010.
5. Lori Montgomery and Scott Wilson, "Obama Targets Overseas Tax Dodge," http://www.washingtonpost.com/wp-dyn/content/article/2009/05/04/AR2009050400703.html, accessed October 14, 2010.
6. Eurostat, "Eurostat yearbook 2010," *European Commission*, February 2011.
7. National Association of Manufacturers, *The Facts about Modern Manufacturing*, Manufacturing Institute, 8th ed., 2009, www.nam.org/AboutUs/TheManufacturingInstitute/CenterforManufacturingResearchandInnovation/TheFactsAboutModernManufacturing.aspx?DID=%7BE9F34396-247D-4475-A518-518FE3CBE638%7D, accessed October 13, 2010.
8. Survey of registered voters by the Mellman Group, "Decline of Manufacturing Jobs, Loss of Global Economic Standing, and Fears About China are Top Voter Concerns," June 24, 2010, www.americanmanufacturing.org/newscenter/pressreleases/2010/06/24/new-poll-decline-of-manufacturing-jobs-loss-of-global-economic-standing-and-fears-about-china-are-top-voter-concerns/, accessed October 13, 2010.
9. Terence P. Stewart and Elizabeth J. Drake, "Buy America: Key to America's Economic Recovery," Alliance for American Manufacturing, February 2009.
10. "Buy America Brouhaha: What Are the EU and Canada Hollering About? Their WTO Procurement Exceptions Are (Wisely) Much Broader Than U.S. Stimulus Proposal," Public Citizen, February 5, 2009, www.citizen.org/documents/BuyAmericaMemo-FINAL.pdf, accessed October 13, 2010.
11. Keith Bradsher, "China Builds High Wall to Guard Energy Industry," *New York Times*, July 14, 2009, www.nytimes.com/2009/07/14/business/energy-environment/14energy.html?_r=3&ref=business, accessed October 13, 2010.
12. Keith Schneider, "Talk About a Window of Opportunity," *Apollo News Service*, March 21, 2009, http://apolloalliance.org/new-apollo-program/talk-about-a-window-of-opportunity/, accessed October 13, 2010.

Green For All:
1. Sacramento Mayor Kevin Johnson will release his Regional Action Plan on January 20, 2011, and it will include the specifics of the plan. Green For All obtained this information prior to the plan's official release as a member of the Mayor Johnson's Leadership Team.
2. http://green.blogs.nytimes.com/2009/06/10/study-cites-strong-green-job-growth, accessed November 4, 2010.
3. "Rebuilding Green: The American Recovery and Reinvestment Act and the Green Economy," The Economic Policy Institute and the BlueGreen Alliance. February 2011.
4. www.usmayors.org/pressreleases/uploads/GreenJobsReport.pdf, accessed January 26, 2011.
5. The Apollo Alliance, "The New Apollo Plan: Clean Energy & Good Jobs," October 1, 2008. http://apolloalliance.org/programs/apollo-14/.
6. R. Pollin et al., "Green Recovery: A Program to Create Good Jobs and Start Building a Low-Carbon Economy," Center for American Progress and Political Economy and Research Institute (PERI), University of Massachusetts-Amherst, September 2008, www.americanprogress.org/issues/2008/09/pdf/green_recovery.pdf, accessed May 27, 2011.
7. www.prnewswire.com/news-releases/dep-three-exciting-projects-in-pa-show-momentum-progress-toward-clean-energy-future-106146893.html, accessed November 4, 2010.
8. www.greenforall.org/resources/greencorps-chicago, accessed January 9, 2011.
9. American Community Survey, 2005-2007 data in G. Yakimov & L. Woolsey, *Innovation and Product Development in the 21st Century*, Hollings Manufacturing Extension Partnership Advisory Board, February 2010.
10. Good Jobs First, "High Road or Low Road? Job Quality in the New Green Economy," February 3, 2009, apolloalliance.org/downloads/gjfgreenjobsrpt.pdf, accessed May 27, 2011.
11. www.marketwatch.com/story/pelosi-gms-initial-public-offering-a-sign-of-progress-for-americas-auto-industry-and-our-nations-workers-2010-11-18-18300, accessed May 27, 2011.
12. US Census Bureau, *Current Housing Reports: American Housing Survey for the United States, 2005*, Washington: Government Printing Office, August 2006.
13. Apollo Alliance, "Make It in America: The Apollo Clean Transportation Manufacturing Action Plan," October 2010, http://apolloalliance.org/tmap/.

BALLE:
1. www.portfolio21.com/, accessed January 9, 2011.
2. www.livingeconomies.org/aboutus/research-and-studies/studies, accessed January 27, 2011.
3. www.stateofworkingamerica.org/charts/view/52, accessed November 3, 2010.

4. seattletimes.nwsource.com/html/opinion/2008936833_opinb29jacoby.html, accessed November 3, 2010.

5. www.evergreencoop.com/, accessed January 26, 2011.

6. www.time.com/time/business/article/0,8599,1947313,00.html, accessed November 3, 2010.

Get America Working!:

1. There are many more Americans who want, but don't have, jobs than the official unemployment rate implies. As of February 2011, the potential workforce in the United States composed of civilian, non-institutionalized adults (not in school, the military or other institutions) ages 17 to 74, numbered 221 million people. These are Americans who, given reasonable opportunity, would overwhelmingly like to have and would be able to do a job if one were available. Of that 221 million, just over half (112 million) have full-time jobs. 27.4 million only work part time, 67.7 million don't work at all, and only 13.9 million are acknowledged in the official unemployment rate (9% at present writing) as being out of work. That official rate has lots of exclusionary criteria as to who is and is not considered officially unemployed, and the definitions keep tightening over time. But the true, raw number of jobless Americans is not 13.9 million; it's closer to 80 million.

2. www.getamericaworking.org/europeanexperience, accessed March 3, 2011.

3. Economist Daniel S. Hamermesh, whose books include *Labor Demand* (Princeton University Press, 1993), *The Economics of Work and Pay* (with R. Filer, Harper and Row, 1996), and *Economics Is Everywhere* (Worth Publishers, 2010), in an April 8, 1997 letter to Josh Gotbaum, then Assistant Secretary for Economic Policy, U.S. Treasury Department, wrote that "cutting payroll taxes by ten percentage points would increase employment roughly three percent in the short term and perhaps as much as ten percent in the long term."

Editor's Boxes Notes

Slows BarBQ

1. Johnny Knoxville, "Detroit Lives," 2010, http://www.palladiumboots.com/video/detroit-lives#part1, accessed July 3, 2011.

Measuring National Happiness & Well-being

1. Allegra Stratton, "David Cameron aims to make happiness the new GDP, The Guardian, November 14, 20101, www.guardian.co.uk/politics/2010/nov/14/david-cameron-wellbeing-inquiry, accessed February 15, 2011.

2. Office of National Statistics, www.ons.gov.uk/well-being, accessed February 16, 2011.

3. Allegra Stratton, "David Cameron aims to make happiness the new GDP, The Guardian, November 14, 20101, www.guardian.co.uk/politics/2010/nov/14/david-cameron-wellbeing-inquiry, accessed February 15, 2011.

4. Laura Stoll, "Beyond GDP: UK to Measure Well-Being," Yes!, January 27, 2011, www.yesmagazine.org/happiness/beyond-gdp-uk-to-measure-well-being?utm_source=wkly20110128&utm_medium=yesemail&utm_campaign=titleStoll, accessed February 16, 2011.

5. Laura Stoll, "Beyond GDP: UK to Measure Well-Being," Yes!, January 27, 2011, www.yesmagazine.org/happiness/beyond-gdp-uk-to-measure-well-being?utm_source=wkly20110128&utm_medium=yesemail&utm_campaign=titleStoll, accessed February 16, 2011.

6. Scott Gast, "Maryland Launches Genuine Progress Indicator," Yes!, April 2, 2010, www.yesmagazine.org/new-economy/maryland-launches-genuine-progress-indicator, accessed February 16, 2011.

Closing Tax Loopholes and Funding Key Priorities

1. Melissa Boteach, Seth Hanlon, "Bait and Switch," June 2, 2011, Center for American Progress, www.americanprogress.org/issues/2011/06/bait_and_switch.html, accessed June 24, 2011.

2. Melissa Boteach, Seth Hanlon, "Bait and Switch," June 2, 2011, Center for American Progress, www.americanprogress.org/issues/2011/06/bait_and_switch.html, accessed June 24, 2011.

3. Melissa Boteach, Seth Hanlon, "Bait and Switch," June 2, 2011, Center for American Progress, www.americanprogress.org/issues/2011/06/bait_and_switch.html, accessed June 24, 2011.

4. Scott A. Hodge, "Who Benefits from Corporate 'Loopholes'?" March 2, 2011, http://taxfoundation.org/publications/show/27081.html, accessed June 24, 2011.

5. http://www.nytimes.com/2011/02/01/business/01oil.html, accessed July 13, 2011.

6. http://www.nytimes.com/2011/03/25/business/economy/25tax.html?pagewanted=1&_r=2&hp, accessed July 13, 2011.

7. http://www.marketwatch.com/story/chevron-profit-tops-5-billion-beats-target-2011-01-28, accessed July 13, 2011.

8. http://1cu2.com/business/corporations-that-got-massive-tax-breaks-spent-millions-in-2010-elections/, accessed July 13, 2011.

9. http://www.ctj.org/pdf/boeing0211.pdf, accessed July 13, 2011.

0. http://www.publicampaign.org/reports/artfuldodgers/banks#_ftn4, accessed July 13, 2011.

Job Training For the New Green Economy

1. "Green Opportunities Annual Impact Report," Asheville GO Annual Report, October 2010.

2. "Green Opportunities Annual Impact Report," Asheville GO Annual Report, October 2010.

3. "Green Opportunities Annual Impact Report," Asheville GO Annual Report, October 2010.

4. "Green Opportunities Annual Impact Report," Asheville GO Annual Report, October 2010.

four

Numbers Pages Notes

1. 'only 8 percent confidence, 18 percent no confidence' Project for Excellence in Journalism, www.stateofthemedia.org/2009/narrative_overview_publicattitudes.php?cat=3&media=1, accessed March 1, 2010.

2. '1 in 5 independent' see Free Press, *Making Coverage Count*, p. 130.

3. 'Public media' "New Public Media," p. 5 http://www.freepress.net/files/New_Public_Media.doc.pdf.

4. 'Iraq 393' Fairness and Accuracy in Reporting, "In Iraq Crisis, Networks Are Megaphones for Official Views," 2003, www.fair.org/index.php?page=1628, accessed October 13, 2010.

5. 'Half of states' Project for Excellence in Journalism, "State of News Media 2009," 2009, www.stateofthemedia.org/2009/narrative_overview_keyindicators.php?media=1, accessed October 13, 2010.

6. '30,000 fired' Olivia Loyd, "My Industry is Hemorrhaging," 2009, http://www.thewip.net/contributors/2009/01/my_industry_is_hemorrhaging_jo.html

7. 'CNN.com/Commondreams' see Free Press, *Making Coverage Count*, p. 129.

Essay Notes

Amy Goodman:

1. He has since admitted, "I have a blot on my record" because of the speech, with its dire warnings about Saddam Hussein's weapons of mass destruction.

2. "In Iraq Crisis, Networks Are Megaphones for Official Views," *Fairness and Accuracy in Reporting*, 2003, www.fair.org/index.php?page=1628, accessed October 13, 2010.

3. Julie Hollar and Isabel Macdonald, "Media Quarantine of Single-Payer Continues," *Fairness and Accuracy in Reporting*, June 2009, www.fair.org/index.php?page=3793, accessed October 13, 2010.

4. www.stateofthemedia.org/2009/narrative_overview_publicattitudes.php?cat=3&media=1, accessed March 1, 2010.

5. http://pewresearch.org/pubs/557/public-blames-media-for-too-much-celebrity-coverage, accessed March 1, 2010.

6. http://people-press.org/report/543/, accessed March 1, 2010.

7. www.indypendent.org/?pagename=about, accessed February 22, 2010.

8. Sheri Fink, "The Deadly Choices at Memorial," *New York Times Magazine*, August 27, 2009, www.propublica.org/article/the-deadly-choices-at-memorial-826, accessed July 1, 2010.

9. www.propublica.org/about/, accessed July 1, 2010.

Free Press:

1. Project for Excellence in Journalism, 2008, "Winning the Media Campaign: How the Press Reported the 2008 General Election," www.journalism.org/analysis_report/winning_media_campaign, accessed October 13, 2010.

2. Snyder and Stromberg, "Press Coverage and Political Accountability," *NBER*, March 2008.

3. Project for Excellence in Journalism, 2009, "State of News Media 2009," www.stateofthemedia.org/2009/narrative_overview_keyindicators.php?media=1, accessed October 13, 2010.

4. Doug Gross, "Survey: More Americans Get News from Internet Than Newspapers or Radio," CNN, March 1, 2010, http://articles.cnn.com/2010-03-01/tech/social.network.news_1_social-networking-sites-social-media-social-experience?_s=PM:TECH, accessed September 21, 2010.

5. Martin Kaplan and Matthew Hale, "Local TV News in the Los Angeles Media Market: Are Stations Serving the Public Interest?" The Norman Lear Center, USC Annenberg School for Communications & Journalism, March 11, 2010.

6. www.pbs.org/roperpoll2010/, accessed March 2, 2010.

7. Steve Coll, "Notes About Public Policy," *The New Yorker*, October 2, 2009, www.newyorker.com/online/blogs/stevecoll/2009/10/public-media.html, accessed September 21, 2010.

8. The Economist Intelligence Unit's Index of Democracy 2010, http://graphics.eiu.com/PDF/Democracy_Index_2010_web.pdf, accessed January 23, 2011.

Solutions Journal:

1. J. Gripsrud, 2001, "Television: General," *International Encyclopedia of the Social & Behavioral Sciences.*
2. James L. Baughman, 2001, *Henry R. Luce and the Rise of the American News Media,* John Hopkins University Press.
3. W.M. Johnston & G.C. Davey, 1997, "The Psychological Impact of Negative TV News Bulletins: The Catastrophizing of Personal Worries," *British Journal of Psychology,* pp. 85-91.
4. A.H. Miller, E.N. Goldenberg & L. Erbring, 1979, "Type-Set Politics: Impact of Newspapers on Public Confidence," *The American Political Science Review,* 73(1), pp. 67-84.
5. Lawrence Street, 2001, *Law of the Internet,* Lexis Law Publications.
6. www.goodnewsnetwork.org/about-us.html, accessed January 26, 2011.
7. http://peace.ashoka.org/michael_gleich_interview, accessed January 26, 2011.
8. Johan Galtung, 2000, "The Task of Peace Journalism," *Ethical Perspectives* 7 (2-3), p. 165.

Editor's Boxes Notes

Covering More of What Matters

1. http://pewresearch.org/pubs/1725/where-people-get-news-print-online-readership-cable-news-viewers, accessed December 10, 2010.
2. www.rasmussenreports.com/public_content/lifestyle/people/july_2010/87_feel_media_covers_celebrities_too_much, accessed December 10, 2010.

More Good News

1. www.educationnation.com/index.cfm?objectid=993A0F30-BA60-11DF-A380000C296BA163, accessed October 18, 2010.
2. www.cbsnews.com/stories/1998/07/08/60minutes/main13503.shtml, accessed October 18, 2010.
3. www.pbs.org/newshour/bb/media/july-dec09/pbsnewshour_12-04.html, accessed December 9, 2010.

five

Numbers Pages Notes

1. 'School district funding' Education Intelligence Agency, www.eiaonline.com/districts/Pennsylvania.pdf, 2010.
2. '40% lack skills' Peter D. Hart Research Associates/Public Opinion Strategies, "Rising to the Challenge: Are High School Graduates Prepared for College and Work? A Study of Recent High School Graduates, College Instructors, and Employers" 2005, *Achieve, Inc.*
3. '75% students' see Community Schools, *A School and Community Strategy for the 21st Century* p. 163.
4. '90% of HCZ' Harlem Children's Zone, http://www.hcz.org/our-results, accessed June 20, 2011.
5. '100-360$ billion and $15 billion' David Goldman, "Obama's School Patchwork Project," CNN Money, 2009, http://money.cnn.com/2009/01/14/news/economy/school_stimulus/index.htm, accessed May 6, 2010.
6. '26 seconds' http://www.26seconds.com/PDF/press_release_20110318.pdf, accessed July 11, 2011.
7. '$900 million' The White House, "President Obama Announces Steps to Reduce Dropout Rate," http://www.whitehouse.gov/the-press-office/president-obama-announces-steps-reduce-dropout-rate-and-prepare-students-college-an, accessed July 5, 2011.
8. '$400-$670 billion' Based on 2008 study, with inflation factored in, www.mckinsey.com/App_Media/Images/Page_Images/Offices/SocialSector/PDF/achievement_gap_report.pdf, accessed May 6, 2010.
9. 'Median earnings' www.bls.gov/emp/ep_chart_001.htm, accessed May 4, 2010.
10. '2x more likely' de Vise and Chandler, "Washington Region's Poorest Areas Have an Abundance of Beginning Teachers," April 27, 2009.

Essay Notes

Geoffrey Canada:

1. Dobbie & Fryer, "Are High-quality Schools Enough to Close the Achievement Gap? Evidence from a Bold Social Experiment in Harlem," Harvard University, 2009, www.economics.harvard.edu/faculty/fryer/files/hcz%204.15.2009.pdf.
2. Sandy Baum, Jennifer Ma & Kathleen Payea, "Education Pays 2010," College Board Advocacy and Policy Center, trends.collegeboard.org/files/Education_Pays_2010.pdf, accessed October 14, 2010.
3. New York State Office of Children & Family Services, "Empty Beds, Wasted Dollars," 2008, www.ccf.state.ny.us/Initiatives/CJRelate/CJResources/Feb28Summit/EmptyBeds.pdf.

4. Jennifer Steinhauer, "To Cut Costs, States Relax Prison Policies," *New York Times,* March 24, 2009, www.nytimes.com/2009/03/25/us/25prisons.html.

Campaign for Educational Equity:

1. www.eiaonline.com/districts/Pennsylvania.pdf, accessed April 22, 2010.
2. According to *The Condition of Education 2008,* high-poverty schools had a 21 percent rate of turnover versus only 14 percent for low-poverty schools. Much of the difference between the two turnover rates is due to the higher transfer rate among teachers in high- versus low-poverty schools (11 vs. 6 percent) (see M. Planty, et al., *The Condition of Education 2008* (NCES 2008-031), Washington, DC: National Center for Education Statistics, Institute of Education Sciences, US Department of Education). See also, R. M. Ingersoll, *Why Do High-Poverty Schools Have Difficulty Staffing Their Classrooms with Qualified Teachers?* Washington, DC: Center for American Progress, 2004; H.G. Peske and H. Haycock, *Teaching Inequality: How Poor and Minority Students Are Shortchanged on Teacher Quality,* Washington, DC: Education Trust, 2006.
3. www.washingtonpost.com/wp-dyn/content/article/2009/04/26/AR2009042602861.html, accessed April 22, 2010.
4. B. Berry, et al., *Creating and Sustaining Urban Teacher Residencies: A New Way to Recruit, Prepare, and Retain Effective Teachers in High-Needs Districts,* Hillsborough, NC: Center for Teaching Quality, August 2008.
5. The Aspen Institute, "Strategic Staffing for Successful Schools," April 2010.
6. US Department of Education, *Impact of Inadequate School Facilities on Student Learning,* April 3, 2000, retrieved on October 22, 2009, from www.ed.gov/offices/OESE/archives/inits/construction/impact2.html.
7. G.I. Earthman, *School Facility Conditions and Student Academic Achievement,* Los Angeles: UCLA Institute for Democracy, Education and Access (IDEA), 2002; J. Oakes & M. Saunders, *Access To Textbooks, Instructional Materials, Equipment, and Technology: Inadequacy and Inequality in California's Public Schools,* Los Angeles: UCLA Institute for Democracy, Education and Access (IDEA), 2002; US Department of Education, *Impact of Inadequate School Facilities on Student Learning,* April 3, 2000, retrieved on October 22, 2009, from www.ed.gov/offices/OESE/archives/inits/construction/impact2.html.
8. www.infrastructurereportcard.org/sites/default/files/RC2009_schools.pdf, accessed May 7, 2010.
9. David Goldman, "Obama's School Patchwork Project," *CNN Money,* January 15, 2009, available at: http://money.cnn.com/2009/01/14/news/economy/school_stimulus/index.htm, accessed May 6, 2010.
10. A. Vanneman, L. Hamilton, J. Baldwin Anderson & T. Rahman, *Achievement Gaps: How Black and White Students in Public Schools Perform in Mathematics and Reading on the National Assessment of Educational Progress,* (NCES 2009-455), National Center for Education Statistics, Institute of Education Sciences, US Department of Education, Washington, DC, 2009; R. Weiner, *Confounding Evidence on Achievement Gaps: Understanding Opportunity Gaps that Undermine School Success for Students from Poverty,* prepared for the UNC Symposium on High Poverty Schooling in America, October, 2006.
11. Low-income students in this study are defined as those students who qualify for federally subsidized free lunches, www.mckinsey.com/App_Media/Images/Page_Images/Offices/SocialSector/PDF/achievement_gap_report.pdf, accessed May 4, 2010.
12. www.bls.gov/emp/ep_chart_001.htm, accessed May 4, 2010.
13. www.mckinsey.com/App_Media/Images/Page_Images/Offices/SocialSector/PDF/achievement_gap_report.pdf, accessed May 6, 2010.
14. M.E. Goertz, *Assessing the Success of Adequacy Litigations: The Case of New Jersey,* Campaign for Educational Equity, New York, November, 2009.
15. www.education.ky.gov/kde/homepagerepository/proof+of+progress/kentucky+progress+in+p12+education.htm, accessed April 22, 2010.

Campaign for Environmental Literacy:

1. Matthew Williams, "Obama Calls L.A. Charter School a Model for Learning," KCET Local, April 15, 2010. Available at: http://kcet.org/local/shows/web_stories/2010/04/obama-names-echs-a-model-high-school-for-learning.html, accessed May 6, 2010.
2. OECD, "Green at Fifteen? How 15-year-olds perform in environmental science and geoscience in PISA," 2006. Available at: www.oecd.org/document/58/0,3343,en_2649_35845621_42473722_1_1_1_1,00.html, accessed November 12, 2010.
3. www.calepa.ca.gov/Education/EEI/FAQs.htm, accessed November 12, 2010.

Coalition for Community Schools:

1. Cincinnati Public Schools, "CPS Community Learning Centers Community Partnerships Transforming Schools and Neighborhoods." Available at: www.cps-k12.org/community/CLC/CLC.htm, accessed August 30, 2010.
2. SUN Community Schools, www.sunschools.org/Public/EntryPoint?ch=87a9e54564f22110VgnVCM1000003bc614acRCRD, accessed August 30, 2010.
3. Harlem Children's Zone, http://www.hcz.org/our-results, accessed June 20, 2011.
4. Obama, Barack, remarks as prepared for announcement of Secretary of Education, Chicago, IL, December 16, 2008, http://change.gov/newsroom/entry/president_elect_obama_nominates_arne_duncan_as_secretary_of_education/, accessed August 30, 2010.
5. www.quotegarden.com/back-to-school.html, accessed August 30, 2010.

Education Trust:

1. OECD, "Education at a Glance 2010: OECD Indicators, Indicator A1, Table A1.2a," www.oecd.org/document/52/0,3343,en_2649_39263238_45897844_1_1_1_1,00.html, accessed May 27, 2011.
2. National Center for Education Statistics, "Public School Graduates and Dropouts from the Common Core of Data: School Year 2008-09," May 2011, Table 1. http://nces.ed.gov/pubs2011/2011312.pdf.
3. Peter D. Hart Research Associates/Public Opinion Strategies, *Rising to the Challenge: Are High School Graduates Prepared for College and Work? A Study of Recent High School Graduates, College Instructors, and Employers* (Washington, D.C.: Achieve, Inc., February 2005).
4. OECD, "Education at a Glance 2010: OECD Indicators, Indicator A1, Table A1.3," http://www.oecd.org/document/52/0,3343,en_2649_39263238_45897844_1_1_1_1,00.html, accessed May 27, 2011.
5. The Nation's Report Card, "Reading: Summary of Major Findings," http://nationsreportcard.gov/reading_2009/summary.asp, accessed June 20, 2011.
6. The Nation's Report Card, "Math: Summary of Major Findings," http://nationsreportcard.gov/math_2009/summ.asp, accessed June 20, 2011.
7. William L. Sanders and June C. Rivers, "Cumulative and Residual Effects of Teachers on Future Student Academic Achievement." Knoxville, Tenn.: University of Tennessee Value-Added Research and Assessment Center, November 1996. See analysis in Haycock, K. (1998). "Good Teaching Matters…A Lot." "Thinking K-16," 3(2), 1-14.
8. Clotfelter, C.T., H. F. Ladd, and J. L. Vigdor. "How and Why Do Teacher Credentials Matter for Student Achievement?" Washington, D.C.: National Center for the Analysis of Longitudinal Data in Education Research, January, 2007.
9. http://nationsreportcard.gov/math_2009/context_5.asp?subtab_id=Tab_2&tab_id=tab2#chart , accessed May 27, 2011.
10. www.edtrust.org/sites/edtrust.org/files/publications/files/SASSreportCoreProblem.pdf, accessed May 27, 2011.
11. https://www.nystart.gov/publicweb/Home.do?year=2011, accessed May 27, 2011.

Editor's Boxes Notes

Environmental Education Improves Learning and Behavior

1. www.seer.org/pages/research.html, accessed December 15, 2010.

Why Art is Essential in our Public Schools

1. www.americansforthearts.org/public_awareness/artsed_facts/001.asp, accessed February 15, 2011.
2. www.americansforthearts.org/public_awareness/spotlights/case_studies/001.asp, accessed February 15, 2011.

Stopwatch: Dropout Rates

1. http://www.26seconds.com/PDF/press_release_20110318.pdf, accessed July 11, 2011.

Re-Thinking Teacher Tenure

1. "Empowering Effective Teachers," February 2010, www.gatesfoundation.org/united-states/Documents/empowering-effective-teachers-empowering-strategy.pdf, accessed March 2, 2011.
2. Alan Greenblatt, "Is Teacher Tenure Still Necessary?" NPR, April 29, 2010, www.npr.org/templates/story/story.php?storyId=126349435, accessed March 2, 2011.
3. Sam Dillon, "A School Chief Takes On Tenure, Stirring a Fight," *New York Times*, November 12, 2008, www.nytimes.com/2008/11/13/education/13tenure.html, accessed March 2, 2011.
4. Trip Gabriel and Sam Dillon, "G.O.P. Governors Take Aim at Teacher Tenure," *New York Times*, January 31, 2011, www.nytimes.com/2011/02/01/us/01tenure.html, accessed March 2, 2011.

Making Higher Education Affordable

1. Anthoy P. Carnevale, Nicole Smith and Jeff Strohl, "Help Wanted: Projections of Jobs and Education Requirements Through 2018." 2010. DC: The Georgetown University Center of Education and the Workforce.
2. www.gatesfoundation.org/postsecondaryeducation/Pages/why-college-completion.aspx, accessed March 2, 2011.
3. www.gatesfoundation.org/postsecondaryeducation/Documents/theirwholelivesaheadofthem.pdf, accessed March 2, 2011.
4. The National Center for Public Policy and Education, "Measuring Up 2008" Report; "Work less, Study More, & Succeed: How Financial Supports Can Improve Postsecondary Success," Demos, 2009.
5. Bureau of Labor Statistics, "Employment and Earnings Report," August 2009.
6. www.gatesfoundation.org/postsecondaryeducation/Documents/theirwholelivesaheadofthem.pdf, accessed March 2, 2011.
7. www.gatesfoundation.org/postsecondaryeducation/Documents/theirwholelivesaheadofthem.pdf, accessed March 2, 2011.

Numbers Pages Notes.

1. 'Half electricity comes from coal' see Union of Concerned Scientists, A Blueprint for a Clean-energy Economy, p. 210.
2. '10x wind' www.eia.doe.gov/oiaf/aeo/aeoref_tab.html, accessed September 20, 2010.
3. '84% saved' see Jeff Barrie, Building a Conservation Nation: What Is the Real Potential of Saving Energy?, p. 194.
4. '450 mountaintops' www.ilovemountains.org/resources/, accessed February 17, 2010.
5. '½ solar PV' Solar Energy Industries Association (SEIA). 2004. Our solar power future: The U.S. photovoltaics industry roadmap through 2030 and beyond.
6. '1 million' see Union of Concerned Scientists, A Blueprint for a Clean-energy Economy, p. 210.
7. 'Energy wasted = used & 11 plants' see Jeff Barrie, Building a Conservation Nation: What Is the Real Potential of Saving Energy?, p. 194.
8. 'Apollo Alliance' (all three): Apollo Alliance, "The New Apollo Program: Clean Energy, Good Jobs," September 2008, p. 6, http://apolloalliance.org/downloads/fullreportfinal.pdf, accessed February 17, 2010.
9. '33% and 60%' N. Lutsey & D. Sperling, "Greenhouse Gas Mitigation Supply Curve for the United States for Transport Versus Other Sectors," Transportation Research Part D14 (2009): 222-229.
10. '10.4 billion gallons' Based on a driving population of 208 million people, the average driver driving 29 miles per day, the average driver would take public transportation 50 weeks per year, (www.bts.gov/programs/national_household_travel_survey/daily_travel.html) and public transit systems using the equivalent of 57 miles per gallon of gasoline (www.publictransportation.org/facts/).
11. '$2,700' Based on oil consumption statistics from Energy Information Administration, "Oil FAQs," http://tonto.eia.doe.gov/ask/crudeoil_faqs.asp#foreign_oil, 2008.

Essay Notes

Jeff Barrie:

1. Shaila Dewan, "Tennessee Ash Flood Larger Than Initial Estimate," New York Times, December 26, 2008, www.nytimes.com/2008/12/27/us/27sludge.html, accessed October 19, 2010.
2. www.ilovemountains.org/resources/, accessed February 17, 2010.
3. www.crmw.net/staff_pics.php?staff=Judy+Bonds, accessed February 17, 2010.
4. www.eia.doe.gov/cneaf/coal/page/special/feature.html, accessed October 19, 2010.
5. www.apsenergyconservation.org/PDF/EnergyFactsforTeachers.pdf, accessed October 19, 2010.
6. www.ucsusa.org/clean_energy/coalvswind/brief_coal.html, accessed February 11, 2010.
7. http://ga.water.usgs.gov/edu/wupt.html, accessed February 11, 2010.
8. www.nrdc.org/health/effects/fasthma.asp, accessed February 17, 2010.
9. www.reuters.com/article/idUSTRE57J01420090820, accessed October 19, 2010.
10. www.epa.gov/hg/effects.htm, accessed October 19, 2010.
11. Christopher Hawthorne, "Turning Down the Global Thermostat," Metrolis Magazine, October 1, 2003, www.metropolismag.com/story/20031001/turning-down-the-global-thermostat, accessed February 11, 2010.
12. Apollo Alliance, "The New Apollo Program: Clean Energy, Good Jobs," September 2008, p. 6, http://apolloalliance.org/downloads/fullreportfinal.pdf, accessed February 17, 2010.
13. Peter Behr, "Austin seeks a new blueprint for power utilties," Renewable Energy World, April 7, 2010, www.eenews.net/public/climatewire/2010/04/07/1, accessed October 19, 2010.

Institute for Transportation Studies:

1. P.S. Hu & T.R. Reuscher, Summary of Travel Trends: 2001 National Household Transportation Survey, US Department of Transportation and Federal Highway Administration, Washington, DC, December 2004.
2. AAA, "Your Driving Costs, 2010 Edition," http://www.aaaexchange.com/Assets/Files/201048935480.Driving%20Costs%202010.pdf, accessed June 21, 2011.
3. National Highway Traffic Safety Administration, http://www.nhtsa.gov/PR/NHTSA-05-11, accessed June 21, 2011.
4. Center for Disease Control and Prevention, "Motor Vehicle Safety," http://www.cdc.gov/motorvehiclesafety/index.html, accessed June 21, 2011.
5. Environmental Protection Agency (EPA), 2005, Health and Environmental Impacts of Ground-Level Ozone, Washington, DC, www.epa.gov/air/urbanair/ozone/hlth.html, accessed 11/7/05. ftp://ftp.eia.doe.gov/pub/oiaf/1605/cdrom/pdf/ggrpt/057308.pdf, accessed March 22, 2010.

6. N. Lutsey & D. Sperling, "Greenhouse Gas Mitigation Supply Curve for the United States for Transport Versus Other Sectors," *Transportation Research Part D* 14 (2009): 222-229.

7. Pew Center on Climate Change, "Comparison of Passenger Vehicle Fuel Economy and GHG Emission Standards Around the World," 2004, www.pewclimate.org/docUploads/Fuel%20Economy%20and%20GHG%20Standards_010605_110719.pdf, accessed March 22, 2010.

8. The International Council on Clean Transportation, "Passenger Vehicle Greenhouse Gas and Fuel Economy Standards: A Global Update," July 2007, p. 9.

9. Todd Woody & Clifford Krauss, "Cities Prepare for Life with the Electric Car," *New York Times*, February 15, 2010, www.nytimes.com/2010/02/15/business/15electric.html?hpw=&pagewanted=all, accessed March 2, 2010.

10. International Energy Agency (IEA), 2008a, Energy Technology Perspectives 2008: Fact Sheet – Transportation, Organization for Economic Co-Operation and Development, Paris, France, http://www.iea.org/techno/etp/fact_sheet_ETP2008.pdf, accessed December 11, 2009.

11. National Research Council, Transitions to Alternative Technologies: A Focus on Hydrogen. Committee on Assessment of Resource Needs for Fuel Cell and Hydrogen Technologies, 2008, Washington, DC.

12. Chuck Squatriglia, "Hydrogen Cars Won't Make a Difference for 40 Years," *Wired*, May 12, 2008, www.wired.com/cars/energy/news/2008/05/hydrogen?currentPage=1, accessed April 7, 2010.

13. International Energy Agency (IEA), Energy Technology Perspectives 2008: Fact Sheet – Renewables. Organization for Economic Co-Operation and Development, 2008b, Paris, France, www.iea.org/techno/etp/fact_sheet_ETP2008.pdf, accessed December 11, 2009.

14. S.C. Rajan, "Climate Change Dilemma: Technology, Social Change or Both? An Examination of Long-term Transport Policy Choices in the United States," *Energy Policy* 34 (2006,): 664-679; Lutsey and Sperling, op. cit.; Christopher Yang, David McCollum, Ryan McCarthy & Wayne Leighty, "Meeting an 80% Reduction in Greenhouse Gas Emissions from Transportation by 2050: A Case Study in California," *Transportation Research Part D* 14 (2009): 147-156.

15. John Pucher & Ralph Buehler, , "Making Cycling Irresistible: Lessons from the Netherlands, Denmark, and Germany," *Transport Reviews* 28(4) (2008): 495-528.

16. S.D. Beevers & D.C. Carslaw, "The Impact of Congestion Charging on Vehicle Emissions in London," *Atmospheric Environment* 39(1) (2005): 1-5.

17. G. Santos & B. Shaffer, "Preliminary Results of the London Congestion Charging Scheme," *Public Works Management & Policy* 9(2) (2004): 164-181.

18. Transport for London, 2008, Cycling in London: Final Report.

19. ICLEI, 2002, Orienting Urban Planning to Sustainability in Curitiba, Brazil, www3.iclei.org/localstrategies/summary/curitiba2.html, accessed December 11, 2009.

20. John Pucher, Jennifer Dill and Susan Handy, "Infrastructure, Programs, and Policies to Increase Bicycling: An International Review, *Preventive Medicine* (2010).

21. Dylan Rivera, "Bike Commuting Surges in Portland, Census Finds," *The Oregonian*, September 23, 2009, www.oregonlive.com/news/index.ssf/2009/09/bike_commuting_surges_in_portl.html, accessed March 2, 2010.

22. "City Council OKs $613 Million Bike Plan," *Portland Business Journal*, February 11, 2010, http://portland.bizjournals.com/portland/stories/2010/02/08/daily43.html, accessed March 11, 2010.

Public Citizen:

1. Van Suntum, "Spinning Nuclear Power into Green," *Center for Media and Democracy*, 2005, www.prwatch.org/prwissues/2005Q1/nuke2.html, accessed October 13, 2010.

2. Department of Energy, "Price-Anderson Indemnification," www.ne.doe.gov/publicInformation/nePublicInfomationPriceAnderson2.html, accessed October 13, 2010.

3. Congressional Budget Office, "Cost Estimate S.14: Energy Policy Act of 2003," April 30, 2003, accessed August 13, 2010, from www.cbo.gov/ftpdocs/42xx/doc4206/s14.pdf.

4. "Oglala Sioux Tribe, Environmental Groups and Concerned Citizens Join to Fight Cameco, Inc. Uranium Mine Lease Renewal and Exp," www.commondreams.org/newswire/2008/10/10-3, accessed February 11, 2010.

5. Winona LaDuke, "Uranium Mining, Native Resistance, and the Green Path," February 7, 2009, www.commondreams.org/view/2009/02/07-5, accessed February 11, 2010.

6. www.citizen.org/cmep/energy_enviro_nuclear/nuclear_power_plants/articles.cfm?ID=15210, accessed February 11, 2010.

7. Ibid.

8. Public Citizen, "Renewable Energy is Capable of Meeting Our Energy Needs," April 2006, www.citizen.org/documents/RenewableEnergy.pdf, accessed February 11, 2010.

9. Christina L. Archer and Mark Z. Jacobson, "Evaluation of global wind power," *Journal of Geophysical Research*, Vol. 110, June 30, 2005, www.stanford.edu/group/efmh/winds/2004jd005462.pdf, accessed October 13, 2010.

10. Assuming 15% panel efficiency and a conservative estimate of at least 7,854 million available residential and commercial rooftop space. This does not include other distributed forms of PV electric generation, such as ground-mounted PV, PV shingles, covered parking lots, windows, awnings and sides of buildings. It also does not take into account additional improvements in panel efficiency.

11. Maya Chaudhari, Lisa Frantzis and Tom E Hoff, "PV Grid Connected Market Potential Under a Cost Breakthrough Scenario," September 2004, *The Energy Foundation and Navigant Consulting*, p. 33.

12. John O. Blackburn and Sam Cunningham, "Solar and Nuclear Costs: The Historic Crossover," July 2010, Duke University, www.ncwarn.org/wp-content/uploads/2010/07/NCW-SolarReport_print.pdf, accessed October 13, 2010.

13. Gul Timur and Till Stenzel, "Variability of Wind Power and Other Renewables: Management Options and Strategies," International Energy Agency (IEA), June 2005.

14. Annual Wind Market Report, www.Windpoweringamerica.gov, October 13, 2010.

Union of Concerned Scientists:

1. www.energystar.gov/index.cfm?fuseaction=find_a_product.showProductGroup&pgw_code=LB, accessed March 30, 2010.

2. Department of Energy, 2009, www1.eere.energy.gov/femp/pdfs/WeatherizTF.pdf, accessed March 30, 2010.

3. www.eia.doe.gov/oiaf/aeo/aeoref_tab.html, accessed September 20, 2010.

4. Rachel Cleetus, Steven Clemmer and David Friedman, May 2009, *Climate 2030: A National Blueprint for a Clean Energy Economy*, www.ucsusa.org/global_warming/solutions/big_picture_solutions/climate-2030-blueprint.html, accessed September 20, 2010.

5. National Renewable Energy Laboratory, "American Energy," 2010, Worldwatch Institute and Center for American Progress.

6. Stephen Lacey, 2011, "Green Jobs Are Real: German and American Solar Industry Both Employ More People Than U.S. Steel Production," Think Progress.

7. Monique Hannis, et al., 2008, "Industry Leaders Forecast Dramatic Growth in the U.S. Solar Market by 2016 with Extension of Credit," Solar Energy Industries Association, www.seia.org/cs/news_detail?pressrelease.id=217, accessed October 19, 2010.

8. The California Energy Commission, 2010, "Geothermal Energy in California," www.energy.ca.gov/geothermal/index.html, accessed October 19, 2010.

9. U.S. Geological Survey, 2008, "Assessment of Moderate- and High-Temperature Geothermal Resources of the United States," Department of the Interior, http://pubs.usgs.gov/fs/2008/3082/pdf/fs2008-3082.pdf, accessed October 19, 2010.

10. "Interim Joint Technical Assessment Report: Light-Duty Vehicle Greenhouse Gas Emission Standards and Corporate Average Fuel Economy Standards for Model Years 2017-2025," Office of Transportation and Air Quality, U.S. Environmental Protection Agency, Office of International Policy, Fuel Economy, and Consumer Programs National Highway Traffic Safety Administration, U.S. Department of Transportation, California Air Resources Board, California Environmental Protection Agency, September 2010. And, "THE TECHNOLOGY TO REACH 60 MPG BY 2025: Putting Fuel-Saving Technology to Work to Save Oil and Cut Pollution," Union of Concerned Scientists and NRDC, 2009.

11. David Friedman and Marshall Goldberg, 2008, *Creating Jobs, Saving Energy, and Protecting the Environment: An Analysis of the Potential Benefits of Investing in Efficient Cars and Trucks, A 2007 Update*, Union of Concerned Scientists, www.ucsusa.org/assets/documents/clean_vehicles/fueleconomyjobs.pdf, accessed December 2, 2010.

12. Office of Management and Budget (2003), *Informing Regulatory Decisions: 2003 Report to Congress on the Costs and Benefits of Federal Regulations and Unfunded Mandates on State, Local, and Tribal Entities*. Available at: www.whitehouse.gov/sites/default/files/omb/assets/omb/inforeg/2003_cost-ben_final_rpt.pdf.

Editor's Boxes Notes

Atmospheric CO2 Concentrations

1. "Last Time Carbon Dioxide Levels Were This High: 15 Million Years Ago, Scientists Report," October 9, 2009, *Science Daily*, www.sciencedaily.com/releases/2009/10/091008152242.htm, accessed June 14, 2011.

2. www.350.org/about/science, accessed June 14, 2011.

3. www.350.org/sites/all/files/science-factsheet-updated2011.pdf, accessed June 14, 2011.

4. www.350.org/en/mission, accessed June 24, 2011.

Youth Activism: Getting Serious About Climate Change

1. "Kids vs. Global Warming: Suing the government for the environment," June 22, 2011, www.pri.org/business/social-entrepreneurs/kids-vs-global-warming-suing-the-government-for-the-environment4539.html, accessed June 24, 2011.

2. "Kids vs. Global Warming: Suing the government for the environment," June 22, 2011, www.pri.org/business/social-entrepreneurs/kids-vs-global-warming-suing-the-government-for-the-environment4539.html, accessed June 24, 2011.

3. "Why 16 Year-Old Alec Loorz Is Suing the Government," March 4, 2011, www.good.is/post/why-16-year-old-alec-loorz-is-suing-the-government/, accessed June 24, 2011.

4. http://imattermarch.org/lawsuit/, accessed June 24, 2011.

5. "Why 16 Year-Old Alec Loorz Is Suing the Government," March 4, 2011, www.good.is/post/why-16-year-old-alec-loorz-is-suing-the-government/, accessed June 24, 2011.

6. "Why 16 Year-Old Alec Loorz Is Suing the Government," March 4, 2011, www.good.is/post/why-16-year-old-alec-loorz-is-suing-the-government/, accessed June 24, 2011.

The 100-MPG Car

1. http://move.rmi.org/markets-in-motion/case-studies/automotive/hypercar.html, accessed April 6, 2010.
2. http://move.rmi.org/move-news/bright-automotive-turns-rmi-s-lightweight--hyper-efficient-vehicle-concept-into-reality.html, accessed April 6, 2010.
3. www.plugin.com/2010/09/move-over-nissan-leaf-coda%E2%80%99s-electric-sedan-is-here/, accessed February 3, 2011.
4. Njiguna Kabugi, "Electric Vehicles Shine at the Washington Auto Show," The Washington Informer, February 3, 2011, www.washingtoninformer.com/index.php?option=com_content&view=article&id=5419:electric-vehicles-shine-at-the-washington-auto-show&catid=53:business&Itemid=162, accessed February 3, 2011.

Carsharing: An Alternative to Owning a Vehicle

1. Doug Pibel, "Yes! But How? Car Sharing," Yes!, November 2, 1998, www.yesmagazine.org/issues/education-for-life/yes-...-but-how, accessed October 18, 2010.
2. Jeremy Adam Smith, "Share Your Stuff," Yes!, September 17, 2010, www.yesmagazine.org/issues/a-resilient-community/share-your-stuff?icl=sample_yesnews_yesemail_sepoct10&ica=ShareYourStuff, accessed October 18, 2010.
3. http://ecoplan.org/carshare/general/cities.htm#latest, accessed October 18, 2010.

An Urban Design Movement that Reduces Vehicle Usage

1. www.forestcity.net/properties/mixed_use/property_listing/Pages/Stapleton.aspx, accessed March 2, 2010.

Drive Less, Save More

1. Based on a driving population of 208 million people, the average driver driving 29 miles per day, the average driver would take public transportation 50 weeks per year, (www.bts.gov/programs/national_household_travel_survey/daily_travel.html) and public transit systems using the equivalent of 57 miles per gallon of gasoline (www.publictransportation.org/facts/).
2. www.publictransportation.org/facts/, accessed March 11, 2010.
3. Based on a driving population of 208 million people and walking five miles/week would save 12.5 gallons/year/person.
4. Calculated using the EPA's conversion rates: "CO2 emissions from a gallon of gasoline = 2,421 grams x 0.99 x (44/12) = 8,788 grams = 8.8 kg/gallon = 19.4 pounds/gallon."
5. Based on a driving population of 208 million people and biking 25 miles/week/person would save 63 gallons/year, using an average gas mileage of 20.6.
6. Calculated using the EPA's conversion rates: "CO2 emissions from a gallon of gasoline = 2,421 grams x 0.99 x (44/12) = 8,788 grams = 8.8 kg/gallon = 19.4 pounds/gallon.

Alternative Fuels: Focusing on Smart Solutions

1. Environmental Working Group, www.ewg.org/reports/Free-Pass-for-Oil-and-Gas/Oil-and-Gas-Industry-Exemptions, accessed October 12, 2010.
2. "Corn-based ethanol not cheap, not green," Seattle PI, April 11, 2007, www.seattlepi.com/opinion/311225_ethanol12.html, accessed October 12, 2010. C. Ford Runge & Benjamin Senauer, "How Biofuels Could Starve the Poor," Foreign Affairs, May/June 2007, www.nytimes.com/cfr/world/20070501faessay_v86n3_runge_senauer.html?pagewanted=print, accessed October 12, 2010.

Nuclear in Japan and Germany

1. Christopher Johnson, "Japan told of more radiation exposure," July 28, 2011, The Washington Times, www.washingtontimes.com/news/2011/jul/28/japan-told-of-more-radiation-exposure/, accessed July 29, 2011. Erich Pica, "Waking Up to a Nuclear Nightmare," July 25, 2011, Huffington Post, www.huffingtonpost.com/erich-pica/waking-up-to-a-nuclear-ni_b_907421.html, accessed July 29, 2011.
2. Gerry Hadden, "Germany's Anti-Nuclear Shift," July 20, 2011, PRI's The World, www.theworld.org/2011/07/germanys-anti-nuclear-shift/, accessed July 29, 2011.

China's Solar Thermal City

1. www.epa.gov/oms/climate/420f05004.htm, accessed December 10, 2010.
2. Alex Pasternack, "Almost Everyone Has a Solar Water Heater in Dezhou, China," May, 29, 2009, www.treehugger.com/files/2009/05/china-solar-city-dezhou-video.php, accessed October 15, 2010.
3. www.sciencedaily.com/releases/2007/11/071114163448.htm, accessed February 4, 2011.

Creating a Sustainable Energy Future With a Smart Grid

1. Brian Vestag, "White House pushes policies to upgrade nation's aging electrical network," June 13, 2011, The Washington Post, www.washingtonpost.com/national/white-house-pushes-policies-to-upgrade-nations-aging-electrical-network/2011/06/13/AGM4nUTH_story.html, accessed June 14, 2011.
2. Brian Vestag, "Whate House pushes policies to upgrade nation's aging electrical network," June 13, 2011, The Washington Post, www.washingtonpost.com/national/white-house-pushes-policies-to-upgrade-nations-aging-electrical-network/2011/06/13/AGM4nUTH_story.html, accessed June 14, 2011.

Being Smart About Biomass

1. Thomas Walker, et al. "Biomass Sustainability and Carbon Policy Study," Manomet Center for Conservation Sciences, 2010.
2. Richard Wiles, "EPA Public Hearing on Three Year Permitting Deferral for Biomass Facilities," Partnership for Policy Integrity, 2011.

seven

Numbers Pages Notes

1. 'Level of health' The World Health Report 2000, "Health Systems: Improving Performance, World Health Organization," Geneva, 2000, Annex Table 1, p. 152, www.who.int/whr/2000/en/whr00_en.pdf, accessed May 25, 2011.
2. '100% French' The World Health Report 2000, "Health Systems: Improving Performance, World Health Organization," Geneva, 2000, Annex Table 1, p. 152, www.who.int/whr/2000/en/whr00_en.pdf, accessed May 25, 2011.
3. '1 out of 3' Bryan Walsh, "Child Obesity Rate Levels Off," TIME, May, 27, 2008, www.time.com/time/health/article/0,8599,1809829,00.html, accessed March 7, 2011.
4. '42 states' http://www.cspinet.org/nutritionpolicy/improved_school_foods_without_losing_revenue2.pdf, accessed February 2, 2011.
5. '1.5 trillion and number of mayors' http://blogs.suntimes.com/sweet/2011/02/michelle_obama_lets_move_anniv.html, accessed March 7, 2011.
6. 17% of GDP: Kerry Capell, "Is Europe's Health Care Better?" BusinessWeek.com, June 13, 2007.
7. '$12 billion' Health Care for America Now!, "Analysis Shows Health Insurers Pocketed Huge Profits in 2010 Despite Weak Economy," 2011, p.1.
8. '$10 million' Joe Light, "Health Care CEO's Earn Top Pay," http://blogs.wsj.com/health/2010/11/16/health-care-ceos-bring-home-the-bacon/, 2010.
9. '$166,700 salary' Executive Order, "Adjustments of Certain Rates of Pay," http://www.opm.gov/oca/compmemo/2001/2001-15A1.txt, accessed July 5, 2011.
10. '4 healthy habits' E.S. Ford, M.M. Bergmann, J. Kroger, A. Schienkiewitz, C. Weikert & H. Boeing, "Healthy Living Is the Best Revenge," Archives of Internal Medicine, 2009, 169(15), p. 1355.
11. '1 in 2' T.C. Campbell & J. Chen, "Diet and Chronic Degenerative Diseases: Perspectives from China," American Journal of Clinical Nutrition, 1994, 59, pp. 1153S–1161S.

Essay Notes

Dr. Holly Atkinson:

1. CIA World Fact Book, accessed at https://www.cia.gov/library/publications/the-world-factbook/rankorder/2102rank.html, accessed January 26, 2011.
2. M. Pollan, "Big Food vs. Big Insurance," New York Times, September 10, 2009.
3. CDC Chronic Disease Control and Prevention, accessed at www.cdc.gov/chronicdisease/overview/index.htm, accessed January 26, 2011.
4. K.E. Thorpe, C.S. Florence, D.H. Howard & P. Joski, "The Impact of Obesity on Rising Medical Spending," Health Affairs, October 20, 2004, W4-480-486.
5. Eric A. Finkelstein, Justin G. Trogdon, Joel W. Cohen & William Dietz, 2009, "Annual Medical Spending Attributable to Obesity: Payer- and Service-Specific Estimates," Health Affairs, September 2009, 28 (5), W822-W831; published ahead of print July 27, 2009, doi:10.1377/hlthaff.28.5.w822.
6. S.A. Schroeder, "We Can Do Better: Improving the Health of the American People," New England Journal of Medicine, 2007, 357(12), pp. 1221-1228.
7. E.S. Ford, M.M. Bergmann, J. Kroger, A. Schienkiewitz, C. Weikert & H. Boeing, "Healthy Living Is the Best Revenge," Archives of Internal Medicine, 2009, 169(15), p. 1355.
8. Department of Health and Human Services, 2000, "Healthy People 2010," 2nd ed., Washington DC, www.healthypeople.gov.
9. Institute of Medicine, 2006, "Preventing Medication Errors," National Academy of Sciences.
10. H.K. Koh & K.G. Sebelius, 2010, "Promoting Prevention through the Affordable Care Act," New England Journal of Medicine, 363(14), pp. 1296-1299.

Dr. Baxter Montgomery:

1. T.C. Campbell & J. Chen, "Diet and Chronic Degenerative Diseases: Perspectives from China, American Journal of Clinical Nutrition, 1994, 59, pp. 1153S–1161S. C.B. Esselstyn, Jr., S.G. Ellis, S.V. Medendorp & T.D. Crowe, "A Strategy to Arrest and Reverse Coronary Artery Disease: A 5-year Longitudinal Study of a Single Physician's Practice," Journal of Family Practice, 1995, 41, pp. 560-568. F. Salie, "Influence of Vegetarian Food on Blood Pressure," Med Klin, 1930, 26, pp. 929-931.
2. T.C. Campbell & T.M. Campbell, 2006, The China Study, Dallas, TX: Benbella Books, pp. 109-110.
3. B. Davis & V. Melina, 2000, Becoming Vegan, Summertown, TN: Book Publishing Company, pp. 20-21.

4. Ibid., pp. 24-25.
5. http://abcnews.go.com/Health/Diabetes/wireStory?id=2244647&page=2, accessed February 2, 2011.
6. www.fns.usda.gov/wic/fmnp/fmnpfaqs.htm
7. http://www.foodproductdesign.com/news/2010/08/healthy-vending-machines-enter-schools.aspx, accessed February 2, 2011.
8. Ibid.
9. http://www.cspinet.org/nutritionpolicy/improved_school_foods_without_losing_revenue2.pdf, accessed February 2, 2011.
10. See note 7.
11. See note 9.

Safer Chemicals Healthy Families:

1. Government Accountability Office, 2009, "Chemical Regulation: Options for Enhancing the Effectiveness of the *Toxic Substances Control Act*," www.gao.gov/new.items/d09428t.pdf, accessed November 12, 2010.
2. Rebecca Ruiz, 2010, "Industrial Chemicals Lurking In Your Bloodstream," *Forbes*, www.forbes.com/2010/01/21/toxic-chemicals-bpa-lifestyle-health-endocrine-disruptors.html, accessed November 12, 2010.
3. Barbara A. Cohn, et al., 2007, "DDT and Breast Cancer in Young Women: New Data on the Significance of Age at Exposure," *Environmental Health Perspectives*, 115 no. 10, 1406-14.
4. Steven G. Gilbert, "The Scientific Consensus Statement on Environmental Agents Affiliated with Neurodevelopmental Disorders," (Bolinas, CA: Collaborative on Health and the Environment, 2008) abstracted in *Neurotoxicology and Teratology*, 31 no 4, 241-42. National Institute of Mental Health, "NIMH's Response to New Autism Prevalence Estimate," www.nimh.nih.gov/about/director/updates/2009/nihmresponse-to-new-autism-prevalence-estimate.shtml, accessed November 4, 2009. Catherine Rice, 2009, "Prevalence of Autism Spectrum Disorders: Autism and Developmental Disabilities Monitoring Network, United States, 2006, National Center on Birth Defects and Developmental Disabilities," MMWR *Surveillance Summaries*, 58 no. SS10 (December 18), 1-20.
5. Anjani Chandra & Elizabeth Hervey Stephen, 1998, "Impaired Fecundity in the United States: 1982-1995," *Family Planning Perspectives*, 30 no. 1, 34-42.
6. Thomas G. Travison, et al., 2007, "A Population-Level Decline in Serum Testosterone Levels in American Men," *Journal of Clinical Endocrinology & Metabolism*, 92 no. 1.
Mona Shah, et al., 2007, "Trends in Testicular Germ Cell Tumours by Ethnic Group in the United States," *International Journal of Andrology*, 30, 206-13. Shanna Swan, Eric P. Elkin & Laura Fenster, 2000, "The Question of Declining Sperm Density Revisited: An analysis of 101 Studies Published 1934-1996," *Environmental Health Perspectives*, 108 no. 10, 961-66.
7. US EPA, America's Children and the Environment, www.epa.gov/economics/children/.
8. For more information on Wal-Mart's removal of BPA bottles, please visit www.washingtonpost.com/wpdyn/content/article/2008/04/14/AR2008041704205.html, accessed November 12, 2010.
9. For a complete list of the businesses and other organizations that have endorsed the Business-NGO Guiding Principles for Chemicals policy, go to www.BizNGO.org.
10. To see how states are safeguarding health, go to www.saferstates.org.
11. On the benefits to downstream users of chemicals policy reform, see International Chemical Secretariat, 2005, "*What We Need from REACH: Views on the Proposal for a New Chemical Legislation within the EU*," http://chemsec.org/images/stories/publications/ChemSec_publications/What_we_need_from_REACH.pdf, accessed November 9, 2010.
12. Marsman, Daniel, et al., 1995, "NTP Technical Report on Toxicity Studies of Dibutyl Phthalates: Administered in Feed to F344/N Rats and B6C3F Mice," National Toxicology Program, no. 30, 1-93. Centers for Disease Control, 2009, "Fourth National Report on Human Exposure to Environmental Chemicals," 1-519.

Steven Hill:

1. The World Health Report 2000 -- Health Systems: Improving Performance, World Health Organization, Geneva, 2000, Annex Table 1, p. 152, www.who.int/whr/2000/en/whr00_en.pdf, accessed May 25, 2011.
2. Using the CIA World Factbook's 2010 data, the US ranks 29th in the world in infant mortality, at 7 deaths per 1000 live births, and 31stth in life expectancy, our 78 years lagging behind Italy (81 years), France (81 years), Japan (82 years), Sweden (81 years) and Germany (80 years), and about the same level as Bosnia (77 years) and Cuba (77 years). According to Holly Sklar, "Time for Health Care for All," *Progressive Populist*, September 1, 2005 and the Organization for Economic Cooperation and Development (OECD) Health Data 2005, "How Does the United States Compare," www.oecd.org/dataoecd/15/23/34970246.pdf, the US has fewer physicians, nurses and hospital beds per person, and fewer MRI and CT scanners, than the average for other advanced nations. The US also has the highest rate of medical errors (receiving the wrong medication, incorrect test results, a mistake in treatment, or late notification about abnormal results), and had more difficulty making physician appointments quickly, or getting care after hours, though Americans generally had easier access to specialists and shorter waits for elective surgery than Canadians or Britons, though longer waits than Germans. Gaps in coverage and high out-of-pocket costs hindered patients' access to care, with nearly a third of US patients reporting spending more than $1000 in out-of-pocket expenses, far outpacing all other nations (Canada and Australia came next with only 14% of patients spending that much). Greatly due to the high out-of-pocket expenses, Americans also were much more likely than residents of the other nations to skip recommended follow-up care, fail to fill prescriptions, or even forgo doctors' visits, even though a lack of timely care can exacerbate health problems and lead to preventable suffering, death and more expensive treatment down the road, as noted in Rob Stein, "For Americans, Getting Sick Has Its Price," *Washington Post*, November 4, 2005, p. A2 and Paul Krugman, "Pride, Prejudice, Insurance," *New York Times*, November 7, 2005.
3. Martin Sipkoff, "Do We Really Have Best Health Care in the World?" *Managed Care*, April 2004, www.managedcaremag.com/archives/0404/0404.worldsbest.html, accessed May 25, 2011.
4. Associated Press, "Lawmakers far outpace most Americans in benefits," *USA Today*, April 19, 2006, www.usatoday.com/news/washington/2006-04-19-congressbenefits_x.htm, accessed May 25, 2011.
5. Kerry Capell, "Is Europe's Health Care Better?" BusinessWeek.com, June 13, 2007, www.businessweek.com/globalbiz/content/jun2007/gb20070613_921562.htm?chan=globalbiz_europe+index+page_economics+%2Bamp%3B+policy, accessed May 25, 2011, US Census, "Per Capita Consumer Expenditures, 2000-2008," http://www.census.gov/compendia/statab/2011/tables/11s0133.pdf.
6. Dmitri Iglitzin and Steven Hill, "A Fair Way to Shrink the Wealth Gap," *Christian Science Monitor*, January 24, 2007.

Editor's Box Notes

Advancing the Nation's Perspective on Health and Healing

1. www.health.com/health/gallery/0,,20307333_8,00.html, accessed June 13, 2011.
2. http://health.discovery.com/fansites/dr-oz/bios/oz.html, accessed June 20, 2011.
3. http://health.discovery.com/fansites/dr-oz/bios/oz.html, accessed June 20, 2011.

The End of Childhood Obesity

1. www.letsmove.gov/, accessed February 3, 2011.
2. www.google.com/hostednews/canadianpress/article/ALeqM5jDFPnFuz8bh8QybMfgg9K8l7TljQ?docId=5786436, accessed February 3, 2011.

2010 CEO Compensation of Top Health Insurance Companies

1. http://seekingalpha.com/news-article/918185-united-ceo-s-pay-rises-21-percent.
2. http://seekingalpha.com/news-article/918185-united-ceo-s-pay-rises-21-percent.
3. http://seekingalpha.com/news-article/918185-united-ceo-s-pay-rises-21-percent.
4. http://www.signonsandiego.com/news/2011/mar/07/humana-ceo-sees-2010-compensation-slide-6-percent/.
5. http://www.chicagobusiness.com/article/20110618/ISSUE01/306189984/blue-cross-profits-surge.
6. http://www.forbes.com/lists/2011/12/ceo-compensation-11_Allen-F-Wise_8TS1.html
7. http://www.chicagobusiness.com/article/20110618/ISSUE01/306189984/blue-cross-profits-surge#ixzz1Q2l7WGmk.
8. http://www.washingtonpost.com/national/calif-health-insurer-to-refund-millions-cap-profits/2011/06/08/AGNGWjMH_story.html.
9. Executive Order, "Adjustments of Certain Rates of Pay," http://www.opm.gov/oca/compmemo/2001/2001-15A1.txt, accessed July 5, 2011.

Numbers Pages Notes

1. '14.3% below poverty' US Department of Commerce, "Income, Poverty, and Health Insurance Coverage in the United States: 2009," *Census Bureau*, 2010.
2. '4 points & 12 million' US Census, "Historical Poverty Tables," 2010.
3. '1.6 million homeless' US Department of Housing and Urban Development, "The 2010 Annual Homeless Assessment Report to Congress," 2011.
4. '$3,500 saved / $1.4 billion' "Based on a study in Wichita, KS where housing 12 women saved $41,000 a year, see www.endhomelessness.org/content/article/detail/2601, accessed November 29, 2010."
5. '$22,000' "Based on increasing the $7.25 minimum to $10.80, working 40 hours a week for 52 weeks."

eight

6. '14.5 million / 1 in 5' Vanessa Wight, "Who are America's Poor Children?," *National Center for Children in Poverty*, 2010.

7. '50% reduction UK' Kate Bell, "The Experience of the U.K. Child Poverty Target, Center for American Progress," 2008.

8. '880 million people' The Growing Connection, "Cultivating Food, Connecting Minds, Harvesting Hope," *Food and Agriculture Association of the United Nations*, 2010.

9. '.2% of GDP' see United Nations Millenium Campaign, *0.7 Percent of Wealth: A Small Price to End Global Extreme Poverty*, p. 268.

10. '33,000 millennium villages' "Based on each .1 percent increasing foreign aid by roughly $10 billion, with Millennium Villages costing $300,000 and serving 5,000 people, according to Millennium Project, "Sustainability and Costs," http://www.unmillenniumproject.org/mv/mv_cost.htm, accessed July 5, 2011.

Essay Notes

Center for American Progress:

1. US Department of Commerce, Income, Poverty, and Health Insurance Coverage in the United States: 2009, Census Bureau, 2010. Available at: www.census.gov/hhes/www/poverty/index.html, accessed September 20, 2010.

2. www.threedoctorsfoundation.org/about, accessed April 18, 2010.

3. For more information, refer to John Andrew, *Lyndon Johnson and the Great Society*, 1999.

4. For a fuller discussion of the Clinton administration record on poverty reduction, refer to Rebecca Blank and David Ellwood, "The Clinton Legacy for America's Poor," *American Economic Policy in the 1990s*, 2002.

5. Rebecca Blank and Brian Kovak, Helping Disconnected Single Mothers, Center on Children and Families, 2008.

6. US Census, Historical Poverty Tables, available at www.census.gov/hhes/www/poverty/data/historical/hstpov2.xls, accessed September 28, 2010.

7. To learn more about the UK's child poverty goal, resulting, policies and outcomes, refer to Kate Bell, The Experience of the U.K. Child Poverty Target, Center for American Progress, 2008, available at www.americanprogress.org/issues/2008/11/pdf/uk_child_poverty.pdf.

8. US Department of Commerce, Income, Poverty, and Health Insurance Coverage in the United States: 2009, Census Bureau, 2009.

9. Adrienne Fernandes & Thomas Gabe, Disconnected Youth: A Look at 16- to 24-Year Olds Who Are Not Working or in School, Congressional Research Service, 2009.

10. William Sabol, Heather West & Matthew Cooper, Prisoners in 2008, Bureau of Justice Statistics, 2009.

11. Caroline Wolf Harlow, Education and Correctional Populations, Bureau of Justice Statistics, 2003.

12. Devah Pager, *Marked: Race, Crime, and Finding Work in an Era of Mass Incarceration* (Chicago: University of Chicago Press, 2007).

13. Richard Wetheimer, Poor Families in 2001: Parents Working Less and Children Continue to Lag Behind, *Child Trends*, 2003.

14. Government Accountability Office, "Multiple Factors Could Have Contributed to the Recent Decline in the Number of Children Whose Families Receive Subsidies," 2010.

15. US Department of Labor, A Profile of the Working Poor, 2009, Bureau of Labor Statistics, 2011.

16. United States Department of Labor, Minimum Wage Laws in the States, July 1, 2010, available at http://www.dol.gov/whd/minwage/america.htm, accessed September 1, 2010.

17. National Institute for Early Education Research, The State of Preschool 2009, 2009.

18. Organisation for Economic Co-operation and Development, www.oecd.org/document/24/0,3343,en_2649_39263238_43586328_1_1_1_1,00.html#Findings, accessed April 18, 2010.

19. US Department of Education, "The Early Learning Challenge Fund," July 2009, www2.ed.gov/about/inits/ed/earlylearning/elcf-factsheet.html, accessed April 18, 2010.

20. President Obama's Remarks to the Hispanic Chamber of Commerce, available at: http://www.nytimes.com/2009/03/10/us/politics/10text-obama.html?pagewanted=1&_r=1&adxnnl=1&adxnnlx=1283373046-YUEBa3Xa67Sms5sWPJLy2A, accessed April 18, 2010.

21. Mary Beth Marklein, "Free-college programs multiply," *USA Today*, July 1, 2008. Available at: www.usatoday.com/news/education/2008-07-01-Kalamazoo_N.htm, accessed April 19, 2010.

National Alliance to End Homelessness:

1. US Department of Housing and Urban Development, June 2011, "The 2010 Annual Homeless Assessment Report to Congress," pp. i-ii, available at www.hudhre.info/documents/2010HomelessAssessmentReport.pdf, accessed June 14, 2011.

2. Ibid., p. ii.

3. Ibid., p. 9.

4. www.endhomelessness.org/content/article/detail/585, accessed November 29, 2010.

5. US Department of Housing and Urban Development, June 2011, "The 2010 Annual Homeless Assessment Report to Congress," pp. 13, available at www.hudhre.info/documents/2010HomelessAssessmentReport.pdf, accessed June 14, 2011.

6. www.usich.gov/PDF/OpeningDoors_2010_FSPPreventEndHomeless.pdf, accessed November 29, 2010.

7. www.endhomelessness.org/content/article/detail/2993, accessed November 29, 2010.

8. www.everyonehome.org/plan_what.html, accessed November 29, 2010.

9. www.endhomelessness.org/content/article/detail/2983, accessed June 14, 2011.

10. www.endhomelessness.org/content/article/detail/2601, accessed November 29, 2010.

11. www.endhomelessness.org/content/article/detail/1440, accessed June 14, 2011.

U.N. Millennium Campaign:

1. *The Millennium Development Goals Report*, 2010, www.un.org/millenniumgoals/pdf/MDG%20Report%202010%20En%20r15%20-low%20res%2020100615%20-.pdf, accessed February 21, 2011.

2. Official Development Assistance is defined by the Organization for Economic Cooperation and Development (OECD) as "flows of official financing administered with the promotion of the economic development and welfare of developing countries as the main objective."

3. OECD, *Development Aid Rose in 2009 and Most Donors Will Meet 2010 Aid Targets*, April 2010.

4. www.state.gov/r/pa/prs/ps/2009/05/123160.htm, accessed February 21, 2011.

The Hunger Project:

1. Food and Agriculture Organization of the United Nations, "1.02 Billion People Hungry," United Nations, 2009, www.fao.org/news/story/en/item/20568/icode/, accessed September 1, 2010.

2. Food and Agriculture Organization of the United Nations, "The State of Food Insecurity in the World," 2006, www.fao.org/docrep/009/a0750e/a0750e00.HTM, accessed September 1, 2010.

3. Food and Agriculture Organization of the United Nations, "Rural Women and the Right to Food," United Nations, www.fao.org/docrep/w9990e/w9990e10.htm, accessed September 1, 2010.

4. "Women Farmers' Productivity in Sub-Saharan Africa," www.unep.org/training/programmes/Instructor%20Version/Part_2/Activities/Human_Societies/Agriculture/Supplemental/Women-Farmers_Productivity_in_Sub_Saharan_Africa.pdf, accessed June 7, 2011.

5. International Center for Research on Women, Foreign Aid Reform, www.icrw.org, accessed September 1, 2010.

6. As of June 2011.

7. As of June 2011.

8. Megan Tady, "Who Does US Food Aid Benefit?" *In These Times*, September 12, 2007, www.inthesetimes.com/article/3342/who_does_us_food_aid_benefit/, accessed September 1, 2010.

9. Food and Agriculture Organization, "FAO Welcomes G8 Food Security Initiative," United Nations, 2009, ftp://ftp.fao.org/docrep/fao/009/a0800e/a0800e.pdf, accessed September 1, 2010.

Editor's Boxes Notes

Cincinnati Works is Finding Answers to Unemployment

1. CincinnatiWorks, "Job Skill Training & Employment Assistance: About Us," http://www.cincinnatiworks.org/index.php?option=com_content&view=article&id=26&Itemid=31, accessed June 29, 2011.

Solving the World's Water Supply Crisis

1. "Matt Damon, Co-Founder of Water.org, Speaks Out About Global Water Crisis (Video)," March 3, 2011, Huffington Post, www.huffingtonpost.com/2011/03/03/matt-damon-water-org_n_830930.html, accessed June 24, 2011.

2. water.org/about/vision-and-mission, accessed June 24, 2011.

3. Ellen McGirt, "Can Matt Damon Bring Clean Water To Africa?", June 20, 2011, Fast Company, www.fastcompany.com/magazine/157/can-this-man-save-this-girl, accessed June 24, 2011.

4. Ellen McGirt, "Can Matt Damon Bring Clean Water To Africa?", June 20, 2011, Fast Company, www.fastcompany.com/magazine/157/can-this-man-save-this-girl, accessed June 24, 2011.

Ensuring Effective Aid

1. http://www.wired.com/techbiz/people/magazine/17-10/ff_smartlist_moyo.

2. http://www.guardian.co.uk/society/2009/feb/19/dambisa-moyo-dead-aid-africa.

nine

Numbers Pages Notes

1. '122 products from 58 countries' Bureau of International Labor Affairs, "List of Goods Produced by Child Labor or Forced Labor," *US Department of Labor*, 2009.
2. '6,000 fair trade' Fairtrade Labeling Organizations International, "Annual Report: 2008-2009," 2010.
3. '41 million' Lifestyles of Health and Sustainability, http://www.lohas.com/about, accessed July 5, 2011.
4. '30 million acres, 25 million families, 460 million pounds' see Rainforest Alliance, *Supplying the Demand for a Livable Planet*, p. 291–292.
5. 'Deforestation 17%, 334 million' see Rainforest Alliance, *Supplying the Demand for a Livable Planet*, p. 291–292.
6. '1% for the planet' see 1% for the Planet at http://www.onepercentfortheplanet.org/en/.
7. 'TOMS' see Tom's Shoes at http://www.toms.com/.
8. 'Newman's Own' see Newman's Own at http://www.newmansown.com/.
9. 'New Leaf' see New Leaf Paper at http://www.newleafpaper.com/.
10. 'Impact Investing' see the Global Impact Investing Network at: http://www.thegiin.org/.

Essay Notes

Environmental Defense Fund:

1. Osman Can Ozcanli, "Products that Heal Themselves," October 30, 2009, *Forbes*, www.forbes.com/2009/11/30/battle-jacket-goodyear-technology-breakthroughs-materials.html, accessed October 13, 2010.
2. Alan Deutschman, "There's Gold in Them Thar Smelly Hills," July 1, 2006, *Fast Company*, www.fastcompany.com/magazine/107/landfill.html, accessed August 13, 2010.
3. US Energy Information Administration, Emissions of Greenhouse Gases Report, www.eia.doe.gov/oiaf/1605/ggrpt/carbon.html, accessed August 13, 2010.
4. Ariel Schwartz, "SurPLUShome's Solar Skin Produces 200% of the Energy It Needs," October 14, 2009, *Fast Company*, www.fastcompany.com/blog/ariel-schwartz/sustainability/surplushomes-solar-skin-produces-more-energy-it-needs, accessed July 26, 2010.
5. ww.biomicryinstitute.org/case-studies/case-studies/termite-inspired-air-conditioning.html, accessed October 13, 2010.
6. www.biomimicrynews.com/research/Blueprint_for_artificial_leaf_mimics_Mother_Nature.asp, accessed July 26, 2010.
7. www.ferc.gov/about/com-mem/wellinghoff/5-24-07-technical-analy-wellinghoff.pdf, accessed October 13, 2010.
8. www.volans.com/volans-solutions/pathways/, accessed July 26, 2010.

Rainforest Alliance:

1. Food and Agriculture Organization, "Assessing agriculture's potential to mitigate global warming," www.fao.org/news/story/en/item/51042/icode/, accessed July 7, 2011.
2. Intergovernmental Panel on Climate Change, 2007, "Summary for Policymakers. Climate Change 2007: The Physical Science Basis. Contribution of Working Group I to the Fourth Assessment Report of the Intergovernmental Panel on Climate Change."
3. Rainforest Alliance, "Coffee," www.rainforest-alliance.org/agriculture/crops/coffee, accessed July 7, 2011.
4. Food and Agriculture Organization, "Spotlight: Livestock impacts on the environment," www.fao.org/ag/magazine/0612sp1.htm, accessed July 7, 2011.
5. Valentin Bellassen et. al., "Reducing Emissions from Deforestation and Degradation: What Contribution from Carbon Markets?" September 2008, www.cdc-climat.com/IMG/pdf/14_Etude_Climat_EN_Deforestation_and_carbon_markets.pdf, accessed July 29, 2011.

International Labor Rights Fund:

1. United Nations Mission to Liberia (2006), "Human Rights in Liberia's Rubber Plantations: Tapping into the Future," *United Nations*.
2. Elegant, Simon, "Slave Labor in China Sparks Outrage," *Time*, June 20, 2007.
3. Martinez, Helda, "Flower Power – But Not for the Workers," *InterPress Service*, August 7, 2006.
4. The Department of Labor's List of Goods Produced by Child Labor or Forced Labor. Bureau of International Labor Affairs, US Department of Labor, Washington, DC, September 2009. Available at: www.dol.gov/ilab/programs/ocft/PDF/2009TVPRA.pdf, accessed August 30, 2010.
5. Cynthia Enloe, "The Globe-Trotting Sneaker," *Ms. Magazine*, March/April 1995; Thuyen Nguyen, "Nike in Vietnam: An Eyewitness Account," report issued by Campaign for Labor Rights, March 2004; William Greider, "The Global Sweatshop," *Rolling Stone Magazine*, June 30, 1994.

6. "Salvadoran Maquila Workers Producing for Gap Under Attack," report by National Labor Committee, May 2005.
7. Lynne Duke, "The Man Who Made Kathie Lee Cry," *Washington Post*, July 31, 2005.
8. Anand Giridharadas, "Boycotts Minus the Pain," *New York Times*, October 11, 2009.
9. Nadia Mustafa, "Fair Trade Fashion," *Time Magazine*, February 27, 2007.
10. "Bono and Bobby Shriver Launch Product Red to Harness Power of the World's Iconic Brands to Fight Aids in Africa," World Economic Forum press release, January 26, 2006. Available at: www.weforum.org/en/media/Latest%20Press%20Releases/PRESSRELEASES66, accessed August 30, 2010.
11. Forest Stewardship Council, www.fsc.org, accessed August 30, 2010.
12. Marine Stewardship Council, www.msc.org, accessed August 30, 2010.
13. VeriFlora, www.veriflora.com, accessed August 30, 2010.
14. Fairtrade Labeling Organizations International, Annual Report 2008-2009.
15. Matthew Saltmarsh, "Strong Sales of Organic Foods Attract Investors," NY Times, 2011, available at: http://www.nytimes.com/2011/05/24/business/global/24organic.html, accessed June 21, 2011.
16. Michael J. Hiscox and Nicholas F. B. Smyth, "Is There Consumer Demand for Improved Labor Standards? Evidence from Field Experiments in Social Product Labeling," Department of Government, Harvard University, 2007.
17. www.goodweave.org/, accessed May 11, 2010.
18. www.unionwear.com, accessed August 30, 2010.
19. www.workersrights.org/dsp/, accessed August 30, 2010.
20. www.transfairusa.org/content/certification/apparel_program.php, accessed May 14, 2010.
21. www.goodguide.com, accessed August 30, 2010.
22. www.free2work.org, accessed August 30, 2010.

Editor's Boxes Notes

World-changing Innovations

1. Tom McNichol, "Tech Pioneers Who Will Change Your Life," Time Magazine, www.time.com/time/specials/packages/article/0,28804,1948486_1948485_1948479,00.html #ixzz1PCNFaR5e, accessed June 13, 2011.
2. Karl Burkart, "Hype buildings around mysterious Bloom Box," Mother Nature Network, August 30, 2010, www.mnn.com/green-tech/research-innovations/blogs/hype-builds-around-mysterious-bloom-box, accessed October 12, 2010.
3. Megan Phelps, "Why We Need Mushrooms," January 13, 2008, Mother Earth News, www.motherearthnews.com/Natural-Health/Mushrooms-Health-Benefits.aspx#ixzz1PCUZFCtW, accessed June 13, 2011.
4. James Trimarco, "Can Mushrooms Rescue the Gulf?", Yes!, October 1, 2010, www.yesmagazine.org/issues/a-resilient-community/can-mushrooms-rescue-the-gulf, accessed October 12, 2010.
5. Mahesh Basantani, "The Maglev: The Super-powered Magnetic Wind Turbine," Inhabitat, November 26, 2007, www.inhabitat.com/2007/11/26/super-powered-magnetic-wind-turbine-maglev/, accessed October 14, 2010.
6. American Wind Energy Association, www.awea.org/faq/wwt_basics.html, accessed October 14, 2010.
7. Alex Pasternack, "Chinese Maglev Turbines Enter Mass Production, November 6, 2007, www.treehugger.com/files/2007/11/chinese_mag_lev.php accessed October 14, 2010.
8. "Maglev Wind Turbine Technologies to Start Operations," July 26, 2007, www.businesswire.com/news/home/20070726005081/en/Maglev-Wind-Turbine-Technologies-Start-Operations, accessed June 13, 2011.

Seeing the Full Value of Ecosystems

1. Costanza, et al. "The Value of the World's Ecosystem Services and Natural Capital," Nature, 1997.
2. TEEB, "The Economics of Ecosystems and Biodiversity: Mainstreaming the Economics of Nature," UNEP, 2010.
3. Joint Ocean Commission Initiative, "Changing Oceans, Changing Worlds," Joint Ocean Commission Initiative, 2009.
4. Mark Schleifstein, "Environmentalists link oil spill response, coastal restoration," 2011, http://www.nola.com/news/gulf-oil-spill/index.ssf/2010/07/environmentalists_link_oil_spi.html, accessed July 7, 2011.

A Look at the Niger River:

1. Energy Information Administration, "US Imports by Country or Region," 2011.
2. Tom O'Neill, "Curse of the Black Gold," National Geographic, 2007.
3. Alan Taylor, "Nigeria: the Cost of Oil," The Atlantic, 2011, http://www.theatlantic.com/infocus/2011/06/nigeria-the-cost-of-oil/100082/, accessed June 28, 2011.
4. Ploughshares, "Nigeria," 2011, http://www.ploughshares.ca/content/nigeria-1990-first-combat-deaths, accessed June 28, 2011.

Businesses Tackling Tough Social Problems

1. Figures as of September 2010.

2. www.toms.com/movement-one-for-one.

3. www.bogolight.com/SearchResults.asp?Cat=60, accessed December 20, 2010.

4. http://philanthropy.com/blogs/philanthropytoday/newmans-own-donations-total-300-million/28574, accessed November 30, 2010.

ten

Numbers Page Notes

1. '1,002 hate groups' Southern Poverty Law Center, http://www.splcenter.org/get-informed/news/us-hate-groups-top-1000, accessed July 5, 2011.

2. '48 not in our town' Not in Our Town, http://www.niot.org/get-local, accessed July 5, 2011.

3. '11 million un-doc immi / $200 billion / $66 billion' "Deporting the Undocumented: A Cost Assessment," Center for American Progress, 2005, available at http://www.americanprogress.org/issues/2005/07/b913099.html, accessed March 28, 2011.

4. 'Fortune 500, # states, 1000 benefits' see Human Rights Campaign, Envisioning an Inclusive World: The Importance of the Gay Civil Rights Movement, p. 337–338.

5. '2.3 million prisoners' Bureau of Justice Statistics, http://bjs.ojp.usdoj.gov/content/glance/tables/corr2tab.cfm, accessed June 15, 2011.

6. '33% drop' see Justice Policy Institute, Reforming Prisons, Saving Billions, Creating Opportunity, p. 348.

7. '$3 billion' Justice Policy Institute, "Pruning Prisons: How Cutting Corrections Can Save Money and Protect Public Safety," 2009.

8. 'Reservation incomes' Chris McGreal, "Obama's Indian Problem," The Guardian, January 11, 2010. www.guardian.co.uk/global/2010/jan/11/native-americans-reservations-poverty-obama, accessed April 26, 2010.

9. '15% of electricity' Lizana K. Pierce, "DOE's Tribal Energy Program," US Department of Energy Office of Energy Efficiency and Renewable Energy.

10. '110,000 jobs' Based on wind power job estimates from Virinder Singh, "The Work That Goes into Renewable Energy," Renewable Energy Policy Project, 2001.

11. '20 cents of $1' Joel McNally, "Green Giant," March 22, 2010, Milwaukee Magazine, www.milwaukeemagazine.com/currentissue/full_feature_story.asp?NewMessageID=25407, accessed March 24, 2011.

12. '$10 / $60 billion' Based on a study conducted in Black Hawk County, Iowa, see Land Stewardship Project, The Next Generation of Family Farming, p. 324.

Essay Notes

Majora Carter:

1. Reuters, "New York using 'green carts' in lastest obesity fight," February 28, 2008. Available at: www.reuters.com/article/idUSN2738591320080228, accessed August 31, 2010.

2. Gregory Dicum, "Meet Robert Bullard, the father of environmental justice," Grist, March 16, 2006. Available at: www.grist.org/article/dicum/, accessed April 17, 2010.

3. Kenneth R. Fletcher, "Robert Bullard: Environmental Justice Advocate," Smithsonian, June 2008. Available at: www.smithsonianmag.com/arts-culture/atm-qa-bullard.html?c=y&page=1#ixzz0lPEiKJjZ, accessed April 17, 2010.

4. Alternatives for Community & Environment, "Environmental Justice and the Green Economy," 2010.

Growing Power:

1. Joel McNally, "Green Giant," March 22, 2010, Milwaukee Magazine, www.milwaukeemagazine.com/currentissue/full_feature_story.asp?NewMessageID=25407, accessed March 24, 2011.

2. Ibid.

3. Charles Wilson, "5 Years After Katrina, Teacher Tills Soil of Lower 9th Ward," January 15, 2011, The New York Times, www.nytimes.com/2011/01/16/education/16blair.html?_r=1&ref=us, accessed March 24, 2011.

Land Stewardship Project:

1. Katherine Gustafson, "Rise Up, Young Farmers!" Change.org, April 13, 2010, available at: http://food.change.org/blog/view/rise_up_young_farmers, accessed August 31, 2010.

2. http://nfu.org/issues/economic-policy/resources/heffernan-report, accessed June 2010.

3. Reynold P. Dahl, "New Growth in Flour Milling," Minnesota Extension Service, 1993. Available at: http://ageconsearch.umn.edu/bitstream/13197/1/mae672b.pdf, accessed August 31, 2010.

4. US EPA, "Nonpoint Source Pollution: The Nation's Largest Water Quality Problem," www.epa.gov/nps/facts/point1.htm, accessed August 31, 2010.

5. Natural Resources Defense Council, "Atrazine: Poisoning the Well," www.nrdc.org/health/atrazine/, accessed August 31, 2010.

6. http://water.epa.gov/drink/contaminants/basicinformation/nitrate.cfm, accessed August 31, 2010.

7. Ryan Hargitt, "The Nitrate Contamination of Private Well Water in Rural Northwest," Cantaurus Vol.9, (May 2001): 12–17. Available at: www.mcpherson.edu/science/cantaurus/Vol9/01-hargitt.pdf, accessed August 31, 2010.

8. Organic Trade Association, "2011 Organic Industry Survy," April 6, 2011.

9. www.ams.usda.gov/AMSv1.0/getfile?dDocName=STELPRDC5080175&acct=frmrdirmkt, accessed August 31, 2010.

10. www.landstewardshipproject.org/pdf/lsp_25.pdf, accessed August 31, 2010.

11. Dave Swenson, "Estimating the Production and Market Value-Based Impacts of Nutritional Goals in NE Iowa," Iowa State University, February 2008. Available at: www.leopold.iastate.edu/research/marketing_files/NEIowa_042108.pdf, accessed August 31, 2010.

Winona LaDuke:

1. Chris McGreal, "Obama's Indian Problem," The Guardian, January 11, 2010. www.guardian.co.uk/global/2010/jan/11/native-americans-reservations-poverty-obama, accessed April 26, 2010.

2. Brian Halweil, "Home Grown: The Case for Local Food in a Global Market," 2002. Available at: www.worldwatch.org/node/827, accessed August 31, 2010.

3. Thomas Starrs, "The SUV in the Pantry," Sustainable Business, October 25, 2005. Available at: www.sustainablebusiness.com/index.cfm/go/news.feature/id/1275, accessed August 31, 2010.

4. Energy Star, "Partnerships for Home Energy Efficiency," 2008. Available at: www.energystar.gov/ia/home_improvement/PHEE_Report_final.pdf, accessed August 31, 2010.

5. Department of Energy, Energy Information Administration-Energy Consumption and Renewable Energy Development Potential on Indian Lands, April 2000.

6. Roger Bezdek, "Renewable Energy and Energy Efficiency: Drivers for the 21st Century," American Solar Energy Society, 2007. Available at: www.greenforall.org/resources/renewable-energy-and-energy-efficiency-economic, accessed August 31, 2010.

7. Virinder Singh, "The Work That Goes into Renewable Energy," Renewable Energy Policy Project, 2001. Available at: www.repp.org/articles/static/1/binaries/LABOR_FINAL_REV.pdf, accessed August 31, 2010.

8. Ibid.

9. Lizana K. Pierce, "DOE's Tribal Energy Program," US Department of Energy Office of Energy Efficiency and Renewable Energy. Availabel at: www.harvestcleanenergy.org/conference/HCE9/Post-conference/PPT/LizanaPierce.pdf, accessed August 31, 2010.

10. Onell R. Soto, "Wind-farm Project Set for Campo Reservation," San Diego Union-Tribune, June 11, 2009. Available at: www.signonsandiego.com/news/2009/jun/11/wind-farm-project-set-for-campo-reservation/, accessed April 26, 2010.

11. Marjorie Childress, "Jemez Pueblo Developing First Utility Scale Solar Plant on Tribal Land," 2010. Available at: http://newmexicoindependent.com/44424/jemez-pueblo-developing-first-utility-scale-solar-plant-on-tribal-land, accessed April 26, 2010.

12. US Department of Energy, Projects on Tribal Lands, http://apps1.eere.energy.gov/tribalenergy/projects.cfm, accessed April 28, 2010.

13. Zachary Shehan, "Native American Tribe Going for Solar, and Money," CleanTechnica, January 13, 2010. Available at: http://cleantechnica.com/2010/01/13/native-american-tribe-going-for-solar-and-money/, accessed April 26, 2010.

14. Susan Montoya Bryan, "Indian Tribe Sees Bright Future in Solar Power," Christian Science Monitor, January 13, 2010. Available at: www.csmonitor.com/Environment/2010/0114/Indian-tribe-sees-bright-future-in-solar-power, accessed April 28, 2010. And http://cleantechnica.com/2010/01/13/native-american-tribe-going-for-solar-and-money/, accessed April 28, 2010.

15. Jeff Biggers, "Green Jobs March On: Navajos Lead First Nations with Historic Green Jobs Legislation," Commondreams.org, July 22, 2009. Available at: www.commondreams.org/headline/2009/07/22-2, accessed April 26, 2010.

Human Rights Campaign:

1. "Coretta Scott King givers her support to gay marriage," March 24, 2004, USAToday, www.usatoday.com/news/nation/2004-03-24-king-marriage_x.htm, accessed February 2, 2011.

2. Julie Bolcer, "NAACP Pres. to Speak at LGBT Center," Advocate, September 20, 2010, www.advocate.com/News/Daily_News/2010/09/20/NAACP_Leader_to_Speak_at_NY_LGBT_Center/, accessed February 2, 2011.

3. Human Rights Campaign, "Degrees of Equality," 2009, www.hrc.org/documents/HRC_Degrees_of_Equality_2009.pdf, accessed February 2, 2011.

4. Human Rights Campaign, "Corporate Equality Index," 2010, www.hrc.org/documents/HRC-CEI-2011-Final.pdf, accessed February 2, 2011.

5. Human Rights Campaign, "Degrees of Equality," 2009, www.hrc.org/documents/HRC_Degrees_of_Equality_2009.pdf, accessed February 2, 2011.

Opportunity Agenda:

1. Robert W. Fairlie, "Kauffman Index of Entrepreneurial Activity, 1996-2010," April 2011, available at http://www.kauffman.org/uploadedFiles/KIEA_2011_report.pdf, accessed June 16, 2011.

2. Council of Economic Advisers, "Immigration's Economic Impact," June 20, 2007, http://georgewbush-whitehouse.archives.gov/cea/cea_immigration_062007.html, accessed February 21, 2011.

3. "The Economic Impacts of Immigration on US Dairy Farms," June 2009, www.nmpf.org/files/file/NMPF%20Immigration%20Survey%20Web.pdf, accessed February 21, 2011.

4. Daniel González, "US Not Cracking Down on Immigrants with Expired Visas," Arizona Republic, May 10, 2010, www.azcentral.com/news/articles/2010/05/10/20100510illegal-immigrants-overstay.html, accessed March 28, 2011; and Ted Robbins, "Nearly Half of Illegal Immigrants Overstay Visas, National Public Radio, June 14, 2006, www.npr.org/templates/story/story.php?storyId=5485917, accessed February 21, 2011.

5. "Money for Nothing: Immigration Enforcement without Immigration Reform Doesn't Work," Immigration Policy Center, May 22, 2008, available at www.immigrationpolicy.org/just-facts/money-nothing-immigration-enforcement-without-immigration-reform-doesn, accessed March 28, 2011.

6. "Secretary Napolitano Announces Record-breaking Immigration Enforcement Statistics Achieved under the Obama Administration," Department of Homeland Security, October 6, 2010, available at http://www.dhs.gov/ynews/releases/pr_1286389936778.shtm.

7. "Deporting the Undocumented: A Cost Assessment," July 26, 2005, Center for American Progress, available at http://www.americanprogress.org/issues/2005/07/b913099.html, accessed March 28, 2011.

8. Ibid.

9. "In Play: African American, Hispanic, and Progressive White Voters on Immigration Reform," April 2010, The Opportunity Agenda.

10. "The Economics of Immigration Reform: What Legalizing Undocumented Immigrants Would Mean for the U.S. Economy," April 2009, Immigration Policy Center, available at http://immigrationpolicy.org/just-facts/what-immigration-reform-could-mean-us-economy, accessed March 28, 2011.

Justice Policy Institute:

1. Roy Walmsley, "World Prison Population List (Eighth Edition)," King's College London International Centre for Prison Studies, 2008. Available at: www.kcl.ac.uk/depsta/law/research/icps/downloads/wppl-8th_41.pdf, accessed August 31, 2010.

2. Bureau of Justice Statistics, http://bjs.ojp.usdoj.gov/content/glance/tables/corr2tab.cfm, accessed June 15, 2011.

3. Bruce Western, Punishment and Inequality in America, Russell Sage Foundation, New York, 2006.

4. Incarceration rates are from June 2007. *Prisons and jails form one integrated system. ** Illinois data from December 2006. Sources: William J. Sabol and Heather Couture, Prison Inmates at Midyear 2007, Bureau of Justice Statistics, Washington, DC, 2008; D.K. Gilliard, Prison and Jail Inmates at Midyear 1998, Bureau of Justice Statistics, Washington, DC, 1999); FBI Uniform Crime Reports, Crime in the United States, Table 4.

5. Pew Center on the States, One in 31: The Long Reach of American Corrections, Pew Public Safety Performance Project, Washington, DC, 2009. Available at: www.pewcenteronthestates.org/uploadedFiles/PSPP_1in31_report_FINAL_WEB_3-26-09.pdf, accessed August 31, 2010.

6. Pew Center on the States, One in 100: Behind Bars in America 2008, Pew Public Safety Performance Project, Washington, DC, 2008. Available at: www.pewcenteronthestates.org/uploadedFiles/8015PCTS_Prison08_FINAL_2-1-1_FORWEB.pdf, accessed August 31, 2010.

7. Philip Beatty, Amanda Petteruti and Jason Ziedenberg, The Vortex: The Concentrated Racial Impact of Drug Imprisonment and the Characteristics of Punitive Counties, Justice Policy Institute, Washington, DC, 2007.

8. Associated Press, "As Calif. prison spending rises, so do concerns," August 23, 2009, www.msnbc.msn.com/id/32529970/, accessed August 31, 2010.

9. Charles B. Reed, "California Values Prisoners over Students," San Francisco Chronicle, July 27, 2009. Available at: www.sfgate.com/cgibin/article.cgi?f=/c/a/2009/07/27/ED3018UPP1.DTL, accessed November 2009.

10. Patrick A. Langan & David J. Levin, Recidivism of Prisoners Released in 1994, Bureau of Justice Statistics, Washington, DC, 2002. www.ojp.gov/bjs/pub/pdf/rpr94.pdf

11. Bureau of Justice Statistics, Reentry Trends in the United States. Available at: http://bjs.ojp.usdoj.gov/content/reentry/reentry.cfm, accessed August 31, 2010.

12. Steve Aos, Marna Miller & Elizabeth Drake, Evidence-based Public Policy Options to Reduce Future Prison Construction, Criminal Justice Costs, and Crime Rates, Washington State Institute for Public Policy, Olympia, 2006. www.wsipp.wa.gov, accessed August 31, 2010.

13. Justice Policy Institute, Education and Public Safety; Employment and Public Safety, Housing and Public Safety, and Substance Abuse Treatment and Public Safety, Washington, DC, 2007. Available at: www.justicepolicy.org/contenthmID=1811&smID=1582&ssmID=30.htm, accessed November 2009.

14. Lauren E. Glaze & Thomas P. Bonczar, Probation and Parole in the United States, 2007 Statistical Tables, Bureau of Justice Statistics, Washington, DC, 2008, Table 7. Available at: www.ojp.gov/bjs/pub/pdf/ppus07st.pdf, accessed November 2009.

15. James J. Stephan, State Prison Expenditures, 2001 Bureau of Justice Statistics, Washington, DC, 2004. Available at: www.ojp.usdoj.gov/bjs/pub/pdf/spe01.pdf, accessed November 2009.

16. This is a rough high estimate for the average a state would spend on parole by using California as the high limit. JPI has been unable to find a single national cost estimate for parole. The cost of parole also varies widely from state to state. California Department of Corrections and Rehabilitation, "Third Quarter 2008 Facts and Figures." Available at: www.cdcr.ca.gov/Divisions_Boards/Adult_Operations/Facts_and_Figures.html, accessed November 2009.

17. Council of State Governments Justice Center, Justice Reinvestment State Brief: Kansas, New York, 2007. Available at: http://justicereinvestment.org/files/KansasStateBrief.letter.pdf, accessed November 2009.

18. Justice Policy Institute, Education and Public Safety, 2007.

19. Ibid.

20. Alliance for Excellent Education, Saving Futures, Saving Dollars: The Impact of Education on Crime Reduction and Earnings, Washington, DC, 2006. Available at: www.all4ed.org/publications/SavingFutures.pdf, accessed November 2009,

Editor's Boxes Notes

Navajo Green Jobs

1. Down2Earth, "Nikki Alex," http://www.youtube.com/watch?v=9l62cEj5t8o&feature=player_embedded#at=227, accessed July 7, 2011.

Numbers Pages Notes

1. '43% and 50%' Stockholm International Peace Research Institute, "World military expenditure increases despite financial crisis," June 2, 2010.

2. '$1 trillion' "Debt, Deficits, and Defense: A Way Forward," Sustainable Defense Task Force, 2010.

3. '800 bases / $102 billion / 392 Japan and Germany' David Vine, "Too Many Overseas Bases," Foreign Policy in Focus, February 25, 2009, www.fpif.org/articles/too_many_overseas_bases, accessed April 20, 2010.

4. '200-300 Rumsfeld' see New America Foundation, Cutting and Reallocating Military Spending, Taking Care of Soldiers and Increasing National Security, p. 367.

5. '21.1% and 16.6%' Robert Faturechi, "Young Veterans Face Steep Unemployment," Los Angeles Times, March 12, 2010, http://articles.latimes.com/2010/mar/12/nation/la-na-vet-unemployment13-2010mar13, accessed March 19, 2010.

6. '25% new hires' Feds Hire Vets, "Employment of Veterans in the Federal Executive Branch: Fiscal Year 2010," Office of Personnel Management, 2011.

7. 'Iraq and Afghanistan fatalities' www.cnn.com/SPECIALS/war.casualties/index.html, accessed June 6, 2011.

8. '76 years / 71 reps' http://studentpeacealliance.org/learn/about-dop/dop, accessed March 8, 2011.

Essay Notes

New America Foundation:

1. Office of Management and Budget, "Outlays by Function and Subfunction," http://www.whitehouse.gov/omb/budget/Historicals/, accessed June 21, 2011.

2. Stockholm International Peace Research Institute, "World military expenditure increases despite financial crisis," June 2, 2010, www.sipri.org/media/pressreleases/2010/100602yearbooklaunch, accessed February 21, 2011.

3. Roxana Tiron, "Panel Recommends Nearly $1 Trillion in 'Defense' Cuts, CommonDreams.org, June 11, 2010, www.commondreams.org/headline/2010/06/11-10, accessed June 14, 2010.

4. Government Accountability Office, "Defense Acquisitions: Assessment of Selected Weapons Systems," 2008, www.gao.gov/new.items/d09326sp.pdf

5. Our Documents, www.ourdocuments.gov/doc.php?flash=true&doc=90&page=transcript, accessed April 17, 2010.

6. Congressional Budget Office, "The Budgetary Effects of Selected Policy Alternatives Not Included in CBO's Baseline," www.cbo.gov/ftpdocs/100xx/doc10014/BudEffects.pdf, accessed June 14, 2010.

7. David Vine, "Too Many Overseas Bases," Foreign Policy in Focus, February 25, 2009, www.fpif.org/articles/too_many_overseas_bases, accessed April 20, 2010.

eleven

8. Arms Control Association, "Nuclear Weapons: Who Has What at a Glance," 2011, http://www.armscontrol.org/factsheets/Nuclearweaponswhohaswhat, accessed June 21, 2011.
9. Stephen Schwartz & Deepti Choubey, "Nuclear Security Spending: Assessing Costs, Examining Priorities," 2009, www.carnegieendowment.org/files/nuclear_security_spending_low.pdf.
10. Government Accountability Office, "Assessments of Selected Weapons Programs," 2008, http://www.gao.gov/highlights/d08467sphigh.pdf, accessed June 21, 2011.
11. National Priorities Project, "Security Spending Primer," www.nationalpriorities.org/Publications/NPP_Security_Spending_Primer.pdf, accessed April 17, 2010.
12. Mark Thompson, "V-22 Osprey: A Flying Shame," Time, September 26, 2007, www.time.com/time/politics/article/0,8599,1665835,00.html, accessed June 15, 2010.
13. Carl Conetta, "Forceful Engagement: Rethinking the Role of Military Power in US Global Policy," Project on Defense Alternatives, December 2008. Available at: www.comw.org/pda/081201FE-ExecSum.htm, accessed September 1, 2010.
14. Based on 23 million veterans living in the US, www4.va.gov/budget/docs/summary/Fy2011_Volume_1-Summary_Volume.pdf, accessed March 24, 2010.
15. Robert Faturechi, "Young Veterans Face Steep Unemployment," Los Angeles Times, March 12, 2010, http://articles.latimes.com/2010/mar/12/nation/la-na-vet-unemployment13-2010mar13, accessed March 19, 2010.
16. Solar Energy Industries Association, www.seia.org/cs/about_solar_energy/industry_data, accessed June 15, 2010.
17. Iraq and Afghanistan Veterans of America, http://iava.org/blog/hvac-turns-bills-impacting-veterans-housing-employment, accessed March 22, 2010.
18. Apollo Alliance, "Apollo 5-Point Plan for Boosting US Clean Energy Job Growth," Available at: www.apolloalliance.org/wp-content/uploads/2009/12/apollojobsbillproposal.pdf, accessed September 1, 2010.

Nuclear Age Peace Foundation:
1. "Treaty Between the United States of America and the Russian Federation on Measures for the Further Reduction and Limitation of Strategic Offensive Arms," April 8, 2010, www.state.gov/documents/organization/140035.pdf, accessed July 1, 2011.
2. Barack Obama, April 5, 2009, Prague, Czech Republic, http://prague.usemlllassy.gov/obama.html.

Peace Alliance:
1. www.studentpeacealliance.org/images/stories/documents/statistics-on-violence_013009.pdf, accessed June 20, 2011.
2. Ibid.
3. Leitenberg, Milton. "Deaths in Wars and Conflicts in the 20th Century," Cornell University Peace Studies, 2006.
4. Institute For Economics & Peace, United States Peace Index, 2011, www.visionofhumanity.org/wp-content/uploads/2011/04/U.S.-Peace-Index-2011-3.pdf, accessed June 21, 2011.
5. Susie Shutts, "Costa Rica Creates Department of Peace," September 22, 2009, Yes! Magazine, www.yesmagazine.org/peace-justice/costa-rica-creates-department-of-peace, accessed May 25, 2011.
6. Ibid.

Editor's Boxes Notes

If we didn't waste $295 billion:
1. Based on the US's $7,100 per capita spending on healthcare, see Steven Hill, Tackling the Profit Problem in Healthcare, p.243.
2. Based on the Bureau of Labor Statistics "Occupational Outlook Handbook," 2010-2011.
3. Based on an installed cost of $1.7 million per MW at Windustry, "How much do wind turbines cost, 2007 building 173,000 MW of wind power, which powers roughly 300 homes per MW according to the Department of Energy's "Wind Energy Development Programmatic."

Essay Notes

Kenny Ausubel:
1. Matthew L. Wald, "Two Large Solar Plants Planned in California," August 14, 2008, The New York Times, www.nytimes.com/2008/08/15/business/15solar.html, accessed March 24, 2011.
2. "Governor Patrick Signs Bills to Reduce Emissions and Boost Green Jobs," August 13, 2008, www.mass.gov/?pageID=gov3pressrelease&L=1&L0=Home&sid=Agov3&b=pressrelease&f=080813_green_jobs&csid=Agov3, accessed March 24, 2011.
3. Megan Treacy, "World's largest wind farm completed in Texas," October 2, 2009, http://green.yahoo.com/blog/ecogeek/1207/world-s-largest-wind-farm-completed-in-texas.html, accessed March 24, 2011.
4. Tiffany Hsu, "Wind farm 'mega-project' underway in Mojave Desert," July 27, 2010, Los Angeles Times, http://articles.latimes.com/2010/jul/27/business/la-fi-windfarm-20100727, accessed March 24, 2011.
5. David Oates, "Imagine," April 16, 2007, High Country News, www.hcn.org/issues/344/16957, accessed March 24, 2011.

Ashoka:
1. Nicholas D. Kristof, "Talia for President," November 16, 2008, New York Times, www.nytimes.com/2008/11/16/opinion/16kristof.html, accessed April 12, 2011.

index

Page numbers appearing in italic type refer to pages that contain illustrations, graphics and/or photographs. None of the information contained in the end-notes has been indexed.